1 & 2 KINGS

Brazos Theological Commentary on the Bible

Series Editors

R. R. Reno, General Editor
Creighton University
Omaha, Nebraska

Robert W. Jenson
Center of Theological Inquiry
Princeton, New Jersey

Robert Louis Wilken
University of Virginia
Charlottesville, Virginia

Ephraim Radner
Ascension Episcopal Church
Pueblo, Colorado

Michael Root
Lutheran Theological Southern Seminary
Columbia, South Carolina

George Sumner
Wycliffe College
Toronto, Ontario

1 & 2 KINGS

PETER J. LEITHART

Brazos Press
Grand Rapids, Michigan

©2006 by Peter J. Leithart

Published by Brazos Press
a division of Baker Publishing Group
P.O. Box 6287, Grand Rapids, MI 49516-6287
www.brazospress.com

Printed in the United States of America

Library of Congress Cataloging-in-Publication Data
Leithart, Peter J.
    1/2 Kings / Peter J. Leithart.
        p.   cm. — (Brazos theological commentary on the Bible)
    ISBN 10: 1-58743-125-4 (cloth)
    ISBN 978-1-58743-125-8 (cloth)
    1. Bible. O.T. Kings—Commentaries. I. Title. II. Title: First-Second Kings.
III. Title: 1st-2nd Kings. IV. Series.
    BS1335.53.L45 2006
    222′.507—dc22   2006011984

CONTENTS

SERIES PREFACE

Near the beginning of his treatise against Gnostic interpretations of the Bible, *Against the Heresies,* Irenaeus observes that Scripture is like a great mosaic depicting a handsome king. It is as if we were owners of a villa in Gaul who had ordered a mosaic from Rome. It arrives, and the beautifully colored tiles need to be taken out of their packaging and put into proper order according to the plan of the artist. The difficulty, of course, is that Scripture provides us with the individual pieces, but the order and sequence of various elements are not obvious. The Bible does not come with instructions that would allow interpreters to simply place verses, episodes, images, and parables in order as a worker might follow a schematic drawing in assembling the pieces to depict the handsome king. The mosaic must be puzzled out. This is precisely the work of scriptural interpretation.

Origen has his own image to express the difficulty of working out the proper approach to reading the Bible. When preparing to offer a commentary on the Psalms he tells of a tradition handed down to him by his Hebrew teacher:

> The Hebrew said that the whole divinely inspired Scripture may be likened, because of its obscurity, to many locked rooms in our house. By each room is placed a key, but not the one that corresponds to it, so that the keys are scattered about beside the rooms, none of them matching the room by which it is placed. It is a difficult task to find the keys and match them to the rooms that they can open. We therefore know the Scriptures that are obscure only by taking the points of departure for understanding them from another place because they have their interpretive principle scattered among them.[1]

As is the case for Irenaeus, scriptural interpretation is not purely local. The key in Genesis may best fit the door of Isaiah, which in turn opens up the

---

1. Fragment from the preface to *Commentary on Psalms 1–25*, preserved in the *Philokalia* (trans. Joseph W. Trigg; London: Routledge, 1998), 70–71.

meaning of Matthew. The mosaic must be put together with an eye toward the overall plan.

Irenaeus, Origen, and the great cloud of premodern biblical interpreters assumed that puzzling out the mosaic of Scripture must be a communal project. The Bible is vast, heterogeneous, full of confusing passages and obscure words, and difficult to understand. Only a fool would imagine that he or she could work out solutions alone. The way forward must rely upon a tradition of reading that Irenaeus reports has been passed on as the rule or canon of truth that functions as a confession of faith. "Anyone," he says, "who keeps unchangeable in himself the rule of truth received through baptism will recognize the names and sayings and parables of the scriptures."[2] Modern scholars debate the content of the rule on which Irenaeus relies and commends, not the least because the terms and formulations Irenaeus himself uses shift and slide. Nonetheless, Irenaeus assumes that there is a body of apostolic doctrine sustained by a tradition of teaching in the church. This doctrine provides the clarifying principles that guide exegetical judgment toward a coherent overall reading of Scripture as a unified witness. Doctrine, then, is the schematic drawing that will allow the reader to organize the vast heterogeneity of the words, images, and stories of the Bible into a readable, coherent whole. It is the rule that guides us toward the proper matching of keys to doors.

If self-consciousness about the role of history in shaping human consciousness makes modern historical-critical study critical, then what makes modern study of the Bible modern is the consensus that classical Christian doctrine distorts interpretive understanding. Benjamin Jowett, the influential nineteenth-century English classical scholar, is representative. In his programmatic essay "On the Interpretation of Scripture," he exhorts the biblical reader to disengage from doctrine and break its hold over the interpretive imagination. "The simple words of that book," writes Jowett of the modern reader, "he tries to preserve absolutely pure from the refinements or distinctions of later times." The modern interpreter wishes to "clear away the remains of dogmas, systems, controversies, which are encrusted upon" the words of Scripture. The disciplines of close philological analysis "would enable us to separate the elements of doctrine and tradition with which the meaning of Scripture is encumbered in our own day."[3] The lens of understanding must be wiped clear of the hazy and distorting film of doctrine.

Postmodernity, in turn, has encouraged us to criticize the critics. Jowett imagined that when he wiped away doctrine he would encounter the biblical text in its purity and uncover what he called "the original spirit and intention of the authors."[4] We are not now so sanguine, and the postmodern mind thinks interpretive frameworks inevitable. Nonetheless, we tend to remain modern

---

2. *Against the Heretics* 9.4.

3. Benjamin Jowett, "On the Interpretation of Scripture," in *Essays and Reviews* (London: Parker, 1860), 338–39.

4. Ibid., 340.

in at least one sense. We read Athanasius and think him stage-managing the diversity of Scripture to support his positions against the Arians. We read Bernard of Clairvaux and assume that his monastic ideals structure his reading of the Song of Songs. In the wake of the Reformation, we can see how the doctrinal divisions of the time shaped biblical interpretation. Luther famously described the Epistle of James as a "strawy letter," for, as he said, "it has nothing of the nature of the Gospel about it."[5] In these and many other instances, often written in the heat of ecclesiastical controversy or out of the passion of ascetic commitment, we tend to think Jowett correct: doctrine is a distorting film on the lens of understanding.

However, is what we commonly think actually the case? Are readers naturally perceptive? Do we have an unblemished, reliable aptitude for the divine? Have we no need for disciplines of vision? Do our attention and judgment need to be trained, especially as we seek to read Scripture as the living word of God? According to Augustine, we all struggle to journey toward God, who is our rest and peace. Yet our vision is darkened and the fetters of worldly habit corrupt our judgment. We need training and instruction in order to cleanse our minds so that we might find our way toward God.[6] To this end, "the whole temporal dispensation was made by divine Providence for our salvation."[7] The covenant with Israel, the coming of Christ, the gathering of the nations into the church—all these things are gathered up into the rule of faith, and they guide the vision and form of the soul toward the end of fellowship with God. In Augustine's view, the reading of Scripture both contributes to and benefits from this divine pedagogy. With countless variations in both exegetical conclusions and theological frameworks, the same pedagogy of a doctrinally ruled reading of Scripture characterizes the broad sweep of the Christian tradition from Gregory the Great through Bernard and Bonaventure, continuing across Reformation differences in both John Calvin and Cornelius Lapide, Patrick Henry and Bishop Bossuet, and on to more recent figures such as Karl Barth and Hans Urs von Balthasar.

Is doctrine, then, not a moldering scrim of antique prejudice obscuring the Bible, but instead a clarifying agent, an enduring tradition of theological judgments that amplifies the living voice of Scripture? And what of the scholarly dispassion advocated by Jowett? Is a noncommitted reading, an interpretation unprejudiced, the way toward objectivity, or does it simply invite the languid intellectual apathy that stands aside to make room for the false truism and easy answers of the age?

This series of biblical commentaries was born out of the conviction that dogma clarifies rather than obscures. The Brazos Theological Commentary on the Bible advances upon the assumption that the Nicene tradition, in all its

---

5. *Luther's Works*, vol. 35 (ed. E. Theodore Bachmann; Philadelphia: Fortress, 1959), 362.
6. *On Christian Doctrine* 1.10.
7. *On Christian Doctrine* 1.35.

diversity and controversy, provides the proper basis for the interpretation of the Bible as Christian Scripture. God the Father Almighty, who sends his only begotten Son to die for us and for our salvation and who raises the crucified Son in the power of the Holy Spirit so that the baptized may be joined in one body—faith in *this* God with *this* vocation of love for the world is the lens through which to view the heterogeneity and particularity of the biblical texts. Doctrine, then, is not a moldering scrim of antique prejudice obscuring the meaning of the Bible. It is a crucial aspect of the divine pedagogy, a clarifying agent for our minds fogged by self-deceptions, a challenge to our languid intellectual apathy that will too often rest in false truisms and the easy spiritual nostrums of the present age rather than search more deeply and widely for the dispersed keys to the many doors of Scripture.

For this reason, the commentators in this series have not been chosen because of their historical or philological expertise. In the main, they are not biblical scholars in the conventional, modern sense of the term. Instead, the commentators were chosen because of their knowledge of and expertise in using the Christian doctrinal tradition. They are qualified by virtue of the doctrinal formation of their mental habits, for it is the conceit of this series of biblical commentaries that theological training in the Nicene tradition prepares one for biblical interpretation, and thus it is to theologians and not biblical scholars that we have turned. "War is too important," it has been said, "to leave to the generals."

We do hope, however, that readers do not draw the wrong impression. The Nicene tradition does not provide a set formula for the solution of exegetical problems. The great tradition of Christian doctrine was not transcribed, bound in folio, and issued in an official, critical edition. We have the Niceno-Constantinopolitan Creed, used for centuries in many traditions of Christian worship. We have ancient baptismal affirmations of faith. The Chalcedonian definition and the creeds and canons of other church councils have their places in official church documents. Yet the rule of faith cannot be limited to a specific set of words, sentences, and creeds. It is instead a pervasive habit of thought, the animating culture of the church in its intellectual aspect. As Augustine observed, commenting on Jeremiah 31:33, "The creed is learned by listening; it is written, not on stone tablets nor on any material, but on the heart."[8] This is why Irenaeus is able to appeal to the rule of faith more than a century before the first ecumenical council, and this is why we need not itemize the contents of the Nicene tradition in order to appeal to its potency and role in the work of interpretation.

Because doctrine is intrinsically fluid on the margins and most powerful as a habit of mind rather than a list of propositions, this commentary series cannot settle difficult questions of method and content at the outset. The editors of the series impose no particular method of doctrinal interpretation.

8. *Sermon* 212.2.

We cannot say in advance how doctrine helps the Christian reader assemble the mosaic of Scripture. We have no clear answer to the question of whether exegesis guided by doctrine is antithetical to or compatible with the now-old modern methods of historical-critical inquiry. Truth—historical, mathematical, or doctrinal—knows no contradiction. But method is a discipline of vision and judgment, and we cannot know in advance what aspects of historical-critical inquiry are functions of modernism that shape the soul to be at odds with Christian discipline. Still further, the editors do not hold the commentators to any particular hermeneutical theory that specifies how to define the plain sense of Scripture—or the role this plain sense should play in interpretation. Here the commentary series is tentative and exploratory.

Can we proceed in any other way? European and North American intellectual culture has been de-Christianized. The effect has not been a cessation of Christian activity. Theological work continues. Sermons are preached. Biblical scholars turn out monographs. Church leaders have meetings. But each dimension of a formerly unified Christian practice now tends to function independently. It is as if a weakened army had been fragmented, and various corps had retreated to isolated fortresses in order to survive. Theology has lost its competence in exegesis. Scripture scholars function with minimal theological training. Each decade finds new theories of preaching to cover the nakedness of seminary training that provides theology without exegesis and exegesis without theology.

Not the least of the causes of the fragmentation of Christian intellectual practice has been the divisions of the church. Since the Reformation, the role of the rule of faith in interpretation has been obscured by polemics and counterpolemics about *sola scriptura* and the necessity of a magisterial teaching authority. The Brazos Theological Commentary on the Bible series is deliberately ecumenical in scope, because the editors are convinced that early church fathers were correct: church doctrine does not compete with Scripture in a limited economy of epistemic authority. We wish to encourage unashamedly dogmatic interpretation of Scripture, confident that the concrete consequences of such a reading will cast far more light on the great divisive questions of the Reformation than either reengaging in old theological polemics or chasing the fantasy of a pure exegesis that will somehow adjudicate between competing theological positions. You shall know the truth of doctrine by its interpretive fruits, and therefore in hopes of contributing to the unity of the church, we have deliberately chosen a wide range of theologians whose commitment to doctrine will allow readers to see real interpretive consequences rather than the shadowboxing of theological concepts.

Brazos Theological Commentary on the Bible has no dog in the current translation fights, and we endorse a textual ecumenism that parallels our diversity of ecclesial backgrounds. We do not impose the thankfully modest inclusive-language agenda of the New Revised Standard Version, nor do we insist upon the glories of the Authorized Version, nor do we require our commentators to create a new translation. In our communal worship, in our private devotions, in our theological scholarship, we use a range of scriptural translations. Precisely as Scripture—a living, functioning text in the present life of faith—the Bible is not semantically fixed. Only a modernist, literalist hermeneutic could imagine that this modest fluidity is a liability. Philological precision and stability is a consequence of, not a basis for, exegesis. Judgments about the meaning of a text fix its literal sense, not the other way around. As a result, readers should expect an eclectic use of biblical translations, both across the different volumes of the series and within individual commentaries.

We cannot speak for contemporary biblical scholars, but as theologians we know that we have long been trained to defend our fortresses of theological concepts and formulations. And we have forgotten the skills of interpretation. Like stroke victims, we must rehabilitate our exegetical imaginations, and there are likely to be different strategies of recovery. Readers should expect this reconstructive—not reactionary—series to provide them with experiments in postcritical doctrinal interpretation, not commentaries written according to the settled principles of a well-functioning tradition. Some commentators will follow classical typological and allegorical readings from the premodern tradition; others will draw on contemporary historical study. Some will comment verse by verse; others will highlight passages, even single words that trigger theological analysis of Scripture. No reading strategies are proscribed, no interpretive methods foresworn. The central premise in this commentary series is that doctrine provides structure and cogency to scriptural interpretation. We trust in this premise with the hope that the Nicene tradition can guide us, however imperfectly, diversely, and haltingly, toward a reading of Scripture in which the right keys open the right doors.

R. R. Reno

ACKNOWLEDGEMENTS

By their very nature, commentaries are extratexts that depend for their sense on the text commented upon, but this commentary risks being clinically diagnosed as codependent. It will be well-nigh nonsensical to readers unfamiliar with the general outlines of 1–2 Kings and perhaps will make sense only to readers who have an open Bible in front of them and are willing to pause occasionally to examine the passages cited and discussed. More than that, this commentary has an unconscionably narrow focus. I deal only occasionally with the synoptic problems of coordinating Chronicles and Kings; I make only a few passing references to problems of the internal chronology of the book or the even more complex problems of harmonizing the data of 1–2 Kings with extrabiblical information; I skip many verses of the text that contain fascinating and edifying details. All that is to say: anyone reading this book without the Scriptures handy is likely to be lost, and anyone using this commentary without the assistance of other commentaries is likely to receive a severely limited view of 1–2 Kings. The notes scattered through the commentary, and the bibliography, will alert the reader to the additional reading that I found most profitable, and I urge use of those works.

Even on the issues I have chosen to attend to, I am aware that my effort is deeply inadequate and incomplete. The oversights and weaknesses are too numerous to mention, but a few examples will give the reader a sense of where some of the most gaping potholes might be: I treat Solomon's reign far too much as a separate narrative, isolated from the whole of 1–2 Kings; I *know* that more is going on in 1 Kgs. 3:15–28 than I have been able to discern; the temple is far more complicated and fascinating than I have space or talent to communicate; I have not been able to do justice to the meaning of Aram in Israel's history; Elijah and Elisha remain opaque mysteries to me in many ways; the treatment of the latter part of the kingdom of Judah is far more superficial

13

than I would like; and so on. Beyond the remaining mysteries of this particular text, I cannot pretend to comprehend fully how 1–2 Kings fits into the canon of Scripture and especially its integral role in the story of Jesus, which is the Bible's master story. No matter: the Scriptures are the revelation of an infinite God, whose depths we will never fathom. If I have at least alerted the reader to profundities I cannot plumb, this book may yet have some part in edifying the church of Christ.

I owe thanks to many people who contributed to the writing of this book. Thanks first to Rusty Reno for honoring me with an invitation to contribute a volume to this series, for forcing me to return to a manuscript I fondly hoped was finished, and for providing honest and helpful feedback on earlier drafts. Michael Root also offered encouragement and editorial guidance on the early drafts of the commentary. Thanks also to Rodney Clapp, Rebecca Cooper, and the editorial staff of Brazos for stylistic and substantive improvements. For research help, I thank Nate Smith and Michael Saville, former students at Covenant Seminary in Saint Louis, who tracked down and photocopied articles for me. I would never have been able to finish the manuscript in a timely way without the assistance of Tim Enloe, who brought a very rough first draft into conformity to the Brazos style sheet, and Vicki Church, who helped to prepare a subsequent draft.

I have taught on 1–2 Kings at two Biblical Horizons Summer Conferences, and I wish to thank James B. Jordan, director of Biblical Horizons, for those opportunities and, as ever, for continuing inspiration. I first began studying 1–2 Kings in depth several years ago while teaching through the book in a Sunday school class sponsored by Christ Church in Moscow, Idaho. To Pastor Douglas Wilson and the elders of Christ Church, and to those who faithfully attended that class, my thanks. I have also been preaching through 1–2 Kings at Trinity Reformed Church for over a year, and I thank elders Patch Blakey and Chris Schlect, as well as the congregation at Trinity, for their permission and encouragement. My family has, as always, displayed something close to condescending forbearance with my occasional (regular?) desperation as deadlines approached, and I am grateful to all of them, particularly to my wife, Noel, whose courage and perseverance have left me in awe for nearly a quarter century.

Finally, I am very grateful to the members of the Pesher Group—Joshua Appel, Josh Davis, Toby Sumpter, Brent Harken, and Peter Roise—for stimulating discussions of 1–2 Kings over the last couple of years. They all know, better than I do, how much this commentary owes to their insights and suggestions. Those Thursday afternoons sitting on the edge of Friendship Square outside Zume Bakery, sipping coffee in the afternoon sun with 1–2 Kings open before us, provided some of the most intense anticipations of eschatological glory I expect to know. The new earth, surely, will be something like that, only the coffee will be infinitely better. While knowing that I cannot adequately compensate their assistance by giving proper attribution at every point, I dedicate this commentary to them with gratitude and love.

It is wholly a happy gift of providence that I finished the first draft of this book on October 31, Reformation Day 2005. In my reading, 1–2 Kings both confirms the Reformers' proclamation of the utter gratuity of grace and their stringent demand for exclusive devotion to the Triune God and also pointedly reminds us of the unhappy divisions that so early and so deeply vitiated the Reformation's power. It is also something of a providential "accident" that this book ended with forty chapters (including the introduction), but this too is a happy providence. This structure will remind the Christian reader of the forty days of Lent in which the church journeys through the wilderness of repentance toward the promised land of Easter. The book of Kings recounts a history of schism and ultimate exile; of a temple ignored and abused and finally destroyed; of cross and tomb. There are golden moments, but overall the story is very much a Lenten story, a story of the suffering and alienation of Israel, which serves as a figure of the passion—and the longed-for restoration—of the new Israel.

Peniel Hall
Christmas 2005

ABBREVIATIONS

Acts	Acts	Judg.	Judges
Amos	Amos	1 Kgs.	1 Kings
1 Chr.	1 Chronicles	2 Kgs.	2 Kings
2 Chr.	2 Chronicles	Lam.	Lamentations
Col.	Colossians	Lev.	Leviticus
1 Cor.	1 Corinthians	Luke	Luke
2 Cor.	2 Corinthians	Mal.	Malachi
Dan.	Daniel	Mark	Mark
Deut.	Deuteronomy	Matt.	Matthew
Eccl.	Ecclesiastes	Mic.	Micah
Eph.	Ephesians	Nah.	Nahum
Esth.	Esther	Neh.	Nehemiah
Exod.	Exodus	Num.	Numbers
Ezek.	Ezekiel	Obad.	Obadiah
Ezra	Ezra	1 Pet.	1 Peter
Gal.	Galatians	2 Pet.	2 Peter
Gen.	Genesis	Phil.	Philippians
Hab.	Habakkuk	Phlm.	Philemon
Hag.	Haggai	Prov.	Proverbs
Heb.	Hebrews	Ps.	Psalms
Hos.	Hosea	Rev.	Revelation
Isa.	Isaiah	Rom.	Romans
Jas.	James	Ruth	Ruth
Jer.	Jeremiah	1 Sam.	1 Samuel
Job	Job	2 Sam.	2 Samuel
Joel	Joel	Song	Song of Songs
John	John	1 Thess.	1 Thessalonians
1 John	1 John	2 Thess.	2 Thessalonians
2 John	2 John	1 Tim.	1 Timothy
3 John	3 John	2 Tim.	2 Timothy
Jonah	Jonah	Titus	Titus
Josh.	Joshua	Zech.	Zechariah
Jude	Jude	Zeph.	Zephaniah

INTRODUCTION

1–2 Kings as Gospel

Christians generally regard 1–2 Kings, which forms a continuous narrative and single book, as a historical book, and since the work of Noth in the early 1940s many scholars have operated on the assumption that 1–2 Kings forms the conclusion to a larger narrative known as the "Deuteronomistic History" that covers Deuteronomy, Joshua, Judges, 1–2 Samuel, and 1–2 Kings.[1] The rationale for this classification of these books as historical is obvious, given the author's evident interest in chronology, his effort to recount Israel's monarchy, and his attention to the relations between Israel and various Gentile peoples.

Yet, not all readers assume that Kings is primarily historical. Jews have long classified the book of Kings among the Former Prophets, and this understanding, though more subtle than the typical Christian one, is suitable to the book's contents. The book of Kings is prophetic in the obvious sense that it centers attention on the words and works of Yahweh's prophets. Nathan is the mastermind behind Solomon's ascension to David's throne (1 Kgs. 1:5–53); Ahijah the prophet informs Jeroboam I that he is chosen to lead ten tribes (11:26–40); a lengthy prophetic narrative interrupts the account of Jeroboam's reign (13:1–32); Micaiah prophesies Ahab's death (22:5–28); Isaiah is a prominent figure during the reign of Hezekiah (2 Kgs. 18–20); and King

---

1. Noth's original argument may be found in Noth 1957. Since then, a number of specifics of Noth's original thesis have been challenged, and there has been considerable debate about the various redactions of the work. Some have raised questions about the existence of a Deuteronomistic History (Knaut 2000). For a recent survey of the development of the thesis and its various permutations, see Romer and de Pury 2000. The present commentary treats 1–2 Kings as a literary and theological whole and does not enter into any discussion of the sources for the text. I assume that the book was written during the exile for a mainly exilic audience.

Josiah consults the prophetess Huldah when his priest, Hilkiah, discovers the book of the law in the temple (22:14–20). Lesser prophets dot the landscape throughout (1 Kgs. 12:21–24; 16:1; 20:35–43; 2 Kgs. 9:4; 14:25), and groups of prophets are referred to repeatedly—both true prophets (1 Kgs. 18:3–4; 20:35; 2 Kgs. 2:3–7; 4:1, 38) and false (1 Kgs. 18:19–20; 22:6, 12; 2 Kgs. 3:13). By my reckoning, ten prophets or prophetesses are named: Nathan, Shemaiah, Ahijah, Jehu, Elijah, Micaiah, Elisha, Jonah, Isaiah, and Huldah. The structural arrangement of 1–2 Kings reinforces this prophetic emphasis. Eleven chapters at the beginning of the book record the reign of a single king, Solomon, but then the book skims over the surface of several decades, devoting no more than a chapter to any single king, until we reach the dynasty of Omri, to which the author devotes the entire central section of the narrative (1 Kgs. 16:21–2 Kgs. 11:20). In these chapters, kings recede into the background as the prophets Elijah and Elisha take center stage.

Treatment of prophets and the kings' response to the prophetic word determine the rise and fall of dynasties and kingdoms. Yahweh enlists Jehu to destroy the house of Ahab in order to avenge the blood of his prophets (2 Kgs. 9:7), and both Israel and Judah fall because they refuse to listen to the voice of Yahweh's prophets (17:13, 23). Equally important, the prophetic word shapes the destinies of the various kingdoms, a point the narrator makes by repeatedly noting occasions of prophetic fulfillments (1 Kgs. 14:18; 15:29; 16:12, 34; 22:38; 2 Kgs. 1:17; 9:26; 10:17; 14:25; 23:16; 24:2). For those who trust and honor the prophets, the word of Yahweh is a word of life and health (1 Kgs. 17:5, 15–16; 2 Kgs. 2:22; 4:44; 5:14; 7:16; 8:2); those who renounce the prophets face his wrath.

The book of Kings is prophetic in a more particular sense as well. According to Gowan (1998), the prophets to ancient Israel did not preach a legalistic message of moral reformation but an evangelical message of faith in the God who raises the dead. From the first days of the human race in Eden, the curse threatened against sin is "dying you shall die," and the same curse hangs over Israel after Yahweh cut covenant with it at Sinai. The message of the prophets is not, "Israel has sinned; therefore, Israel needs to get its act together or it will die." The message is, "Israel has sinned; therefore, Israel must die, and its only hope is to entrust itself to a God who will give it new life on the far side of death." Or even, "Israel has sinned; Israel is already dead. Cling to the God who raises the dead." This is precisely the prophetic message of 1–2 Kings, which systematically dismantles Israel's confidence in everything but the omnipotent mercy and patience of God.

The opening chapters of 1 Kings, for instance, highlight the wisdom of Solomon. Wisdom is the royal virtue par excellence (1 Kgs. 3:3–14; Prov. 4:7–9; 8:1–11), yet Solomon's wisdom does not prevent him from falling into sustained idolatry and leaving the Davidic kingdom disrupted and truncated (see the commentary on 1 Kgs. 11:1–43 and 12:1–24). After Solomon, wisdom simply disappears from 1–2 Kings. The words "wise" or "wisdom" occur twenty-one times in 1 Kgs. 1–11, but never again after those chapters. Never again does Israel or Judah have a philosopher-king, a sage on the throne. Royal wisdom, touted so heavily at the opening of the book, fails to deliver, showing that Israel's hope for restoration, blessing, and life does not lie in human wisdom, no matter what heights it attains.

The book of Kings can thus be fruitfully read as wisdom literature, albeit in a rather counterintuitive way. Proverbs describes wisdom as the way to life and prosperity: those devoted to Lady Wisdom are told that "riches and honor" as well as "enduring wealth and righteousness" come with her (8:18). According to Proverbs, there are stable patterns in the world, a moral cause-and-effect overseen by a just God, who rewards those who fear him. Yet, much of the wisdom literature of the Old Testament teaches an apparently contradictory message. Job is blameless in all his ways, yet suffers such excruciating loss that he concludes that Yahweh has abandoned him, and Ecclesiastes seems to directly challenge Proverbs with its recurring message that the wise and the foolish are both teetering toward the grave (Eccles. 2:14–16). Proverbs and Ecclesiastes are not contradictory, but rather highlight two poles of the biblical understanding of wisdom: if Proverbs teaches that Yahweh operates by a moral calculus, Ecclesiastes teaches that this calculus is as much beyond our grasp as Yahweh himself is, and as a result we experience the world as "vapor" (הֶבֶל, often mistranslated "vanity") that slips away when we try to understand or control it.

The book of Kings might be read as a historical endorsement of the viewpoint of Proverbs. Good and faithful kings achieve unbelievable wealth and notoriety (Solomon) and are miraculously delivered from enemies (Hezekiah) (2 Kgs. 18–19). Bad kings brace themselves for stinging rebukes from prophets, die randomly in battle (1 Kgs. 22:34–36), and are devoured by wild dogs and scavenging birds (14:11; 2 Kgs. 9:36–37). Though the judgment of the wicked is doubtless a strong theme in 1–2 Kings, the overall effect of the narrative is the opposite, closer to Ecclesiastes than to Proverbs. Wicked kings are delivered as frequently as righteous ones: Ahab defeats the Arameans twice (1 Kgs. 20) before falling to a "chance" Aramean arrow, and Ahab's son also defeats the Arameans twice (2 Kgs. 6–7). Wicked Jehoash of Israel trounces righteous Amaziah of Judah (14:8–14), and Yahweh leads Israel in triumph over Aram during the reigns of Jehoahaz and the equally wicked Jeroboam II (13:22–25; 14:23–27). The book of Kings, especially 1 Kgs. 1–11, narrates the limitations of royal wisdom, while the book as a whole demonstrates the wisdom of Ecclesiastes, a wisdom that finds history elusive, unfathomable, uncontrollable. In its treatment of wisdom, then, 1–2 Kings is prophetic literature, demonstrating that wisdom is essential yet ultimately ineffectual to secure the health and salvation of Israel.

The prophetic thrust of 1–2 Kings is also evident in its treatment of the Mosaic Torah. Deuteronomy 17:18–20 requires that the king of Israel keep the Torah before him "all the days of his life," and Josh. 1:8 promises conquest, prosperity, and success to Joshua if he is "careful to do according to all that is written" in the Torah. Especially if we read 1–2 Kings as part of a Deuteronomistic History, we would expect its kings to be responsive to Torah. Yet, the only king connected to Torah in 1–2 Kings is Josiah, and we are no sooner assured that he keeps Torah to perfection (2 Kgs. 23:25) than we learn that Yahweh still intends to destroy Judah: "However, the LORD did not turn from the fierceness of his great wrath with which his anger burned against Judah" (23:26). Throughout the history of Israel's monarchy, Torah is neglected and forgotten, and when it was finally recovered, even the most thorough obedience imaginable does not work. Once Israel sins, wisdom cannot save Israel and Judah; nor can Torah obedience. The curse still hangs over north and south: "Dying, you shall die."

First Kings 8 is a critical chapter in the book, recording the dedication ceremony for Solomon's temple in Jerusalem. The temple is an important addition not only to the daily life of Jerusalem and the liturgical life of Israel, but to the covenant arrangements between Yahweh and his people. By Solomon's assessment, the temple is a haven for Israel when it falls under judgment. As detailed in the commentary on 1 Kgs. 8:1–66, Solomon mentions many of the covenant curses listed in Deut. 28 and asks Yahweh to intervene to deliver from the curse when Israel turns to the temple in prayer. Solomon's temple serves as a mediator between Yahweh and his people, and Yahweh responds by promising that his eyes and heart will be in the temple to see and respond (1 Kgs. 9:3). After 1 Kgs. 9, however, the temple recedes from view, serving mainly as a source for gold and silver for Davidic kings to pay off invading Gentiles (15:18). Solomon's temple is a refuge for the young prince Joash, who later repairs its ruins (2 Kgs. 11–12), but no Davidic king ever prays in or toward the temple until Hezekiah is threatened by the Assyrians (19:1), and in the following generation Hezekiah's son, Manasseh, defiles the sanctuary more than any other king of Judah when he places a sacred pole for Asherah in the temple precincts. After a history of neglect and abuse, 2 Kings ends with an account of Nebuchadnezzar's destruction of the house (25:8–24).

Wisdom cannot save Israel from division; Torah cannot save Judah from destruction; and the last refuge of hope, the temple, is torn apart and burned by a Babylonian king. All that made Israel Israel—king and priest, Torah and temple—is destroyed. As prophetic narrative, 1–2 Kings makes it clear that there is no salvation for Israel from within Israel. Having broken covenant, it faces the curse of the covenant: in the day you eat, you will be driven from the garden. Dying, you shall die.

To end our consideration here, however, would do an injustice to 1–2 Kings and particularly to a Christian reading of 1–2 Kings. Ultimately, for a Christian reading, 1–2 Kings is prophetic because it points to, anticipates, and foreshadows the gospel of Jesus the Christ, and a Christian reading of 1–2 Kings must regard it not primarily as historical, prophetic, or sapiential but as evangelical.

The book of Kings is a gospel text in several respects. On the one hand, it reveals the God and Father of Jesus Christ, the God who is long-suffering and patient, who so loved the world that he gave his only begotten Son. This, to be sure, is not how the theology proper of 1–2 Kings is often read, and there is of course plenty of evidence that Yahweh of Israel is a God of righteous jealousy and wrath. From early in the history of the monarchy, the Lord warns that Israel and Judah have provoked him to anger with their idols (1 Kgs. 14:9, 15; 15:30; 16:2). After hearing the book of the law, Josiah knows that the Lord's wrath was "great" (2 Kgs. 22:13), and the narrator plunders the Hebrew vocabulary of wrath to describe the Lord's reasons for sending Judah into exile: "Yahweh did not turn from fierceness of his great wrath with which his anger burned against Judah" (23:26). Nebuchadnezzar's invasion comes about "through the anger of Yahweh" (24:20), and the fire that burns Jerusalem is not finally from Babylon but from the God who is a consuming fire. Dynasty after dynasty falls in the north, each fall more savage than the last (1 Kgs. 15:25–28; 16:8–14), and this history of failure comes to a crescendo with Jehu's obliteration of Ahab's family (2 Kgs. 9–10). Yahweh sends Elijah to unleash the Arameans against Israel (1 Kgs. 19:15–18), and the Arameans drive the residents of Samaria to cannibalism (2 Kgs. 6:24–31), burn fortresses, slaughter the young men, and rip open pregnant women (8:12). Superficially, 1–2 Kings seems to lend support to the Marcionite view that the God of Israel is a different God from the Father of Jesus; 1–2 Kings seems to reveal a petulant God of wrath, rather than the merciful God of the gospel.

In fact, 1–2 Kings as a whole puts the lie to Marcionite theology. Though 1–2 Kings reveals God's judgment against unfaithful Israel, the God revealed in this book is not peevish and vindictive, a God quick to fly off the handle. On the contrary, a careful reading of 1–2 Kings reveals a God who is always giving more than people ask, imagine, or deserve (1 Kgs. 3:10–14; 2 Kgs. 3:17–18; 4:8–17), a God of infinite, uncanny, unnerving patience.

As soon as Solomon finishes the temple, Yahweh appears in a dream to warn him that he has to remain faithful if he wants the temple to stand: "If you or your sons shall indeed turn away from following me and shall not keep my commandments and my statutes that I have set before you and shall go and serve other gods and worship them, then I will cut off Israel from the land that I have given them, and the house that I have consecrated for my name I will cast out of my sight" (1 Kgs. 9:6–7). Solomon turns from Yahweh and is infatuated with other gods (11:1–8), and Yahweh is provoked to anger (11:9). Yet the temple stands. Shishak of Egypt takes away pieces of it to Egypt (14:25–28), yet the temple stands. Judah's kings get worse and worse: the temple is neglected and plundered, and Ahaz replaces the altar of Moses with an altar of his own design and remodeled the temple furnishings (2 Kgs. 16:10–18); still the temple stands.

In the north, Jeroboam I no sooner erects his shrine to golden calves than a man of God from Judah confronts him, performs a predictive sign by splitting the altar, and warns that a king from the line of David, named Josiah, will rise in Judah to destroy the altar of Jeroboam (1 Kgs. 13:1–5, 32). We turn to 1 Kgs. 14, expecting a Davidic king named Josiah, but he is nowhere to be found. History continues decade after decade, and still no Josiah. By the time we finally get to Josiah (2 Kgs. 22–23), our minds are so numbed by the details of the chronicle that we have likely forgotten all about the prophecy of the man of God. Every king but Shallum (15:13–16) continues in the sins of Jeroboam son of Nebat, who caused Israel to sin, and yet no Josiah. If we are reading attentively, each reference to Jeroboam's calf shrine (and there are over sixty of them) reminds us that Yahweh threatened to destroy Bethel's sanctuary. And each time, we wonder: How can he let them get away with this? Where *is* Yahweh? Is there a God who judges in the earth?

Yahweh gives Elijah the commission to anoint three destroyers—Hazael of Aram, Jehu of Israel, and Elisha son of Shaphat—to carry out his judgment against Israel (1 Kgs. 19:15–18). The first two do not appear for ten chapters, and meanwhile Yahweh helps Ahab win several battles with the Arameans (1 Kgs. 20). Yahweh announces the final destruction of the house of Ahab (21:17–24), but relents and gives Ahab a reprieve when the king wears sackcloth and acts despondent. Yahweh threatens to destroy the house of Ahab in the reign of Ahab's son—but then Ahaziah son of Ahab dies in bed, and the dynasty continues to another son of Ahab (2 Kgs. 1).

The impression we get from 1–2 Kings is not that God is a stingy disciplinarian with an anger problem. If anything, the God of 1–2 Kings is irresponsibly indulgent toward his people, a God who does not seem to realize he cannot run the world without a dose of law and order. By the time Judah is sent into Babylonian exile in 2 Kgs. 25, we are not saying, "My, what a harsh God"; if we read attentively, we are saying, "It's about time! What took him so long?" The offense of the theology proper of 1–2 Kings is not that God is angry with the innocent. The offense is the offense of Jonah—the offense of God's mercy, the offense of Yahweh's unearthly patience with the irascible and unresponsive.

Yahweh's patience is especially evident in his treatment of the Davidic dynasty. As von Rad suggests (1953), the promise that David will have a perpetual dynasty in Israel (2 Sam. 7) forms an important part of the background to 1–2 Kings, and this theme is underscored by the structure of the book.[2] Structurally, 1–2 Kings is constructed as a series of embedded narratives, and the various narratives within the Chinese box of the book all have essentially the same shape. David-Solomon form an analogous pair to Omri-Ahab, and Jeroboam I shares certain biographical details with both David and Omri. The book of Kings also depicts the destruction of the Omride dynasty, Samaria, and Jerusalem as a triad of parallel events (see the commentary on 2 Kgs. 23:31–25:30). The Omride dynasty ends with a bloodbath and the destruction of the temple of Baal in Jerusalem (2 Kgs. 9–10); after the fall and deportation

2. For details, see the remainder of this commentary and Leithart 2005a.

of the northern kingdom, Josiah destroys the principal shrine of the north, Jeroboam's shrine at Bethel (23:15–20); and the Babylonians deport the people of Judah and Jerusalem and burn the temple of Solomon. Significantly, each of these destructive acts is immediately followed by a revival of the Davidic dynasty. The house of Ahab falls, and the devastation nearly engulfs the house of David (11:1), but Yahweh preserves Joash and places a son of David back on the throne (11:4–20). Assyria conquers the northern kingdom and its capital Samaria (17:1–6), and threatens Jerusalem (2 Kgs. 18–19), but just in time Yahweh sets the righteous king Hezekiah on the throne, through whose prayers Jerusalem is delivered. After Babylon takes Judah into exile, the final scene of 1–2 Kings shows Jehoiachin of Judah elevated from prison to a place at the table of the king of Babylon (2 Kgs. 25:27–29). The following chart provides a blueprint for the architecture of the book as a whole:

united kingdom	destruction of temple	fall of Judah → Davidic revival
Jeroboam I	destruction of Bethel	fall of Israel → Davidic revival
Omri	destruction of house of Baal	fall of Omrides → Davidic revival

When we view this structure through the lens of the prophetic perspective described above, we arrive at one of the most deeply evangelical perspectives on 1–2 Kings. David's sons sin, and they and their kingdom must die, but Yahweh does not allow death to have the final word. Though the Davidic kingdom is executed, Yahweh's promise to David remains. The book of Kings tells the story of the death and resurrection of David's dynasty, the death and resurrection of David's son.

In two senses, then, 1–2 Kings offers a justification of God that is brought to completion in the gospel. On the one hand, God's justice is shown in that he does not wink at sin forever. He will wait until the sins of the Amorites develop to maturity (Gen. 15:16), but he will not leave the guilty unpunished. On the other hand, 1–2 Kings shows that the reason for the apparent delay of justice lies in Yahweh's faithfulness to his covenant with Abraham, Isaac, Jacob, and David: his compassion is always just (2 Kgs. 13:22–25; 14:26–27). The book of Kings reveals the glory of Yahweh revealed to Moses on Sinai: "Yahweh, Yahweh God, compassionate and gracious, slow to anger, and abounding in loving-kindness and truth, who keeps loving-kindness for thousands, who forgives iniquity, transgression, and sin; yet he will by no means leave the guilty unpunished, visiting the iniquity of fathers on the children and on the grandchildren to the third and fourth generations" (Exod. 34:6–7). The book of Kings reveals the glory of Yahweh, which is incarnate in Jesus.

Even the critique of wisdom and Torah and temple is ultimately fulfilled in the gospel. What Paul sees in the history of Israel is already obvious to the deeply Pauline author of 1–2 Kings. Wisdom cannot preserve the Davidic dynasty, nor can Torah, nor can the temple. But what wisdom, what the law, what the temple cannot do, God has done in fulfillment of all his promises (Rom. 8:1–4). In the end, David lives only through his death, and David's kingdom is preserved only on the far side of the grave of exile. And while it demonstrates that royal wisdom fails, the book hints that Israel needs—and will get—a king who not only possesses but is wisdom. When it shows that perfect Torah obedience cannot undo centuries of flagrant unfaithfulness, it proclaims the promise of an incarnate Torah, whose Spirit will write the law on tablets of human hearts. When we see the temple reduced to smoldering ruins, we are encouraged to hope for a living temple, a temple in flesh, who gathers an Israel that is itself a living temple.

Israel's history is not only evangelical, but ecclesial, the history of the *people* of God. During the Reformation, 1–2 Kings was an important text for ecclesiological reflection (Radner 1998, chap. 1), with the divided Israel of 1–2 Kings serving as a figure of the divided Christendom of post-Reformation Europe. Of course, various readings of church history might arise from this narrative of 1–2 Kings. Catholics identify themselves with Judah and challenge Protestants for recalcitrantly refusing to submit to the See of Peter, as Israel refused to submit to the Davidic king. Catholics may charge Protestants with idolizing Scripture or the individual interpreter of Scripture. For their part, Protestants see Catholic venerations as a species of the sin of Jeroboam son of Nebat who caused Israel to sin and perhaps await a Josiah to tear down the calves and burn bones on the altars. On many issues, I side with Luther and Calvin, but this is not the place to recount my reasons, and in any case 1–2 Kings actually offers an alternate, far more sobering yet far more hopeful, perspective on the division and reunion of the church, one in which it becomes impossible and probably inappropriate to identify Israel and Judah with some segment of the post-Reformation Christian church. In place of partisan readings of 1–2 Kings, I wish to offer a reading that places the story of divided Christendom within an evangelical framework.

For starters, 1–2 Kings helpfully focuses the question of ecclesial division on the issue of idolatry. When the story of post-Reformation church history is told as if it were little more than a debate over the fine points of justification, the Reformation can seem to be motivated by a tedious form of theological precisionism. No one who has read a paragraph of Luther or Calvin would make that mistake, but their heirs have not always captured the breadth or the focus of the Reformers' proclamation. Luther and Calvin both protested the idolatry of late medieval Christianity, an idolatry that crept into synergistic soteriologies and flourished in a host of human-created devotional and liturgical practices. As Radner points out, for 1–2 Kings division was not the cause of eventual exile; rather, division was itself a punishment for a more fundamental apostasy (1998, 36–37). The book of Kings focuses ecumenical efforts on the central issue of idolatry and issues a warning that myriads of joint declarations on justification, important as they may be, fail to address the causes of ecclesiastical division.

The liturgical differences that divided Israel are not a matter of adiaphora. The idolatries of the north are a temptation for the southern kings, a temptation to which they eventually succumb, and the narrator explicitly and implicitly criticizes Davidic kings who participate in the idolatrous worship in the north, seek alliances with Israel's kings, or follow the ways of the kings of Israel. When Yahweh sends a man of God from Judah to confront Jeroboam I at his freshly built shrine in Bethel, he prohibits him from eating or drinking there and severely judges him when he disobeys (1 Kgs. 13). Jehoshaphat of Judah twice cooperates with kings of the Omride dynasty (1 Kgs. 22; 2 Kgs. 3), and both expeditions end badly (1 Kgs. 22:29–36; 2 Kgs. 3:27). Though the narrator generally approves of Jehoshaphat, he criticizes him for making peace with the king of Israel (1 Kgs. 22:44–45). Jehoshaphat's son marries the daughter of Ahab (2 Kgs. 8:16–19), one of several signs that Ahab is making a bid to reunite Israel under an Omride king, and this nearly destroys the Davidic line (9:26; 11:1–3). As long as Israel persists in idolatry, Judah's kings are wise to keep their distance.

Yet, it is clear throughout 1–2 Kings that both Israel and Judah, despite their multiple apostasies, continue to be objects of Yahweh's attention and care. Israel and Judah together, and Israel and Judah as separated nations, remain the people of God. This is the more obvious with regard to Judah, as Yahweh preserves a "lamp for David" through threat after threat (1 Kgs. 11:36; 15:4; 2 Kgs. 8:19), but it is also evident in Yahweh's patience and faithfulness to the north. A prophet intervenes to prohibit Rehoboam from attacking his "brothers" to the north (1 Kgs. 12:21–24), and the very fact that Yahweh continues to send prophets to call Israel's kings to repentance is a sign of his continuing mercy. Yahweh chooses and rejects dynasties, but he remains attentive to the people they rule, and late in the history of Israel, after generations of kings have committed the sins of Jeroboam I and after the Omride dynasty pledged allegiance to Baal and declared war on the prophets of Yahweh, Yahweh is still reluctant to abandon his people (2 Kgs. 13:22–25; 14:23–27), so deep is his affection for them and for their fathers. Yahweh considers this rebellious people his own, bound to him by covenant, and he shows mercy "because of his covenant with Abraham, Isaac, and Jacob" (13:23). Even though they are divided politically and liturgically, Yahweh views both Israel and Judah through the one lens of the covenant.

Not only does Yahweh continue to regard Israel as his people, but 1–2 Kings describes his program for restoring Israel to himself and reuniting the divided people of God. It is a paradoxical program in many ways. Yahweh's Spirit enters the divided kingdom and begins to restore it, counterintuitively, by dividing it again, as the Spirit's sword, the word of the prophets, separates husband from wife, brother from brother, mother from daughter, father from son. At the heart of 1–2 Kings is the lengthy narrative of the prophetic ministries of Elijah and Elisha, who not only challenge the idolatries of the Omride kings but lead a renewal movement in the north, the communities of the "sons of the prophets." Through Elijah and Elisha, Yahweh forms a community within Israel that does not kiss Baal (1 Kgs. 19:18) and enjoys life and fruitfulness by clinging to the prophet, the bearer of the presence and life of Yahweh.

As will be explained at length in the commentary on 1 Kgs. 17:1–24, it is misleading to describe these prophetic communities as a "remnant," and this title is especially misleading when the nation of Israel as a whole is displaced by a remnant, which is then viewed as "true Israel." The notion that the prophetic communities constitute the true Israel and the deduction that some particular ecclesial community in the contemporary church is the true church have powerfully supported sectarian ecclesiologies of withdrawal since the Reformation, among both Catholics and Protestants, but such an ecclesiology cannot be sustained by the narrative of 1–2 Kings.

Elijah and especially Elisha form an alternative community within Israel, which functions as an *ecclesiola in ecclesia* alongside the idolatrous national church of Israel. In the commentary on 2 Kgs. 4:1–44, I show that Elisha is a living temple of sorts, who offers the people of the northern kingdom what the temple provides in the south, and there are hints that the sons of the prophets function as a kind of alternative to the corrupted priesthood at the shrines of the Omride kings. Within the overall narrative of 1–2 Kings, however, this "free-church" dimension of the prophetic community is qualified by several factors. Contrary to some remnant ecclesiologies, Yahweh does not turn away from the palace to attend exclusively to the sons of the prophets. On the contrary, Elijah repeatedly confronts the Omride kings and calls them to repentance (1 Kgs. 18:16–19; 21:17–24; 2 Kgs. 1:1–16), and, though Elisha leads the sons of the prophets, he also, despite his evident disgust at idolatry, repeatedly advises and assists the Omride king Jehoram (3:13–20; 6:8–14; 7:1). Yahweh does not give up easily on the northern kingdom, and neither do his prophets. Further, the sons of the prophets disappear after 2 Kgs. 6, apart from the sole prophet who anoints Jehu (9:1–10), demonstrating that their renewal movement is no more an ultimate solution to Israel's fall into idolatry than was royal wisdom, Torah keeping, or the temple. When the Assyrians invade to destroy Samaria, they make no distinction between those who are faithful to the prophets and those who are not. Israel as a whole—sons of the prophets along with the sons of apostate nobles and kings—suffers exile together. As Israel is carried into exile, the members of the renewal movement are in many respects indistinguishable from the rest of Israel.

But not in all respects: those who listen to the prophets in Judah are equipped to resist the temptations and face the challenges of exile, surviving the Babylonian invasion by submitting to Nebuchadnezzar (as Jeremiah instructs), maintaining their identity and worship as the people of God, and refusing assimilation among the Gentiles. The Israel that Yahweh brings from exile is the remnant, the survivors, who survive not only physically but culturally and religiously; they survive *as Israel*. Elijah and Elisha prepare the way for this remnant Israel by preserving faith during a corrupt generation.

By preserving faith within the northern kingdom, the prophetic communities also preserve the hope for reunion. Brief moments of reunion of the kingdoms occur throughout the latter history of the divided kingdom. It is likely that the dynasty of Jehu reunited Israel and Judah after a fashion (see the commentary on 2 Kgs. 14:1–29), but the narrative of ecclesiastical division and reunion comes to a climax after the fall of Samaria in 722 BC. Though understated in 1–2 Kings, it is clear from the whole canonical witness that the Davidic kings reunite the kingdom in the waning days of Judah. According to the account of 2 Chr. 30, Hezekiah invites "all Israel from Beersheba even to Dan"—the author uses a merism that traditionally describes the limits of the united kingdom—to celebrate the Passover, and couriers are sent "throughout all Israel and Judah" with the invitation (30:5–6). Not everyone responds (30:10), but "some men of Asher, Manasseh, and Zebulun humbled themselves and came to Jerusalem" (30:11), and no doubt those who responded to Hezekiah's invitation maintained faithful worship of Yahweh by clinging to the communities of the sons of the prophets. The book of Kings ignores Hezekiah's Passover to enhance the achievements of Josiah, but Josiah's iconoclast reformation extends to Bethel and "all the cities of Samaria" (2 Kgs. 23:15–20), and 1–2 Kings strongly suggests that Josiah's Passover is an all-Israel celebration (2 Kgs. 23:21–23; cf. 2 Chr. 35:16–19).

Like everything else that Josiah attempts, his bid at reuniting Israel under a Davidic king is futile. Josiah reunites the kingdom just in time for Babylonian exile, and when Nebuchadnezzar besieges Jerusalem, he attacks the capital of an Israel that has lately been liturgically if not politically reunited. Neither Josiah's Torah observance nor his ecumenical efforts save Israel from exile. Josiah's effort to reunite Israel is as right as his dutiful but doomed adherence to Mosaic law, but Josiah is not to be the one to tie together the stick of Judah with the stick of Israel in an enduring unity; Yahweh is, and Israel and Judah go into exile with the promise of Ezekiel ringing in their ears: "Behold, I will take the stick of Joseph, which is in the hand of Ephraim, and the tribes of Israel, his companions; and I will put them with it, with the stick of Judah, and make them one stick, and they will be one in my hand. . . . And I will make them one nation in the land, and on the mountains of Israel; and one king will be king for all of them; and they will no longer be two nations, and they will no longer be divided into two kingdoms" (37:19, 22). When Israel returns to the land, they are a very different people from the people who are driven from the land. There is no king, and the second temple seems a pathetic replica of Solomon's (Hag. 2). But they are recognizably one people, known as "all Israel" or, more simply, as "Jews." The division of Judah and Israel no longer exists. The Passover gatherings of the faithful from north and south during the reigns of Hezekiah and Josiah are gatherings of the "remnant," those who remain in the land after the Assyrians destroy Samaria, and they anticipate the regathering of the remnant "all Israel" at the second temple following the exile (Ezra 10:5; Neh. 7:73).

The ecclesiology of 1–2 Kings is thus profoundly evangelical, and Israel's history of division becomes a figure of *sola gratia*.[3] Imitating the zeal of Josiah, Christians in a divided church must make every effort to reunite, but 1–2 Kings makes it clear that our hope for union does not lie in human efforts to unify. Ultimately, no matter how diligent and faithful the church's efforts are, only the Lord can tie together Rome with Wittenberg and Geneva, not to mention Constantinople and Moscow. Hope for reunion of the church is thus the same as the hope of the gospel. Hope for a future single body lies with the God who has committed himself by oath to bless all nations in Abraham's seed, who has promised to gather from every tribe, tongue, nation, and people to form a body where there is neither Jew nor Greek, neither slave nor free, and, surely, neither Presbyterian nor Methodist, neither Protestant nor Catholic. The hope for union for a divided church is in a God who always calls Israel back from exile, who always raises the dead.

---

3. Thanks to Rusty Reno for suggesting this formulation.

1 KINGS 1:1–53

In contemporary scholarship, 1 Kgs. 1–2 is often viewed as the conclusion of a "Succession Narrative" or "Court History" that begins in 2 Sam. 9 (e.g., Ackerman 1990). The continuity of these chapters with 2 Samuel is evident: 1 Kgs. 1–2 concludes the biography of David, the dominant character in 2 Samuel, and the characterization of David as an exhausted and impotent lame duck is consistent with the portrait of 2 Sam. 11–20, where David is acted upon rather than acting, a pale vestige of the robust ruddy youth of 1 Samuel. As reported in 1–2 Samuel, David's life follows the life story of Jacob (Leithart 2003d), and that typology continues into 1 Kgs. 1, as he bows like Jacob on his deathbed after making arrangements for the future (1:47; cf. Gen. 47:31). The links between 1 Kgs. 1 and 2 Sam. 11–12 are particularly strong. Between 2 Sam. 12 and 1 Kgs. 1, Bathsheba, Nathan the prophet, and Solomon are never mentioned, but in 1 Kgs. 1 they are all reunited one last time. David's adultery began with David in bed while his armies were fighting at Rabbah (2 Sam. 11:1–2), and near the end of his life David lies in bed with the beautiful Abishag while a succession crisis rages around him (1 Kgs. 1:1–4). In the aftermath of David's sin, Absalom challenged David's throne (2 Sam. 15), and in this new situation Adonijah, a new Absalom (1 Kgs. 1:5–6), challenges Solomon.

Canonically, however, 1 Kgs. 1 does not conclude the narrative of 1–2 Samuel but begins a new narrative. In this, 1–2 Kings differs markedly from other biblical and extrabiblical ancient literature. Genesis leads up to the death of Jacob, while Deuteronomy ends with the death of Moses, Joshua with the death of its title character, 1 Samuel with the death of Saul, and the *Iliad* with the death of Hector. Many of the beds mentioned in 1–2 Kings are deathbeds (1 Kgs. 17:19; 2 Kgs. 1:6; 4:32; 20:1–11), and the biographies of many of the kings end with the king being laid to "rest" with the fathers (1 Kgs. 2:10; 11:43; 14:20, 31; 15:8, 24). Other narratives *end* at a deathbed or a funeral pyre, but, remarkably, 1–2 Kings *begins* there, with Judah's great lion "old, advanced in age" (1 Kgs. 1:1; cf. Josh. 23:1). Does this foreshadow the eventual death of the Davidic monarchy and of Israel, thrown into the grave of exile? Is Israel, represented by the Davidic king, doomed to die even before the story begins? Or does 1–2 Kings *begin* at a deathbed to show that history moves on after death, to suggest a hope for resurrection?

Sick or injured kings and princes appear repeatedly in 1–2 Kings (Cohn 1985), symbolizing the sickness or weakness of the kingdom (Hobbs 1985, xxxvi) and highlighting the inseparability of private and public life. While 1 Kgs. 1:1–4 is the first such scene of this type, the language also suggests a more specific weakness in David in that several of the terms used in the opening verses are used elsewhere in the Old Testament with sexual connotations (Provan 1995, 27–28). Sexual potency is symbolically and actually connected with political potency, for an ancient king not only manifested his political virility by fathering sons but also needed an heir to ensure the continuity of his kingdom (Nelson 1987, 16; Walsh 1996, 5). David's servants find a beautiful woman to "warm" him, but his passivity with regard to Abishag foreshadows his lassitude in responding to the plot of Adonijah. The verb "know," first used with reference to sexual potency (1:4), echoes throughout the chapter, reminding us of all the things that David does not know.[1]

As David dallies with a beautiful maid, Adonijah initiates a political crisis. Following Absalom's death, Adonijah son of Haggith is the oldest remaining son (2 Sam. 3), and it is not unreasonable for him to expect to succeed David. Handsome like his half-brother Absalom (1 Kgs. 1:6; 2 Sam. 14:25), Adonijah follows Absalom's example by organizing a team of horses and fifty runners who surround him as he travels the streets of Jerusalem (1 Kgs. 1:5; 2 Sam. 15:1), an entourage that replicates Yahweh's glory-chariot, surrounded on four sides by myriads of living creatures (Ezek. 1). Adonijah campaigns, in short, as one for whom the title "son of Yahweh" (2 Sam. 7:14) is appropriate. He actively seeks the position, conferring repeatedly with Joab and Abiathar.[2] David's weakness leaves an opening for the ambitious son: even when Adonijah begins to organize his supporters, still David does nothing to "pain" him. Ironically, Adonijah means "Yah is master." In spite of his efforts to make himself master, Adonijah's life history demonstrates that Yah is indeed Master. Adonijah, an Adam figure, attempts to seize the forbidden fruit of the kingdom and is cast out as a result.

Adonijah begins his bid for the throne at a feast, and his guest list (1 Kgs. 1:9–10) is repeated several times in the chapter, so that the word "invite" or "call" (קרא) becomes a leitmotif. The people who were *not* invited are as

---

1. The verb ידע is used four times (1 Kgs. 1:4, 11, 18, 27), and in addition there are repeated references to Benaiah's father Jehoiada ("Yah knows"), whose name contains the same verb.

2. So Mulder 1998, 46, who takes this as implied by the plural "his words" (ויהיו דבריו) in 1 Kgs. 1:7.

important as those who were, and a neatly ordered chiasm in 1:9b–10 places the emphasis on the exclusion of Solomon, first mentioned in 1:10:

A and he *called* all his *brothers*, sons of the king
 B and to all the men of Judah, the servants of the king
 B′ but Nathan the prophet and Benaiah and the mighty men
A′ and Solomon his *brother* he did not *call*

Table companionship is a sign of political alliance, and a review of Adonijah's guest list indicates that his conflict with Solomon is a conflict between old and new. Adonijah, the pretender to the throne, is thoroughly a man of the old regime, choosing as his allies Joab and Abiathar, David's subordinates—not to say henchmen—throughout his reign. Solomon's allies are also men from David's past—Nathan the prophet, Benaiah, and Zadok—but of more recent vintage. The transition from David to Solomon is not only a transition from one king to another, but a shift in administration, the formation of a new regime (Provan 1995, 25; Walsh 1996, 8).

Adonijah has powerful allies, but he does not have access to David or his bedroom, and that private access is a key to political success. Nathan plans a response in cooperation with Bathsheba, offering to "save" her and her son (Mulder 1998, 53) and developing his plan in two stages to convince David with a "double witness." Bathsheba first goes to appeal to David, humbling herself as a "maidservant" and appealing to David not as her husband but as her "lord the king."[3] Nathan instructs Bathsheba to base her appeal on an earlier oath. Commentators sometimes suggest that this oath is fictitious (Nelson 1987, 20) and that David is fooled into a false memory (1 Kgs. 1:30). First Chronicles, however, records that David appoints Solomon while remaining on the throne (1 Chr. 23:1; 29:22). From the perspective of Chronicles, Adonijah is not attempting to fill a power vacuum but to overthrow a prince who already serves with David as crown prince. Bathsheba, whose name means "daughter of oath," reminds David of his promise and asks him to keep it. After Bathsheba leaves, Nathan is to enter the king's chambers to confirm her words.

To this point in the narrative, David has said only two words: מַה־לָּךְ ("what to you?") (1 Kgs. 1:16), a pun on מֶלֶךְ ("king") (Walsh 1996, 12), and the text emphasizes what he has *not* said (1:6, 27). In a scene that will be enacted elsewhere in Kings (e.g., 2 Kgs. 20:1–11), the prophet's intervention rouses a king from bed, and as soon as David speaks the direction of events begins to shift. His first word is "call" (קִרְאוּ־לִי) (1 Kgs. 1:28), and David's invitation answers and unravels Adonijah's, as David gathers those excluded from the feast of Adonijah: Bathsheba, and later Zadok, Nathan, and Benaiah (1:32).[4] He acknowledges his

---

3. This phrase recurs throughout the text, punning on Adonijah's name (Walsh 1996, 11).
4. This is the first time in the narrative that someone enters David's presence with his permission. Abishag was "caused to enter" David's presence, and Bathsheba and Nathan came

prior oath to give Solomon the kingdom and reinforces that oath with a second oath, a double oath in answer to the double witness of queen and prophet.

Private words are not enough. In a power struggle of this kind, ceremony has to be met with ceremony. David issues a public invitation to answer Adonijah's invitation (1:32) and instructs his servants concerning the coronation ceremony. Solomon rides on David's own mule, a sign that Solomon will sit in David's place (1:38). Riding an animal was a common ancient image of rule; just as a rider directs the powerful animal beneath him, so a king directs the nation. Mules are mixed-breed animals, and this perhaps points to Solomon's kingdom including Jews and Gentiles. As mixed-breed animals, further, mules are cherubic, reflecting the composite character of those creatures that draw the chariot of Yahweh (cherubim have four faces: ox, lion, eagle, human; Ezek. 1). Adonijah attempted to capture the high ground by presenting himself as "son of Yahweh," traveling in a glory-chariot, but in the end David designates Solomon as son of Yahweh, riding on a cherubic animal just as his divine father does. David directs his servants to take Solomon down to the spring of Gihon, immediately to the east of the city and the main source of water for the city of David (1 Kgs. 1:33). Both Adonijah and Solomon hold their coronation ceremonies in valleys, alongside springs, in quasi-Edenic settings (Gen. 2:13; Mulder 1998, 65). The narrator adopts virtually the same language as David's speech to describe the enactment of the ceremony (1 Kgs. 1:33–40), emphasizing that they fulfill the king's word to the letter.

David's instructions might suggest a private ceremony, but in 1:39 "all the people" suddenly appear.[5] Solomon is not made king in secret, installed on the throne by a few aged men, nor is his guest list, like Adonijah's, limited to "men of Judah" (1:9). Rather, "all the people" acclaim Solomon as king, as Zadok anoints him from a horn of oil kept in "the tent" (1:39). This could be a reference to the Mosaic tabernacle, housed in Gibeon (3:4), or the tent that David sets up in Jerusalem after bringing the ark into the capital city (2 Sam. 6:17). In either case, the oil comes from the tent of Yahweh and represents a heavenly anointing of the Spirit poured from above. As Solomon ascends in procession to the throne, the people are "fluting with flutes and rejoicing with great joy" (1 Kgs. 1:40). Like a greater son of David anointed by the Spirit of his Father (Matt. 21:1–11), Solomon's entrance into the city (riding on a mule!) is greeted with celebration. Solomon enters Jerusalem to be enthroned as the temple builder, while Jesus enters Jerusalem in order to preenact the temple's destruction (21:12–17).

The narrator follows the echoes of rejoicing down the Kidron Valley to En-rogel, where Adonijah and his compatriots are finishing their meal (1 Kgs.

---

in without invitation. But Bathsheba now "entered" at the king's call. Instead of bowing and prostrating herself, Bathsheba stood (replacing Abishag; 1:28 uses the same verb as 1:2), restored to her status as queen, to the bedroom of the king, and to her status as queen mother.

5. A procession from the city to Gihon led by Zadok, Nathan, and Benaiah, who leads the king's son riding on the king's mule—no doubt that spectacle attracted some attention from the citizens of Jerusalem.

1:41–48). Adonijah and Joab both hear the noise, the blast of eschatological doom from the shofar in particular, and are wondering at its meaning, when Jonathan son of Abiathar arrives. Jonathan's description provides the third account of Solomon's coronation ceremony, and Jonathan adds several details to the story, confirming Adonijah and his allies in their dread. By that time, Solomon's enthronement is an accomplished fact. Jonathan also reports the good wishes that David's servants bring to the king. Following Benaiah's lead, David's servants express their hope that Solomon's name and throne will surpass even his great father's. Jonathan recounts David's response, an act of worship, blessing God not only for putting a successor on his throne but for preserving him alive to see that successor. Adonijah's coronation dissolves. All the "called ones" of Adonijah disappear, slipping back to their homes, without attempting a counterattack. Each goes "to his way" (1:9).

In a terse series of clauses, the narrator describes Adonijah's flight to the horns of the Mosaic altar at Gibeon: he fears, he rises, he goes, he takes hold (1:50). According to the Torah, a murderer might be taken even from the horns of the altar to receive punishment (Exod. 21:14). But Solomon begins his reign with an act of clemency, promising that Adonijah will not suffer retribution, so long as he does nothing provocative. In response, Adonijah himself takes the position that Bathsheba, Nathan, and all David's servants are taking: he prostrates himself before Solomon. The man who attempted to "lift himself up" comes low.

As this book's ancient and modern names indicate (English: Kings; Septuagint: Βασιλειῶν; Masoretic Text: מלכים), 1–2 Kings concerns the political history of the kingdoms of Israel and Judah. It thus intersects with the concerns of the growing body of literature that goes under the heading "political theology." Much recent political theology, however, is conducted in the rarefied idiom that is second nature to academic theologians who have never been engaged in any political struggle more serious than annual departmental budget battles.[6] In her contribution to the *Blackwell Companion to Political Theology*, for instance, Tanner considers the political import of the Christian confession of the Trinity, arguing that theologians should not focus on modeling the Trinity in social and political life but rather on how participation in the Trinity shapes human relations: "Human relations, which remain fully human, only image the Trinity as they are joined up with its own life. Humans do not attain the heights of trinitarian relations by reproducing them, but by being incorporated into them as the very creatures they are" (2004, 329). Tanner's point is, in itself, perfectly unobjectionable, and her formulation highlights the ways that God's life enters into actual social history. But the precise impact of that "incarnation" of trinitarian relations on practical politics remains extremely vague.

---

6. Though I differ with the politics of the book at several levels, Cavanaugh's 1998 book is an outstanding exception to this generalization, in that Cavanaugh pays close attention to concrete particulars of political life.

When theologians attempt to do political theology "on the ground," they frequently adopt some variation of Niebuhrian realism, which attends to the specific concerns and actions of socially and politically situated persons. In particular, realists readily concede the necessity of coercion and conflict in political life. For Niebuhr, all political actors are servants of interest, and therefore justice cannot be achieved simply by persuasion. Battles are inescapable, and justice can be achieved only by the exercise of power (Niebuhr 1932, xv). As Milbank points out, however, Niebuhrian realism rests often on assumptions about the nature of reality that conflict with Christian convictions. Niebuhr supposes "that there is some neutral 'reality' to which Christians bring their insights." Christians, however, must assume that "the *entire* Christian narrative tells us how things truly are," and if this is true "we have no other access to how things truly are, nor any additional means of determining the question." In assuming, on the contrary, that reality can be empirically and neutrally assessed, Niebuhrian realists are too often betraying the entire Christian reading of history (Milbank 1997, 250). In short, "for the Christian, a realistic apprehension of the world does not consist in factual survey and surmise, but in an evaluative reading of its signs as *clues to ultimate meanings and causes*" (1997, 244 [emphasis original]).

Issues of political theology are invariably connected with the problems of historiography. Secular historiography, which necessarily treats all events as products of purely immanent factors and causes, cannot but yield a secular political theory, and if the church is to offer a theological account of politics it must also offer a theological historiography, which is to say, a doctrine of providence. Unfortunately, doctrines of providence, when developed at all in modern theology, manifest the same tendency toward generalization and abstraction found in political theology. Calvinists like the great nineteenth-century Princetonian Charles Hodge have no hesitation in saying that "God uses the nations with the absolute control that a man uses a rod or a staff. They are in his hands, and he employs them to accomplish his purposes" (1986, 1.588) or in insisting that even sinful acts "are so under the control of God that they can occur only by his permission and in execution of his purposes. He so guides them in the exercise of their wickedness that the particular forms of its manifestation are determined by his will" (589). Once those generalizations are made specific, however, they stick in the throats of all but the highest of the high Calvinists. Substitute "the Pol Pot regime" for "the nations," and theologians begin running for cover. Substitute "the abortionist's scalpel" for "them" in Hodge's final sentence, and few theologians will follow.

The Bible's own providential historiography is able to absorb these challenges. While Scripture teaches in various ways that God rules and overrules and orchestrates all things, even injustice and violence, for the good of his people and the world (e.g., Rom. 8:28), Scripture does not present his governance as an abstraction. A biblically grounded political theology will be a political theology from below. Trust in providence is not necessarily consoling but provokes the Lamentations of Jeremiah, the book of Job, and the prophet Habakkuk, as well as the assurance of Rom. 8. Recognition of providence evokes both anguish in the face of evil and exultation at Yahweh's triumph over evil. A scriptural historiography cannot be written in stoic calm; it must be written with sackcloth and ashes and with dancing and singing.

Such is the political theology and the theological historiography implicit in 1 Kgs. 1. The narrative is utterly realist in its unblinking depiction of conflict, interest, manipulation, and sexuality in political life, yet at the same time the author insists that Yahweh fulfills his purposes for Israel and the nations through these very strategies of *realpolitik*. For most of the chapter, Yahweh remains, as in Esther, the *Deus absconditus*. The only references to Yahweh are found in speeches from characters in the narrative (1:17, 29–30, 36–37), climaxing in 1:48, where David describes Solomon's accession to the throne as a gift of Yahweh. This last reference, reported by Jonathan, has been interpreted as cynical propaganda, as if David is giving a pious gloss to what is really nothing more than a sordid tale of court intrigue. But the author of 1–2 Kings is free of such cynicism and is able to see within the struggle for succession "clues to ultimate meanings and causes" (Milbank 1997, 244). For the author of 1–2 Kings, Yahweh really does employ the timely tactics of a shrewd court prophet, the rhetorical and sexual appeal of a queen, the democratic weight of an acclamation by "all the people" to place Solomon on the throne.

One of the important lacunae in much political theology is an inadequate account of the interplay of private and public life. Even at its most particular and refined, political theology is often forced by the limits of its sources to deal with the public surface of political life, which emerges from a hidden, impenetrable, and densely complex network of private circumstances, interests, influences, desires, and hopes. Because he works out political theology in narrative form, the author of 1–2 Kings displays a Shakespearean sense of the interplay of public and private, recognizing that great public events often arise from intimate and tenuous private concerns. Fittingly, 1 Kings begins indoors, initially in the intimacy of David's bed and bedroom, and then moves into the public space where kings are anointed and acclaimed. The key decision is made in secret, though things done in secret are finally proclaimed on the rooftops.[7]

Ultimately, this political narrative of a crisis transition from one regime to another foreshadows a greater transition from an old to a new regime. It foreshadows the coronation of David's still greater Son, a king sent to fulfill the Lord's oath to Israel, a king anointed not with oil but with the abundance of the Spirit, a king who rides into Jerusalem on a donkey to take his cruciform throne. Jesus's kingdom emerges, like Solomon's, from the midst of political conflict and self-interest in a world of sin, and his Father turns and overrules raging sinners and their vain plots to install Jesus as both Lord and Christ.

7. Beds and bedrooms play an important role in 1–2 Kings and frequently bring out the interplay of private and public; see, for instance, 1 Kgs. 17:19; 21:4; 2 Kgs. 1:4; 4:29–37.

1 KINGS 2:1–46

First Kings 2 consists of two sections, each is marked by multiple inclusions. The first section, 2:1–11, is bracketed by reference to David's immanent death and his "sleep with his fathers" (2:1, 10), as well as by the repetition of the word "days" (2:1, 11).[1] Within this frame is David's final speech to Solomon. The second major section (2:12–46) is enclosed by references to Solomon's rule as king (וַתִּכֹּן מַלְכֻתוֹ מְאֹד) (2:12) and the establishment of the kingdom (וְהַמַּמְלָכָה נָכוֹנָה בְּיַד־שְׁלֹמֹה) (2:46) as he fulfills the instructions of David.

David's charge to Solomon is one of several key farewell speeches in Scripture (e.g., John 13–17), but the closest analogy is Moses's speeches to Joshua. Moses encouraged Israel, Joshua especially, to be "strong and courageous" as it entered the land (Deut. 31:1–8), and Yahweh repeated this exhortation (Josh. 1:7–8). David says the same to Solomon. Hence: Moses is to Joshua as David is to Solomon. Solomon is a "new Joshua," who spends the early part of his reign wiping out the "Canaanites" that remain in David's kingdom, bringing "rest" to the land, and building a sanctuary for Yahweh, recapitulating the sequence of events in Joshua (which climax in Josh. 18:1). Because building the temple completes the conquest, replacing the Canaanite shrines with the house of Yahweh, that project in particular demands a Joshua-like strength, courage, and determination.

David's repetitive description of the law that Solomon must follow was, in some respects, boilerplate Deuteronomistic exhortation, but that David describes Torah in *seven* phrases (1 Kgs. 2:3) suggests a connection with the seven-day structure of the creation narrative. The Edenic allusion is strengthened by the verb "succeed" (שׂכל) (2:3), which is used in Gen. 3:6 to describe the

---

1. In the Hebrew, the opening verse reads "and the days drew near for David to die," while 2:11 begins with "the days that king David reigned over Israel."

power of the tree of knowledge to "make one wise" (cf. 1 Sam. 18:5, 14–15). Torah is a tree of knowledge to those who keep it, a tree that gives wisdom to discern between good and evil. If Solomon follows David's words he will, as a new Adam, establish a "new creation" in Israel.[2] As will be evident later (see the commentary on 2 Kgs. 17:1–41 and 22:1–23:30), Israel fails to keep Torah either in letter or spirit and is driven from the land as a result.

As noted above, this section is enclosed by references to Solomon (1 Kgs. 2:12, 46), the "throne of David" (2:12, 45), and the verb "establish" (כון) (2:12, 45–46). In addition to the three uses of this latter verb at the outer limits of the text, there is a fourth in 2:24. This fourfold repetition hints at the four corners of the earth or the four cornerstones of a house, indicating that Solomon's work sets the foundation stones of the "house of Israel." Elsewhere, the verb sometimes describes Yahweh's creative work: he establishes the heavens by wisdom (Prov. 3:19; Jer. 33:2), as the heavenly king of all creation (Ps. 93:1; 103:19); he establishes David's house as a new creation (Ps. 89:37), and human kings must strive to establish their thrones on righteousness (Prov. 16:12). Solomon imitates his heavenly Father in establishing his kingdom, and the fourfold establishment serves as another image of creation, indicating again that Yahweh places Solomon as a new Adam over a new world.

The transition from 1 Kgs. 2:4 to 2:5 occasions consternation among commentators, and many opt for the theory that 2:1–4 was interpolated to balance the negative portrayal of David in 2:5–9. First Kings 2:5 begins with a disjunctive particle and an emphatic pronoun, but unless we attribute an anachronistic degree of ironic detachment to the narrator (or redactor), we must conclude that he means 2:5–9 as a sequel to 2:1–4. Keeping the sevenfold Torah to establish the four corners of the world *as a king* means employing the sword against evildoers. The connection is not only evident from the sheer juxtaposition, but also from a conceptual link that binds the two sections together. The Edenic associations of "succeed" indicate that by coercively eliminating the violent from his kingdom, Solomon is acting as a true Adam, carrying out vengeance against Adonijah, who tried to become king at the "stone of the serpent" ("Zoheleth" in 1:9 means "slithering").[3] Strikingly, in the narrator's one great illustration of Solomon's wisdom in judgment, he pictures Solomon calling for a sword (3:24).

David knows that as Solomon takes the throne, the garden house of Israel is threatened by "satans" from the previous generation. First among these

---

2. Another striking thing about this list is the predominance of priestly terminology in an exhortation to a future king (Mulder 1998, 89). Through much of the list the implied imperative is "guard." Solomon is going to be a king, but like a priest he will have to do guard duty, preventing incursions on the "holy space" of the land or violations of the "holy word" of the Mosaic Torah. On priestly guarding, see Milgrom 1970.

3. Elsewhere, 1–2 Kings makes the same point from the opposite direction. A prophet denounces Ahab's *unwillingness* to employ the sword against an enemy: "Your life shall go for his life, and your people for his people" (1 Kgs. 20:42).

threats is Adonijah, who, satanically enough, attempts to seize the king's bride (2:13–18). Using Bathsheba as an intermediary, he asks Solomon for Abishag. Since Abishag was David's last bed partner, though David never "knew" her, she is undoubtedly part of the household that Solomon inherits from his father (2 Sam. 12:8), and Adonijah's request renews his efforts to lay claim on the kingdom (Walsh 1996, 50; Mulder 1998, 108). "Kingdom" (מלוכה) is feminine symbolically as well as grammatically, and during the succession crisis Israel acted, in Adonijah's account, like a lover torn between different suitors (1 Kgs. 2:15). The king is husband to his nation-bride, and the actual brides of the king represent the land and kingdom. Solomon certainly sees Adonijah's request as a renewal of his earlier plot (2:22), an effort to seize the "bride" of Israel that Solomon protects.[4] First Kings 2:24 includes some significant allusions to the Davidic covenant (2 Sam. 7), suggesting that Solomon's vow to put Adonijah to death is crucial for preserving what Yahweh has achieved, for preserving Solomon on his throne, and for preserving the house of David.

Solomon also perceives a connection between Adonijah's request and renewed efforts by David's old guard to regain control of the kingdom, and he immediately sets about protecting the house of David from Abiathar and Joab. Abiathar he treats gently, exiling him to Anathoth (1:26; cf. Jer. 1:1), using a verb used of the exodus from Egypt (Exod. 12:39), the exile of Adam and Eve from Eden (Gen. 3:24), and the dismissal of Cain from the land (4:14). Abiathar's banishment fulfills the threat that Yahweh made against the house of Eli the priest (1 Sam. 2–3), the first of many prophetic fulfillments in 1–2 Kings.

Joab, the last prominent member of the conspiracy, flees to the altar seeking sanctuary, as Adonijah did. When Joab refuses to come down from the altar, Solomon treats him as the murderer he is and takes him from the altar for execution (Exod. 21:14). David says that Joab is guilty because he "shed the blood of war in peace" (וישם דמי־מל חמה בשלם) (1 Kgs. 2:5). Normally blood is "poured out," but here the Hebrew translated "shed blood" uses the verb שים (normally translated "set" or "place"), and this usage is elsewhere found only in Deut. 22:8, which warns that accidents resulting from negligence will "bring bloodguilt upon the house" (תשים דמים בביתך) (Mulder 1998, 93–97, 119–20). When the author turns to describing Solomon's fulfillment of David's instructions, he uses language that again stresses the Mosaic justice of Solomon's actions. According to Solomon's assessment, Joab receives what he deserved: Solomon gives Benaiah the execution order, but it is Yahweh who "returned his blood on his own head" (והשיב יהוה את־דמו על־ראשו) (1 Kgs. 2:32).

4. Some commentators sentimentally psychologize the passage to suggest that Bathsheba is a born matchmaker or perhaps too naïve to understand the implications of what Adonijah requests. Neither of these is likely. Bathsheba proves a shrewd enough operator in 1 Kgs. 1, and the custom of inheriting the previous king's harem was too widely practiced for her to be ignorant of it. Given her cryptic response to Adonijah, she knows what she was doing. She does *not* say that she would speak to Solomon "on your behalf," but "about you" (Walsh 1996, 51).

The chiastic structure of Solomon's speech in 2:31–33 reinforces the connection between the execution of Joab and the cleansing of guilt from David's house, graphically displaying the "turning" that the text describes (Walsh 1996, 58):

A fall upon him and bury him to remove blood from me and my father's house
  B Yahweh returns blood on him
    C because he killed two better and more righteous men
      D David was ignorant
    C′ Abner and Amasa
  B′ blood will be on Joab and seed
A′ but to David and seed peace of Yahweh forever

Solomon's execution of Joab is a cleansing sacrifice that saves Solomon from the consequences of Joab's sins.

To Shimei, Solomon likewise declares that Yahweh "shall return your evil on your own head" (2:44). Shimei's offense was cursing David by calling down Saul's blood on his head, claiming that "Yahweh has returned upon you all the blood of the house of Saul" (השיב עליך יהוה כל דמי בית־שאול) (2 Sam. 16:8). In punishing Shimei, Solomon performs a double turning: the blood that Shimei hoped would turn on David is turned back on his head.[5] Solomon's execution of Shimei is an application of Mosaic justice. At the same time, Solomon demonstrates a knowledge of the "weightier matters" of Torah (Matt. 23:23) by giving Shimei a reprieve and placing him under house arrest. Shimei "stoned" David symbolically, but Solomon counts him as guilty of manslaughter rather than murder, confining him in Jerusalem as a "city of refuge" (Num. 35:9–34). When his slaves later flee to Achish, where David found refuge during his flight from Saul (1 Sam. 27), Shimei, a Benjamite relative of Saul, repeats Saul's pursuit of David by chasing his slaves into Philistine territory (1 Kgs. 2:39–40). Saul's house comes to an end in the "third year" (2:39), the year of transition, judgment, and resurrection, and Saul's house disappears from history in an event that recapitulates Saul's persecution of the anointed David (Ackerman 1990, 54). Solomon plays the role of the avenger of blood, and as soon as Shimei leaves the city, he carries out the execution (2:41–45).

Solomon imitates the creator Yahweh in "establishing" his political world, but he does it through a violent application of Mosaic justice. Deadly violence is a part of the "creative" act of establishing Israel as a "garden land," flowing with milk and honey, just as Joshua's earlier violence against the Canaanites established Israel in the land. Under the influence of feminist critiques of atonement theories that imply that the Father is an abusive parent, Anabaptist theologians

---

5. Though generally taking a negative view of Solomon's actions in 1 Kgs. 2, Walsh recognizes (1996, 64) that Shimei's execution is justified by an appeal to the *lex talionis*.

who make nonviolence programmatic to their entire theology, and postmodern philosophy, much recent theology blanches at texts of this sort. Wink (1998) entirely rejects what he describes as "redemptive violence," and theologian Weaver attempts to construct a nonviolent conception of the atonement. In place of the supposedly violent and ahistorical satisfaction theory of Anselm and others, which deletes the devil from the atonement, as well as theories that reduce Jesus to a passive victim of injustice, Weaver outlines a "narrative Christus Victor" version of the atonement. Drawing on the Gospels and Revelation, Weaver insists that the reign of God is on earth and yet both "make quite clear that the triumph occurred not through the sword and military might but nonviolently, through death and resurrection." The battle imagery of Revelation refers to a "confrontation" between Christ and Satan that "was not an actual battle waged in the cosmos," but rather "events of the first century in the world that we live in." Jesus is no passive victim, but "an activist, whose mission was to make the rule of God visible" and whose embodiment of the rule of God was so threatening to the violent powers that they killed him (Weaver 2001).

Examined in the light of postmodern analyses that revel in unmasking the dagger in every smile, however, Weaver's nonviolent atonement appears naïve and arbitrary. On the one hand, he defines violence flexibly enough to include not only "overt violence (exercised in war and in capital punishment)" but also "systemic violence (such as racism, sexism, and poverty)" (2001). Yet, on the other hand, somehow Jesus's confrontation with the powers of the world remains nonviolent. Violence in the end seems to mean little more than "action of which Weaver disapproves." As Boersma argues, "violence need not necessarily be physical," and he charges that "insistence on absolute nonviolence is often based on an arbitrary understanding of violence as something physical, so that we are willing to accept our involvement in other forms of coercion and force that often are no less invasive" (2004, 44).

Christian theology cannot, however, accept the analysis of violence offered by postmodern thinkers such as Emmanuel Levinas and Jacques Derrida. For Derrida, violence is a pervasive evil. All efforts to judge or classify the "other" constitute violence against individual uniqueness, and love and justice require absolute openness, unconditional acceptance. Yet, absolute openness is an impossible ideal. Derrida knows that all social and cultural orders classify, and by his theory they all contain the seeds of violence as a result (Boersma 2004, 28–39). Human beings are inevitably locked within a violent order that can at best only be ameliorated, usually by acts of counterviolence. As Milbank (1990b) and Hart (2003) powerfully argue, this postmodern analysis of violence depends on an "ontology of violence" similar to the pagan myths of Mesopotamia and Greece. Ancient myths depict a world of ultimate conflict, whether between various petty deities or between metaphysical principles of order and chaos. In the creation mythologies of Babylon or Hesiod, creation itself is an act of violence, the ruling God triumphing over rivals through cunning or castration or both. By contrast, Christianity confesses that the transcendent source of all things is a perfectly loving, perfectly peaceful communion of Father, Son, and Spirit and that creation came into being through a peaceful act of giving through speech.

Yet, 1–2 Kings and other portions of Scripture endorse violence in certain settings, and, as Boersma argues, there is an ineradicable element of violence in the atonement. For Scripture, though violence is an intrusion in an originally peaceful world, violence may be redemptive. In our current postlapsarian and preeschatological condition, violence is not only (at times) a necessary evil but also (at times) a positive good. First Kings 2 gives a particularly important gloss on this claim by showing that in the postlapsarian and preeschatological world, violence is necessary for establishing the conditions of social flourishing that the Bible describes as "peace." Violent execution of justice is one of the means for establishing conditions of the new creation. As Boersma puts it, "God's hospitality requires violence, just as his love necessitates wrath," and "divine violence . . . is a way in which God strives toward an eschatological situation of pure hospitality" (2004, 49). As 1 Kgs. 2 makes clear, violence (like wrath) is not God's monopoly. Solomon serves as a "minister of wrath" (Rom. 13:4) to establish an Israel that is a preview of the continual rejoicing and pure hospitality of the eschaton (1 Kgs. 4–5). Yet, the violent establishment of Solomon is but a faint shadow of the greater Solomon, who establishes a new creation first of all by suffering violence rather than deploying it.[6]

Most of 1 Kgs. 2 recounts the "establishment" of Solomon's kingdom, which can be done only by eliminating the enemies of the kingdom. But what is he protecting? What is the kingdom that he establishes? In the midst of encouraging his son to deal vigorously with old enemies, David tells Solomon to reward Barzillai the Gileadite, who fed David when he fled Jerusalem during the rebellion of Absalom (2 Sam. 17:27–29) (Provan 1995, 35). Barzillai blessed the Lord's anointed, the true Abrahamic seed, and receives a blessing. He fed David, and so his sons are fed. This provides a clue to the goal of Solomon's violent justice. Executing enemies is obviously not the ultimately aim of political action, nor is it designed merely to establish power and exercise control and maintain a degree of decent order. Enemies must be removed in order to open up space for a table; fear must be eliminated in order to give place to joy; the boundaries of the kingdom must be secured so that the people of the kingdom can eat and drink and rejoice before the Lord. Solomon executes the enemies of the kingdom so that the friends of the kingdom can eat and drink in security, peace, and joy. For Solomon as for Jesus, the table is the heart of the kingdom.

---

6. But a Christ who does *no* violence, a Christ who *only* suffers violence, is not the Christ of the New Testament. Solomon and Jehu (see the commentary on 2 Kgs. 9:1–10:36) are types of Christ as much as the Suffering Servant is, and the Christ of Revelation is no passive victim of violence (Rev. 19:11–21).

1 KINGS 3:1–28

Near the beginning of the *Summa theologiae* (1920, part I Q. 1 art. 6), Thomas Aquinas asks whether sacred doctrine is wisdom. The question has an intricate history. Though the distinction of *scientia* and *sapientia* is found in ancient philosophical texts, Augustine offers the most important theological treatment. Augustine describes *scientia* as rational knowledge concerning history and experience, which plays a role in theology because theology has to do with the historical events of the Christian story (1998, 13.24). The knowledge of *sapientia*, by contrast, aspires to delight in God and can be defined as piety, worship, or love (14.1; 12.22). As Charry, one of the most articulate contemporary defenders of "sapiential" theology, notes, the distinction "comes down to a distinction between the knowledge of faith and the wisdom of love, and the greater of these is love." The whole point of pursuing "scientific" knowledge is to ascent to love of God, to *sapientia*: "Together the knowledge and love of God constitute proper Christian piety" (1993, 94).

By the time of Thomas Aquinas, the Augustinian distinction in union of *scientia* and *sapientia* was disrupted, and Thomas's conception of sacred doctrine as a form of wisdom depends more on Aristotle than Augustine, and he explicitly cites Aristotle's *Metaphysics* in discussing the sapiential character of Christian doctrine (Thomas Aquinas 1920, part I Q. 1 art. 6). Aristotle explains the difference between knowledge and wisdom as the difference between knowledge of effects and knowledge of causes (*Metaphysics* 1.1), and sacred doctrine is a form of wisdom because it penetrates from effects to underlying causes. A wise person is able "to arrange and to judge" and is wise in a particular sphere when he or she "considers the highest principle in that order." In the order of building, the architect is wise, while the laborers who cut wood and stone possess a lesser kind of knowledge, and in the order of ethics a person is wise who knows how to direct his or her actions toward a "fitting end." Sacred doctrine considers the cause and end of all things, which is God, and therefore the student of sacred doctrine is most wise, not wise in only one particular order but wise "absolutely" (Thomas Aquinas 1920, part I Q. 1 art. 6).[1]

In large part, the historical discussions miss the point of biblical wisdom. Augustine assumes something like a Platonic epistemological dualism of sensible and intelligible that rests on the metaphysical dualism between the world of forms and the world of experience, while Thomas's conception, though preferable in many ways, remains too intellectualist to capture the biblical conception. In Scripture, wisdom is often more closely associated with the skill of the woodcutter than with the ecstasies of the mystic. The Hebrew word for wisdom (חכמה) often means "artistic skill" (Exod. 28:3; 31:3; 35:31; 1 Kgs. 7:14), and even where the reference is not directly to art, the esthetic and practical dimension is not left behind. A furniture maker displays wisdom in craftsmanship, not only by knowing "causes" but by excellence in the sheer physical activity of the craft. A musician displays wisdom in making music, a parent in training and guiding children. There is a craft or art to these endeavors, and overall Proverbs is a book of instruction concerning skillful living, teaching how to construct a life that is attractive, fitting, and beautiful. Jesus, the incarnate wisdom, is wisdom in just this sense, the one who embodies, as Nicolas of Cusa said, the art of the Father, the craftsman who shapes the raw and ruined matter of this world into the kingdom of God, the teacher who instructs his disciples how to build well (Matt. 7:24–27).

First Kings 3 is one of the great biblical treatments of wisdom and sets wisdom firmly in this practical—and in this case political—context. Yet, the chapter appears to begin ominously, with Solomon committing what some see as a breach of Deuteronomic law. Solomon "became son-in-law to Pharaoh" (ויתחתן שלמה את־פרעה), in apparent violation of Deut. 7:3, which forbade the Israelites to "become sons-in-law" to Canaanites (ולא תתחתן). By becoming Pharaoh's son-in-law, it is argued, Solomon effectively puts himself in a subordinate position to the Egyptian king, reversing the exodus (Walsh 1996, 70). Yet (contra Provan 1995, 44–45), the suggestion that his marriage is sinful is undercut when we are immediately told that he "loved Yahweh" (1 Kgs. 3:3). This stands in contrast to the judgment of 11:1–8, where Solomon loves foreign women who turn his heart from Yahweh. The author is hardly an uncritical admirer of Solomon, but he does not criticize the king for his marriage to Pharaoh's daughter (3:2). Solomon's marriage to Pharaoh's daughter instead fulfills the Abrahamic promise to bless the nations. Yet, that Solomon later commits himself to multiply sinful marriages hints that the complete fulfillment of this promise awaits a new covenant, a covenant of the spirit and not of the letter. Solomon's marriage to Pharaoh's daughter points to Jesus,

---

1. For further discussion, see Marshall 2005.

who, like Solomon, covenants with a bride from the nations, but who, unlike Solomon, remains faithful to his Father.[2]

First Kings 3 is dominated by Solomon's request for wisdom, recounted in 3:4–15, a section framed by references to two shrines where Solomon worships Yahweh: in Gibeon at the Mosaic tabernacle and in Jerusalem before the Davidic shrine for the ark. Solomon's movement from one to the other is a second enthronement, as he ascends from the old Mosaic system to the new capital of Jerusalem. In Jerusalem, Solomon becomes the first man in the Old Testament to *stand* before the ark (3:15). Once he receives wisdom, Solomon has a standing before the ark/throne of Yahweh, as royal servant ready to "stand and serve" Yahweh, as Solomon's servants "stand and serve" before him.

Typical of Yahweh's revelations to kings, he appears to Solomon in a dream, the first of two recorded dreams (see also 9:2). Yahweh invites Solomon to choose a gift, and Solomon's request is set out in a parallel sequence (Walsh 1996, 74):

A   Yahweh's kindness to David (3:6a)
  B   David's faithfulness (3:6b)
    C   Yahweh gave David a son (3:6c)
A′ Solomon king in place of David (3:7a)
  B′ Solomon's inexperience and youth (3:7b–8)
    C′ give a hearing heart (3:9)

Framing this structure are two references to "heart": David's "uprightness of heart" (3:6)[3] and Solomon's request for a "hearing" or "listening" heart (לב שמע) (3:9). The heart of Solomon's concern with wisdom is the state of his heart (Walsh 1996, 73). Genuine wisdom is not only cunning or the slick ability to get one's way, but arises from a heart directed to Yahweh and to his ways. It is no accident that Solomon's eventual fall occurs when his heart goes awry (11:4).

Solomon asks for wisdom, more specifically for "discernment of good and evil" (להבין בין־טוב לרע) (3:9), using a phrase similar to that found in Gen. 2–3 to describe the tree in the garden (עץ הדעת טוב ורע), a tree that gives wisdom (Deurloo 1989, 12). Solomon's request can thus be described as a request for access to the tree forbidden to Adam. Like Adam, Solomon goes into "deep sleep" in order to receive a bride, but Solomon awakes in the

---

2. The reference to Solomon's worship at the high places (1 Kgs. 3:3) is also seen as a criticism. Yet, when Solomon worships at the "great high place" at Gibeon (3:4), Yahweh appears to him and offers wisdom. During the early part of Solomon's reign, when the central sanctuary is not functioning, high places such as Gibeon are tolerated. As soon as Solomon receives the wisdom necessary to build the temple, however, he moves to the ark-shrine in Jerusalem and never returns to Gibeon.

3. Perhaps all three descriptions of David's faithfulness are modified by "of heart." That is, David not only shows uprightness of heart, but also "truth and righteousness" of heart.

company of Lady Wisdom. As in 1 Kgs. 2, Solomon is a new and improved Adam. In asking for wisdom to "judge" (3:9), Solomon seeks the skill to rule well; he wants to be a royal Bezalel (Exod. 31:2–5) so that his nation will, like the tabernacle, become a place of glory. Carried out with wisdom, politics is a craft, the product of which is social harmony and beauty. Yahweh's promise to add to Solomon all the things he does not request (1 Kgs. 3:10–14) no doubt inspires Solomon's teaching in Proverbs, where he emphasizes that wisdom is the chief thing to seek and that honor, riches, and supremacy come through pursuit of wisdom (e.g., Prov. 8:12–21). Yahweh, as Paul writes, gives abundantly beyond what we can ask or imagine (Eph. 3:20). He is the giving God.

Solomon demonstrates the wisdom that Yahweh gives in his judgment of the prostitutes (1 Kgs. 3:16–28). At one level, this is a straightforward story demonstrating Solomon's uncanny ability to unravel a judicial riddle: he is Solomon Holmes, Hercule ben David. But the passage is too unusual in style and too rich in typological resonance to leave it at that. Nowhere in the story is Solomon named (Walsh 1996, 78). He is always "the king" (הַמֶּלֶךְ, which is used ten times in 3:16–28), and the women are identified only as nameless "prostitutes" (3:16) or, more frequently, "women" (seven times in the passage). English translations identify the women as "the first" and "the other" (3:22), but the Hebrew leaves them indistinguishable: Solomon summarizes the argument of "this" and of "this" (3:23). The characters take on archetypal dimensions, and the two rival women become indistinguishable "mimetic rivals" for the living child.[4]

Much of the story is dialogue, and repetitive dialogue at that. The women are not only indistinguishable, but their testimony quite literally goes in circles. First Kings 3:22 is chiastically arranged (Nelson 1987, 38; Walsh 1996, 81), and in the following verse Solomon repeats the two claims in reverse order. Solomon's verdict is another quotation: the mother says, "Give her the living child, and by no means kill him" (3:26); and Solomon responds with almost identical words: "Give her the living child, and by no means kill him" (3:27). Armed with divine wisdom, he cuts through the repetitive testimony and countertestimony, demonstrating that Yahweh gave him a new, "hearing" heart (3:9), a heart attuned to the confession of the Shema ("Hear, O Israel") (Deut. 6:4). Solomon's wisdom is not "outside law," yet neither is it a simple application of a rule. Unlike Adam, who took the fruit from his wife, Solomon listens to the women with discernment and judges rightly. Even more, Solomon enacts a judgment that exposes the hearts of the two women, showing his divine ability to "distinguish good and evil." The genuine mother responds with "compassion" or, more colorfully "wombliness" (רַחֲמֶיהָ, related to "womb").[5]

4. This passage is a classic case of the phenomenon often described by Girard.
5. The sequence of 3:26 makes it appear that the mother speaks first and then the false mother. This would indeed be an alarming turn of events: the two women are disputing custody

In its context in 1–2 Kings, the story is similar in important respects to the events recorded in 1 Kgs. 1–2:

1 Kings 1–2	1 Kings 3
two mothers: Haggith and Bathsheba	two mothers
two sons: Adonijah and Solomon	two sons
Bathsheba pleads for life of child	mother pleads for child
Bathsheba pleads for Adonijah, who dies	one mother accepts death of a son
Adonijah dies	one son dies
Solomon rescued from threat	son rescued from threat
David passes judgment in favor of Bathsheba	Solomon passes judgment

Solomon enacts the cunning divine wisdom that gives him the throne over the rival, Adonijah. No wonder Israel "saw that the wisdom of God was with him" (1 Kgs. 3:28).

Further, the story told by the prostitutes has an eerie resemblance to Passover. The exchange of sons takes place at night, as does Passover (Exod. 12:29), and as at Passover one male child dies while another is delivered. This suggests that the false mother is Egypt, a Pharaoh-like woman who smothers her own children and then seeks to toss Israelite children into the Nile. Endowed with Yahweh's wisdom, the king comes with a sword to kill, as the angel of Yahweh frees the sons of the Israelites, under threat from Pharaoh. Passover is itself a reenactment of the Aqedah, the binding of Isaac (Gen. 22), and 1 Kgs. 3 is redolent with allusions to that story as well. Both the true mother and the false are willing to "sacrifice" the living son, but the true mother "sacrifices" the son in order to save him while the other sacrifices to destroy. Through his test, Solomon discerns which woman is the true Israelite, the true daughter of Abraham, who, like Abraham, gives up her child in faith to save him. Following Abraham's offer of Isaac, Gen. 22:17 records Yahweh's first promise to multiply Israel like the sand on the sea. A similar sequence appears in 1 Kgs. 3–4: a prostitute acts like an Abraham by giving up her own son, and in the following chapter we read that Israel became "as numerous as the sand that is on the seashore" (4:20), the first time that this phrase is applied to Israel as it actually exists (rather than as a promise of what it would be).

Harlots and harlotry are mentioned elsewhere in 1–2 Kings only in connection with the idolatries of Ahab (1 Kgs. 22:38; 2 Kgs. 9:22), and the image of unfaithful Israel as a prostitute is common in prophetic tradition (Hos. 1–3; Jer. 3; Ezek. 16), most spectacularly in Ezekiel's allegory of the twin harlots, Jerusalem and Samaria (Ezek. 23). Two prostitutes represent the two portions of the divided kingdom, struggling over claims to the seed. Harlot Israel, like

---

of the living child, and the real mother concedes her claim to her rival. And, *at the very moment she's won*, the false mother callously calls on Solomon to kill the child. For the sake of realism, we should understand the women's responses to be simultaneous. But the sequence is intriguing and truly renders the false mother's envious motivations.

Egypt, kills its children, but there will always remain a bride who will protect the seed (2 Kgs. 11:1–3). That Solomon chooses between two women reminds us of Proverbs, where the prince must choose between wisdom and folly, both depicted as women (though only folly is a prostitute).

First Kings 3:18 refers to the "third day," suggesting a connection with other third-day events in the Bible, particularly the resurrection of Jesus. This also relates to the theme of the "replacement son" already introduced in 1 Kgs. 1 and very common in Genesis. Looking toward the New Testament, the two competing mothers anticipate the two mothers of Gal. 4, the wives of Abraham who represent the old Judaism and the new Israel attached to Jesus. When the first Israel, the Israel of the flesh, has died, only those who seek the living child, the child of the Spirit, the child delivered from death on the third day, are saved.

1 KINGS 4:1–5:18

As noted above, 1 Kgs. 2 begins with a Solomon-Joshua typology. David urges Solomon to be "strong and courageous" and to follow the law of Moses (2:2–3), just as Moses urged Joshua to be strong and courageous in the invasion of Canaan (Deut. 31:6–7, 23; Josh. 1:6). As Joshua's spies stayed with the prostitute Rahab, so Solomon passes judgment in the case of the two prostitutes. Joshua led Israel in the conquest of Jericho and Ai, while Solomon rules the kings west of the Euphrates River (1 Kgs. 4:21). Solomon divides the land into administrative districts (4:7–19), as Joshua earlier divided the land into tribal areas (Josh. 13–21). The Gentile Gibeonites tricked Joshua into forming an alliance with them (Josh. 9), and Hiram of Tyre, a Gentile ruler, forms an alliance with Solomon (1 Kgs. 5). Between these two events, Israel never cuts covenant with Gentiles. Solomon tells Hiram the land is at "rest" (ועתה הניח יהוה) (5:4), a condition that Joshua achieved by defeating Canaanites in the north and south (Josh. 11:23). At the climax of his conquests, Joshua set up the tabernacle at Shiloh (18:1), and the high point of Solomon's reign comes with the building of the temple (1 Kgs. 6–7).

Joshua led Israel into a land flowing with milk and honey, a land with abundant food, and this too is brought to greater fulfillment in Solomon's reign. The structure of 1 Kgs. 4 centers on the rich provision of Solomon's table:

> A   Solomon's officials and deputies (4:1–19)
> 　B   Judah and Israel eat, drink, and rejoice (4:20)
> 　　C   Solomon rules over the kingdoms from the River to Egypt (4:21)
> 　　　D   provisions of Solomon's table (4:22–23)
> 　　C′   Solomon rules over everything west of the River (4:24)
> 　B′   Judah and Israel are living in safety (4:25)
> A′   deputies provide for Solomon's household (4:26–28)

Solomon's reign not only fulfills the promise of Joshua's conquest, but also demonstrates Yahweh's faithfulness to his promises to Abraham. Under Solomon,

Israel's life is a utopia of peace, harmony, safety, and joy. Israel finally becomes as numerous as the sand on the seashore (4:20; cf. Gen. 22:17), a description that between Abraham and Solomon is applied only to Israel's enemies, false Israels (Josh. 11:4; Judg. 7:12; 1 Sam. 13:5; 2 Sam. 17:11). The phrase "like sand on the seashore" is repeated in 1 Kgs. 4:29, where it describes Solomon's breadth of "heart." The king has a "hearing heart" (3:9), a heart of wisdom broad enough to rule a people that cannot be counted. Solomon's kingdom stretches between the waters of the Mediterranean and the waters of the Euphrates, north to Dan and south to Beersheba (4:25; cf. Gen. 15:18), spreading to the four corners of the earth. Moreover, the kings who rule in the territory of Solomon become tributary states, bringing their glories to Solomon (1 Kgs. 4:21; cf. Rev. 21:24). Under Solomon, Israel becomes the head and not the tail (Deut. 28:13).

Behind these analogies, 1 Kgs. 4 shows again that Solomon is also a greater Adam. Beyond Adam, he eats from the tree of wisdom and demonstrates his wisdom by organizing the kingdom, in his relations with Hiram of Tyre, and in building the temple (Exod. 31:3). All these displays of wisdom bring him glory beyond the glory of any kings of his time, a partial restoration of the bright radiance of Eden. In 1 Kgs. 4:21, the narrator uses מושל ("ruled"), while in 4:24 the verb is רדה ("have dominion"). The former puns on the word for "proverb" or "riddle" (משל) in 4:32 and highlights that Solomon has dominion over this empire through wisdom, the same wisdom that enables him to speak proverbs and untie riddles. The latter verb is used in Gen. 1:26 to describe Adam's commission in the world. By "having dominion" over the nations surrounding Israel, Solomon fulfills the Adamic mandate to rule and subdue the earth. Consistent with this portrait, Solomon's knowledge of the natural world encompasses all created categories of living things: beasts, birds, creepers, and fish (1 Kgs. 4:33: cf. Gen. 2:19–20). Israel is called to be an Adamic race, and Solomon is the chief exemplar of that calling, the greater Adamic man, who reigns over an Adamic race, countless as the stars and sand.

For much of the Christian theological tradition, the image of God has been understood as a quality of individual human beings primarily or exclusively located in the soul. For Thomas Aquinas, "the image of God belongs to the mind only," and the "image" evident in human beings is distinct from the "trace" of godlikeness found in the rest of the creation. As image, humanity represents God "by likeness in species," while a trace merely "represents something by way of an effect," as a footprint is a trace of an animal. Rational creatures are like God in species in that they not only participate in life and being "but also in intelligence," while "other creatures do not understand, although we observe in them a certain trace of the Intellect that created them, if we consider their disposition." Further, human beings reflect the triune processions of word and love: "In rational creatures . . . we find a procession of the word in the intellect, and a procession of the love in the will," and this forms a "certain representation of the species" of the Trinity (Thomas Aquinas 1920, part I Q. 93 art. 6).

Calvin claims that the image of God has its "proper seat" in the soul. Though acknowledging that "the outward form" of human beings "in so far as it distinguishes and separates us from brute animals, at the same time more closely joins us to God," yet "the image of God, which is seen or glows in these outward marks, is spiritual." Calvin reasons backward from the New Testament's teaching about the restoration of the image of God to explain the substance of the *imago*. Citing Col. 3:10 and Eph. 4:24, he concludes: "In the first place [Paul] posits knowledge, then pure righteousness and holiness. From this we infer that, to begin with, God's image was visible in the light of the mind, in the uprightness of the heart, and in the soundness of all the parts" (Calvin 1960, 1.15.3–4). Calvin explicitly rejects the traditional Augustinian notion that the image consists in the imprint of the Trinity on the soul that participates in triune life, as well as the suggestion that the image consists of human dominion over the animals. Rather, "whereas God's image is properly to be sought within him, not outside him, indeed, it is an inner good of the soul" (1.15.4). Calvin does not explain or defend the force of this statement, and his insistence that the image is located within humans rather than in relation perhaps provides grounds for seeing continuity between Calvin and the "self-present subject" of Descartes. For Calvin, humans are fully the image of God standing alone in a barren landscape. Imaging God is at best tangentially related to one's engagement with the world or even engagement with other human beings.

Few today would find Calvin's treatment of the image adequate either to the biblical evidence or human experience, and for that dissatisfaction Barth is largely responsible. Barth recovers the Augustinian insight that humanity images a Triune God and gives it a fresh twist. Being the image, Barth argues, means that "in God's own sphere and being, there exists a divine and therefore self-grounded prototype to which this being [i.e., humanity] can correspond." Within God there is an I-Thou, "a genuine but harmonious self-encounter and self-discovery; a free co-existence and co-operation; an open confrontation and reciprocity." Humanity is "the repetition of this divine form of life; its copy and reflection." Only in humanity does God create a "true counterpart to God," a counterpart that can enter into a personal I-Thou relationship with him (Barth 1939–69, 3.1.183–87).

Within the context of Gen. 1, the God imaged by the "image of God" is the God whose creative speech is recounted in the creation narrative. When the creator makes a creature in his image and likeness, he forms a creature who speaks and creates as well. Humans are made in the image of the Triune God insofar as they are created for relationship with God and with one another and insofar as they recapitulate the creative work of Yahweh, his word, and Spirit. Human beings are not images of God apart from relationship with God and with other humans or apart from their embedded lordship over the creation. In speech and creative *poiesis*, human beings image the eternally creative God who is word. Solomon is image of the creator God in his rule over Israel, his wise proverbial speech, his scientific study of animals, and the creative impulse of his poetry and songs.

Solomon's administration of the kingdom is also described to emphasize that he is the image of Yahweh. First Kings 4:1–19 describes Solomon's administrative of the kingdom, both his cabinet (4:1–6) and the regional administrators who supply the court (4:7–19). The men listed in 4:1–6 are described as "officials," "captains," or "chiefs." The wider usage of the term (1 Chr. 24:3; Dan. 10:20; 12:1) suggests analogies between Solomon's household, the "house" of Yahweh and its servant-priests, and the heavenly council, where Yahweh sits enthroned, surrounded by myriads of heavenly beings (1 Kgs. 22:19). Solomon's house is overseen by "priests" (כהנים), just like Yahweh's (4:2, 4, 5). The second list includes twelve names, a numerical allusion to the tribal structures of Israel's earlier history. Each official is in charge of a district that supplies food to Solomon's table one month of the year.[1] Solomon's organization does not suppress but enhances Israel's flourishing and joy: the dry list of administrators is followed immediately by the assertion that Israel and Judah are "eating, drinking, and rejoicing" (4:20). The sequence "eating, drinking, and rejoicing" is typically associated with the activities of the central sanctuary and of worship (Deut. 12:7, 18; 14:26; 27:7). Even before the construction of the temple, the whole land turns into a forecourt for the Yahweh's house, a place of feasting. Solomon's judicial and administrative wisdom finds its *telos* in joy, the joy of a table.

Solomon rules a sizable empire of tributary kingdoms.[2] The "river" of 1 Kgs. 4:21 is the Euphrates (Josh. 24:15; 2 Sam. 8:3), and Solomon's power extends as far as the "border of Egypt." Gentiles are incorporated, albeit at a distance, into the life of the new Adamic race. The narrator lists seven animals that are eaten daily at Solomon's table: oxen, pasture-fed oxen, sheep, deer, gazelles, roebucks, and "fowls of the feed trough" (1 Kgs. 4:23). The numerology hints again at a creation theme: the sevenfold creation is given to Solomon as food, as it was originally given to Adam as food (Gen. 1:29–30). Solomon's menu includes meat that is not part of Israel's sacrificial feasting. Sacrificial animals represent Israel, while clean wild animals symbolize Gentile "God-fearers" (Jordan 1990b, 18–23). As Gentile nations are incorporated into the body of Solomon's kingdom, so "Gentile" animals are incorporated into his physical body. Those who "come to Solomon's table" (1 Kgs. 4:27) include visitors to whom Solomon extends hospitality. Solomon's table, like Yahweh's, is open to all, and Solomon is a new Joseph, offering bread to hungry nations. The Gentiles eat the crumbs that fall from his table, and this typifies the greater Solomon who sets up a table in the center of the world, one so abundant that it feeds humanity.

Glory is not a zero-sum game. Because the wise new Adam sits on the throne, the entire kingdom basks in his riches. Solomon has his own wondrous table and

---

1. It is doubtful that these districts exactly match the tribal areas of the former Israel. Even if they do, more than half of the districts are identified otherwise, mostly by the major cities in the districts. Solomon redistricts the land so that it functions as a twelve-state monarchy rather than a tribal amphictyony.

2. "Tribute" here translates מנחה, the normal word for "grain offering" (Lev. 2). Solomon, like his father Yahweh, receives the "worship" of the nations of the earth.

garden of plenty, but each Israelite too has their own Edenic vineyard and orchard (4:25). Vine and fig tree are associated with Israel, especially during its Solomonic splendor (Mic. 4:4; Zech. 3:10), and when the prophets mourn the withering of the vine and the fig tree they are lamenting Israel's fall from the glories of Solomon (Isa. 34:4; Jer. 5:17; 8:13; cf. the ironic temptation of Isa. 36:16).

First Kings 4:29 begins a new section, organized as a chiasm:

> A   Solomon's wisdom (4:29–34)
> > B   Hiram sends servants to Solomon (5:1)
> > > C   Solomon's message to Hiram (5:2–6)
> > B′   Hiram's response to Solomon (5:7–11)
> A′ Solomon's wisdom (5:12)

The section begins with a sevenfold description of the wisdom of Solomon and ends with another statement about Solomon's wisdom. Within this inclusio, the narrator describes Solomon's wisdom in his diplomatic relations with Hiram of Tyre. Solomon enlists the aid of Gentiles to build the house of Yahweh, a sign that the temple from its beginning is a "house of prayer for all nations." Solomon again plays an Adamic role, moving out from the "Eden" of Israel to gather goods from the outlying lands, as Adam is to spread out from the garden to gather riches and goods to glorify the garden dwelling of Yahweh in Eden (Jordan 1988a, 147–48). Gentiles join Israel in building a temple that connects heaven and earth, the true tower of Babel that unites the scattered nations.[3]

3. By Walsh's account (1996, 96–99), Hiram's letter to Solomon is a cunning and successful effort to change the terms of the deal. Instead of allowing Solomon's servants to work alongside Hiram's in Lebanon, Hiram offers to float the wood down to Israel by sea, and instead of allowing Solomon to pay his workers their wages, thus implicitly claiming them as his employees, Hiram asks that Solomon supply his court. Walsh's interpretation is overly subtle. According to 5:14–15, Solomon's servants work in Lebanon, presumably alongside Hiram's servants, just as Solomon had originally proposed. To sustain his interpretation, Walsh has to resort to saying that a compromise is reached. It is simpler to conclude that Hiram's terms are never so radically opposed to Solomon's as Walsh imagines. Further, Walsh is forced to take 5:12 as a deeply sarcastic comment on Solomon's wisdom. But that is hard to sustain, given the undiluted enthusiasm that the narrator has shown for Solomon's wisdom up to this point and given that the result of the exchange is peace and a covenant of brothers between Israel and Tyre. Hiram's response to Solomon suggests some changes in the specifics of Solomon's proposal, but all of them are advantageous to Solomon. In response to a request for cedar, Hiram offers cedar and cypress (5:8); in response to a request that Solomon's servants come to Lebanon to work, Hiram offers to bring the wood down to Solomon (5:9), taking over responsibility for transport that would otherwise have fallen to Solomon. The narrator indicates that Hiram fulfills Solomon's desire (5:10), so that it is clear he is not displeased with the deal. Hiram offers to do what Solomon desires (5:8) in the hopes that Solomon will do him pleasure in return (5:9). This is underhanded only to the cynical, for to the cynical all things are cynical. On the face of it, however, this is simply the way that honest people do business, each party seeking benefit. What is striking is that Hiram pursues the pleasure and benefit of Solomon, rather than seeking only his own. This is the way that godly people do business.

1 KINGS 6:1–38; 7:13–51

Solomon dispenses justice like a god and administers a small empire with skill, but his greatest work is building a house for the name of Yahweh.[1] The same is true for the greater Solomon, Jesus, who builds his church on the rock of confessing Peter and promises that the gates of hell will not prevail against it (Matt. 16:17–18). In theological terms, the central chapters of the Solomon narrative, which recount the building of the temple, center on ecclesiology.

In the opening pages of his classic *Images of the Church in the New Testament*, Minear suggests that the New Testament manifests "a way of thinking dominated by pictures, analogies, and images" and that each image of the church is the product of "communal imagination" that is "deeper than the images." In the

---

1. Frisch (1991) shows that the Solomon narratives are structured to focus attention on the temple:

    A the beginning of Solomon's reign (1:1–2:46)
      B Solomon and the Lord, loyalty and reward (3:1–15)
        C the glory of Solomon: wisdom, rule, riches, and honor (3:16–4:34)
          D toward the building of the temple: Hiram (5:1–18)
            E the building and dedication of the temple (6:1–9:9)
          D′ in the wake of the temple: Hiram (9:10–25)
        C′ the glory of Solomon: trade, riches, wisdom, and honor (9:26–10:29)
      B′ Solomon and the Lord: disloyalty and punishment (11:1–13)
    A′ the end of Solomon's reign (11:14–12:24)

Frisch's outline runs contrary to scholarly consensus by including 1 Kgs. 12 as part of the Solomonic storyline, but this, I suggest below, is a very illuminating conclusion. He highlights the structural centrality of the temple texts, but shows that the temple texts extend further than is usually recognized. Solomon's intention to build a house for Yahweh is first announced in 5:5, as Solomon enlists Hiram's assistance. Solomon deals with Hiram again in 9:10–14, so that the Tyrean king's appearances form an inclusio around the temple texts. Frisch describes 9:1–9 as the Lord's response to Solomon's dedication prayer and notes the similarities of that text with 6:11–13. The final statement of the temple's completion does not occur until 9:25. The temple is the central concern of 1 Kgs. 5–9.

modern church, by contrast, biblical images are difficult to recover because the images do not come naturally, and any attempt to explain the meaning of an image is inherently counterproductive, a sign that "*rigor mortis* has set in, and that full rapport between the eye and the picture has been lost" (2004, 16–18; cf. Dulles 1987). Modern thought, including modern theology, distinguishes between figurative and nonfigurative expressions, and "we assume that clarity in thought and expression demand that we discriminate sharply between the two. But this demand is quite absent from the New Testament." New Testament writers use words in both figurative and literal senses and often fail to explain which they mean in any particular context. In some cases (Minear cites the example of "sonship"), the figurative meanings virtually displace the nonfigurative (2004, 18).

It is thus a mistake for modern interpreters to begin their consideration of scriptural images by disentangling the figurative from the literal meanings. For instance, "the word 'temple' . . . may refer to a specific building located in one place and one time, and, simultaneously, to the divine-human traffic that takes place there," but "the building does not become a temple apart from the actualities of that traffic, nor can that traffic be wholly separated from a particular assembly of men at a specific place." Instead of attempting to separate literal and metaphorical, Minear argues that "it is wise to expect that vital figures of speech will have a more literal referent than is at first apparent and that apparently literal terms will have a larger cargo of figurative meanings" (2004, 19–20).

Not only is it often impossible to separate the literal and figurative meanings, but Scripture often makes it impossible to distinguish images neatly from one another. When Paul talks about the "body of Christ" growing up into its "head" (Eph. 4:12, 15), he has conflated images impossibly, but such conflations are not original with Paul. The temple of Solomon has multiple dimensions of significance, none of which could be isolated as the basic meaning of temple. When we attempt to move from the temple imagery into ecclesiology, we should make every effort to leave these layers of meaning undisturbed. A temple ecclesiology brings into play a host of other associations that inhere in the concept of temple.

Sacred architecture is one of the Bible's chief idioms for revealing the character of the church. Long passages of the Torah, the historical texts, and the prophetic literature describe, in sometimes numbing detail, the features of the various sanctuaries of Israel (Exod. 25–40; 1 Kgs. 6–8; 2 Chr. 1–7; Ezek. 40–48). These are doubly daunting for Christian readers, first, because Christian architects no longer use these biblical blueprints and, second, because many of the details of these descriptions are obscure, employing various *hapax legomena* or giving unfamiliar connotations to familiar terms. Few if any of Israel's sanctuaries could be constructed architecturally from the biblical record. But that is not the point. These biblical sanctuaries are all verbal sanctuaries, and these texts are given to the church not to enable it to rebuild a temple but to edify—the construct—the body of Christ.

In many respects, the temple and tabernacle all share the same multiple dimensions of meaning and symbolism,[2] but the temple is no restoration of the tabernacle. It is a permanent building rather than a tent, suitable for a period when Israel settles in the land and rests from its enemies (1 Kgs. 5:4; Deut. 12:10). The terminology used for the temple, further, differs from the terminology used for the tabernacle. The three areas of the tabernacle were the courtyard, holy place, and most holy place. Only once in 1 Kgs. 6 is the phrase "holy of holies" or "most holy place" used (6:16), and there is no reference to a courtyard until 6:36, which obscurely describes an "inner court." In place of the tabernacle terminology, 1 Kgs. 6 describes three sections of the temple, using the words הָאוּלָם ("porch") (6:3), הֵיכַל ("nave" or "palace") (6:3), and דְּבִיר ("inner sanctuary") (6:23).

The temple is far larger than the tabernacle. The tabernacle was 10 cubits x 30 cubits, but the temple is 60 cubits long, 20 cubits wide, and 30 cubits high. In the tabernacle, the most holy place was a cube 10 cubits on each side, but the "inner sanctuary" of the temple is 20 cubits on a side (6:20). Solomon covers much of the interior of the temple, including the floor, with gold (6:20–22, 28, 30, 32), a significant upgrade from the curtain walls and dust floor of the tabernacle. The tabernacle was glorious, but Solomon builds a more glorious house. With the building of the temple, Israel moves from glory to greater glory. In this way, Solomon's temple reaches toward the resurrection. While in the fleshly body, we are in tents, but we long to cast off these temporary vestments in order to be clothed with the permanent house of the resurrection body, the body/house of which the Spirit is a pledge and down payment (2 Cor. 5:1–10).

One feature of the literary arrangement of 1 Kgs. 6–7 is important. First Kings 6:1 says that Solomon begins building the house of Yahweh in his fourth year, and 7:51 announces, with a pun on Solomon's name, that Solomon "finished all the work" (וַתִּשְׁלַם כָּל־הַמְּלָאכָה). Hence, the building of Yahweh's house covers both chapters. Within these two chapters, however, the narrator also includes information about Solomon's palace, the "house of the forest of Lebanon," the hall of the throne, the hall of judgment, and a house for Pharaoh's daughter (7:1–12). Solomon, as Yahweh's son (2 Sam. 7:14), builds his house next door to his heavenly Father's. During the period of the monarchy, Yahweh's house extended to the palace of the king and other public buildings of the monarchy, as later, after the exile, Yahweh's house expands to encompass the entire city of Jerusalem (Jer. 3:16–17; Ezek. 40–48).

What does the temple mean? Many things. Israel's sanctuaries are houses for Yahweh, palaces of the divine king of Israel. Throughout 1 Kgs. 6, the word for "temple" is "house" (הַבַּיִת), and the large room of the temple is called a "palace" (הֵיכַל) (Ezra 4:14). Solomon's temple thus fulfills Yahweh's promise

---

2. Much of the following is inspired by Jordan 1988a, chaps. 15–16.

to "dwell in the midst of the sons of Israel" (1 Kgs. 6:13). The book of Kings, like Deuteronomy, says that the "name" of Yahweh—rather than Yahweh himself—dwells in the house (1 Kgs. 5:5). This terminology might represent an acknowledgement of the transcendence of God, who cannot be confined to houses built by human hands (8:27), but from a Christian perspective "name" takes on a heightened significance. The name is both identified with and distinguished from Yahweh himself, a hint of differentiation within the being of God unfolded in the gospel of Jesus. "Name" identifies the mode of Yahweh's presence in the temple, and the same name now dwells in Jesus and with those who dwell with him.

Sanctuaries are also architectural recapitulations of the garden of Eden. In Solomon's temple, the interior of the house is covered with wood, and the walls carved with fruits, vegetables, and flowers (6:14–18), while cherubim guard the inner sanctuary of the temple (6:23–28), as they guarded the return route to Eden (Gen. 3:24). This Edenic theme is reinforced by the verb "finish" (כלה), used multiple times in 1 Kgs. 6–7 (6:9, 14, 38; 7:1, 40) and alluding to the creation narrative (ויכלו השמים והארץ) (Gen. 2:1) and the tabernacle texts of Exod. 40:33 (ויכל משה את־המלאכה). Tabernacle and temple are both "world models," and Moses and Solomon are "creators" who imitate the divine creator.

The monumental pillars Jachin and Boaz are a prominent Edenic symbol (1 Kgs. 7:15–22).[3] Stationed at the doorway, they resemble cherubim, guardians of the holy place, and, like the temple itself, contain garden motifs—a lily-shaped capital and pomegranates. Pomegranates, along with figs, symbolize the fruitfulness of the Edenic land of Canaan (Num. 13:23; 20:5; Deut. 8:8), and Solomon refers to pomegranates and lilies in the Song of Songs as adornments of a love garden (pomegranates in 4:3, 13; 6:7, 11; 7:12; 8:2; lilies in 2:1–2, 16; 4:5; 5:13; 6:2–3; 7:2). The giant bronze lilies, adorned with pomegranates, identify the temple as the "trysting place" for Yahweh and his bride.[4]

Eden is a "well-watered" place (Gen. 13:10), and the temple is full of water. There is a basin of water in the courtyard of Moses's tabernacle (Exod. 30:17–21), but the amount of water is small compared to the water in the temple. The Bible's use of water imagery is extensive and complex. In creating the world,

---

3. For more detailed discussion, see Jordan 1988b.

4. Pillars are symbolic of people (Ps. 144:12; Isa. 19:10), and the association with human beings is strengthened by their names (1 Kgs. 7:21): Boaz is an ancestral name in the Davidic line (Ruth 4), and Jachin means "he will establish," pointing to the establishing function of the priesthood in Israel. The link between pillar and priest is strengthened by details of the pillar construction. The high priest has pomegranates at the end of his robe (Exod. 28:33), and there are pomegranates on the capitals of the pillars (1 Kgs. 7:18). The high priest wears chains around his neck, holding the breastplate to the ephod (Exod. 28:14; 39:15), and there are networks of chains around the base of the capital of each pillar. The pillars are a vertical representation of the temple itself, just as the priestly garments themselves are. There are chains around the capital of the pillar (1 Kgs. 7:17) and at the entrance into the most holy place (6:21).

Yahweh separates waters above the firmament and waters below the firmament (Gen. 1:6–8) and divides the lower waters from land to make the sea (1:9–13). Waters from above are heavenly waters coming from God, while waters below often represent dangerous waters of death (though the flood represents a partial exception to this symbolism; cf. 7:11). Water is also for cleansing (e.g., Lev. 15) and, especially in the form of rivers, serves as a boundary. Israel crosses out of Egypt into the wilderness through the Red Sea and crosses from the wilderness to the land through the Jordan. The sea is frequently a symbol of the Gentile nations in the Old Testament, surrounding and threatening the solid ground of the promised land (Ps. 46; Jonah 1–2).

Much of this symbolism is evident in the temple. Because the water in the bronze sea is lifted up from the ground, it represents the heavenly sea stretching out before the throne of God (Rev. 4–5), who is enthroned above the cherubim in the "inner sanctum." The sea itself is a "firmament" standing between the worshipers below and the waters above, and the twelve bulls holding the sea obviously represent Israel, particularly in its priestly capacity (Lev. 4:3; cf. Ps. 22:12). Israel has a global ministry, stretching to the four corners of the earth, symbolized by the bulls who face toward each point of the compass (1 Kgs. 7:25). Israel is "Atlas," with the sky resting on its shoulders. Since the sea is particularly associated with the Gentile nations, the sea also symbolizes the arrangement of the political world under the old covenant. Contrary to all appearance, the restless sea of Gentiles is supported by the obscure priestly nation living on a small seaside corner of the world.

In addition to the bronze sea, Hiram of Tyre makes ten water stands or "chariots" for the temple (7:27–39), an architectural depiction of water flowing out of the temple. The stands are arranged in two lines stretching eastward from the face of the temple toward the entrance to the court, five on each side. They form a gauntlet, a water passage, so that anyone approaching the house of the Lord relives the crossing of the Red Sea, journeying toward Yahweh's presence on Sinai (in the temple), as well as passing through the Jordan, entering the garden land symbolized by the temple. Living water is not confined to the temple courts, but flows to the corners of the earth, just as water goes out from Eden (Gen. 2:10–14; cf. Ezek. 47). Israel's temple is the source of living water for the nations.

Sanctuaries are architectural "holy mountains," as Eden itself was. The tabernacle became what Sarna (1986) calls a "portable Sinai" when the glory cloud that had been on top of the mountain rested in the most holy place (Exod. 40:34–38). With Solomon's temple, the building itself is built in pyramid shape, a stylized mountain.[5] By alluding to the exodus (1 Kgs. 6:1), the narrator makes the connection of exodus and temple explicit, implying that

---

5. This is evident from the side chambers, which get wider as they go higher (1 Kgs. 6:5–6), and this can be the case only if it gets narrower. See Wiseman 1993, 108.

Yahweh's purpose in the exodus is to bring Israel out to serve him in the land promised to Abraham at the "new Sinai" in Jerusalem.[6]

Solomon's temple has a "face" (עַל־פְּנֵי הֵיכָל) (6:3), "ribs" (צְלָעוֹת) (6:5, 8), and "shoulders" (כָּתֵף) (7:39). It is an architectural "body," and this metaphorical relation between body and building is pervasive in the Song of Songs. That the temple is equipped with "ribs" particularly suggests that the temple building is analogous to the creation of Eve in Gen. 2, "built" (בנה) from Adam's rib (2:21–22). The temple/body is specifically a bridal body: Yahweh the husband of Israel dwells in the temple as a man lives in his bride. This is the flow of redemptive history: Yahweh "builds" a woman for Adam, and Solomon, a new Adam, builds a bride for Yahweh.[7]

Much of 1 Kgs. 7 is taken up with lists of bronze utensils used in the temple service (7:40–47) and the gold furnishings and utensils (7:48–50). The bronze utensils are used in the courtyard, and the gold within the temple proper. Thus, the materials of the utensils match the gradation of holiness in the temple; the less holy courtyard is furnished with the less valuable and glorious bronze, while the holy temple is adorned with gold. These temple utensils picture the people of Israel, each gifted in a unique way to contribute to the service of God. Paul says that the church too is a "body with many members," and he can equally describe the church as a "house with many utensils" (2 Tim. 2:20). Those who are shovels in the temple of God should shovel with all their might; those who are snuffers should snuff to the glory of God; the basins and the bowls devote themselves wholly to God's service.

A temple ecclesiology is simultaneously an Eden ecclesiology, a holy mountain ecclesiology, a body and bride ecclesiology. The church is Eden because in Christ it is the place well watered with the Spirit poured from heaven at Pentecost, the source for living waters that flow to the corners of the earth (John 7:37).

6. Reference to the "second month" (1 Kgs. 6:1) suggests another typology. Twice in the flood narratives, events happen in the "second month" (Gen. 7:11; 8:14). Nor is this the only allusion to the flood narrative in 1 Kgs. 6. The dimensions given in 6:3 use standard terms for width and length, but both of these are found in Gen. 6:15, which describes Noah's construction of the ark. In 1 Kgs. 6:4, the word "window" alludes to the window of the ark through which Noah receives the dove (Gen. 8:6). Solomon has already noted to Hiram that he reigns over "Noachic" conditions (1 Kgs. 5:4), and now he begins to build an ark that will provide shelter to all nations in the house of prayer.

7. First Kings 7:46–47 informs us that the casting for the bronze furnishings and tools of the temple worship was done in the "plain of the Jordan between Succoth and Zarethan." As Yahweh makes Adam outside the garden and brings him in (Gen. 2:7–8), so Solomon, imitating Yahweh, makes bronze items outside the garden land and outside the area of the garden house and brings them across the river. This association is hinted at by two verbal echoes of the creation account. Solomon casts the bronze items in the clay of the ground (הָאֲדָמָה בְּמַעֲבֵה), just as Adam is made from and takes his name from the "ground" (הָאֲדָמָה). Further, 1 Kgs. 7:47 says that Solomon "left all the utensils unweighed" (New American Standard Bible), but the Hebrew actually says "Solomon caused to rest all the instruments" (וַיַּנַּח שְׁלֹמֹה אֶת־כָּל־הַכֵּלִים), alluding to the rest that God gave Adam when he first placed him in the garden (וַיַּנִּחֵהוּ בְגַן־עֵדֶן) (Gen. 2:15).

The church is the true holy mountain, where the Spirit is present in cloud and fire, where the living word of the Lord is heard in thunder, where we can draw near to stand face to face with the glory of the Lord and be transformed into an image of that glory, where we ascend to joy with the joyful assembly of saints and martyrs around the throne of God (Heb. 12:22–24). The church is the house/bride of Christ, in whom he dwells by his Spirit, and the church is the house/body of Jesus, who is the true temple of God, the diversely unified communion of saints.

Interrupting the account of Solomon's construction, 1 Kgs. 6:11–13 places the temple within a Deuteronomic context.[8] Yahweh repeats his promises to "dwell" within Israel and never to "forsake" it, yet Yahweh makes clear that his presence is not automatic. If the king permits Israel to turn the temple into a den of thieves, Yahweh threatens to abandon the house and leave it to be desolated, as he abandoned the tabernacle at Shiloh (1 Sam. 4–5; Jer. 7). Strikingly, the verbs in 1 Kgs. 6:12 are all second-person singular, addressed to Solomon, an indication that the Lord's presence among his people and in his house depends on the conduct of the king in particular. This is one of the key differences between the Mosaic and Davidic phases of Israel's history. Under Torah, Yahweh's presence was contingent on Israel's faithfulness; under the Davidic system, Yahweh's presence is contingent on the faithfulness of Israel's king.

Yet, as we shall see (in the commentary on 2 Kgs. 22:1–23:30), ultimately even a faithful king will not be able to undo the idolatries of generations. The Davidic system is an instantiation of God's covenant with an Adamic humanity, and humanity can be saved only by becoming the humanity of the last Adam, the humanity of God. The Davidic covenant is the basis for this promised new covenant. What the law cannot achieve, the Davidic promise ultimately brings to pass, for the church serves a king who obeys and guards all the commandments of the Lord and who secures the Lord's perpetual presence with his church. Because of Yahweh's faithfulness to Abraham and David, from now to the eschaton, the world will always have an Eden, a holy mountain, a bride and a body, a sanctuary where the Triune God dwells in the Spirit.

---

8. First Kings 6:11–13 is surrounded by a double inclusion: 6:9 states that Solomon "built the house and finished it" (ויבן את־הבית ויכל הו), and 6:14 repeats the declaration in virtually the same words (ויבן שלמה את־הבית ויכל הו).

1 KINGS 7:1–12

As noted in the previous chapter, Solomon's house is included in the larger reality of the "house of Yahweh" (1 Kgs. 6:1; 7:51). A greater Adam, Solomon takes his throne alongside his heavenly Father's and rules with him, a type of the greater Davidic King, Jesus. This point is reinforced in 7:1–12, which shows how Solomon's house replicates the house of Yahweh.

Solomon spends a total of twenty years in building (9:10), seven years on the temple (6:38) and thirteen years on his own house (7:1). Commentators sometimes suggest that the time that Solomon spends on his own house, nearly double the time he spends on the temple, is an early sign of his later apostasy (Provan 1995, 63, 69–70). Yet Solomon is nowhere criticized for this. Apparently the logic is similar to the logic of the tithe: once Solomon pays his firstfruits, his time is "desanctified" so that he can devote his attention to building his own house. The objection that Solomon's glory challenges Yahweh's assumes a false doctrine of God. God's glory does not compete with human glory, nor does God glorify himself by siphoning glory from his people. He glorifies himself by freely and abundantly bestowing glory, just as the Father glorifies himself in the Son through the Spirit, and the Son in the Father through the same Spirit. Yahweh gives Solomon glory, but this makes the name of Yahweh glorious among the Gentiles, precisely because it makes the name of Solomon glorious.

First Kings 7:8 mentions a "house where he lived" (וּבֵיתוֹ אֲשֶׁר־יֵשֵׁב שָׁם), but this is only one of several buildings that constitute the complex known as "the king's house." Most are public buildings, built for service to Israel and not for Solomon's personal use. There are several separate buildings in the complex, and each corresponds to a section of the temple:

1. The first building is the "house of the forest of Lebanon" (בית יער הלבנון) (7:2–5). Both the house of the forest and Yahweh's house are paneled with cedar (6:15; 7:3); both have "ribs" (6:5; 7:3); and both have windows (6:4; 7:4–5). Specifically, the house of the forest corresponds to the היכל or "nave" of the temple.

2. Both the temple description and the description of Solomon's house begin with the nave, and both move on to describe a "porch" or "vestibule" (6:3; 7:6). Like the porch of the temple, "vestibule of pillars" (אולם העמודים) extends from the front of the house of the forest outward an additional fifty cubits, a colonnade stretching out from the front of the house of the forest, which itself is columned.

3. The third building is the "hall of the throne" (אולם הכסא) or the "hall of judgment" (אלם המשפט) (7:7). Both refer to the same building, as is evident from the hall of the throne being the place where Solomon passes judgment (אשר ישפט־שם) (7:7). It is "paneled with cedar from floor to floor," a phrase that also describes the nave and inner sanctuary of the temple (6:16–17). Yahweh's house also has a throne room, the inner sanctuary built to house the ark of the covenant (6:19). The portico of the throne, the portico of judgment, corresponds to the most holy place of the temple.

The temple and the palace have some of the same architectural features, the same materials, and the same triple structure. Solomon's house is like Yahweh's: like father, like son. By residing in the temple complex in a house modeled on the temple, Solomon makes clear that his kingship has divine sanction. His kingship is, in some sense, a sacral kingship.

Sacral kingship is standard fare in the ancient world. Kings are often believed to be virtual incarnations of a deity or at least sacred personages. Israel's politico-religious system differs form this common ideology at crucial points. The Israelite king is not considered a god, and Israel's kings are not priest-kings with access to the sanctuary. Uzziah's attempt to usurp a priestly privilege ends with his complete exclusion from the temple because of leprosy (2 Chr. 26). A "separation of church and state," or better of king and priest, was built into Israel's monarchy. Yet, as is evident in 1 Kgs. 8, Israel's kings preside at religious festivals, and the architectural arrangements of Solomon's palace show that the king is a human representative of Yahweh. Though he was not a priest, the king of Israel is not a secular figure either.

Weigel argues that the church's claim to authority is a challenge to the totalitarian aspirations of empire and "desacralized" political life. For Christianity, no human authority can claim divine status, and hence "the 'reach' of public authorities was understood to be circumscribed (at least in principle), the cultural ground on which a politics of consent could be built was prepared, and an antitotalitarian vaccine was injected into Europe's civilizational bloodstream." At the same time Christianity taught Europe "about the proper dignity of the secular: according to the Church, which took this from its Jewish parent, the human task was to humanize the world, which in Christian terms meant learning to be 'at home' in the world even as one prepared for the world to come" (Weigel 2005, 104). For Weigel, this does not mean that Christianity endorses a secular politics, for his entire essay is a passionate plea for Europe to acknowledge its roots in Christian civilization and to abandon the project of removing the Christian God from political life.

Many, most especially the Lockean founders of the American republic, pushed genuine insights like Weigel's into a Christian defense of secular politics, as if the political genius of Christianity found its fulfillment in a politics wholly emancipated from religious sanctions. Christian though he was, Locke defined the goals of civil order in purely immanent terms:

> The commonwealth seems to me to be a society of men constituted only for the procuring, preserving, and advancing their own civil interests. Civil interests I call life, liberty, health, and indolence of body; and the possession of outward things, such as money, lands, houses, furniture, and the like. It is the duty of the civil magistrate, by the impartial execution of equal laws, to secure unto all the people in general, and to every one of his subjects in particular, the just possession of these things belonging to this life. . . . Now that the whole jurisdiction of the magistrate reaches only to these civil concernments; and that all civil power, right, and dominion, is bounded and confined to the only care of promoting these things. (Locke 1963, 9–10)

Locke's secular politics was, importantly, linked to a low church ecclesiology that reduced the church to a voluntary society:

> I say, it is a free and voluntary society. Nobody is born a member of any church; otherwise the religion of parents would descend unto children by the same right of inheritance as their temporal estates, and every one would hold his faith by the same tenure he does his lands; than which nothing can be imagined more absurd. Thus therefore that matter stands. No man by nature is bound unto any particular church or sect, but every one joins himself voluntarily to that society in which he believes he has found that profession and worship which is truly acceptable to God. The hope of salvation, as it was the only cause of his entrance into that communion, so it can be the only reason of his stay there. For if afterwards he discover any thing either erroneous in the doctrine, or incongruous in the worship of that society to which he has joined himself, why should it not be as free for him to go out as it was to enter? No member of a religious society can be tied with any other bonds but what proceed from the certain expectation of eternal life. A church then is a society of members voluntarily uniting to this end. (Locke 1963, 9–10)

A secular order can no more accept a public church than it can tolerate religious ends or theological norms for politics.

As Milbank shows, the secular realm is not the natural product of Christian development but was constructed from materials borrowed from heretics and outright pagans (Milbank 1990b, part 1). In the beginning, and for many centuries, there was no secular. Nor was the secular realm a shining political jewel waiting to be discovered once the layers of sacralization were scraped away. At least, if Christianity has an inherent drive toward secular politics, Christians themselves took a long time to realize it, since the division of Christendom into church and state was a fairly late development.[1] Prior to the investiture controversy, the whole of Christendom was viewed as an ecclesia, presided over jointly by king and priest (Leithart 2003b; cf. Gierke 1987, 22–23).

It is doubtful that modern politics is any healthier for purging politics of religious input and not at all clear that Christian political thought can fundamentally challenge totalitarianism and secularism without recognizing that political authority is accountable to theologically grounded demands. Molnar's warning about the impotence of secularized power reflects the regression of modern political life:

> Soon after political power emancipates itself from spiritual authority it loses its own stability and, in short order, its legitimacy. The downward trend cannot be arrested. Individualism then anarchy appear as the natural consequence. This was also the view of the Roman historians and of the Greek Polybius, the chronicler of Roman grandeur after the war with Carthage. The monarchy, they wrote, gave way to the government of a few, who unseated the king out of jealousy. This oligarchy was dispossessed in turn by a popular revolution, which brought the masses to power. Soon a generalized anarchy ensued, shored up again by quasimonarchs, the emperors who followed Caesar. We have no proof that such cycles have been broken. (Molnar 1988, 104–5)

The remnants of Christendom within our political order (the President's hand is on the Bible—not the Qu'ran—during the inauguration) are brittle remnants and provide neither standards of conduct nor accountability to those standards. O'Donovan writes that "the political doctrine that emerged from Christendom is characterized by a notion that government is responsible. Rulers, overcome by Christ's victory, exist provisionally and on sufferance for specific purposes" (1996, 231). The palace of Solomon, adjacent to the temple of Yahweh, is a mark of that responsibility, a sign that however high the king's throne, another throne is higher and another king has authority to render final judgment.

At the same time, it is an overstatement to suggest that notions of sacredness have been expunged from modern politics. Sacrality has not been so much

---

1. Shakespeare's Richard II expresses what was an unquestioned article of faith for medieval and early modern Christians: "Not all the water in the rough rude sea / Can wash the balm off from an anointed king. / The breath of worldly men cannot depose / The deputy elected by the Lord" (*Richard II*, 3.2).

removed as relocated. Property rights, individual autonomy, and especially the constitutional boundary separating church and state are all protected with sacred zeal. As Bauman comments:

> In most of its descriptions, modernity is presented as a time of secularization ("everything sacred was profaned," as young Marx and Engels memorably put it) and disenchantment. What is less often mentioned, however, though it should be, is that modernity also deified and enchanted the "nation," the new authority—and so by proxy the man-made institutions that claimed to speak and act in its name. "The sacred" was not so much disavowed as made the target of an "unfriendly takeover": moved under different management and put in the service of the emergent nation-state. (Bauman 2005, 44)

Christian capitulation to secular politics—more the rule than the exception in the modern church—is nothing less than apostasy, a denial of the gospel that announces Jesus as Lord. Solomon's residence in the temple complex stands as a scriptural figure indicating that all earthly rule, not only Israel's, is overshadowed by heaven and a reminder that the gospel we preach is good news about a king of all kings.

1 KINGS 8:1–66

In the previous chapter, we saw that the temple provides a useful entrée into ecclesiology, but a temple ecclesiology exists only because Christ himself is the human temple of Yahweh (John 2:21). First Kings 8 provides a starting point for a templar Christology.

That such a temple Christology is worth pursuing is evident from some of the problems raised in traditional Christology, which has been worked out using categories of substance, nature, and personhood taken mainly from Greek philosophy rather than from Scripture. This is not to say that the Greek categories falsify the theology, but to suggest that some of christological tensions might be avoided by rigorously working through Christology using biblical categories.

In an article on the incarnation, for instance, theologian Coakley highlights a critical theological problem with Chalcedonian Christology:

> [Richard] Norris concludes that [Chalcedon] "appears to insist upon a synthesis or union of *incompatibles* precisely because it takes its physical models too seriously." In other words, the concretization of thought about the "natures" leads, he avers, to the supposition of their "incompatibility." And whereas in the patristic debate this false disjunction resulted in an overemphasis (claims Norris) on Christ's divinity, the modern form of this aberrant perception of Chalcedon's intent has been the opposite: "a new type of Monophysitism"—a tendency, in the face of its own strong sense of the incompatibility of divine and human agencies, to reduce the Christ not to a God fitted out with vestiges of humanity but to a human being adorned with the vestiges of divinity. (Coakley 1996, 147)

As Coakley explains, "both these alternatives, however, suffer from a misconception of the 'natures' as 'interchangeable contraries'—as 'differing items of the *same* order,' competing against one another for the same space." In place of this assumption, she argues, "we need a 'negative theology' here in a particular sense, one that *denies* that the difference between God and humanity is a matter either of 'contrariety' or of 'contradiction'" (1996, 147). Ultimately, Norris claims, the question is not "how to fit two logical contraries together into one, as its ancient and modern interpreters have all but uniformly supposed, but how to dispense with a binary logic in figuring the relation between God and creatures" (147).

In Thomist terms, the problem that Coakley identifies is that Chalcedonian Christology might be taken to imply that God (or divine "nature") is a member of a genus, the genus "nature." Within the general metaphysical category of "nature," there are (at least) two species: divine and human. But Thomas Aquinas (1993, 16–18) is surely right that God is not a member of a genus, and it follows that "divine nature" should not be conceived as a member of the genus "nature." It is likely that the Chalcedonian use of nature is meant analogically, so that divine nature is the original of which human nature is a copy, which implies that there is similarity despite the distance between creator and creature. Even if this is the sense of the Chalcedonian formula, it needs to be emphasized that the incarnation is not about two natures competing for the same space.

Contrary to many scholars, Wright suggests that first-century Jews did have a notion of incarnation, one that offers a starting point for thinking about the incarnation. After all, "the Temple, from the beginning, had as its whole *raison d'etre* the dwelling of Israel's God in the midst of his people, and the daily and yearly sacrifices through which fellowship with this God, and forgiveness from this God, were assured." According to Wright, "the Temple has for too long been the forgotten factor in New Testament Christology," and he urges its centrality (1996b, 56).

Elsewhere, Wright emphasizes that Jesus's ministry is a counter-temple movement. What Jews normally expected from the temple—an encounter with the presence of their God, festivity and food, forgiveness and cleansing, instruction in Torah—the disciples come to expect from Jesus himself (1996a, 435–37). Wright joins many recent scholars in recognizing the central importance of Jesus's "cleansing of the temple" (Matt. 21). In this confrontation, the incarnate temple of God enacts the coming judgment on the architectural temple, a judgment that he spells out at length in the Olivet Discourse (Matt. 24). When the true temple arrives in human form, the stone temple of Herod gives way. Luke develops this templar Christology in a distinctive way, emphasizing that Jesus receives the Spirit, as the Spirit-glory of Yahweh had once been enthroned above the cherubim in the temple. For John, Jesus's death is a temple destruction (John 2:19–22), a fact underscored by the verbal and conceptual parallels between Mark's account of the crucifixion and his record of the Olivet Discourse (Horne 2003, 166–68). In the course of 1–2 Kings, the northern kingdom of Israel, once Jeroboam I and then Ahab reject Solomon's temple and erect their own, will see its own version of this counter-temple movement in the prophetic ministries of Elijah and Elisha.

For 1 Kgs. 8, a temple Christology is simultaneously a corporate or ecclesial Christology. The passage has an obviously liturgical character. Israel gathers in Jerusalem, offers prayers and sacrifices, feasts, and returns home. The noun "assembly" and the related verb "assemble" (קהל) dot the passage. The verb is used in 8:1–2 to announce the beginning of the assembly, and when the glory of Yahweh fills the most holy place Solomon "faced about and blessed all the assembly" (8:14). As he starts to pray, he turns toward the altar "in the presence of all the assembly" (8:22), and for the next forty verses, he prays in the presence of the assembly facing the altar. At the end of the prayer, he turns and blesses the "assembly" (8:55). This use of this word suggests connections with the assembly of Israel at Sinai (Exod. 35:1; Deut. 4:10), and the Septuagint translation of "assembly" as ἐκκλησία anticipates New Testament usage. The temple is the site of an assembly, as Christ the temple is the central point around which the *totus Christus* assembles.

One key moment in the dedication ceremony occurs when Solomon transfers the ark from the fortress of Zion to the temple mount. During David's reign, the palace and the tent for the ark are both in this portion of the city, but in 1 Kgs. 8, the Zion system of worship is incorporated, with the Mosaic tabernacle (8:4), into the temple (Leithart 2003a). Solomon reunites the divided worship of Israel into a single location. Starting from 1 Sam. 4, the story of the ark is a story of death and resurrection: the "body" of the tabernacle is divided and then reunited, and this points to the ultimate tabernacle of God in the flesh of Jesus, who is torn on the cross before he is raised and ascends to the "house" of his Father in heaven.[1] The emphasis on the ark and the tablets of the law inside demonstrates the continuity between the order of Solomon and the Mosaic covenant (אשר כרת יהוה עם־בני ישראל) (1 Kgs. 8:9). The temple becomes an architectural emblem of the nation and the individual with the Torah of Yahweh written on his or her heart. Once the ark is in the temple, Yahweh descends in a cloud and consecrates the temple as his holy place. The temple is the place of Yahweh's enthronement, again pointing to the human temple at the center of the Father's kingdom.

Though highlighted in the dedication, the ark hereafter disappears from 1–2 Kings and is not even listed among the furniture seized by Nebuchadnezzar (2 Kgs. 25) or among the furnishings brought back from exile. It is apparently lost at some point in Israel's history, since Pompey found the most holy place empty when he came to the temple. The understated treatment of the ark in 1–2 Kings seems to indicate that its role is already envisioned to be temporary. If its loss is a tragic mistake, one would expect some mention of the tragedy, but there is none. The ark serves as the transportable throne of Yahweh until he takes his rest in the temple, but once there the temple itself is seen as the "throne" of Yahweh. Jeremiah makes this point in Jer. 3:11–18, where he refers

---

1. There was a literal ascent in Solomon's dedication ceremony, since the "city of David" is on a lower hill of Jerusalem than Mount Moriah, the temple mount (1 Kgs. 8:3–4).

to the days after the exile when the ark will be forgotten. Instead of the ark serving as Yahweh's throne, the entire city of Jerusalem will become a throne. The dedication of the temple is the beginning of this shift of attention from the ark to the temple and city. During the Mosaic period, the ark was the throne of Yahweh; during the Davidic/Solomonic period, the temple serves that purpose; but in the restoration, Jeremiah said, the whole city will serve as the throne of Yahweh.

The dedication service links to the Mosaic covenant in a number of other ways. It takes place at the "feast of booths," the Mosaic feast of the seventh month (1 Kgs. 8:2, 65). In this, it contrasts with the Sinai covenant, established at Pentecost in the third month. In agricultural terms, Pentecost was a firstfruits festival, the beginning of the harvest, but not yet the end of the harvest. The temple completes the process of maturation begun at Sinai. With the Mosaic covenant came the firstfruits, but with Solomon the full corn appears.

In part, the harvest is a harvest of nations. The temple is built as a cooperative venture of Israelites and Gentiles and thus is a "house of prayer for all nations," a fact signaled by the use of the Phoenician name for the seventh month in 1 Kgs. 8:2 (אתנים).[2] The temple marks a moment in the history of the Gentiles, not merely in the history of Israel. Further, Gentiles are included in the worship offered "toward" the temple (8:41–43). Solomon expects Gentiles to hear of the Lord's great fame, his "great arm and mighty hand" (again an exodus motif: Exod. 3:20; 6:1; 13:3), and turn to Jerusalem in prayer. Isaiah, much less Jesus, is not the first to see the temple as a place of worship for the world. Christologically, the temple as a place of assembly for prayer points to the future incorporation of Gentiles and Jews into one new body.

A number of the curses mentioned in Solomon's prayer appear in the great Deuteronomic list of curses in Deut. 28:

1. defeat before an enemy (1 Kgs. 8:33; Deut. 28:25, 48)
2. heavens shut up without rain (1 Kgs. 8:35; Lev. 26:19; Deut. 28:24)
3. famine, pestilence, blight, mildew, locust, grasshopper, plague, siege (1 Kgs. 8:37; Deut. 28:21–22, 38, 59)
4. exile (1 Kgs. 8:46–51; Deut. 28:58–63)

Importantly, both Deut. 28 and 1 Kgs. 8 end with a reference to exile. As Nelson suggests (1987, 54), the chapter employs a running pun on שׁבה ("take captive") and שׁוּב ("return" or "repent") in 1 Kgs. 8:46–48. The former, which refers to the exile, is used four times, and the latter, translated "turn" and referring to repentance and return, is used three times, for a total of seven.

2. Chronological references in 1–2 Kings are always pregnant with significance. For most of 1–2 Kings, Israel functions according to the years of the kings of Israel and Judah, but at the end of Kings everything is dated by reference to the reign of Nebuchadnezzar. In a very literal sense, the "times of the Gentiles" begin with the destruction of Jerusalem and the temple (see the commentary on 2 Kgs. 23:31–25:30).

The two verbs alternate chiastically, and the arrangement of the text solidifies the connection between captivity and repentance, indicating that the solution to שבה ("exile") is שוב ("return"), both literally (return to land) and, more important, figuratively (return to Yahweh). In 1 Kgs. 8, the "turning" has a specific focus: Israel is urged to turn not toward Torah but "toward [Yahweh] in this place" (ושבו אליך . . . בבית הזה) (8:33). The repentance that ends Israel's exile is a turning toward the temple, ultimately the living temple that is Jesus. Repentance in 1–2 Kings is not a matter of moral improvement, but of turning in faith toward the Lord who alone heals the land. This, as we shall see throughout this commentary, is what Israel fails to do.

The allusions to Deut. 28 provide a further indication that the Solomonic order of things is built on the Deuteronomic order. Beyond the Mosaic order, however, the temple dedication provides a double mediator for Israel. King and temple function as co-mediators for Israel. Solomon begins his prayer with a review of Yahweh's promise to David, and his entire prayer is rooted in 2 Sam. 7, where David's "son" is figured as Yahweh's son, the representative Israelite (Exod. 4:23). This is reflected in the subtle interplay between the prayers of the king and the prayers of the people: 1 Kgs. 8:28 refers to the prayer of "your servant" (עבדך), while 8:30 uses what in Hebrew is an alliterative phrase: "your servant and your people" (עבדך ועמך). Israelites are permitted to approach Yahweh individually without the mediation of the king, but Solomon's entire prayer appeals to Yahweh to hear the prayers of the people. Individual Israelites and even individual foreigners address Yahweh about personal as well as national afflictions (8:38, 41–43), but first the anointed king, the Christ, opens a channel of communication.

Additionally, the temple itself functions as mediator, a communications switchboard connecting heaven and earth. Yahweh promises, in keeping with the language of Deut. 12, that his "name" would dwell in the house, less a way of distancing Yahweh from the temple (Provan 1995, 79) than an indication of the mode of his presence. From the New Testament perspective, the "name" is associated with the second person of the Trinity (Nelson 1987, 59), the specific "address" of God. Yet, prayer is not offered to Yahweh but "toward the house" or "toward the city" (1 Kgs. 8:33, 35, 38, 42, 44, 48). Once prayer is offered toward the house, it will be delivered to Yahweh who "hears from heaven," a phrase repeated in each of the seven petitions of the prayer. To say that Jesus is the temple of God is not only to say that he is the earthly address of God, but also that he is the one toward whom we address our prayers and through whom our prayers are heard by our Father in heaven.

Though sacrifices are included in the dedication ceremony, the accent is on prayer. At the end of Exodus, the cloud fills the tabernacle, and the Lord begins to give instructions about sacrificial procedures (Lev. 1–7). In 1 Kgs. 8, *Solomon* (not Yahweh) speaks, and he prays instead of instructing Israel in sacrificial procedures. The prayer is partly an instruction about prayer. Prayer does not replace sacrifice by any means, but it begins to displace it from the center of Israel's worship. Sacrifice is transformed into a sacrifice of prayer and praise, a liturgical move in the direction of the nonbloody worship of the new covenant.[3] In the temple, Yahweh comes near; he does not remain at a distance to hear prayer and to flick a distant switch. He enters into Israel's space to open his eyes and ears to their cries and to stretch out the arms of his temple toward his people. For such a God, coming in human flesh is the most natural thing in the world.

First Kings 8 is the climax of the Solomonic narratives in 1–2 Kings and stands out as an event of world-historical importance. Yahweh, the creator of heaven and earth, settles in Jerusalem, in the nation of Israel, and the seven petitions at the center of the passage offer a rough preview of the trials that Israel will face in the subsequent centuries:

oath before altar	reign of Solomon
defeat by enemies	division of the kingdom
no rain	Elijah and Omrides
famine, siege, plagues	siege and famine in Samaria
foreigner prays	fall of northern kingdom
sent out to battle	last days of Judah
exile	exile of Judah

Though many of the plagues that Solomon mentions in the prayer happen in the course of 1–2 Kings, few kings ever resort to prayer or the temple for forgiveness and healing. Occasionally kings pray or ask for prayer, and Hezekiah actually goes into the temple during the Assyrian siege of Jerusalem (2 Kgs. 19), but such examples are few and far between. More often, kings plunder the temple for gold and silver to pay off Gentile invaders. When the Babylonians come to destroy the temple, the Jews treat it as a talisman whose mere physical presence will save them from national destruction (Jer. 7).

Yahweh establishes his house at the center of Israel and stretches his arms out in invitation to a stubborn people, who refuse to turn to him and be healed. This too is christologically significant, for when the human temple appears, the Jews refuse to turn toward him as well. The story of 1–2 Kings is the story of a rejected temple, a rejected and suffering Messiah and mediator, a temple destroyed but destined to be raised on the third day. A temple Christology thus works out in a narrative of cross and empty tomb.

---

3. 2 Chr. 6:13 makes the point in a brilliantly understated fashion. There, Solomon kneels on a platform the dimensions of which are the same as the dimensions of the Mosaic altar (Exod. 27:1). Solomon prays on the altar as a sacrifice, and his prayer is a sacrifice of the lips. It has the same effect as sacrifice, offering a sweet savor to Yahweh, who responds by forgiving sin. A similar point may be made with reference to music (see Leithart 2003a).

1 KINGS 9:1–28

Frisch (1991, 12) suggests that 1 Kgs. 9:1–9 records Yahweh's response to Solomon's prayer of dedication and is part of the temple section of 1 Kings.[1] The chapter opens with an account of the "second dream" of Solomon (9:2), a second witness, a "Deuteronomy." At the end of the earlier dream, Solomon moved from Gibeon to Jerusalem to stand before the ark (3:15); once the temple is finished, Solomon is permanently installed in Jerusalem. Solomon functions within a new covenantal order, one in which he goes three times each year to offer ascensions and peace offerings before Yahweh (9:25), as he once offered ascensions and peace offerings before the shrine that held the ark (3:15). At the temple dedication, Solomon requested that the Lord hear prayers at the temple, and in this second dream Yahweh promises to keep his eyes open in the house perpetually. The Lord's answer shows that Yahweh's relationship to the temple is not "distant" or "reserved." Yahweh promises to put his "name" at the temple (9:3, using the triple pun: לשום־שמי שם), as well as his "eyes" and "heart."[2] By these, Yahweh "consecrates" (הקדשתי) the house, which shows that Yahweh is present in the temple, since sanctuaries are consecrated by his advent in glory (Exod. 29:43). Yahweh "hears" (שמעתי) Solomon, and the narrator employs the verb used in the great Mosaic confession of Deut. 6. In the Mosaic confession, Israel was urged to "hear" that Yahweh is one and to devote itself to the Lord with singleness of heart; in the Solomonic dedication of the temple, Solomon calls on Yahweh to "hear."

Like the earlier dream, the second includes conditional promises. Yahweh promises long life if Solomon keeps the Lord's statutes and commandments

---

1. The following discussion overlaps with Leithart 2000b.
2. The reference to Yahweh's "eyes" is important. Eyes have to do with judgment (Job 34:21; Ps. 66:7; 94:9; Amos 9:4), and a number of passages of Scripture emphasize the comprehensive vision of the heavenly judge (Prov. 15:3; 2 Chr. 16:7–9; Jer. 16:16–17; Zech. 4:10).

(1 Kgs. 3:14), and in 9:4–5 he promises that the Davidic kingdom will endure if Solomon walks as his father walked. Israel's fate is dependent on Israel's faithfulness, but Israel's faithfulness is linked with the faithfulness of the king, not merely with Solomon but his sons (9:6; cf. 2 Sam. 7:14). In the light of 2 Sam. 11–12, it is curious that David provides the standard by which Solomon will be measured. Using David as a standard of uprightness focuses attention on the issue of idolatry, as does the remainder of the warning. "Turning away from walking after me" means "going and serving other gods and prostrating yourself before them" (1 Kgs. 9:6), something that David never did. What God requires of Solomon is an upright orientation: he must keep his face turned in Yahweh's direction, his feet walking in the path of Yahweh's statutes and ordinances.

In words resonant of the flood narrative, Yahweh threatens to "cut off" Israel from the face of the ground if Solomon or his sons fail to follow him (9:7). Since land is the source of all of Israel's blessings—the gift of life, the gift of food, the great public sign of Yahweh's favor to Israel—removal from the land would be an equally public removal of favor. Covenants are "cut" in Scripture, terminology that refers to the literal cutting that occurs in most covenant-making ceremonies (cutting of animals for sacrifice or a meal) and also points to the threat that hangs over the covenant breaker. Cutting is also associated with circumcision, again a literal cutting of the flesh. Those who are cut by circumcision live "under the curse," under the threat that they will be "cut off" if they turn from Yahweh and serve other gods.

Yahweh also threatens to "send" the temple from before his face. The verb "send out" (שלח) is used of the exile of Adam and Eve from the garden (Gen. 3:23) and can be used to describe the "letting free" involved in divorce (Deut. 22:19, 29; Isa. 50:1). The specific object of the "sending" is the house, not the people, and in the event, the temple is sent away into exile with the people (2 Kgs. 25:13–17). By expelling the "house" from before his face, Yahweh divorces Israel and sends the bride from the garden land where he placed it. In this way, Israel will become a "proverb and a byword" (1 Kgs. 9:7), its history a parable of judgment for the nations. This combination of terms appears only a few times in the Old Testament, most relevantly in Deut. 28:37, within a list of the curses that Yahweh threatens to bring on Israel if it does not keep covenant. In Deut. 28, Yahweh threatens to bring these curses if Israel as a whole turns from him to follow other gods, but with Solomon, the threat is focused: "If you or your sons shall indeed turn away . . . [then] Israel will become a proverb and a byword among all peoples" (1 Kgs. 9:6–7).

A good deal of the chapter describes Solomon's achievements as a king. The chapter ends with Solomon's seafaring, the first time in Scripture that an Israelite goes sailing. Through much of the Old Testament, the sea represents the Gentile world, and Israelites are normally land-based shepherds and herders rather than fishers.[3] Solomon, however, extends his reach to the sea and like Yahweh is able to divide the waters and pass through. Solomon specifically goes to Ophir for gold, and in Gen. 10:29, Ophir is associated with Havilah, the original land of gold in Gen. 2. Solomon collects gold from Ophir as a greater Adam, moving out from the garden to collect the resources of the outlying lands and bringing them back to adorn the house of the Lord.

Yahweh's warning to Solomon enables us to clarify the nature of Solomon's creativity. When he reviews his building projects in Eccl. 2:4–7, he describes them as repetitions of Yahweh's original acts of creation. Solomon, like Yahweh, first forms a garden (Gen. 2:8) and then fills it with fruit trees (2:9). Water flowing from the land of Eden irrigates the garden (2:10), so that it could become a forest. Yahweh places a man in the garden, along with all animals (2:15–20), and climactically forms Eve as a companion for Adam (2:21–25). Solomon follows the same procedure, as an Adam imitating his creator. In constructing the temple, Solomon is a new Adam who follows his heavenly Father's example in constructing a world/house and planting a "garden."

The language of 1 Kgs. 9 is consistent with the notion that Solomon's creativity is analogous with the creativity of God. The chapter is framed by references to Solomon "finishing" the house (9:1, 25), employing the clause ויהי ככלות שלמה לבנות, an echo of Gen. 2:1–4. After Solomon "plants" his own garden, Pharaoh's daughter moves into Jerusalem (1 Kgs. 9:24), like Eve entering the garden, so that Solomon makes a place for his bride as Yahweh made a place for his. Between his completion of the building and the coming of the bride, Yahweh instructs Solomon about his responsibilities in regard to the house. There is a similar sequence in Gen. 2: the heavens and earth are "finished," and Yahweh places Adam in the garden, commands him with regard to the tree of knowledge, and then presents his bride to him.

In describing his achievements, Solomon is not boasting with ungodly hubris but fulfilling the potentials of human nature. Humans are created in the image of a God who creates, and humans are therefore created to be subcreators. Human making and creativity are not secular concerns in Scripture, but central to humanity's imaging of the transcendent God. According to Milbank, a fundamental assumption of modernity is that what is humanly constructed (the "made" or *factum*) is secular or religiously neutral (1990b, 10–11). With the Renaissance discovery that culture is a thoroughly human construction, historical "all the way down," the whole of culture was conceived as secular, and religion was pushed out of the arena of culture into a closet of inner piety. Rehabilitation of a theological concept of "making" or *poiesis* thus plays a central role in any antimodernist reconstruction of theology (Williams 2005).

To challenge the identification of the *factum* with the secular, Milbank resuscitates a "countermodern" thread of philosophy and theology rooted in

---

3. The inclusion of Gentiles in the new covenant is signaled symbolically by many of the apostles being fishermen.

the work of Nicholas of Cusa and Giambattista Vico and developed further in
the metacritical philosophies of Hamann and Herder (Milbank 1999). At the
center of Vico's thought is the axiom that *verum et factum convertuntur*, that
"truth and the made are convertible" (1991, 5). This axiom has epistemological
and cultural dimensions, but for Vico the convertibility of *verum* and *factum* is
applicable not only to created reality, but is true absolutely, finding its ontological ground in the intertrinitarian relations. Earlier, Cusa had speculated about
the second person of the Trinity as the "art" of God, so that, without denying
the Nicene formula, he could speak of a kind of eternal "making" or artistry
in the Father's begetting of the Son, which rendered "God's inner creativity
definatory of the divine essence." Since all truth and wisdom is contained
in the word of the Father, who is generated by the Father, *verum* and *factum*
are convertible even in the Godhead. In this way, *factum* became one of the
transcendentals. "Making" or creativity is among the leading attributes of the
Trinity; a "creation" *ad intra* grounds the *ad extra* (Milbank 1991, 27–30,
82–84, 126–32). On Milbank's reading, Cusa makes creation rather than *esse*
the principal philosophical concept (1991, 22).

Made in God's image, the human is *homo creator*, and, just as the Father
is never without his eternal "art," so human artifacts are not a secondary reality grafted onto a more basic "natural" existence but "fully equiprimordial"
with humanity itself (Milbank 1991, 22). Since human making reflects the
eternal trinitarian nature and the continually creative work of God, however,
it is not secular or neutral but a reaching for transcendence and an imitation
of and participation in the ongoing creative action of God. Reflecting the
divine making, human art even partakes of the *ex nihilo* of the original divine
creation. Though the original creation is unique, it implies that the essence of
created existence is ongoing origination, a continual bringing-into-existence
of new things and new states of affairs. A table is not "rearranged lumber"; it
is an ontologically new thing, which did not exist before being built. Human
invention brings into being entire new classes of things—lightbulbs, books,
and computer terminals. Thus Milbank, following Cusa and Vico, wishes to
contest modernity *not* by a reactionary rejection of the Renaissance discovery
of the "fictional" (= *factum*) character of cultural life—such as the Cartesian
effort to discover a secure "foundation" for knowledge and culture. Instead,
Milbank extends divine *concursus* to the creative cultural act. God is the ultimate author of cultural "fictions."

Yet, despite the profoundly constructivist note struck here, Milbank does
not grant even a moment of autonomy, for when we are most "self-made"
we are simply carrying out as creatures what is eternally carried out in the
intertrinitarian relations. Thus, as Pickstock points out, this poetic vision not
only blurs the distinction of intransitive *praxis* and transitive *poiesis*, but also
the distinction between active and passive. Modernity, emerging from late
medieval voluntarism, sets an immanent and external power over against a
passive subject, and postmodernity, while attempting to rehabilitate a middle

voice, reduces it to a dialectical "shuttling between action and passion." Earlier theology, because of its understanding of the transcendence of God, was able to speak in a genuine middle voice of God operating through human action without destroying human freedom. Pickstock argues that this middle voice is restored preeminently in worship, for in liturgy one receives in the act of giving, and what one receives is the enablement to offer oneself (Pickstock 1998; Milbank 1995). *Poiesis*, as any poet knows, is as much "happening to" as a "doing."

According to 1–2 Kings, the "way" of creative work is not the way of absolute freedom. Yahweh reveals to Solomon that his kingdom and temple will flourish only if Solomon himself keeps Torah, yet Torah is not so much a constraint on creativity but a condition of its possibility. Solomon's creativity is truly creative only insofar as it conforms to the word of the God whose word created the world. If Solomon abandons Yahweh and creates his own gods, all his creations would come to nothing and his kingdom would come to an end. Making idols is mismaking and can only end in the decreation of exile.

First Kings 9 hints in various ways that some of Yahweh's threats are already coming to pass. Solomon's encounter with Hiram (9:10–14) is a negative counterpart to the smooth and cordial relationship depicted in 1 Kgs. 5. Earlier, the exchanges of the two kings are mutually satisfactory, but now, though Hiram fulfills all Solomon's desire, Solomon fails to satisfy Hiram's (9:12–13). Hiram "came out" (ויצא חירם) (9:12), and the narrator uses a verb that a few verses earlier describes Israel's exodus from Egypt (9:9). Hiram "exits" Tyre in order to "see" a portion of the land that Solomon gives him, but the lands are "not right in his eyes." Hiram judges that Solomon is not dealing straight with him, not giving him a good land, in spite of the "covenant of brotherhood" between them (9:13). When Yahweh brought Israel out of Egypt, he gave them a good land; Solomon brings Hiram out of Tyre to show him a land that Hiram judges to be "worthless" (כבול). Instead of causing Yahweh's name and generosity to be praised among the Gentiles, Solomon damages Yahweh's reputation with Hiram.[4]

A "reverse-conquest" theme is apparent in the brief account of Pharaoh's conquest of Gezer (9:16). Pharaoh destroys a Canaanite city with fire and then kills the Canaanite residents, bequeathing the city to his daughter as a "dismissal gift." Gezer is singled out in Judg. 1:29: "Neither did Ephraim drive out the Canaanites who were living in Gezer, so the Canaanites lived in Gezer among them"—until Pharaoh removes them. Pharaoh acts like Yahweh: he comes out of Egypt at the head of an army, conquers a city, and then gifts it to his

---

4. Alternatively, the gift of cities to Hiram might have been a false move on Solomon's part. The land has been bequeathed to Israel and is so much the possession of Israel that not even other Israelites can possess land belonging to their fellow Israelites (hence the institution of the Jubilee; Lev. 25). Solomon sells twenty cities of Galilee for 120 talents of gold (1 Kgs. 9:14). Instead of extending the conquest, Solomon reverses it, and a portion of the land falls back into the hands of the Gentiles—Canaanites no less.

daughter, the wife of the king of Israel. Just so, Yahweh leads Israel from Egypt in military formation, conquers the land, and then gifts it to daughter Israel. Pharaoh carries on a holy war, conquering the land as Israel was commanded to conquer in the time of Joshua.[5] Israel was not able to put these Canaanites under the ban (לא־יכלו בני ישראל להחרימם) (1 Kgs. 9:21), and Solomon subjects the Canaanite peoples to forced labor rather than destroying them, just as Israel failed to destroy the Canaanites during the times of the judges (Judg. 1:28, 30, 33, 35). Pharaoh proves more an Israelite than Israel, a more diligent son of Yahweh than his son-in-law Solomon. Earlier, Israel's failures give Canaanites a foothold to pester Israel throughout the period of judges, and the presence of Canaanites in the land make it far easier for Ahab's later plans for "re-Canaanitization" to succeed.

Meanwhile, Solomon begins acting like a Pharaoh, not only in the obvious sense that he builds stables for his horses and chariots (1 Kgs. 9:19; cf. Deut. 17:16), but also in that he builds "cities of storage" (כל־ערי המסכנות) (1 Kgs. 9:19), a phrase used elsewhere only in Exod. 1:11, where Hebrews "built for Pharaoh cities of storage Pithom and Raamses" (ויבן ערי מסכנות לפרעה). Solomon returns Israel to an Egyptian-like state, setting up for the "Mosaic" liberation of the northern tribes under Jeroboam I.

---

5. There is also an important typological dimension to this. Solomon's father(-in-law) conquers a town and gives the town to his daughter, which his son-in-law rebuilds. So also, the Father gives the world to the church (Rom. 4:16), the bride of his Son.

1 KINGS 10:1–29

Human beings are made for wisdom, yet reaching for wisdom has been a danger since Eden. Adam would eventually have been permitted to eat from the tree of knowledge of good and evil, as he was permitted to eat from "every tree" that was in the garden (Gen. 1:29). His premature seizure of wisdom introduced sin into the world. Wisdom is the greatest thing, but the great *aporia* of wisdom is that one can gain it only if one pursues it wisely.

Solomon's skill has been on display through several chapters of 1 Kings, and it is again on display before the queen of Sheba. Because of his wisdom, Solomon's throne is exalted above the thrones of the Gentiles, and Gentiles bring their treasures, especially gold (1 Kgs. 9:28; 10:2, 10, 14, 16, 18, 21, 22, 25), as tribute (10:25; cf. Ps. 72:10–11). Sheba's state visit inspires many a later prophetic vision (e.g., Isa. 60:4–14), which are ultimately fulfilled in the magi's gift (Matt. 2:1–12) and the treasures of the world brought into the church and the eschatological incorporation of Gentile treasures into the New Jerusalem (Rev. 21:24). One of the key thematic words of the passage is "hear," and 1 Kgs. 10 begins with a clause that uses the verb twice: woodenly translated, the verse says, "Now the queen of Sheba heard the hearing of Solomon" (וּמַלְכַּת־שְׁבָא שֹׁמַעַת אֶת־שֵׁמַע שְׁלֹמֹה). As the nations "heard" of Solomon (10:1, 6, 7, 8, 24), the king with the "hearing heart" (3:9), they join with Israel in confessing the Shema (Deut. 6:4), praising Solomon's God as the one God.

The queen of Sheba comes skeptically (1 Kgs. 10:7) to "test him with riddles" (10:1; cf. Judg. 14:10–20).[1] Sheba speaks all on her heart (1 Kgs. 10:2), and Solomon is able to tell all her words (stated twice in 10:3). Solomon's wisdom

---

1. Josephus records that Hiram and Solomon engage in a riddle contest (Wiseman 1993, 129), though Wiseman suggests that these were not merely mind games but challenging political and ethical dilemmas.

is made audible, and those words of wisdom that Solomon speaks cause the "word" about Solomon to spread even further. Strikingly, Sheba says she *heard* about Solomon's "word and wisdom," but did not believe it until "my eyes *saw* it" (10:7). Solomon's wisdom is made visible, and this visibility of wisdom finally overwhelms the queen. Though Sheba is satisfied with Solomon's answers to her questions, what takes her breath away is the embodiment of wisdom in the order, abundance, and beauty of Solomon's state dinners.

The description of the order and beauty of Solomon's table is carefully structured (10:4–5):

A the house that he built (presumably, his palace)
   B food of his table
      C seating of servants
      C′ standing of attendants and attire
   B′ cupbearers
A′ ascent to the house of Yahweh

If we add the reference to the things that Sheba "sees" (10:7), we have a seven-fold list. Solomon's wisdom is analogous to the wisdom of Yahweh displayed in the seven days of creation.

The whole description is framed by references to "houses," probably two different houses, the house of Solomon and the house of Yahweh, and the chiastic structure brings them into close conjunction (as do 1 Kgs. 6–7; see the commentary on 1 Kgs. 6:1–38; 7:13–51). Sheba is equally impressed with the liturgy of the house of Yahweh and the choreography of his son's house. At the center of the chiastic structure is a description of two groups of servants at Solomon's table, described with alliterative phrases: "servants" who are seated (ומושב עבדיו) and "attendants" who serve (ומעמד משרתו). Both phrases are at home in temple texts. Worship is often described in the Hebrew Bible as "service," and the priests and Levites are "servants" of the sanctuary (Deut. 10:8; 18:1). Solomon's court is a human replica of the divine court, his table a replica of the banquet of angels. The phrase "his ascent which went up to the house of Yahweh" (1 Kgs. 10:5) is sometimes translated "his stairway by which Solomon went up to the house of Yahweh," but the most natural meaning of עלתו ("his ascent") is "ascension offering." Sheba is astonished at the ascension offering that ascends in the house of Yahweh.

Solomon's wisdom embodied visibly, ritually, and liturgically provokes not only breathless awe but confession. Sheba's speech moves from a confession of the greatness of Solomon's wisdom to recognition of the blessing for those who stand continually (תמיד, another liturgical term) before Solomon (10:8), to a blessing on Yahweh himself, who desires Solomon and who gives Israel such a king out of his love. Sheba is no neutral international observer. She is a convert, won by Solomon's sapiential evangelism. In this, Solomon typifies his successor, Jesus, who is the full embodiment of the wisdom and word of the

Father, who is wisdom made tangible, visible, and audible (1 John 1:1–5), who attracts the nations through the wisdom manifested within his kingdom.

Seen from this typological angle, this passage raises important reflections about the nature of the public in modern life. Modern use of the word "public" is deeply ambiguous. On the one hand, "*the* public" refers to the society as a whole. The phrase "public opinion" uses the word in this sense. When we say that "the public is outraged" by such and such, we mean that the people (or a large subsection of the people) is outraged. In this context, something is private when it is of concern to only an individual or a small group. A public good is something that benefits the society as a whole, and a private good is one that benefits only a few. Law and order is a public good; the fruit in an orchard is a private good. On the other hand, public also means "of, or relating to, civil government." In this sense, a public official is a government employee. Public funds are monies collected and used by civil government. Betraying the public trust means violating the rules of Congress or pilfering from the treasury. Public in this sense is virtually interchangeable with the word "political." In this context, private means nonpolitical.

Public has other meanings as well, and it is of course inevitable that words will develop various shades of meaning. The problem occurs when these meanings are systematically confused, and the two senses of "public" are confounded in the thought of Rousseau. In Rousseau's vision of democracy, all citizens submit themselves to the "general will" of the people (public in the first sense). This general will is not discovered through elections or plebiscites or public-opinion polls, however. Elections, an expression of the "will of all," are always guided by private interest, but the general will seeks common interests. How is the general will to be determined, if not by voting? According to Rousseau, if legislators (public officials in the second sense) act justly, they can be certain that they are following the general will. More pointedly, Rousseau implies that legislators can in some mystical way divine the general will (1968, 2.3, 7). The end result of Rousseau's view, according to Nisbet, is totalitarianism, or at best what de Tocqueville called the tyranny of the majority. Public officials form a kind of gnostic elite capable of making decisions that promote the common good, while the people—the public—because they are dominated by private interest, are unable to make such decisions. Public in the first sense is swallowed by public in the second sense, and it is assumed that the public speaks only through public officials (Nisbet 1988, 52–55). Rousseau's system requires that public officials make decisions without any admixture of private interest. A more realistic view of the activity of public officials was offered by the American founders, who wisely recognized that public officials are as likely to be ambitious and greedy as private individuals and that the destructive effect of their ambition and greed is compounded by their power.

Back to Solomon: competing readings of the Solomon narrative support competing political theologies, different understandings of what constitutes the public. On the one hand, a literal reading suggests that Solomon stands in for "rulers and kings" of the new covenant, who pursue their public foreign policy for the public good. On the other hand, a typological reading locates Solomon's reign ecclesially and implies that the church is its own public existing within but not accountable to the needs of any nation-state. On this reading, the church might pursue, for instance, its own sapiential foreign relations, which depend on its conformity to the incarnate wisdom through the work of the spirit of wisdom, and these are as public as the foreign policies of the nation-state. While not denying that Solomon's reign yields insights into political issues, the typological reading is the one supported by the New Testament, and it supports a public-church ecclesiology. It is precisely this ecclesiology that modern politicians and, too often, theologians have blunted in favor of exclusively state-managed foreign affairs—one reason that moderns have long been hostile to Roman Catholicism and especially the existence of the Vatican states. It is no accident that modern politicians and, too often, theologians have often been hostile both to an ecclesiology of a public church and to typological interpretations of Scripture.

The remainder of 1 Kgs. 10 continues the celebration of Solomon's wisdom, centered on the glory of Solomon's throne, greater than any among the Gentiles. Like a holy mountain, the throne sat on a platform on a seventh level above six steps (10:19). The mountainlike structure (10:17) suggests a connection between Yahweh's enthronement on Zion above the cherubim, while the numerology of the structure suggests a connection with the creation, with Solomon seated in a "sabbatical" position. The literary structure of the description reinforces the sabbatical aspect and the parallels between Yahweh and his king:

A   the king made a throne of tooth (כסא־שן), a great one, and overlaid
    it with gold refined
    B   six ascending steps to the throne
        C   and the head was round to the throne
            D   and hands on this side and on that
                E   to the place of the resting (אל־מקום השבת)
            D′   and a pair of lions standing beside the hands
        C′   now twelve lions standing there
    B′   on six ascending steps on this side and on that
A′   there was not made any such for all the kingdoms

Each step is guarded by two "cherubic" lion figures, representing the twelve tribes of Israel, all of which are like their Judahic king, the "lion's whelp" (Gen. 49:9). Solomon rules lions, showing that he is an Adam who tames wild beasts. Two additional she-lions (the form is feminine) form the "hands" of the throne: Solomon's throne is supported by the she-lion bride of the lion of Judah (or, perhaps, Israel and Judah). The lions are "standing" (עמדים) like the standing servants of 1 Kgs. 10:5. The "round head to the throne" (ראש־עגל לכסה)

(10:19) perhaps represents the firmament canopy above the king. Solomon does not, like Yahweh, sit *on* the circle of the heavens, but he is very close.

Yet, the praise of Solomon is not undiluted, since the narrator records that Solomon violates the laws of kingship by multiplying gold and weapons. Gold is mentioned some ten times in this chapter. The amounts are impressive: 666 talents is equivalent to between thirty and eighty tons, and this is the amount that Solomon accumulates in one, no doubt very good, year; (10:14). Solomon has so much gold that he uses it for drinking vessels and for ceremonial shields, and the abundance of gold drives the value of silver to nothing (10:21). This seems a further encomium to Solomon, but Deut. 17:14–17 specifically forbids Israel's kings from multiplying gold and silver:

> When you enter the land that the LORD your God gives you, and you possess it and live in it, and you say, "I will set a king over me like all the nations who are around me," you shall surely set a king over you whom the LORD your God chooses, one from among your countrymen you shall set as king over yourselves; you may not put a foreigner over yourselves who is not your countryman. Moreover, he shall not multiply horses for himself, nor shall he cause the people to return to Egypt to multiply horses, since the LORD has said to you, "You shall never again return that way." He shall not multiply wives for himself, or else his heart will turn away; nor shall he greatly increase silver and gold for himself.

Solomon also gathers horses and chariots, again in violation of the rules of Deut. 17:16, and even imports them from Egypt, the very place that Israel was *forbidden* to go for horses and chariots. These violations prepare for the climactic violation in 1 Kgs. 11, the multiplication of wives, who seduce Solomon into idolatry. First Kings 10:29 is particularly damning: Solomon not only imports horses from Egypt, but also exports horses and chariots to Hittites and kings of Arameans. Hittites are mentioned in 9:20 as descendants of Canaanites that Israel failed to destroy. Solomon provides horses for Canaanites and apparently contributes to making the Hittites a regional power (2 Kgs. 7:6). Even worse, Solomon exports arms to the Arameans, and during the following century Aram emerges as a constant threat to Israel (1 Kgs. 11:23–25; 20; 22; 2 Kgs. 5; 7). Solomon, the wisest man in the world, funds his enemies. Even here, he displays a kind of wisdom, a skill in geopolitical positioning, but this is not the wisdom that Yahweh approves.

Folly is not a lack of knowledge or skill. As Barth says, "When the Bible speaks of the *nabal* or *kesil* [fool] . . . there can be no question of any lack of intellectual endowment, or of powers of thought and comprehension, or of the erudition which we both need and desire. The biblical dolt or fool may be just as carefully taught and instructed as the average man at any particular cultural level. He may be below the average, but he may also be above it, and even high above it. What makes him a fool has nothing whatever to do with a feebler mind or a less perfectly attained culture or scholarship. It is not in any sense a fate" (Barth 1939–69, 4.2.411–12). Solomon reaches the heights of political and cultural attainments, develops creativity in all spheres of endeavor, yet his cultivation and energy are ultimately directed toward finding new ways to violate the Yahweh's covenant with Israel.

Simplistic moralisms are out of place in this passage, however. Solomon's wisdom and well-deserved fame increase and remain with him at the very time he begins violating the laws of kingship. Wisdom does not flit away as Solomon begins to multiply horses, chariots, and women. The same chapter that documents Solomon's accumulation of gold informs us that he is "greater" than all the kings of the earth in wisdom (1 Kgs. 10:23) and that his wisdom is of such a quality that kings come to hear about it (10:24). These are not ironic evaluations. Assessing Solomon would be infinitely easier if the narrator told us that he became a fool, but Solomon remains wise, and Solomon the sage breaks the word of Yahweh. Wise Solomon remains wise even while he abandons the fear of Yahweh, which is the beginning of wisdom.

Solomon's life does not narrate the simple truism that even a wise person can fail. Rather, it shows a wise man who fails precisely at the height of his wisdom, precisely at the moment when everyone acknowledges his wisdom, indeed, precisely in his exercise of wisdom. To accumulate vast amounts of gold, after all, Solomon has to maintain an efficient trading fleet; trading horses with Egyptians requires developed skills in negotiation and diplomacy; gathering wives from the surrounding nations presupposes that Solomon is powerful enough to attract allies and skillful enough to conclude advantageous alliances with them. Solomon is capable of accumulating gold, guns, and girls precisely because of his wisdom. Had he been a fool, he would be in no position to pursue these projects.

The book of Kings is, among other things, wisdom literature, and the life of Solomon demonstrates that wisdom does not allow the wise to rest on their laurels and coast through life. Wisdom requires guarding one's steps, and the wiser one is, the more skilled one is, the more paths are open, the more options. Folly, Barbara Tuchman says, is a function of power, and power is often the product of skill (quoted in Davis 2005, 206n7). The wise can accomplish things that a fool cannot, and this means that the wise faces peculiar temptations, temptations that are simply not available to the fool. Humans rightly strive for wisdom, strive above all to get wisdom, but there is a kind of skill in living that is no more than a highly refined form of folly.

In the larger scheme of 1–2 Kings, Solomon's failure is nestled within a story of Israel's failure. Successful as he is, Solomon does not bring in a perpetual golden age. Human wisdom cannot bring in salvation for a fallen Israel or a fallen humanity. That can only be done through God's wisdom in flesh, a wisdom that confounds the wisdom of the wise, a wisdom that looks for all the world like folly.

1 KINGS 11:1–43

The book of Kings narrates Israel's fall into idolatry, its seduction by the ways and gods of the Gentiles, which leads to the judgment of exile, and 1 Kgs. 11, which initiates the story of the northern kingdom, displays the logic of 1–2 Kings as a whole. Solomon marries Pharaoh's daughter and continues to love Yahweh (3:1–3), but when he marries other foreign women, he is drawn away to love them. His love for Yahweh leads him to build the temple of Yahweh, but his love for foreign women leads him to build shrines for idols. Instead of "clinging to Yahweh" as the law requires (Deut. 10:20; 11:22; 13:4; 30:20), he "clung to" (בהם דבק שלמה לאהבה) the foreign women and their gods (1 Kgs. 11:2). In the covenant relation of marriage, a man must cleave to his wife (Gen. 2:24), and in the covenant relation with Yahweh the loyal and faithful and righteous person is the one who clings in faith and loyalty to Yahweh. When David "did evil" in seizing a married woman (2 Sam. 11–12), the kingdom was temporarily divided by the rebellion of Absalom. Solomon does evil in taking many women, and the result is a longer-lasting breach in Israel. Solomon's wisdom is guided by his loves, and when his love turns to foreign women and foreign gods, he employs his administrative skills and his creativity to construct what are no doubt magnificent shrines—for false gods.[1] Solomon becomes a multiculturalist, a manager of diversity.[2]

The list of foreign women in 1 Kgs. 11:1 conflates lists of forbidden unions from the Torah. First Kings 11:2 cites Exod. 23:32–33, a warning against covenants with the nations that Israel is supposed to drive out from the land

---

1. The word for "idol" at several places is a substantive form of the adjective "detestable" (1 Kgs. 11:5, 7). As Walsh points out (1996, 135), the very names of the foreign gods have been changed to bring out their shamefulness. The vocalization of Ashtoreth, for instance, suggests the word for "shame."

2. Thanks to Rusty Reno for this way of describing the situation.

of Canaan, but also alludes to Deut. 7:1, 3, which forbids intermarriage with Hittites, Girgashites, Amorites, Canaanites, Perizzites, Hivites, and Jebusites. First Kings 11 slightly changes the wording of the Torah commandments. Exodus 23:32–33 forbids covenants with the Canaanites, and Deut. 7:3 refers explicitly to intermarriage (ולא תתחתן), but 1 Kings uses the much more general terminology "go among" (לא־תבאו בהם והם לא־יבאו בכם—note the chiastic structure of the clause). As interpreted by the writer of 1–2 Kings, Torah warns not only against covenants and marriages but against close associations of any sort between Israel and idolatrous Gentiles. Intriguingly, the Pentateuch does not forbid association or intermarriage with the Sidonians at all, though Sidonians would come under the larger prohibition of intermarriage with "Canaanites," and the reference to Sidonian women in 1 Kgs. 11:1 foreshadows the great Sidonian witch Jezebel (16:31). When the sons of God marry the daughters of men, Yahweh sends a flood that destroys the human race (Gen. 6:1–4). When Solomon son of Yahweh marries the daughters of Canaanites, Yahweh brings a rebellion that splits the new human race, Israel, in two.

Solomon becomes a polytheist, though no doubt he continues to think of Yahweh as the chief of his pantheon. He puts an idolatrous shrine for Molech right on the Mount of Olives, just to the east of the Temple Mount (1 Kgs. 11:7), before the face of Yahweh (Walsh 1996, 187). First Kings 11:4–8 places striking emphasis on the "heart" of Solomon, using the word four times in 11:3–4, twice with the verb "turn away" (ויטו נשיו את־לבו). The same heart in which Yahweh places wisdom (10:24), the heart that the Lord made wise and discerning (3:9, 12), turns away after other gods. Solomon's "hearing heart" (3:9) is no longer attuned to the Shema's confession of the uniqueness of Yahweh. As a result, Solomon's heart is not "wholly devoted" to Yahweh. The writer uses the verb שלם, which puns on Solomon's name, שלמה, implying that Solomon is *himself* only so long as his heart turns in the right direction, in love toward Yahweh. When Solomon's heart turns and is no longer complete with Yahweh, Solomon ceases to be Solomon. His idolatry is a profound self-alienation, not merely an alienation from Yahweh, and Solomon's self-alienation in idolatry leads to a cultural and political dislocation. The Hebrew word for the "mantle" torn by Ahijah (11:30) contains the same consonants of the king's name (שלמה) (Walsh 1996, 143–44). Ahijah symbolically tears not merely Solomon's kingdom, but Solomon himself. The kingdom is torn, becomes double, because of the divided heart of its king.

Post-Cartesian, postmodern philosophers tell us that the self is not, as Descartes believed, "self-present," but radically "decentered." The more one searches for a stable core of identity within the human ego, the more elusive it appears. This would not have come as a surprise to the theologians of the early Christian tradition. As Hart points out, for Gregory of Nyssa the original act of creation is a movement from "the darkness of nonbeing toward the light of God," and creation is nothing other than ceaseless change: "The created dies every moment, writes Gregory, to be reborn the next," and "if it ceased to change, it would cease to exist." An individual is never merely an individual but a nation, and "the whole of humanity is an unfolding 'series,' a successive realization of the creative word (the first Adam) that God uttered in making humanity in his image" (Hart 2003, 189). Trying to locate a stable, unchanging core *within* a temporal being is a quixotic effort.

For Christian faith, however, to say that a self is not self-centered is not to say that it is without a center. To say that created things are in constant motion is to say that they are constantly pulled by something beyond them, by desire for good or evil. Human existence is ecstatic, centered not in self but in a reach for an elusive beauty, ultimately for the beauty of God: "Desire is the energy of our movement, and so of our being." Creation "is a symphonic and rhythmic complication of diversity, of motion and rest, a song praising God, the true, primordial, archetypal music." More succinctly and beautifully, "we are music moved to music," moved to endlessly various variations by our desire for the boundless and eternal music of God (Hart 2003, 190–94). For Gregory, desire can move away from the infinite toward the "evil" of nonbeing. Gregory treats evil as "that purely privative nothingness that lies outside creation's motion toward God" and "never stands in relation to the infinite but is always an impossible attempt at an ending, a constant breaking of the waves of being upon an uninhabitable shore, the ceaseless cessation of time" (194–95). But this turn to evil is not an original decentering. The self is always decentered, clinging to some "other" in love, centered not in itself but in God. The only question is to which beloved one will cling. When Solomon clings to foreign women, and foreign gods, in love, he ceases to be Solomon because he ceases to be Solomon-with-Yahweh.[3]

This notion of selfhood has profound soteriological implications. As noted in the commentary on 1 Kgs. 4:1–5:18, Calvin insists that humanity's created nature as image is strictly something internal, something within our possession. In postmodern lingo, the essence of Calvin's Adam consists in being a "self-present subject," defined by something that one possesses internally. On the other hand, Calvin insists that justification is *extra nos*, dependent on the work of Christ and on our being outside ourselves in Christ. In postmodern lingo, the essence of Calvin's saved person consists in being a "decentered subject," whose center of existence is located outside oneself. Calvin seems to be operating with a nature/supernature distinction he elsewhere renounces. A saved human is not merely a human in a different condition from a cre-

---

3. Psychologically, the self-present self is a disaster site. Stivers (2004) argues that psychology ignores sociological factors in mental illness, and he argues that depression, schizophrenia, compulsive disorders, and other sorts of psychological ills are related to the social dislocations that have created the "technological self"—a self that is outwardly garrulous and inwardly detached and desperately lonely. Loneliness is an underlying social factor in most mental illness. On the other hand, the "diffused self" of postmodern theory and hypermodern practice is hardly an improvement.

ated human; rather, a saved human and a created human are two different sorts of subject, one defined "in oneself" and the other defined "in another." With regard to justification, one can well query Calvin: Is the person justified when taken out of the self and relocated in Christ? Or does the person remain defined by what one is "in the self"? Is the person righteous in Christ, or a dual person—*simul iustus et peccator* not just in fact but in definition? Because of Calvin's anthropological setup, only sanctification can affect the person ("essentially"). Justification, precisely because it is ecstatic, does not affect identity, since the person is defined by standing within oneself rather than outside.

Bonhoeffer is stronger—more Protestant even—when he insists that the image of God is fundamentally ecstatic, fundamentally an *analogia relationis* rather than an *analogia entis*. Bonhoeffer even introduces soteriological language to describe the original condition of Adam: the *relatio* in which Adam stands to God "is not a human potential or possibility or a structure of human existence; instead it is a given relation, a relation in which human beings are set, a *justitia passiva!*" (Bonhoeffer 2004, 65). Some goods, Augustine argues (1997), are such that they can be possessed only when they are given away; they can be possessed rightly and truly only in dispossession, only in recognizing that the self must be centered in God. The self is among these goods. First Kings 11 suggests a similar anthropology: Solomon is himself not in himself but in relation to his Lord, Yahweh, and when he departs from Yahweh he becomes a different Solomon.

Solomon's idolatry not only leads to profound self-alienation, but has devastating political consequences. The first Adam fell when he listened to the tempting voice of the serpent and ate the fruit offered by his wife. Solomon, the new Adam, falls through his devotion to foreign women, and Yahweh's initial judgment is to raise up adversaries ("satans," שׂטן) (11:14, 23), whose heads the idolatrous Solomon is, in contrast to the faithful Solomon of 1 Kgs. 2, powerless to crush. The three adversaries arise from three groups that oppose Israel throughout its history. Hadad is an Edomite, a descendant of Esau, and his conflict with Solomon continues the original enmity of Jacob and Esau. Rezon is a Gentile, who reigns in Damascus, the capital of Syria or Aram.[4] And Jeroboam I is an internal enemy to the house of David, an Israelite. Within 1–2 Kings, the three "satans" who oppose Solomon foreshadow the three adversaries that later oppose Israel and Judah: Aram, Assyria, and Babylon. In his fall from favor into idolatry as well as in Yahweh's judgment against him, Solomon's life lays the pattern for the history of the kingdom. In the Gospels, representatives of these same three groups oppose Jesus: the Idumean/Edomite Herod, the Roman Gentiles, and the Jewish scribes and Pharisees. Solomon faces these opponents because of his sin, while the one greater than Solomon

4. Aram is a Shemite (Gen. 10:22), and Laban the Aramean is Rebekah's brother (28:5). The Arameans thus are nearer to the covenant people than are Assyria or Babylon.

will face these adversaries, these "satans," not for his own sin but because he bears the sins of his people.

First Kings 11 gives a brief biography of each adversary, and each echoes events in Israel's earlier history. Hadad's story (11:14–22) is one of exile and exodus:[5]

1. As a boy, Hadad is carried to Egypt because Edom is occupied by David and Joab (11:14–15). Earlier, Jacob takes his clan to Egypt because of famine.
2. While in Egypt, Hadad is treated kindly by Pharaoh, given a house, bread, and land (11:18). Jacob's family is treated well by Pharaoh and given the fruitful land of Goshen.
3. Hadad marries into the Egyptian royal family (11:19), just as earlier Joseph receives Pharaoh's favor and marries the daughter of an Egyptian priest.
4. Hadad's son is among the sons of Pharaoh, born to the sister of Tahpenes, the queen of Egypt (11:20). Here we seem to have an echo of the story of Moses, who is raised in Pharaoh's house.
5. When David dies, Hadad sought to return to his land, using exodus language to express his desire: "send me out" (שלחני ואלך אל־ארצי) (11:21–22). Similarly, Israel escapes Egypt in the exodus and conquers the land of Canaan and rules it.

In Hadad's biography, Solomon plays the role of the Canaanites. Solomon marries Canaanites (11:1) and becomes a Canaanite, beleaguered by an Edomite leader who had been through an exodus and is pursuing conquest. Hadad has sufficient power in Edom to become an opponent for Solomon, and this indicates that Edom separates from Israel at this point in history, a power shift from earlier in Solomon's reign (9:26–28). Solomon once exercised sufficient control over Edom to have access to the sea, but Solomon's kingdom contracts from the south, just as it shrinks in a much larger way from the north. Whenever Yahweh judges Israel, he chips away pieces from the kingdom of Israel.[6]

Rezon son of Eliada's story also parallels a story from Israel's history (11:23–25):

5. Nelson (1987, 75) sees the parallels without recognizing their significance to the structure of 1–2 Kings.
6. The biography of Hadad the Edomite ends curiously, with the request to be sent back to his own land but without any indication of whether Pharaoh complies with the request. That Hadad becomes an adversary of Solomon implies that he does return to Edom and begin to chip away chunks from Solomon's kingdom, but the text never tells the return story. In this, the story of Hadad is as unfinished as the story of Israel as the writer of 1–2 Kings and as the Old Testament tells it. Like the story of Hadad, the final book in the Tanak, 2 Chronicles, ends inconclusively, with Cyrus's command to "go up."

1. Rezon flees from his lord, Hadadezer (11:23), as David is threatened and flees from his master, Saul.
2. Rezon gathers a band to himself and becomes a leader of a kind of guerilla force (11:24). David too flees into the wilderness and begins to gather the disaffected to himself, forming them into an "Israel-in-exile."
3. Rezon moves to Damascus to become king over Syria (11:24), as David moves from the wilderness into the land to take the throne at Hebron and eventually at Jerusalem.

If Hadad is a counterfeit Israel (or Joseph/Moses), Rezon is a counterfeit David. In this scenario, Solomon plays the role of Saul, challenged by the "Davidic" Rezon. Ironically, Solomon provides arms to the very Arameans ruled by Rezon (10:29). Solomon gives his "satan" the weapons to fight him.

The longest story is that of Jeroboam I (11:26–40), and his biography too follows earlier biblical history:

1. Like Saul and David (Provan 1995, 97), Jeroboam is a "valiant warrior" (גבור חיל) (11:28), a potentially royal figure.
2. Jeroboam faithfully serves Solomon, a rising star of the royal administration (11:28). The original pattern for this scenario comes from the story of Joseph, but this is refracted through the story of David, who faithfully serves Saul.
3. Jeroboam meets a prophet from Shiloh, who tells him he will be king (11:29–39). David is anointed by Samuel, a prophet who grows up with Eli in Shiloh.
4. Ahijah symbolizes the tearing of the kingdom by tearing a "new cloak" that he wears (11:30). Similarly, the kingdom taken from Saul is symbolized by the torn robe of Saul.
5. Once Solomon finds that Jeroboam has been designated as his successor, he attempts to kill him (11:40), just as Saul attempts several times to kill the anointed prince, David.
6. The promises to Jeroboam (11:38–39) are similar to promises that Yahweh made to David.

David's life is itself a typological repetition of the history of Jacob and of Israel (Leithart 2003d), so Jeroboam is typologically both counterfeit David and counterfeit Israel. In 1 Kgs. 12, Jeroboam is a liberating Moses, leading "Israel" out from the oppressive "Egypt" of the kingdom of Solomon.

In 1 Kgs. 11, we have the first example of prophet-as-outsider,[7] the first prophet born of Spirit, blowing where he wills. Ahijah, unintroduced except

---

7. Nathan appears in 1 Kgs. 1, but functions as a court prophet.

with the ominous description of "Shilonite,"[8] appears from nowhere to speak the word of Yahweh and to redirect the course of Israel's history. The word of the Lord delivered through Ahijah decisively shapes the history that follows, and from this point on in Kings, the "word of Yahweh" is fulfilled at every turn (1 Kgs. 13; 14:18; 15:29; 16:12, 34; 17:16). By the word of Yahweh dynasties rise and fall; by the word of Yahweh barren widows become fruitful and their stores of food are not exhausted; by the word of Yahweh arrows find chinks in armor; by the word of Yahweh the price of grain tumbles overnight; by the word of Yahweh Jerusalem and the temple are destroyed. If the word of Yahweh is so effective in bringing destruction, the same word will preserve the house of David forever. Even death cannot triumph over the word of Yahweh. He promises that he will not destroy David's house (11:12–13, 34–36), but instead will leave a lamp burning (הֱיוֹת־נִיר לְדָוִיד) (11:36). Yahweh disciplines the house of David with the rod of humans, but he does not remove his love from David's house as he removed it from Saul's (2 Sam. 7:14–15). Though Solomon turns from Yahweh and departs from him, though Solomon and his kingdom are both torn in two by his double loyalties, yet Yahweh promises to restore David's house, ultimately through another Son of David, torn in two in his sacrifice on the cross, that he might join all Israel into one new person.

8. The reference to Ahijah's place of origin calls attention to parallels between the fall of Solomon's dynasty and the fall of the dynasty of Eli. These parallels will be brought out clearly by the end of 1–2 Kings, when Zedekiah's sons are killed before he is blinded, and then the temple, like the Shiloh sanctuary, is destroyed (Walsh 1996, 148).

1 KINGS 12:1–24

Israel is called to be a unique people, and its uniqueness is particularly to be in its devotion to the one God of creation. Other nations worship false gods, but Israel is to be exclusively devoted to Yahweh, the creator of heaven and earth. Israel rapidly forsakes that calling, immediately after the exodus, after arriving in the land, and after the Lord set up a monarchy. This is a catastrophe for the people of Yahweh: when Israel turns to other gods it ceases to be Israel.

The initial judgment on the kingdom begins with an assembly at Shechem. Shechem is the place where Israel first renews covenant after the conquest (Josh. 24:1) and the place where Joseph's bones are finally laid to rest (24:32). In the time of the judges, Abimelech has himself crowned king at Shechem (Judg. 9:6). Abimelech is the first man in Israel to call himself king, and he is violent, oppressive, bloodthirsty, power hungry. He slaughters his brothers to gain the throne, and he is ruthless with anyone who crosses him. He is eventually killed by a woman who dropped a millstone on his head, a serpent with a crushed head. A king crowned at Shechem might be a second Abimelech, following his example of oppression and political folly. The association with Abimelech is, to put it mildly, no compliment to Rehoboam.

Shechem has more ancient associations as well. In Gen. 12, Abram enters the land and goes to Shechem, before moving on to Bethel to set up an altar (12:6–8). Jeroboam takes the same route, though his altar is not devoted to the true worship of God (1 Kgs. 12:1–5, 25–33). The two itineraries are linked in central ways. Abram's journey around the land is a protoconquest. Centuries before Joshua enters the land to conquer its people, Abram "conquers" the land by setting up places of true worship throughout. Jeroboam follows the same itinerary as Abram, but instead of moving around the land to establish true worship, he moves from Shechem to Bethel to establish an idolatrous altar. This inverts Israel's purpose in conquest: Jeroboam's work is a kind of anticonquest, a return to the wilderness.

As Frisch (1991, 6–9, 11) suggests, 1 Kgs. 12 is an integral part of the Solomon narratives. It follows naturally from 1 Kgs. 11, fulfilling Ahijah's prophecy about the rending of the kingdom, and 1 Kgs. 11–12 shares important themes and structural patterns with 1 Kgs. 1–2:

> Each pair of chapters contains a political narrative about Solomon's rivals which describes the change that takes place in their status: the fall of Adonijah and the rise of Jeroboam respectively. In each case the candidate who loses out is the one with the best chance and the best right to the throne . . . ; and the startling ascent of his rival is perceived as a work of God. . . . These reversals are described in similar terms: "However the kingdom has *turned about*" . . . (2:15), and "So the king did not hearken to the people; *for it was a turn* of affairs . . . brought about by *the Lord*" . . . (12:15). (Frisch 1991, 8–9 [emphasis original])

At the assembly at Shechem, Jeroboam seems to be a hero stepping out from Israel's early history. Jeroboam leads a delegation asking Rehoboam to lighten the "weight" (הככבד) that Solomon had placed on the people (12:4). Solomon's kingdom is full of "glory" (כבד), but while achieving this glory, he makes things "heavy" for the people. Given regional tensions in Israel, we should be a bit skeptical about the demands coming from the northern tribes. Still, Jeroboam's request is similar to the demand that Moses makes before Pharaoh (Exod. 5:1–14; cf. 1:14; 2:23). Solomon turns to Egypt for horses and chariots, worships the gods of the nations, and transforms his kingdom into an Egyptian tyranny from which Israel seeks to be liberated. Ultimately, Jeroboam leads the people out of bondage into the wilderness. Spiritually, the northern kingdom remains in the wilderness throughout the history in 1–2 Kings, until removed from the land entirely by Assyria. They worship golden calves as Israel had at Sinai (Exod. 32:1–5), never entering rest, never entering the land. Not every leader who sounds like Moses is a Moses. Some, like Jeroboam, begin like Moses only to end like Aaron (Provan 1995, 103).

When Jeroboam's delegation approaches, Rehoboam requests three days to consult with his advisors about the people's request. Rehoboam first consults the old men who were with Solomon and know something of his wisdom. They give Rehoboam good advice, repeating the word "serve" (1 Kgs. 12:7). Rehoboam must serve the people one day, and they would be his servants "all the days." Apparently, the old men believe that Jeroboam has a point and that Rehoboam needs to lighten the burden that Solomon placed on the people. They also conceive of a king as a servant rather than master of the people.[1]

---

1. It is possible to interpret the elders' advice more cynically. The word "answer" in 12:7 puns on the word "afflict," used in 11:39. First Kings 12:7 might read, "if today you are a servant and will serve them, and afflict/answer them, and speak good words to them, then they will be your servants forever." On this reading, the elders are cunning, though not wise in the sense

Rehoboam is forty-one years old when he becomes king (14:21), so the "boys" (הילדים) that he consults in 12:10 are in early middle age, yet they are "boys" both in being younger than the "elders" and in their youthful folly and adolescent bravado. Instead of promising to lighten the burden, they advise Rehoboam to make the burden heavier (Exod. 5:1–2), a Pharaoh-like act (Provan 1995, 104). Their advice is phrased in vulgar terms. "My little finger" is literally "my little thing" (קטני), and the comparison with "loins" suggests a phallic reference (Nelson 1987, 79). If Israel feels "raped" by Solomon, Rehoboam plans to give them more of the same. Rehoboam's advisors are "boys" who identify cruelty with leadership, who are flexing their political muscles for the first time, who think that the main thing that people need is a good dose of discipline. The boys would be perfect candidates for Hitler Youth, if only they weren't so old.

Rehoboam follows the advice of the "boys," answering the complaint about "harsh" labor (12:4) by speaking "harshly" (12:13) (Walsh 1996, 164). He displays further stupidity in sending Adoram, head of the corvée, to the northern tribes (12:18). Even after the northern tribes leave Shechem, Rehoboam is *still* determined to impose a harsh discipline on them (Provan 1995, 107). Adoram is killed, and Rehoboam has to flee for his life, but then gathers an army of 180,000 men to try again and only stops when a prophet intervenes. If Solomon's idolatry is the source of the kingdom's division, Rehoboam's folly is the immediate mechanism. Rehoboam's folly is a characteristic folly of a "boy," a young man who chooses advisors full of youthful pride, cockiness, and crudity, the type of companion against whom Proverbs warns repeatedly (13:20; 28:7; cf. Ps. 119:63). The contrast of youth and age is crucial, and Rehoboam's story is a cautionary tale in an age intoxicated as ours is with youth and youth culture.

The history of the divided kingdom was contested territory during the Reformation. As Radner notes, Calvin's *Reply to Sadoleto* "attempts to explain the apparent 'schism' of the Reformers in terms of the figure of the faithful 'remnant' of Israelite prophets and their followers who set themselves 'against' the corruption of the rulers and priests of the nation." The Roman church especially is "figured in the Israel of kings Zedekiah and Jehoiakim, far fallen from the purity of David and Solomon's rule, and prophetically destined for dismemberment and destruction at the hands of avenging agents." This figural rhetoric was also employed by the seventeenth-century English Puritans. John Owen characterizes the Roman church as idolatrous, contemptuous of the word of God, and internally schismatic. Not to be outdone, Catholics refer to the history of Kings to characterize "the Roman Church in the figure of a chosen people victimized by their own children" (Radner 1998, 30).

---

that Solomon was wise. They are shrewd enough to give the appearance of being conciliatory, but not wise enough to actually rule with gentleness (Walsh 1996, 162).

First Kings 12 provides several insights into the causes and nature of Christian division. As noted in the introduction to this commentary, 1–2 Kings points to idolatry as the root cause of division within Israel and within the church, and, at least from the Protestant side, this is borne out by the history of the Protestant Reformation. Underlying *sola fide* was the confession that salvation and justification are found *solo Christo*, and this was for the Reformers simply another way of saying that *sola fide* was inseparable from *sola Dei Gloria*. To say that one is justified and saved by faith alone is to say that salvation is God's work, not the work of humans, and that salvation exalts and glorifies the saving God. The same principle is at the foundation of *sola scriptura*. As Barth and many others note, *sola scriptura* is not *merely* a "formal" principle, as if it were nothing more than a piece of theological method (Barth 1939–69, 1.1.248–75). Behind the affirmation of *sola scriptura* is the question of authority: Whose voice guides the church? Is the church guided by itself *and* God—or by the voice of God alone? Somewhat more modestly but no less radically, *sola scriptura* can be understood as the affirmation that "all church teaching is corrigible."[2] God's godness, his lordship over the church, remains the fundamental issue. From this perspective, then, the dual principles of the Reformation are aspects of a basic challenge to the idolatries that had infiltrated the theology and practices of the medieval church.

The Reformation protest against idolatry expressed itself even more clearly in the Reformation challenge to medieval liturgical practice and piety. Like the great biblical reformations of Hezekiah and Josiah, the practical side of the Reformation was a purging of idolatry, a stripping of the altars. This was especially evident in the Continental Reformed branch of the Reformation. In the Swiss cantons, the coming of Reformation was marked by outbreaks of iconoclasm and emptying of reliquaries, spreading from Bern to Basel to Neuchâtel and Geneva (Eire 1989). Alongside a satiric attack on the idolatrous veneration of relics, Calvin insisted that relics were spiritually destructive because they pointed sinners away from those designated sites where Christ had promised to make himself available—in the water, where God speaks his word, at the table, in the fellowship of saints (Calvin 1983, 1.289–341).

Luther's focus on idolatry is perhaps less visible, but it is no less central to his concerns. In a stimulating essay, Lutheran theologian Yeago argues that the key question that sparked Luther's "Reformation turn" was not "How can I find a gracious God?" but "How can I find the true God?" As Yeago writes, Luther's early writings show an obsession with "the threat of *idolatry*, not a craving for assurance of forgiveness" (1996, 17). Above all, Luther wanted to root out the subtle spiritual idolatry of treating God as a means to the end of one's own spiritual satisfaction. Operating with an Augustinian distinction between *uti*

---

2. This is the formulation of Kevin Vanhoozer, given in a response to a paper read by Stanley Hauerwas at the 2004 American Academy of Religion meeting.

and *frui*,[3] between the use of created things and the enjoyment of God, Luther worried that in his sin he would act as if God were in the category of the "useful" instead of the "enjoyable." In this way, even the sinner's religious devotions can be idolatrous, an expression of the sinner's tendency to "curve in on himself" (*incurvatus in se*).[4] For all these reasons, the Reformers charged that the Roman Catholic tolerance of idolatry, not the Reformers' protests against it, were the root cause of the church's division. If there is something to this Reformation protest, as I believe there is, then Christian reunion will happen through the renunciation of the idols that caused division in the first place.

Yet, 1–2 Kings also shows that a division in government is not necessarily a division among the people (Walsh 1996, 203). When Rehoboam wants to pursue the Israelites and force them back into the house of David, the Lord through the prophet says, "You must not go up and fight against your brothers, the sons of Israel" (1 Kgs. 12:24). Long after this event, when the northern kingdom has promoted Baal worship and attacked the prophets of Yahweh, Yahweh still regards them as his covenant people (2 Kgs. 13:22–25). Likewise, all who are baptized wear the name of Jesus, and we should recognize them as fellow citizens of the church of Christ, yet this does not mean that the various churches can leave each other alone, overlooking genuine error or heteropraxy. Baptists and Episcopalians, Presbyterians and Lutherans, Orthodox and Roman Catholics are siblings, but it does not follow that each accepts the sins and errors of others. A sibling relation does not mean universal affirmation. Quite the contrary: siblings *confront*, albeit as siblings.

A "twist from Yahweh" (כִּי־הָיְתָה סִבָּה מֵעִם יְהוָה): that is what the writer of Kings calls the division of the kingdom (1 Kgs. 12:15). Rehoboam

---

3. "Enjoy" for Augustine means "enjoy for its own sake, as an end in itself." According to Augustine's formulation, therefore, the only "thing" that should be enjoyed is God himself, and all other things should be used as means to achieve this enjoyment. There is thus a twofold potential for idolatry: enjoying anything other than God turns that thing into an idol, and "using" God to enjoy something else is also an idolatrous attempt to master God, thus in effect making a claim to be God (Augustine 1997, 9–10).

4. Luther returned to this theme frequently: "Our nature, by the corruption of the first sin, is so deeply curved in on itself that it not only bends the best gifts of God toward itself and enjoys them (as is plain in the works-righteous and hypocrites), or rather even uses God himself in order to attain those gifts, but it also fails to realize that it so wickedly, curvedly, and viciously seeks all things, even God, for its own sake" (quoted in Yeago 1996, 19). Anyone who believes that he or she can "use" the true God is clearly, Luther thought, not dealing with the true God, who always remains the sovereign Lord. Using God for our own satisfaction is tantamount to worshiping of God of our own making: "By the same steps [of idolatry] people even today arrive at a spiritual and more subtle idolatry, which is now quite common, by which God is worshiped, not as he is, but as he is imagined and reckoned to be. For ingratitude and love of vanity (that is, one's sense of oneself and of one's own righteousness, or, as they say, one's good intention) violently blind people, so that they are incorrigible, and unable to believe otherwise than that they are acting splendidly and pleasing God. And in this way they form a God favorable to themselves, even though he really is not so. And so they more truly worship their fantasy than the true God, whom they believe to be like that fantasy" (quoted in Yeago 1996, 19).

acts willfully, stupidly, brazenly, with foolish bravado, but the division is not ultimately Rehoboam's doing but Yahweh's. As is already evident in 1 Kgs. 1, Yahweh sovereignly rules even in the midst of human stupidity, ensuring that his promise to Jeroboam comes to pass. Yahweh fulfills his word, and even the folly and sin and youthful stupidity of Rehoboam cannot stop it. But the idea of the division of the kingdom as a "twist" not only points to Yahweh's sovereign control of these events, but to the shrewdness and cunning that he displays in these events. Yahweh turns Rehoboam's power play against him. Instead of intimidating the northern tribes into submission, he drives them away; instead of gaining greater authority over Israel, he loses all authority over Israel. To the kind, David writes, Yahweh shows himself kind. To the blameless, he shows himself blameless. But to the crooked, he shows himself twisted (Ps. 18:25–26). This will not be the last time the narrator of 1–2 Kings makes this point.

There is a larger divine intent here as well, an even bigger twist. The whole of 1–2 Kings is overshadowed by Yahweh's fixed intent to fulfill his promise to David. David's son will rule forever, as the Abrahamic seed who will bring blessing to the Gentiles and restore the creation, but the path toward this universal blessing is not easy, nor is the gate wide. Narrow is the gate and hard the way that leads to the Davidic promise. The way lies through death and division; the way is the way of death and resurrection. With Abraham, Yahweh selects one nation from among the nations to be the priestly people, to be the agent of salvation for the world. Life begins to come to the divided human race when Yahweh tears the human race again, into Jew and Gentile. In 1–2 Kings, Israel relives the history of the human race in its own Adamically shaped history, recapitulating the division and reunion of humanity in its own division and ultimate reunion.

The history of Israel is a history of sacrifice: the holy people is torn in two, broken into pieces, and finally immolated in the fire that burned Samaria and Jerusalem. Yet, that sacrifice is fulfilled in a new Israel, the Israel of the restoration. Ultimately, this is the cunning plan, the "twist from God" that the church proclaims as gospel and celebrates as Eucharist. Jesus, the true Israel, reunites the nations in himself by offering himself to be torn and by entrusting himself to his Father, who raises the dead. God's strange plan for salvation has been fulfilled in Jesus, and we are caught up in that plan as the new human race, the true Israel, gathered at his table to break and share bread.

1 KINGS 12:25–13:34

The break between 1 Kgs. 12 and 1 Kgs. 13 obscures the relation of the two chapters. There is a clear inclusio between 12:25–33 and 13:33–34, in that the oracle of the prophet of Bethel in 13:32 mentions the altar in Bethel and the "houses of the high places" mentioned in 12:31, 33. Further, 13:33–34 repeats some phrases from 12:30–31 in reverse order, so that, as Walsh points out, a chiastic inclusio surrounds the passage (1996, 190):

A and this thing was as sin (12:30)
> B and he made the house of the high places (12:31a)
>> C and he made priests from the extremities of the people (12:31b)
>> C′ and he made from the extremities of the people priests (13:33a)
> B′ and there were priests of the high places (13:33b)
A′ and this thing became as a sin (13:34a)[1]

The story of the man of God from Judah is thus a part of the story of Jeroboam I's reign, and the man of God from Judah confronts Jeroboam while he sacrifices at a shrine for the golden calves at Bethel.

Rehoboam is the Pharaoh of the previous chapter, and Jeroboam the liberating savior of Israel, but Jeroboam is no Moses. His golden calves instead recall Aaron's idolatry in Exod. 32, and this association is strengthened by the similarity of Jeroboam's announcement and Aaron's: "Behold your gods, O Israel, who brought you up from the land of Egypt" (1 Kgs. 12:28; cf. Exod. 32:4). Jeroboam even names his two sons after Aaron's sons (1 Kgs. 14:1, 20;

---

1. At the same time, there are also inclusios surrounding 1 Kgs. 13. See Mead 1999, 194–96, who offers a very useful parallel outline of 1 Kgs. 13.

Lev. 10) (Walsh 1996, 173n1). The Moses figure in 1 Kgs. 13 is the "man of God from Judah"[2] who confronts the "Aaronic" Jeroboam and splits the altar as Moses broke the tablets of the covenant at the foot of Sinai (Exod. 32:19–20).

Jeroboam is a sociologist of religion who would have been deeply enamored of Durkheim's notion that society is the true object of worship (Provan 1995, 109–10). Despite Yahweh's assurance that his kingdom would endure, Jeroboam fears that the people will return to David if they continue to worship in Jerusalem (1 Kgs. 12:26–27; cf. 11:34–39) and initiates liturgical innovations to prevent it. In place of the Mosaic feast of booths in the seventh month (Lev. 23), he institutes a feast in the eighth month (1 Kgs. 12:32), and he consecrates priests from outside the family of Aaron (12:31–32). In place of Solomon's temple in Jerusalem, he constructs shrines for golden calves.[3] Though he introduces new elements in Israel's worship, Jeroboam positions himself as an Aaronic restorationist maintaining the true tradition of Israel's worship over against Mosaic and Solomonic innovations. He understands the community-building power of ritual and sets out to exploit it, manipulating religious images to maintain social and political cohesion and attempting to harness the forces of worship in support of his political power. Confronted by the word of Yahweh, that hope is destined to have an ironic outcome. Ahijah warns him: keeping, not breaking, Yahweh's commandments is the way to long-lasting political success (11:38). Rejecting the "way" of Yahweh, Jeroboam walks in his own way and causes Israel to do the same. Because Jeroboam attempts to unify the people through idolatry, his kingdom is eventually subdivided into the faithful prophetic communities and an idolatrous mainline (1 Kgs. 17–2 Kgs. 8). National and religious division are the results of the application of the sociology of religion.

Yahweh does not let Jeroboam get away with it for long. The break at the beginning of 1 Kgs. 13 is abrupt. Normally, Hebrew narrative moves from one verb to another, using the word "and" (ו, *vav*). ו followed by something other than a verb marks a disjunction in the text, and thus 13:1, which uses this disjunctive syntax, might be translated, "Look, see, a man of God coming from Judah by the word of the Lord to Bethel." The courtly liturgical scene is disrupted by a flash across the screen, a man of God coming from Judah, a man of the Spirit who blows where he lists (Walsh 1996, 176).[4] Prophets break into and out of the normal "chronicled" history, the usual progression of kings and successors, as Yahweh slices across the grain of history with his prophetic word.

2. Moses is called the "man of God" in the Pentateuch (Deut. 33:1; cf. Josh. 14:6; Judg. 13:6). The word "sign" (1 Kgs. 13:3, 5) is more often translated "wonder" or "marvel." Though it is often associated with signs, it is different from the specific term for signs. These terms are used to describe the wonders that Moses performed in Egypt (Exod. 7:9). The man of God who confronts Jeroboam is a Mosaic figure, performing signs before an Israelite "Pharaoh."

3. Both Bethel and Dan are traditional centers of religious activity. Jacob named Bethel (Gen. 28:19), while Dan had been a shrine since the time of the judges (Judg. 18:27–31).

4. This same device is used in 1 Kgs. 17:1, with the appearance of Elijah.

The story of the man of God and the old prophet is one of the strangest narrative passages in the Old Testament and deserves a monograph to itself. At the most basic narrative level, it raises many puzzles, even if we eschew (which we cannot) attempting to understand the point of the story. The man of God from Judah prophesies against the altar rather than against Jeroboam. Why is the altar the focus of attention? How does the splitting of the altar confirm his word? Characters are undermotivated (or perhaps overmotivated): Why does Jeroboam invite the man of God to eat and drink with him? Why does the old prophet lie? There are uncanny moments: a hand withered and healed; the altar splits; a man-killing lion springs on the disobedient man of God, but is suddenly tame enough to sit amicably beside a donkey. The moral perspective of the story is unsettling. Jeroboam is clearly a villain, but the man of God, true prophet though he is, falls, and the old prophet who seduces him from the way announces the oracle that condemns him. In the end, the lying prophet survives to a peaceful death while the courageous man of God is mauled by a lion and buried far from his home, an unnerving injustice.

The internal difficulties of the narrative are made more complex by multiple echoes with other parts of 1–2 Kings. The garment "torn" from Solomon (11:30) is linked to the tearing of Jeroboam's altar (13:5, using the same verb: קרע).[5] Jeroboam's "hand" that receives the kingdom (11:12, 31, 34–35) withers (13:4). Ahijah "takes hold" of his robe (11:30), as Jeroboam orders his men to "take hold" of the man of God (13:4), and the "way" first mentioned in 11:29 becomes a leitmotif throughout 1 Kgs. 13. In both 1 Kgs. 13 and 20, two prophets speak, one disobeys, and a lion kills the disobedient. Looking more broadly, 1 Kgs. 13 is one of the structural pillars of 1–2 Kings, linked with two other key texts in 2 Kings—the postmortem of Israel (2 Kgs. 17) and the reforms of Josiah (2 Kgs. 23)—by multiple rare phrases: "cities of Samaria" (1 Kgs. 13:32; 2 Kgs. 17:24–28; 23:19), "priests of the high places" (1 Kgs. 13:33; 2 Kgs. 17:32; 23:9, 20), and "shrines of the high places" (1 Kgs. 12:31; 13:32; 2 Kgs. 17:29, 32; 23:19) (cf. Lemke 1976, 307–13). These three passages surround the history of the northern kingdom and of Jeroboam's liturgical program, and 1 Kgs. 13 reaches over the history of Israel until it comes to fulfillment in 2 Kgs. 23.

Many of the key themes of 1–2 Kings are also developed or initiated here. Walking the "way of Jeroboam" is the recurring sin of northern Kings. Yahweh's word delivered by the man of God from Judah is immediately and dramatically fulfilled. Much of the passage focuses on the conflict of two prophets, one of whom is a lying prophet (1 Kgs. 22), and the miraculous events of the story anticipate the ministries of Elijah and Elisha. Commentators often point out that none of the main characters of the story are named; they are simply "king,"

---

5. "Tearing" and "pouring" (שפך) is an unusual way to describe the destruction of an altar and suggests an analogy between the destruction of the altar and the rending of a human body. It thus foreshadows the lion who tears the man of God (though the verb is not the same).

"man of God," "prophet." One effect of this technique is to highlight geography. By virtue of his designation, the man of God becomes representative of Judah, while the old prophet stands for Bethel and Israel, suggesting that the whole history of Israel and Judah is somehow foreshadowed in this chapter.

Whatever else we might say about this story, the narrator believes that Jeroboam should have taken warning from these events and did not (13:33–34). What is Jeroboam supposed to learn? The man of God demonstrates the power of the word of Yahweh by splitting the altar (13:3, 5), and Jeroboam should reason that his prediction about Josiah is equally accurate (13:2). Altars represent humans and nations (18:30–40), and the tearing of the altar represents the "tearing" of the kingdom from Jeroboam's hand, just as it was torn from Solomon's hand and given to Jeroboam in the first place. Jeroboam sets up an altar to maintain the unity of the northern kingdom, but that altar is split in two, indicating that the sociologist of religion is not going to stand against Yahweh's prophet. On the other hand, at Jeroboam's request, the man of God prays and heals the king's hand (13:6), a sign of what can happen to Jeroboam's kingdom if he seeks Yahweh through his prophet. Instead, however, Jeroboam "does not return" from the way of idolatry (13:33–34). When Moses grounds the golden calf to powder, Aaron has the sense not to make another one. Jeroboam is defiant: in spite of the proofs of the man of God's reliability, he rebuilds the altar and continues to worship calves at Bethel.[6] When Jeroboam later consults a prophet about his sick son (1 Kgs. 14), it is too late. By renewing his perverse covenant, he has chosen his path. An idolatrous king can pray and be healed; but a healed king who sets his restored hand to rebuild his idols is a dog returning to vomit (2 Pet. 2:20–22), and his last state is worse than the first.

The encounter of the old prophet and the man of God likewise serves as a warning to Jeroboam. Yahweh prohibits the man of God from eating and drinking "in this place," probably a reference to Bethel rather than to the whole northern kingdom (Walsh 1996, 180). He is under a food prohibition, like Adam, and the old prophet thus plays the role of Satan. The narrator draws out the implications for Jeroboam by rearranging the characters in different scenes:

	speaker	action	hearer
scene 1	man of God	confronts	king
scene 2	king	tempts	man of God
scene 3	prophet	tempts	man of God
scene 4	prophet	confronts	man of God

Two contrasts emerge from this. At the center of the story, the man of God faces two temptations, successfully resisting the first but succumbing to the

---

6. Moses, by contrast, breaks the tablets of the covenant (Exod. 32:19) and receives a new set of tablets, a sign that Yahweh has renewed covenant (34:1). Jeroboam's rebuilt altar is a perverse covenant renewal, as if Aaron had gathered the dust of his golden calf to make a new one.

second. At the borders of the story are two prophetic confrontations. In the first, the man of God confronts Jeroboam, warning him of destruction, while in the second, the old prophet confronts the man of God, warning him of immediate death. By the time we reach scene 4, the prophet is in the same relation to the man of God as the man of God is to Jeroboam, and as a result what happens to the man of God serves as a warning of what will happen to Jeroboam. The man of God resists the seductions of the king, as Jeroboam appeals for help when his hand withers. But the man of God falls when seduced for a second time, as does Jeroboam. Always, the church's greatest tests come not from kings who call for imprisonment and torture; Christians relish martyrdom. The great tests arise from lying prophets, from wolfish bishops and priests, pastors and preachers.

The man of God's story offers a lesson for Jeroboam and also for all other kings of the north. During the Omride dynasty, the lone lying prophet of 1 Kgs. 13 multiplies to Ahab's hundreds of lying prophets (18:19). The man of God from Judah cannot defend himself by saying he has been lied to. He does not even try, and Israel's kings likewise have no excuse. Even when Ahab is surrounded by hundreds of deceptive prophets, Yahweh still judges him for his idolatries. He has Moses, and that is enough to resist blandishments of false prophets.

The narrator develops this cautionary tale largely through the terms "way" and "return." Deuteronomy frequently describes obedience to Yahweh's commandments in terms of "walking in the way" (5:33; 9:12, 16; 11:28), but this metaphorical usage is set up in Deuteronomy by repeated references to Israel's travels between Egypt and the plains of Moab (1:2, 19, 22, 31, 33, 40). Literal and metaphorical ways are integrated: Israel comes on the way out of Egypt to the promised land, but the way to enter the land and conquer it is not simply a roadway but a way of obedience. When Israel turns from the way of Yahweh's commandments, it will be on the way out of the promised land. When the man of God goes on the way back to Bethel, he is also on the way to destruction and to a grave in a foreign land: the road to Bethel is the road to exile. Once again, the experience of the man of God serves as a warning to Jeroboam. When he refuses to return (or repent) from his way (1 Kgs. 13:33), he leads Israel out of the land flowing with milk and honey into the howling waste, where they again turn to worship of golden calves. The law warns about false prophets (Deut. 12:32–13:5), and the proof that a false prophet is a false prophet is that he encourages disobedience to the commandments of God. In Deut. 13:5, the false prophet spoke about "turning against Yahweh your God," and the repetition of "turning" in 1 Kgs. 13 alludes to this passage in Deuteronomy.

Because the man of God disobeys the word of Yahweh, Yahweh sends a lion to kill him. Lions and other wild animals are instruments of judgment in a number of places in 1–2 Kings. Another prophet is killed by a lion when he fails to obey the word of the Lord (1 Kgs. 20:36), bears attack mocking "boys" (2 Kgs. 2:23–25), and Yahweh sends lions into Israel after the Assyrian deportation (17:24–26). Yahweh "gives" the man of God to the lion, and in a number of places Yahweh himself is depicted as a lion who tears his people as prey or who roars from Zion (Hos. 5:14–15; 11:10; 13:7; Joel 3:16; Amos 1:2). Judah is a lionlike tribe (Gen. 49:9), and in the context of 1 Kgs. 13 Josiah is the promised lion from the house of David who will be roused against Jeroboam's altar and against all the houses of the high places.

As noted above, throughout this chapter the principal characters are anonymous, simply "man of God" and "prophet." Apart from 1 Kgs. 13:1, Jeroboam himself is not named either but is simply "the king." This makes the specific naming of Josiah in 13:2 all the more striking, and the style also suggests that the characters are not being treated as individuals so much as archetypes or roles. Jeroboam becomes generic or representative king, and the two prophets are generic prophets. Further, as noted above, the two prophets are identified by their country of origin or by their actions: the man of God is from Judah, and the old prophet is from Bethel. That the man of God is from Judah does not appear particularly germane to the particular story, but it is repeated so often that it becomes a significant theme. Walsh puts it this way:

> The individuals mirror their kingdoms, and their tragedy portends the tragic destiny awaiting Israel and Judah. Israel has become unfaithful. Judah can speak the word that Israel needs to hear; but if Judah, too, following Israel's lead, compromises its worship (as history shows it will do), then both are doomed to overcome their separation only in death. Judah will be buried in an alien land, and Israel will be saved only so far as it is joined to Judah. (Walsh 1989, 368)

Judah remains for centuries as a prophetic witness against the northern kingdom, but at some time, Israel seduces Judah as the old prophet seduces the man of God from Judah. Eventually, the two nations will be united in death, in the grave of exile. This is the ironic end of Jeroboam's experiment in religious sociology. The ritual, architectural, and iconographic instruments he uses to unite his kingdom destroy it; the kingdom is reunited only under Josiah, when Jeroboam's program is finally brought to an end. Yahweh is not susceptible to partisan manipulation. He is the judge, not the underwriter, of human power, and his prophetic, judging word will triumph. As noted in the introduction to this commentary, this also has ecumenical implications, for it suggests that no amount of maneuvering or shrewd compromise will reunite a divided church. God will reunite the church by raising one church at the far end of the death of exile.

I noted above that the structure of the narrative identifies the man of God with Jeroboam, both recipients of prophetic doom. But the man of God is also identified with the old prophet. He eats and drinks at his house, leaves on the prophet's donkey, and after being carefully distinguished as "man of God" through most of the narrative is suddenly called a "prophet" in 13:23.

The man of God takes on the identity of the lying prophet, but, more than that, he takes the punishment that the lying prophet deserves, just as Judah was willing to give his life for his brother Benjamin (Gen. 43:8–10; 44:18–34). The Israel that centers its worship on Bethel and golden calves is doomed, and Israel will not be saved until Judah dies too. But the death of Judah holds out hope for the restoration and reunion with Israel. By identifying with the man of God in his death, the old prophet hopes that his bones will rest in peace. As he is united with the man of God in his grave, Israel will be reunited with Judah in the grave of death, in the grave of exile. The death of Israel will not save Israel; but when Judah dies, then all Israel will be saved.

And so, the prophetic power of this chapter stretches beyond Josiah. Many centuries later, another man of God condemns the shrines of Israel as "dens of thieves." Another and greater Josiah, a scion of the house of David, throws tables and disrupts the worship of the temple, as the man of God disrupts Jeroboam's worship. Another prophet resists the seductions of dining with demons and holds fast to his Father's word. Ironically, the fate of this faithful prophet is the same as the fate of the unfaithful man of God, and he is mauled and exiled to a grave of another man. But this prophet and this Josiah do not remain in the grave, any more than Israel and Judah do; for he is Judah who dies for the sake of the harlot Israel.

1 KINGS 14:1–31

"In my beginning is my end," writes T. S. Eliot at the beginning of "East Coker," one of the *Four Quartets*. It is a doubly melancholic observation. Every beginning initiates a history that will ultimately end, so that the brightness of the day is overshadowed by the inevitable approach of night. No sooner is Heorot built than the poet is thinking, with grim Anglo-Saxon realism, of its demise:

> Far and wide through the world, I have heard,
> orders for work to adorn that wallstead
> were sent to many peoples. And soon it stood there,
> finished and ready, in full view,
> the hall of halls. Heorot was the name
> he had settled on it, whose utterance was law.
> Nor did he renege, but doled out rings
> and torques at the table. The hall towered,
> its gables wide and high and awaiting
> a barbarous burning. That doom abided,
> but in time it would come: the killer instinct
> unleashed among in-laws, the blood-lust rampant.[1]

Beginnings at the same time appear to set a path for the future from which no real escape is possible. Those who do poorly in grade school are condemned (an apt usage!) to a lifetime of remedial education; marital problems in the first year of marriage are never resolved, and husband and wife spend the rest of their lives grimly repeating the same perverse behaviors; children who are out of control before they are six are beyond recovery at thirteen; careers begin with a dead-end job and never make it out of the basement. Good beginnings often

1. Beowulf, lines 74–85, from the translation of Heaney 2000, 7.

prelude a future of uninterrupted success, but this can be equally depressing for those who were something less than golden children in their youth.

The dynasty of Jeroboam I seems to confirm this tragic wisdom. Jeroboam's reign begins with an exodus. Like Moses, he confronts Solomon's son Rehoboam, calling on the king of Judah to "lighten the burden" and "let my people go" (1 Kgs. 12:4). When Rehoboam brusquely threatens (12:12–15), like Pharaoh (Exod. 5:1–14), to make the burden of Israel heavier, Jeroboam leads a defection from the house of David, which has become no better than another Egyptian house of bondage. Yet, as we have seen, Jeroboam quickly proves to be more Aaron than Moses. Instead of allowing Israel to worship in Jerusalem, he sets up high places in Dan and Bethel, where he leads Israel in worshiping golden calves (1 Kgs. 12:25–33). According to Jeroboam, Israel's worship is still offered to the God of the exodus (12:28), but the Lord sees it as a contemptuous rejection of him (14:9). It is not so much a violation of the first commandment as of the second, by which Yahweh prohibits the use of images in Israel's worship (Exod. 20:4–6). As Yahweh threatened, Israel's dynasties last into only the third and fourth generations. Yahweh sends a man of God from Judah to challenge and confront Jeroboam (1 Kgs. 13), as Moses the man of God confronted Aaron at the foot of Sinai when Sinai was worshiping golden calves (Exod. 32), but still Jeroboam does not turn.

Ahijah prophesies not only the death of Jeroboam's son, but the catastrophe that befalls the entire house of Jeroboam. Children are the future, and this is eminently true of the children of a king. A king needs an heir, a successor, if his kingdom is not to fall into turmoil upon his death. The death of a king's son is the death of the king's house, the death of his dynasty. Despite the favor that Yahweh shows to Jeroboam, he tosses Yahweh behind his back and instead turns toward "other gods," the calves of gold. He does "evil," and so Yahweh will bring "evil" on him (1 Kgs. 14:9–10). Like Egypt, the house of Jeroboam is to be overthrown and decimated.

The prophet announces the end of Jeroboam's house in strikingly harsh language (Walsh 1996, 197), which modern translations have unfortunately Victorianized. The phrase translated "every male" actually means (in the robust Jacobean rendering of the Authorized Version) "him that pisseth against the wall" (משתין בקיר) (Leithart 2001), and 14:10 ends with a warning that Yahweh's wrath will burn away the members of the house of Jeroboam in the way that dung is burned (יבער הגלל).[2] Passages such as these occur with some regularity in historical and prophetic literature. Jezebel's corpse is like "dung upon the ground" (2 Kgs. 9:37), and corpses of those killed by invading Babylonians are like dung (Jer. 8:2; 9:22; 16:4; 25:33). These passages are moderate in comparison with the grotesque sexual imagery of Ezek. 16 and 23, which describe, in graphic detail, the unfaithfulness of Israel toward Yahweh, her husband. Nor is such language confined to the Old Testament. Jesus

2. Dung was used for fuel in the ancient world (Ezek. 4:12, 15).

advises against casting pearls before undeserving "swine" (Matt. 7:6); Paul calls Judaizers "castrati" (Phil. 3:2); and Peter warns of apostates who are like "dogs returning to their vomit" (2 Pet. 2:22). Vulgarity and scatology are weapons in the rhetorical arsenal of prophecy, and, from the perspective of the writer of 1–2 Kings, we cannot find fault with the language without finding fault with God himself, since Ahijah claims to be speaking the words that Yahweh delivered to him (1 Kgs. 14:7, 11). Yahweh uses shocking language when he calls useless men "those who piss against the wall" and speaks of an idolatrous royal house as a pile of shit.[3]

It goes without saying that such language has little place in religious discourse in the early twenty-first century and might even qualify as hate speech in some contexts. Earlier centuries of theologians were not so rhetorically tepid; reformers in both the Middle Ages and the Protestant Reformation attacked the abuses of the church with the rhetorical fervor of a prophet. Irenaeus's response to Gnosticism, *Against All Heresies*, provides a fine example (Irenaeus 1981). Large stretches of his treatise are virtually unreadable today. Most of the first two books consist of intricate retellings of a hundred and one variations on gnostic myth, of interest to almost no one except patristic specialists, modern gnostics, feminists, or any combination of the three. Another major section contains a ponderous proof of the obvious fact that the New Testament teaches that Yahweh is the same God as the Father of Jesus Christ.

In the course of his treatise, however, Irenaeus made some theological moves that have enduring relevance for the church. Against the gnostic denigration of the physical world, Irenaeus insisted on the biblical doctrines of incarnation, resurrection, and Eucharist, demonstrating that the gnostic system was fundamentally inconsistent with cardinal doctrines and practices of Christian faith. Gnostic interpretation of the Bible ignored context and erased the distinction between word and referent with its simplistic assumption that different names for God implied different persons. Brilliant as some of his theological argumentation is, Irenaeus is most effective, and certainly most entertaining, when he resorted, as he frequently did, to irony and outright mockery. In one early passage of the treatise, he lost patience with the wholesale arbitrariness of the gnostic system. If the gnostics can fabricate divine beings *ex nihilo*, Irenaeus concluded, so can anyone else. The bishop of Lyons thus proposed the following account of the origin of the material world:

> There is a certain Proarche, royal, surpassing all thought, a power existing before every other substance, and extended into space in every direction. But along with it there exists a power that I term a Gourd; and along with this Gourd there exists a power that again I term Utter-Emptiness. This Gourd and Emptiness, since they are one, produced (and yet did not simply produce, so as to be apart from themselves) a fruit, everywhere visible, eatable, and

---

3. The reference is probably to the corpses of the men of Jeroboam's house, which will be laid out on the ground with no one to bury them.

delicious, which fruit-language calls a Cucumber. Along with this Cucumber
exists a power of the same essence, which again I call a Melon. These powers,
the Gourd, Utter-Emptiness, the Cucumber, and the Melon, brought forth
the remaining multitude of delirious Melons of Valentinus [a leading gnostic].
(*Against All Heresies* 1.11.4)

A thoroughly biblical theology will consider these biblical and historical prec-
edents carefully, for a truly biblical theology must be biblical not only in
content but in form.

In the story of the death of Abijah, the exodus is systematically reversed.
At Passover, the Lord preserves the firstborn sons of Israel; but Yahweh does
not pass over the son of Jeroboam, apparently the firstborn and heir apparent
of Jeroboam, even though he acknowledges that Abijah is the best that the
house of Jeroboam can offer (1 Kgs. 14:13). There is no doorway sprinkled
with the blood of a substitute, and no angel of Yahweh crossing over to stand
at the threshold of the house (Exod. 12:13). There is only the fateful footfall
of Jeroboam's wife on the threshold that proclaims the doom of her son. As
she passes through the doorway, her son passes from life to death. The doorway, frequently associated with births and renewals (Gen. 18; 2 Kgs. 4:15),
is associated with death, again a sign of an inverted Passover. Later in 1–2
Kings, both Elijah and Elisha bring sons back from the dead and restore them
to their mothers, performing straightforward "Passover" miracles. Ahijah the
prophet brings no such deliverance to Jeroboam. This is an inversion of Passover, a Passover in which the best son dies. Even though Jeroboam seeks out
a prophet, he finds no relief.

Ahijah's prophecy extends beyond the immediate crisis of Abijah's sickness
and the end of Jeroboam's house to encompass the future of the northern
kingdom. Here, the prophecy moves beyond an inverted Passover to an inverted exodus. One day, Israel's clock will be turned back, and Israel's history
will unravel like a movie in reverse. The people who came through the sea of
reeds will be shaken like a reed in the water; the people whom God planted
as his vine and as his oak will be uprooted and scattered; and the people who
long ago left Gentile Egypt, the land of the Nile, to settle in the promised land
will one day return to another Gentile nation, beyond the River Euphrates
(1 Kgs. 14:15).

In short, much that made Israel Israel—the exodus, the gift of land—will
be taken. Ahijah prophesies that Israel itself will be undone, losing what marks
it as Israel. Of course, Jeroboam starts the process of reversion as soon as he
sets up golden calves at Dan and Bethel. Imitating Aaron, he takes the people
back to Sinai and builds some golden calves, symbolically taking the people
back into the wilderness. That is where Israel will stay, Ahijah says, until they
are ready to enter another land that is not Israel on the far side of another
river that is not Jordan. Ahijah names Jeroboam seven times in his oracle (the
name appears twelve times in the whole chapter), and the climactic seventh

use refers to the exile (14:16). Exile is already implicit in Jeroboam's sins. In Israel's beginning is Israel's end.

Throughout this lengthy prophecy, Jeroboam's wife remains silent, and in fact she is silent throughout these events. She follows Jeroboam's instructions without a word. Only her feet have "voice" (14:6), and their voice speaks the death of her son (14:17). A hard word comes to Jeroboam's wife, and she responds with utter silence. Does she accept the prophetic word, or does she reject it? If she believes her son will die at her return, why does she return? Does Jeroboam's wife act out of belief or unbelief? Perhaps she disbelieves Ahijah and is surprised that her son dies. But the more interesting and likely possibility, however, is that she believes him. She knows that Ahijah is a prophet. Like Macbeth's witches, Ahijah predicts that the thane of Shechem will become king, and he does. If Lady Macbeth is convinced by witches, why not the nameless Lady Jeroboam by a prophet? The interesting thing about this possibility is that her silent resignation is as much an act of unbelief as loud rejection. Faith responds to a prophecy of doom like David, who fasts, prays, and mourns for his son, in spite of Yahweh's telling him that his son will die (2 Sam. 12). So long as the child lives, there is hope.

Faith is often confused with resignation. The prophetic word comes, cutting like a double-edged sword, and we respond with tight-lipped silence. This is not faith. Faith responds to God's word, not with silent submission, but with confession, praise, earnest and anguished petition. Faith responds with the desperate cries of a Job, the "my God, my God" of David and Jesus, the "how long, O Lord?" of the Psalms. God's word is not the end of a conversation, but an invitation to renew conversation. God does not judge and condemn to send us slinking away in resigned silence. God judges and condemns so that we can give our "amen" to his judgment, humble ourselves, and be saved. Ultimately, the issues go to theology proper: the Triune God, the God whose life is an eternal conversation, does not create a world as a stage where he performs soliloquies before a respectfully hushed audience. God creates the world and humanity to enter into a dialogue. Ahijah delivers a devastating oracle to Jeroboam, but that is an invitation to repentance, as is Elijah's oracle to Ahab (1 Kgs. 21). The text gives us a hint, if only a hint, that the end is not set out by the beginning, that there is yet hope for Israel.

That hint is expanded when we consider the beginnings of the history of Judah, the southern kingdom ruled by the Davidic dynasty after the separation of Israel. After the announcement of Ahijah's death, the writer turns his attention to the south and resumes the interrupted account of Rehoboam's reign. On the surface, things are not much better in Judah than in Israel. Rehoboam introduces various abominations into the kingdom (14:22–24), and just as Jeroboam's idolatries at Dan and Bethel set the pattern for recurring sin in Israel, so Rehoboam's construction of high places set the pattern for the kings of the south. Kings of the north are consistently condemned for "following in the way of Jeroboam son of Nebat," while kings of the south are consistently condemned for building "high places," sanctuaries that compete with the chosen place in Jerusalem on every hill and under every tree.[4]

The writer characterizes Rehoboam's actions as "abominations" (התועבת) like the actions of the nations whom "Yahweh dispossessed before the sons of Israel" (14:24). Jordan writes: "Basically . . . 'abominable' has to do with the land, while 'detestable' has to do with the sanctuary. Abominations defile the land, while detestable things defile the sanctuary." From Lev. 18:24–29, Jordan concludes that abominations include especially sexual immorality and idolatry: "The sins spoken of here are acts of sexual immorality and idolatry, considered not as cultic acts in God's special sanctuary presence, but as acts of covenantal idolatry committed in his land. If they do these things, they will be vomited out of the land. To spare the nation such general punishment, they are to vomit out any individual who does such things by cutting him off from the people. They are to act as guards, guarding the holiness of the land even as the armed Levite guards secured the holiness of the sanctuary" (Jordan 1991; cf. Klawans 2000). That these abominations are committed by the Canaanites is thus no extraneous detail (1 Kgs. 14:24), for the ultimate result of Judah's abominations is expulsion. Like Israel, then, Judah faces the threat of exodus in reverse.

In the event, Judah does not have long to wait before seeing the outcome of its abominations. In a preview of exile, King Shishak of Egypt attacks Jerusalem, plunders the treasures of the temple and the palace, and steals the ceremonial gold shields of Solomon (14:25–28). A few centuries later, an invader from Babylon, the new Egypt, invades Judah, plunders the temple and the king's palace, and destroys them. Those who commit abominations are spewed out from Yahweh's land and spit out of Yahweh's mouth.[5]

Rehoboam's beginning is as abominable as Jeroboam's, but the pattern of events in Judah is markedly different. Rehoboam's son, Abijam, follows his father's example (15:3), but in the third generation, Asa "did what was right in the sight of Yahweh, like David his father," and his reforms turn Yahweh's wrath from Judah (15:11). This set a pattern that continues throughout the history of Judah: faithful to his promise to David, Yahweh does not permit the house of David to continue in its rebellion for more than a few generations. He interrupts the decline in the third generation. He does not allow Judah to fill up its sins for a week; on the third day, in the middle of the week, he brings Judah back from the dead.

---

4. First Kings 14:24 describes "consecrated ones" (קדש) in the land, and the word is often taken to refer to male cultic prostitutes. See Gen. 38:21, where the feminine form is used to describe Tamar.

5. Rehoboam tries to restore the shields that Solomon made, but his restoration pathetically shows how the mighty are fallen. In place of the brilliant gold shields of Solomon, Rehoboam makes bronze shields, thereby symbolizing the deterioration of glory in his own kingdom. Solomon presides over a united Israel during an age of gold; Rehoboam can do no better than institute a bronze age.

It often appears that Eliot is right and that life's beginnings determine and shape its end, but that is *not* how life goes. Eliot knew it, for "East Coker" ends not with the tragic observation that our beginnings determine our ends, but with a confession of faith in cosmic comedy: "In my end is my beginning." Jesus's death, unlike the death of Jeroboam's good son, does not spell the end of things, but the beginning of things, because Jesus's death is followed by his resurrection. Jesus's death is not an inverted Passover that leads to destruction, but a true Passover that liberates the people of God. Through Jesus, the guilt that plagues us from the past is forgiven, and through forgiveness and the renewing power of the Spirit the world is opened—Israel is opened—to a future for which none had dared to hope. This simply *is* the gospel, the good news that ends are not straight-line extrapolations from beginnings; this is the gospel, that the end reverses the beginning, as tears are washed away, the curse removed, the dead raised. The world is not condemned by its beginnings to a certain ending, for there is no condemnation for those who are in Christ Jesus.

That is the gospel we celebrate at the Lord's Table: this is the blood of the new covenant, Jesus says, which is shed for you and for many for the remission of sins. At the table, we are renewed in covenant, freshly forgiven, so that the past can be put behind us. At the table, we celebrate the opening of a new future, for Christ our Passover is sacrificed for us.

1 KINGS 15:1–16:14

Once Jeroboam I sets the pattern of rebellion and resistance to the prophets, Israel descends into turmoil, and the turmoil is depicted literarily in the acceleration of the narrative. Solomon reigns forty years, and Jeroboam another twenty-two (1 Kgs. 14:20), and these sixty-odd years of Israel's history are recounted in thirteen and a half chapters. Suddenly, with 14:21, we go into hyperdrive, and the text takes us over the next sixty years in a couple of chapters. The writer of Kings captures the whirligig of time with a rapid-fire narrative style.

As a result, 1 Kgs. 15–16 is a schoolchild's nightmare, the kind of chronicle that evokes lifelong loathing of history. A king rises, a king reigns, a king sins, a king dies. His son rises, his son reigns, his son sins, and his son dies. Meaningless and confusing dates for indistinguishable kings, all told in a colorless and repetitive prose. The setting and events are themselves repetitive and boring. It becomes impossible to distinguish between Israel and Judah: both have fallen into idolatry; both are displeasing to Yahweh; both are threatened with exile; and Judah experiences a foretaste of exile in the invasion of Shishak of Egypt. Little is told about Abijam of Judah's life, other than that he does not walk in the ways of David (15:3–5). In fact, the account of Abijam's reign tells us more about David than about Abijam. Even names became indistinguishable: Jeroboam's dead son is named Abijah, but Rehoboam has a son by the same name (Abijam is a variant of Abijah; cf. 2 Chr. 13:1). How are we supposed to keep all this straight? How can we tell one king from another, one kingdom from another?[1]

War continues throughout, wearily year upon year. Four times in the chapter we are reminded of the war between Israel and Judah (1 Kgs. 15:6, 7, 16, 32).

1. Much of my thinking in this chapter was inspired by Davis 2002, 181–82.

At times, the participants in the war do not change, even though one of the participants dies. Rehoboam dies and Abijam succeeds him, but the writer tells us that "there was war between Rehoboam and Jeroboam all the days of his [i.e., Abijam's] life" (15:6). It is the same old inconclusive and enduring war, neither victory nor defeat, and we can imagine war-weary Israelite warriors gathered in gloomy clumps to trade cynicisms, like the Trojan and Greek heroes in Shakespeare's *Troilus and Cressida*.

Things get worse as the chapter moves ahead. In Judah, "Maacah the daughter [or granddaughter] of Abishalom" is the mother of Abijam (15:2). "Abishalom" is a variant of Absalom, David's son, and this text implies that Abijam marries his cousin, the daughter of his father Solomon's half-brother. Nothing in the Torah forbids this degree of consanguinity, but 15:10 is shocking: Asa, Abijam's son (15:8), is also the son of "Maacah daughter of Abishalom" (15:10): that is, Abijam has children by his mother (Provan 1995, 126).[2] Incestuous royal marriages are known elsewhere in the ancient world (e.g., Egypt),[3] but the Torah forbids cross-generational incest in the most strenuous terms (Lev. 18:7; 20:11) and warns that incest is the kind of "abomination" that causes the land to spew out its inhabitants (18:24–29). Abijam is not "complete with" (שלם, reminiscent of שלמה ["Solomon"]) (1 Kgs. 15:3) Yahweh, but instead follows the ways of his father Abishalom (אבישלום). Abijam is a true "son of Absalom," who takes his father's wife (2 Sam. 16:20–23).

Finally, a new dynasty arises in the north, and we hope against hope that Israel can get out of the rut that Jeroboam created. But no: Baasha sins just like Jeroboam, lacking even the demonic creativity to repackage Jeroboamism with fresh new idols. He simply "walked in the way of Jeroboam." Same old, same old. The history of Jeroboam's house replays in the house of Baasha. No sooner has he become king than a prophet confronts him (1 Kgs. 16:2–4, 11), in language very similar to Ahijah's prophecy against Jeroboam (14:7–11). A man of God confronts Jeroboam at the beginning of his reign, and a prophet confronts Baasha as well. Though raised from the dust of the ground (like Adam), Baasha rebels (like Adam) and will lose the kingdom (16:2). Baasha's dynasty mirrors Jeroboam's in its sinfulness (16:7), and it ends in the same catastrophic way as did Jeroboam's dynasty. Elah is doomed before his reign begins, and he and his house rapidly fall to one of his military commanders, Zimri, who destroys the entire household (16:12).

---

2. It is possible that "mother" in 15:10 means "grandmother." Kinship names in Hebrew tend to be quite fluid. But certainly a surface reading of the text implies cross-generational incest.

3. Lewis (1983, 43–44): "When instances of brother-sister marriages first began to appear in the papyri, they were greeted with great skepticism in some quarters, where doubt was expressed that any society would really have countenanced such common violation of the incest taboo. . . . Such arguments [to otherwise explain the evidence] are ingenious, but they collapse completely in the face of the cumulative evidence of scores of papyri, official as well as private documents, in which the wife is unequivocally identified as the husband's 'sister born of the same father and the same mother.'"

Like David in his worst moments (2 Sam. 11:1), Elah stays at Tirzah luxuriating (1 Kgs. 16:9), while the troops besiege Gibbethon (16:15). Elah provokes Yahweh with "vanities" (בהבליהם) (16:13), a word that means "vapor" or "breath" (Ecclesiastes). It refers to idols only a few times in the Old Testament, the most important of which is Deut. 32:21, where Yahweh threatens to abandon Israel for another people when they provoke him to jealousy with their "vanities." Eventually Yahweh carries out his threat, sending the blessing of the prophets to the Gentiles of Sidon rather than to the Israelites (1 Kgs. 17).[4]

As if repetitive events are not bad enough, the writer chooses to report in the numbingly repetitive style of an incantation: "Now in the eighteenth year of Jeroboam son of Nebat, Abijam became king over Judah. He reigned three years in Jerusalem, and his mother's name was Maacah. He reigned three years . . . and there was war . . . now the rest of the acts of Abijam and all that he did, are they not written in the book of the Chronicles of the Kings of Judah? And there was war." Then "Nadab son of Jeroboam became king over Israel in the second year of Asa king of Judah, and he reigned over Israel two years. And he did evil in the sight of Yahweh. . . . Baasha killed him in the third year of Asa. . . . Now the rest of the acts of Nadab and all that he did, are they not written in the book of the Chronicles of the Kings of Israel?" And then, "In the third year of Asa king of Judah, Baasha son of Ahijah became king over all Israel in Tirzah, and he reigned twenty-four years. And he did evil in the sight of Yahweh. . . . Now the rest of the acts of Baasha and what he did and all his might, are they not written in the book of the chronicles of the kings of Israel?"

We learn that kings battle, but never see a single battle up close—no swords disappearing into the guts of a fat king, no tent pegs through heads, no slaughter with the jawbone of an ass, no smooth stones in a sling, not even a bit of clever strategizing and heroism. Homer would have written page after relentless page of graphic, cartoonish violence. Not the author of 1–2 Kings. Only: "there was war" and then again "there was war." The narrator tells us that kings sin, but their sins are told in the most general terms, with no juicy details like those in Josephus or Suetonius or Gibbon.

Rise, reign, sin, die. War and sin, sin and war. Edna St. Vincent Millay seems to have had it right: "It's not true that life is one damn thing after another; it is one damn thing over and over." In fact, it's the *same* damn thing after another.

But, as Davis points out, this is precisely the author's point: idolatry is boring (2002, 181). Idolatry produces nothing new, nothing exciting, nothing fresh, nothing adventurous. Jeroboam pretends to take a walk on the wild

---

4. More subtly, the chronology of Baasha's dynasty repeats Jeroboam's. Jeroboam's reign lasts twenty-two years (14:20), and he is followed by Nadab, who reigns for two years (15:25) before being overthrown. Baasha rules for twenty-four years (15:33), and he is succeeded by his son Elah, who reigns only two years before the dynasty is ended (16:8). This pattern of long reign–short reign–end of dynasty is broken by the Omride dynasty.

side, pretends to be doing something slick and edgy. His wildness is not just tame. It is somnolescent and acts as a soporific for the northern kingdom. Rehoboam permits high places in Judah, but that just leads to drudgery of the same. Solomon's reign, by contrast, is full of excitement: political intrigue to secure the throne, clever sleuthing to determine which prostitute is telling the truth, a continuous party in Israel, adventurous endeavors on the high seas, a court visit from the exotic queen of Sheba. When prophets show up, the world suddenly opens up even wider: hands wither and heal, altars are split, lions leap into the text and onto a prophet but do not eat the donkey, jars of oil never empty, dead children are raised, bears come crashing out of the woods to slaughter mocking young men, and dead bodies thrown into the wrong grave come catapulting out again. The moon turns to blood, the sun is black as sackcloth, stars fall from the sky; dreams, signs, visions; blood, fire, and vapor of smoke.

A great deal of postmodern thought has been a war against the reduction of "difference" or the "other" to the "same." In metaphysics and philosophy generally, this reduction manifests itself in totalizing efforts to pinion all reality together in a theory, ignoring whatever escapes the theoretical framework; in ethics, the totalizing impulse manifests itself in an egoism that attempts to absorb the irreducible other into the self.[5] Along similar lines, several theologians—chiefly Milbank and Pickstock—develop Kierkegaard's essay on repetition into a critique of modernity. Kierkegaard explores the possibilities of reliving an earlier portion of his life, coming to the conclusion that every effort at identical repetition is thwarted so that "the only repetition was the impossibility of repetition" (1983, 170). Modernity attempts the impossible by positing the possibility of identical repetition (e.g., in scientific experiments), but for Milbank and Pickstock every effort at identical repetition expresses an infatuation for death, since only the dead repeat identically. Ultimately, the inevitability of nonidentical repetition is an analogous expression of the triune character of God, who is God as Father and who is eternally and necessarily "repeated differently" as God in the Son and Spirit. The author of 1–2 Kings suggests that identical repetition is, despite its apparent logical and existential impossibility, the reality of idolatrous life and idolatrous communities. Identical repetition is the "impossible possibility" of sin, the collapse of the ecstatic creature into a self-enclosed repetition (see the commentary on 1 Kgs. 4:1–5:18).

Idols are lifeless and therefore cannot impart life. Lifeless idols only make for lifeless people. When the initial titillation has passed, idolatry quickly yields to dryness and death. The signs of this spiritual exhaustion are everywhere in twenty-first-century culture, which has become a culture of "whatever"—not only the whatever of "anything goes," but the whatever of "and who cares anyway?" This is the end result of a culture that has been built on idols of

5. For a powerful theological critique of this theme in Levinas, see Hart 2003, 75–90.

success, money, pleasure, self-indulgence, sex. Such a culture becomes slothful, thoroughly infused with what the Christian tradition calls *acedia*.

Traditionally, sloth is seen as an enemy of faith and hope. The Latin word *acedia* ("lack of concern, lack of care") is used to describe these dimensions of sloth. In her essay entitled "The Other Six Deadly Sins," Sayers defines *acedia* as "the accomplice of the other sins and their worst punishment. It is the sin which believes in nothing, cares for nothing, seeks to know nothing, interferes with nothing, enjoys nothing, loves nothing, hates nothing, finds purpose in nothing, lives for nothing, and only remains alive because there is nothing it would die for" (1949, 81). Sloth is a lack of faith in God's providence and care and a lack of hope that God will keep his promises.

Modern *acedia* is not merely an individual sin, but is a widely accepted cultural norm and has been institutionalized in education and in our sexual mores. In her comments on Canto 18 of Dante's *Purgatorio*, Sayers writes that

> the sin which in English is commonly called *Sloth*, and in Latin *accidia* (or more correctly *acedia*), is insidious, and assumes such Protean shapes that it is rather difficult to define. It is not merely idleness of mind and laziness of body: it is that whole poisoning of the will which, beginning with indifference and an attitude of "I couldn't care less," extends to the deliberate refusal of joy and culminates in morbid introspection and despair. One form of it which appeals very strongly to some modern minds is that acquiescence in evil and error which readily disguises itself as "Tolerance"; another is that refusal to be moved by the contemplation of the good and beautiful which is known as "Disillusionment," and sometimes as "knowledge of the world"; yet another is that withdrawal into an "ivory tower" of Isolation which is the peculiar temptation of the artist and the contemplative, and is popularly called "Escapism." (Sayers 1955, 209)

Sayers also helps to explain how *acedia* or sloth can coexist with frantic activity: "It is one of the favourite tricks of this Sin to dissemble itself under cover of a whiffling activity of body. We think that if we are busily rushing about and doing things, we cannot be suffering from Sloth. And besides, violent activity seems to offer an escape from the horrors of Sloth" (1949, 81). Our culture is a frenetic 24/7 culture precisely as a way of masking the emptiness of it all. It is simply a disguise, Sayers says, "for the empty heart and the empty brain and the empty soul of Acedia" (1949, 82; cf. Reno 2001).

First Kings 15–16 depicts a world of idolatrous, identical repetition. Baasha's coup, however, reveals another dimension of this reality. Baasha is "son of Ahijah" (15:27). Though his father is not the prophet Ahijah (11:29; 14:1–16), the repetition of the name points back to Ahijah's prophecies against Jeroboam, suggesting that Baasha is the "spiritual son" of the prophet, carrying out the prophet's doom against Jeroboam. As Ahijah predicts, Jeroboam's house is completely destroyed, until there is no "breath" in it (15:29). Baasha conspires against and kills Nadab during a siege of the Philistine city of Gibbethon (16:15), formerly a Levitical city in the tribal area of Dan (Josh. 19:44; 21:23) that Philistines recovered.[6] The kingdom of Israel contracts, and Israel's kings fight the same battles that David once won (2 Sam. 5). In one sense, idolatry produces a constant round of static repetition, but from another angle idolatry leads to retreat. Territory conquered long before has to be reconquered; enemies that disappeared into hiding return. Israel's kings begin to lose ground in the most literal sense. This literal loss of ground is profoundly connected with the loss of Israel's tradition, especially liturgical tradition. In a liturgical form of Gresham's Law, bad worship drives out good, and idolatry leaves the northern kingdom with few resources for recovery.

This is the story of Israel and the story of humanity. Adam thinks that seizing the fruit of the tree of knowledge will enrich his life with wisdom; it does not, but instead condemns him to an endless round of sweat and sadness. The wonder is that the Lord does not leave things there. He appears in the garden and promises a savior, and to fallen Israel he speaks through the prophets and carries them by the Spirit, so that wonders follow. He speaks his word in flesh, the Spirit hovers, and the face of the ground is renewed. That part of the story is also evident in this chapter, captured in a wonderful phrase in 1 Kgs. 16:7: "The word of Yahweh came *against* Baasha and his household (דבר־יהוה היה אל־בעשא)."[7] Yahweh's word is an attacking adversary, not merely passively describing what is the case but moving toward Baasha and toward Israel, to do what it proclaims. Yahweh's word is the main participant in the battles of history, and it is Yahweh's (s)word (Heb. 4:12–13) that cuts into the boring round of idolatry and sin to make things new.

In Judah, we see a fuller illustration of the effects of that invading word. Asa is not a perfect king. When Baasha builds Ramah within Judah's territory, he sends money to the Arameans, asking them to attack Baasha from the north and force him to abandon the fortification of Ramah (1 Kgs. 15:18–21).[8] A shrewd move, it might seem, but the prophets regularly condemn kings for relying on Gentiles rather than on the Lord.[9] Further, Asa takes the money from his recently refurbished temple (15:18), plundering his own treasury.[10] It is

6. Note that Israel is still besieging Gibbethon over two decades later (1 Kgs. 16:15, 17)—another example of the inconclusive identical repetition that dominates idolatrous Israel.

7. The preposition אל connotes primarily "motion toward," but in contexts where the motion is hostile, the word is translated "against" (some 150 times in the Hebrew Bible). See the comment of Brown, Driver, and Briggs 1980, 40: "Where the motion or direction implied appears from the context to be of a hostile character, אל = *against*."

8. The background is as follows: Judah and Israel have been at odds for two generations (1 Kgs. 14:30; 15:6–7). Baasha fortifies Ramah, located some ten miles northwest of Jerusalem in the territory of Judah. With a regiment of Israelite soldiers stationed there, Baasha can prevent access in and out of Judah ("going out or coming in" in 15:17 usually refers to military movements).

9. Second Chronicles 16:7–10 includes a prophecy of Hanani that explicitly condemns Asa's action.

10. The Arameans later become one of the great enemies of the northern kingdom, and we know that they were supplied and egged on by Judah. Like Solomon (1 Kgs. 10:29), Asa

perfectly consistent for Asa to rely on physicians rather than Yahweh when his feet become diseased (15:23; cf. 2 Chr. 16:12). Relying on humans is already an established pattern of life.

Despite his failure in this instance, Asa is a righteous king, the first of eight kings in Judah's history who do "right." Asa is the first king of the divided kingdom to be compared favorably with David, and his reforming efforts anticipate both in general and in detail the later reforming efforts of Joash, Hezekiah, and Josiah. By contrast with his father, Asa follows the ways of David (1 Kgs. 15:11), with his heart "complete with" Yahweh (15:14). He reverses many of the evils that Rehoboam instituted (15:12–13; cf. 14:23–24; 22:46; 2 Kgs. 23:7), though he fails to remove the high places (1 Kgs. 15:14; cf. 22:43; 2 Kgs. 12:3). He shows his devotion to Yahweh by taking a stand against his own mother, removing her from being queen mother and destroying the Asherah she makes (1 Kgs. 15:13; cf. 2 Kgs. 23:6). Asa is a true disciple, who hates his mother to follow Yahweh (Luke 14:26). He restores the golden splendor of the temple, which was tarnished under Rehoboam (1 Kgs. 15:15).

One of the striking things about the narrative of Asa is that there is no explanation for his reformation. Heir to three generations of idolatrous tradition, product of an incestuous marriage, child of idolaters, Asa reverses course and turns Judah back to Yahweh. Joash has his Jehoiada; Hezekiah sees the handwriting on the wall when the northern kingdom collapses; Josiah discovers the law in the temple. From what the text tells us, Asa simply begins to do what is right. There is no explanation, no agency is mentioned. Only: "Asa did what was right." But the gap in the story is a pregnant one, a variant of the "divine passive": this interruption of the boring round of sin and idolatry is a gift of God. God's grace, God himself, God's word, erupts in the history of Judah and turns Asa to righteousness and thereby escapes another round of the same.

---

supplies the enemies of Israel.

1 KINGS 16:15–34

"By the transgression of a land many are its princes, / but by a man of understanding and knowledge, so it endures" (Prov. 28:2). The history recorded in the latter part of 1 Kgs. 16 illustrates Solomon's observation as well as any portion of Scripture. Israel indulges in idolatry for generations, as golden calves become the official, state-sanctioned cult of the northern kingdom. That transgression continues from Jeroboam I through his son, and then through the new dynasty of Baasha and his son, and then again to the dynasty of Omri and his descendants. Dynasties come and go, but golden calves remain.

Israel falls into transgression, and the predictable result is many princes in the land. Over the course of about six decades, the dynasty of Jeroboam is destroyed by Baasha; the house of Baasha, by Zimri; and Zimri is rapidly overthrown by Omri. Baasha comes to power by assassinating Jeroboam's son Nadab; Zimri, by assassinating Baasha's son Elah; Omri, by attacking Zimri, who holes himself up in Tirzah for protection. A new dynasty arises every generation, and over the course of a single week, the house of Baasha yields to Zimri, and Zimri is overthrown by Omri (16:8–20). Over time, transgression brings many kings. At times, there are many princes at the same time: after Baasha's dynasty collapses, there is a three-way contest for the throne. Even after Omri takes Tirzah and Zimri died, Omri fights a civil war with Tibni-ben-ginath for four years (16:15 and 16:23 imply that Omri spends four years fighting Tibni before he becomes king without a rival). A kingdom with many princes cannot be a stable or strong kingdom. Without continuity through time, cultural and artistic pursuits are forgotten.[1] Plagued by multiple kings,

---

1. In the words of the Duke of Burgundy from Shakespeare's *Henry V*, 5.2, Israel's peace, like France's, "dear nurse of arts . . . and joyful births," has become "naked, poor, and mangled," with the result that "our vineyards, fallows, meads, and hedges, / Defective in their natures, grow to wildness, / Even so our houses and ourselves and children / Have lost, or do not learn

the faithful in Israel looks for the day when there will be one ruler, a prince who will bring peace.

Three details of this text illustrate the devastation brought by this period of transgression and many princes. When Zimri becomes king, the Israelite army camps at Gibbethon, a city that once belonged to Israel but was lost to Philistia (16:15–16). Israel is already besieging Gibbethon when Baasha becomes king twenty-four years earlier.[2] It is likely that the siege is sporadic, not continuous, though sieges in the ancient world were often brutally long (e.g., the ten-year siege of Troy), yet after twenty-four years of battling to regain ground from the Philistines Israel can no longer hold or regain territory that God gave their ancestors. There are unbeatable giants in the land, as the ten spies said (Num. 13), and the walls of the cities of Canaan are impenetrable—not because they are powerful, but because Israel's idolatry leaves it impotent. Idols are nothing, powerless, incapable of action, and "those who worship them shall be like them"—deaf, dumb, weak, lame, blind (Ps. 115).

When Israel's army at Gibbethon hears that Zimri made himself king, they immediately make Omri king and march off to Tirzah (1 Kgs. 16:16–17). Twenty-four years of siege warfare ends with Israel walking away from the battle, and they never return. Gibbethon is never again mentioned in Kings or in the rest of the Old Testament, and the text leaves us with the distinct impression that Gibbethon remains forever in the hands of the Philistines. Twenty-four years of supplies, death, blood—all wasted. From the Philistine perspective, Gibbethon is saved because there are many princes in Israel. It happened before: while Saul chases David around the country, the Philistines seize the opportunity to make inroads into Israel, unprotected by its distracted king (1 Sam. 23). When the people of God battle among themselves, Gentiles recover territory. Israel's experience shows, as Henry shrewdly comments, that "Philistines are sure to gain when Israelites quarrel" (1708, 2.662).

Not only does each generation bring a new dynasty, but each new dynasty is worst than the last. Nadab continues in the sins of his father Jeroboam, and Baasha kills him. The same happens to Baasha's son Elah, who is assassinated. Nadab is not a righteous man, but at least he acts like a king: Baasha assassinates him while he besieges Gibbethon (1 Kgs. 15:27). Elah's troops are also at Gibbethon, but he is not with them. Instead, he is in Tirzah, "drinking himself drunk in the house of Arza" (16:9), no longer acting the part of a king. Like a drunkard, his dynasty stumbles and falls (Jer. 25). The Omrides are worse still. Jeroboam causes Israel to sin, but the narrator informs us that Omri "acted more wickedly than all who were before him" (ירע מכל אשר לפניו) (1 Kgs. 16:25). Omri is quickly "bettered" by his son Ahab, who "thought it a trivial

---

for want of time, / The sciences that should become our country, / But grow like savages—as soldiers will / That nothing do but meditate on blood."

2. Baasha kills Nadab in the third year of Asa of Judah (15:28), and Zimri becomes king in the twenty-seventh year of Asa of Judah (16:15).

thing for him to walk in the sins of Jeroboam son of Nebat" and "did evil in the sight of Yahweh more than all who were before him" (הרע בעיני יהוה מכל אשר לפניו) (16:30). Idolatry is uncreative and produces the death of identical repetition. Insofar as it moves at all, it degenerates. Idolatry tolerated and indulged breeds more flagrant idolatry.

All of the turmoil of this period is symbolized by the self-destructive reign of Zimri. He reigns for only a week, but during that time continues in the sins of Jeroboam and slaughters the house of Baasha. Instead of building a city, he spends his week of power destroying Tirzah. He closes himself in and burns the royal palace (16:18). Omri inherits a kingdom consumed in flames.

Omri is the phoenix of Israel's history, rising from the ashes of Tirzah to build a new Israel with a new capital. Clearly, he is a vigorous and skilled leader, and extrabiblical evidence confirms that this is the case. The Bible, however, shows interest in only a few details of his reign. The account of his reign takes up eight verses (16:21–28), compared to the thirteen verses that describe Zimri's coup and his week-long reign (16:8–20), and the focus of 1–2 Kings is not Omri's achievements but his idolatry. More subtly, the writer of Kings indicates that Omri is a David-like king who initiates a counterfeit of the Davidic dynasty in the northern kingdom. Virtually everything that is said about Omri here has some parallel in the life of David (Leithart 2005a). Like David, he is an army commander who fights Philistines (16:15). David gains a reputation as a warrior by killing the Philistine giant Goliath and by leading Israel against the Philistines in a series of wars, while Omri commands the troops during the Israelite siege of the Philistine city of Gibbethon. Like David, Omri succeeds a suicidal king (1 Kgs. 16:18; 1 Sam. 31), and like David he becomes king only after a civil war (1 Kgs. 16:21; 2 Sam. 3). Like David he divides his reign between two capitals (1 Kgs. 16:23–24; 2 Sam. 5:5). Omri buys the hill of Shemer for his capital, just as David purchases the threshing floor of Araunah as the site for the temple (1 Kgs. 16:24; 2 Sam. 24). Unlike David, however, he does not walk in the ways of Yahweh but worships idols (1 Kgs. 16:26).

If Omri is a counterfeit, idolatrous David, Ahab is a counterfeit Solomon. Like Solomon (11:1–3), he marries a foreign woman, Jezebel, an idolater (16:31). Jezebel comes from Sidon, the twin city of Tyre, the city of Hiram, Solomon's ally in building the temple (1 Kgs. 5). Like Solomon, Ahab is a temple builder (16:32), though it is a temple for Baal not Yahweh. With this counterfeit Solomon, a new phase of Israel's apostasy begins, as Ahab and especially Jezebel support Baal worship. The name of Baal first appears in 1–2 Kings in the name of Jezebel's father, Ethbaal, and Jezebel's own name plays on one of the titles or names of Baal, the word *zebul*, which is sometimes included in the name of Baal (2 Kgs. 1:3, 6). Walsh says that "the word *zbl*, 'Prince,' is probably pronounced *zābūl* or *zĕbūl*, as in the name Baalzebul or Beelzebul, 'Baal is Prince' (which itself is usually deformed in the Bible to Baalzebub or Beelzebub, 'Baal of Flies'). Pronounced *zebel*, the element resembles a word in other Semitic languages for 'excrement' that may well have existed also in

Hebrew, though it is not attested in the Hebrew Bible" (Walsh 1996, 218n8). Jezebel is both a daughter of Baal and dung, whose corpse is destined one day to litter the ground (9:30–37).

Omri's idolatry is neither accidental nor tangential to his political program. First, Omri and his son Ahab pursue a program of "re-Canaanitization," reinstituting the worship and practices of the Canaanites that Yahweh drove from the land (1 Kgs. 16:31–32). First Kings 16:34 mentions the rebuilding of Jericho, and it is likely that Ahab authorizes this building, since rebuilding an important border city would hardly be done without the king's permission (Walsh 1996, 219). Of course, Jericho was the first city that Joshua conquered (Josh. 6–7), and its rebuilding symbolizes the reversal of the conquest. Instead of destroying Canaanites, Ahab busies himself restoring their cities. Though it is not clear whether Hiel the Bethelite kills his sons or if they die from natural causes, this is perhaps a "foundation sacrifice," a human sacrifice to consecrate the building of a city or temple. Sacrifices of this kind are not uncommon in the ancient world (Cain/Abel; Romulus/Remus). Though Hiel and Ahab sin when they rebuilt Jericho, they participate in the fulfillment of the word of Yahweh, the word of curse spoken centuries before by Joshua (Josh. 6:26). Second, the Omrides aspire to reunite the kingdom under an Omride king. By intermarrying with the house of David, they also evidently want to reunite the kingdom under an Omride king (see the commentary on 1 Kgs. 22:1–40).

Ahab is the seventh king of the northern kingdom (following Jeroboam I, Nadab, Baasha, Elah, Zimri, Omri) and initiates a numerological structure that runs throughout 1–2 Kings. In the south, the seventh king is Ahaziah of Judah (preceded by Solomon, Rehoboam, Abijam, Asa, Jehoshaphat, Jehoram), who is explicitly compared to Ahab for his wickedness (2 Kgs. 8:27; cf. 8:18). The seven Davidic kings that follow Ahaziah culminate in Manasseh (who follows Jehoash, Amaziah, Azariah, Jotham, Ahaz, Hezekiah), who is the most Ahab-like of the southern kings (21:3, 13). In each case, the seventh king in the sequence is the object of prophetic condemnation, and the seventh king's sins bring an interruption or end of the dynasty of which he is a part. The kings in this sabbatical seventh slot bring the sins of Israel and Judah to completion, and the Lord of the Sabbath brings rest through judgment.

In part, the counterfeit Davidic dynasty constitutes a dramatized warning to the Davidic dynasty in the south. The people of Judah see their own history mirrored in the history of the Omride dynasty, and instead of proudly celebrating their superiority to the idolaters in the north, Judah is supposed to be convicted and driven to repentance. When later they see Jehu slaughtering the house of Ahab, the people of Judah are to conclude that the house of David, which is by that time idolatrous as well, is in danger. If the temple of Jerusalem becomes another outpost for the worship of Baal, Judah can expect a Jehu to tear it down. Judah is to learn wisdom from the chastening lesson of the Omride dynasty's dramatic rise and bloody fall.

Theologically, the similarities between the Davidic and Omride dynasties throw into prominence the radically different trajectory of their histories. Ahab makes ungodly marriage alliances, but Solomon did it before him; Ahab builds a temple for an idol, but Solomon also built high places for his wives; Ahab persecutes Yahweh's prophets, but Solomon tried to kill Jeroboam when he learned that Ahijah the prophet had given Jeroboam a portion of the kingdom. Later, the house of David enters marriage alliances with the house of Omri, so that the two dynasties become virtually indistinguishable. Jehu destroys a house of Baal in Samaria, but not long after the people of Judah, led by Jehoiada, destroy a house of Baal in Jerusalem. As Ezekiel portrays at length, Jerusalem becomes a double of its promiscuous older sister Samaria (Ezek. 23). The book of Kings does not highlight the difference of the house of David but its similarities to the house of Ahab.

What then makes the difference? Why does the house of Omri end in total destruction, without any future? Why does the equally idolatrous house of David survive to this day? The answer to this question, ultimately, is the same answer to the question of why Israel survives and Moab does not; why Israel continues to the first century AD when the Amalekites are long gone; why Israel exists and Philistines are forgotten; why the Lord determines, prior to the birth of Esau and Jacob, that the "older will serve the younger" (Gen. 25:23). When Paul sets out to tell the history of Israel, he tells that history in a way that undermines every prop of ethnic pride by showing that from the beginning there has been a division within the fleshly descendants of Abraham, a division between children of promise and children of flesh (Rom. 9:6–13). When Israel turns from the Sinai covenant by erecting a golden calf at the foot of Sinai itself, Yahweh sovereignly determines to have compassion and accompany Israel to the land of promise (Exod. 32–34; Rom. 9:14–15). For the Davidic dynasty as for Israel, "it does not depend on the man who will or the man who runs, but on God who has mercy" (9:16).

Israel's persistence does not have anything to do with what Israel accomplishes, and the persistence of the Davidic royal line has nothing ultimately to do with the faithfulness of that line. David is faithful, to be sure, and the Lord keeps a lamp in Judah for the sake of David. But finally the difference is in the choice and calling of God: "Yahweh did not set his love upon you or choose you because you were more in number than any of the peoples, for you were the fewest of all peoples, but because Yahweh loved you and kept the oath that he swore to your forefathers, Yahweh brought you out by a mighty hand, and redeemed you from the house of slavery, from the hand of Pharaoh king of Egypt" (Deut. 7:7–8). The history of Judah and Israel thus displays the significance of the Christian doctrine of election: ultimately, what makes the difference is a God who makes a difference.

1 KINGS 17:1–24

The book of Kings is structured by the triple repetition of the following sequence:

king builds
> prophet confronts
>> idolatries persist
>>> delayed judgment
>>>> building destroyed and people exiled

First, when Solomon finishes building the temple, Yahweh appears to him to warn him that his holy house will stand only if Solomon and his sons keep Yahweh's commandments (1 Kgs. 9:1–9), a warning eventually unleashed in the invasion of Nebuchadnezzar (2 Kgs. 24–25). Second, when Jeroboam I finishes building his calf shrine at Bethel, the man of God from Judah confronts him with a warning about a Davidic king named Josiah who will destroy Bethel (1 Kgs. 13), a prophecy fulfilled near the end of Judah's history (2 Kgs. 23). Finally, Ahab no sooner constructs his temple for Baal and authorizes the rebuilding of Jericho when the prophet Elijah appears to announce Yahweh's judgment against Israel (1 Kgs. 17:1). Eventually, Elijah prophesies the end of the Omride dynasty (19:15–18; 21:21–24), a threat carried out by Jehu (2 Kgs. 9–10).

The narrator of 1–2 Kings places Elijah and Elisha at the center of his history (1 Kgs. 17–2 Kgs. 13), and the narrative follows the paradigmatic prophetic narrative of the man of God from Judah (1 Kgs. 13). Like the man of God, Elijah erupts into the Omride dynasty without warning or introduction, a prophet blown by the Spirit wherever he wills (18:12; John 3). Like the man of God from Judah, Elijah not only delivers the word of God but receives it and is obligated to obey (1 Kgs. 17:3, 5). Yahweh gives the man of God from Judah a food command, and he gives the same to Elijah (17:4). Unlike the man of God, Elijah obeys the word of the Lord, and as a result he not only eats but is able to feed others (17:9–16). Like the story in 1 Kgs. 13, the Elijah-Elisha narratives end with a prophet's bones in a prophet's grave, though it is a grave, like the grave of exile, that miraculously coughs up its dead (2 Kgs. 13:20–21). It is not surprising that both Elijah and especially Elisha are repeatedly described as "man of God" (1 Kgs. 17:18, 24; 2 Kgs. 1:9–13; 4:7, 9, 16, 21, 22, 25, 27, 40, 42).[1]

A single prophet denounces Jeroboam's sin, and his word is confirmed by the signs of the split altar and the lion. Yahweh sends two prophets to Ahab's house, who perform numerous signs and wonders, a testimony of two witnesses. Yet, the house of Ahab responds as Jeroboam did (1 Kgs. 13:33): even after all these things, Ahab "did not return from his evil way." Ahab's dynasty is Exhibit A of the judgment passed on the northern (and eventually the southern) kingdom as a whole: they are sent into exile because they do not listen to the word of Yahweh or to his prophets (2 Kgs. 17:13–14). For those with ears to hear, however, the prophet and his word are life and health. When Israel's kings indulge idolatry and turn Israel into an Amorite outpost, provoking Yahweh's anger and bringing the curse of drought and famine on Israel, those who cling to the prophets eat and drink. Elijah and Elisha are eucharistic prophets, who provide bread and spread a table before the sons of the prophets. While Israel suffers drought, Elijah feeds the widow of Zarephath (1 Kgs. 17:9–16), and even persecuted prophets hiding in caves receive bread and water (18:3–4). Elisha's ministry is even more centrally concerned with providing food (see the commentary on 2 Kgs. 2:1–25).[2]

The ministries of Elijah and Elisha mark an epochal shift in the focus of Yahweh's work with Israel his people. From the time of Moses through the period of judges, Yahweh works with the tribes of Israel, with the high priest as the central figure. After Saul and especially after David, Yahweh works with Israel as a whole through the king. When the kings reject Yahweh and serve idols, Yahweh begins to work in Israel through prophets and through the community within Israel led by prophets. Each of these transitions is initiated by a prophet: Moses the great prophet leads the tribes of Israel from Egypt and delivers their constitution, the Torah; a new Moses, Samuel, anoints the first two kings and organizes Israel as a monarchical constitution; and the prophetic era is initiated by the work of two prophets, Elijah and Elisha. Ultimately, Yahweh's work through prophets comes to its fruition in the ministry of Jesus, who gathers a community within Israel, redefining the true Israel as those who follow him as disciples (Wright 1996a).

1. The narrator describes Elisha with this title twenty-nine times (Davis 2005, 59).
2. The structure of this section of 1–2 Kings highlights the prophetic gift of food by placing two of Elisha's food miracles at the center of a large chiasm. See Leithart and Jordan 1995.

The community that gathers around the prophets is sometimes described as a "remnant" community, understood as the "true Israel" within a national Israel that forfeited its status as the people of God because of idolatry. Much free-church ecclesiology has been erected on the basis of this conception. As Radner points out, "the polemicists of Christian division have tended to apply [the story of 1–2 Kings] one-sidedly, choosing to identify their particular communities with various righteous 'remnants' alluded to in the course of the narrative" (1998, 36).

It is understandable that the prophetic community would be identified as a remnant, and there is some, albeit slight, textual basis for the identification. When Yahweh promises Elijah he will leave seven thousand who do not bow to Baal, the word translated "leave" is the verbal form of the word for "remnant" (שאר) (1 Kgs. 19:18). Yet, in the main, the word "remnant" does not refer to those few who remain faithful in a time of apostasy but rather to those who remain alive after a time of judgment (Zech. 8:6; Ezra 9:8, 13, 15; Neh. 1:2–3; cf. Herntrich and Schrenk 1967). The few uses of the term שארית in 1–2 Kings suffice to make the point. When the Assyrians threaten Jerusalem during the reign of Hezekiah, the king asks Isaiah to "offer a prayer for the remnant that is left" (2 Kgs. 19:4). Here, the term refers either to all Judah as the remnant left from the divided kingdom after the fall of Samaria or to the remainder of the population of Jerusalem that survives the Assyrian siege. In either case, it refers to those who are still living in the land, and the remnant is not some subdivision of Judah but simply *is* the Judah that still exists. In the same context, Isaiah delivers the Lord's promise that a remnant of Judah would go out of Jerusalem to "take root downward and bear fruit upward" (1 Kgs. 19:30–31). Again, the referent is ambiguous, indicating either the survivors of the Assyrian siege or the survivors of exile or both. It is clear that the term does not refer to some faithful *ecclesiola in ecclesia*, but to the mixed multitude of Judah who will remain when Yahweh has passed judgment. Finally, and decisively, Yahweh threatens to "abandon the remnant of my inheritance and deliver them into the hand of their enemies" because of the idolatries of Manasseh (21:14). Whoever this remnant is, they do not miraculously escape judgment but are, as Radner says, "thrown by God into the same cauldron [with everyone else] and share the same burdens of destruction and enslavement" (1998, 36). Judah itself is the remnant in 21:14, the one tribe that has survived the Assyrians.

Technically, the remnant is the restored Israel that persists through and endures after Yahweh's judgment. The chastening of judgment leaves this new remnant of Israel humbled (Zeph. 3:12–13), cognizant that Israel deserved to be utterly destroyed (Isa. 1:8–9) and that its very existence depends on the mercy of God alone (Mic. 4:7; 5:7–8). Thus, the remnant is righteous, but it is clear from the accounts of the postexilic community in Ezra and Nehemiah that the remnant is far from sinless. In certain groups within Second Temple Judaism, the remnant idea was given a sectarian spin (Herntrich and Schrenk

1967, 212–13), but in its biblical conceptualization, the remnant is Israel as a whole—not an Israel that deftly sidestepped the grave, but an Israel miraculously raised from the grave. Radner puts it well: "The restoration of the remnant is not the unveiling, let alone the vindication, of the 'true church' from amid its travails, but rather the gracious action of recreating a united people out of the dust of their past obliteration. . . . We are dealing, then, with the character and fate of the whole people of Israel; and whatever distinctions are given to members of that people on the basis of their division are not such as to remove them from that general character and fate in which their division lies" (1998, 36).

The ecclesiological implications here are vastly important. American fundamentalists and conservative evangelicals in particular tend to operate with free-church ecclesiologies in which they regard themselves as the remnant, the true Israel, separated from the false church in the mainline. Thinking that they are following Luther, they withdraw from contact with the mainline churches, largely ignoring them and leaving them to their own devices.[3] To be sure Elijah and Elisha set up their own network of prophetic communities, but they remain in regular, if confrontational, contact with Israel's mainline. An ecclesiology of total withdrawal cannot be sustained by 1–2 Kings. Elijah and Elisha do not entertain the comforting illusion that they can carry on happily as the true Israel while the Omrides take the nation further into the cesspool of idolatry. They recognize that they are inevitably bound with the nation as a whole, and their prophetic labors that gather faithful communities within Israel aim not at forming a *permanent* alternative to Israel but at *renewing* Israel.

To put it into contemporary terms: those outside the mainline do not have the luxury of considering mainline confusions and apostasies "their problem" as opposed to "our problem." If the Episcopal Church in the United States of America sanctions homosexual conduct among its bishops, that is as much a problem for believers in a Bible church as it is for Episcopalians themselves.

As the author's focus shifts from kings to prophets, he initiates a sustained parody of royal power. Elijah controls the rains (1 Kgs. 17:1) and has sufficient food and drink, while King Ahab searches ineffectually for water and a modicum of grass (18:3–6). Two sets of Ahaziah's soldiers are burned by Elijah's fireballs (2 Kgs. 1:9–12), and King Jehoram of Israel leads an expedition against Moab but is stranded in a waterless wilderness until saved by a prophet (3:4–12). Israel's king has no power to cleanse Naaman's leprosy, but Elisha does (5:6–7), and Jehoram of Israel cannot provide food for his besieged capital (6:24–31), though through the word of Elisha the people of Samaria receive flour and barley (7:1, 16–20). Kings who follow the prophets prosper (13:14–19), but kings who attack or avoid the prophets are frustrated and impotent.

---

3. My limited experience in England suggests that these sectarian tendencies are equally pronounced among Protestants there.

By the appearance of things, association with the prophets is a bad bet. The northern kingdom of Israel pursues idolatry for generations, first with golden calves at Bethel and Dan and then with Baal worship at the heart of the nation, in the capital city of Samaria. Baalists and calf worshipers hold all the cards. Yahwism is in retreat, or so it appears. While the church may suffer setbacks, however, Yahweh never does, and his word never does. Yahweh is never frustrated, never retreats, never has to regroup and reconsider. He never has too little to work with. His word is always moving forward, whatever the human response (Van't Veer 1980, 111–12). If the word is rejected in Samaria, he finds a place where it will be welcomed in Zarephath; if he is ignored and despised in Los Angeles, he will go to work in Lagos. Yahweh is "impassible," never passively reacting to human action, but always active.

Despite appearances, that is what we find in the early ministry of Elijah. Yahweh sends Elijah to Ahab and then to the wadi Cherith across the Jordan. Sending Elijah out of the land looks like a tactical retreat, but it is first of all a judgment on Israel (Van't Veer 1980, 65). Elijah is not a mere "private believer," but a prophet, a man with an office and a vocation, the representative and bearer of the word and presence of God (Van't Veer 1980, 76–78, who perhaps overplays this point). When Yahweh sends Elijah out of the land, his word is silenced in Israel. To the famine of bread, Yahweh adds a famine of the word. Over a century before, the Philistines had captured the ark, a sign that Yahweh removed himself to Philistia (1 Sam. 4–6). During the reign of Ahab, Yahweh again turns from his unfaithful people, so that Israel, whose whole identity is bound up with the presence and the word of Yahweh, is for a time bereft of both. By sending Elijah out of Israel, Yahweh shows his lordship in judging Israel, removing the word they refuse to hear. Whether Israel is flowing with milk and honey or suffering drought, Yahweh remains Lord, faithful and true and almighty.

The events of Elijah's early ministry are also preparation for greater acts of God. Israel is an Egypt, and it is increasingly a Canaanite nation. It is time for a new exodus out of Egypt/Israel and a new conquest of Canaan/Israel. Yahweh calls a new Moses and a new Joshua: Elijah and Elisha. During Elijah's early ministry, Yahweh prepares him to play the role of Moses and later prepares Elisha as a new Joshua. Elijah single-handedly leads the people to renew the covenant they had made at Sinai (1 Kgs. 17–19). Elijah's life is modeled on Moses, and just as Moses prefigured the history of Israel in his own life (Leithart 2000a, 77) so Elijah recapitulates that history in his life. During the drought, he leaves the land for the wilderness, where Yahweh provides for him with miraculous bread, meat, and water, just as he provided for Israel in their wilderness wanderings after the exodus. Elijah takes the people onto Mount Carmel, a new Sinai, where they renew their commitment to worship Yahweh and Yahweh alone (Exod. 24). Elijah goes to Horeb or Sinai, where Yahweh reveals himself as he had to Moses (Exod. 33–34) and where he pled with Yahweh considering Israel's future (Allison 1993, 39–45). After Elijah's work is finished, it is time for Elisha, a new Joshua. Elijah leaves a double portion of his spirit behind for Elisha, who begins to carry out a conquest of the land through healing and renewal, as well as judgment. When the work of these two prophets is done, there are organized communities of faithful worshipers within Israel.

Like all the other instruments for the renewal of Israel, the renewal movement ultimately fails, for Israel goes to exile despite the ministries of Elijah and Elisha. Here is another dimension of the evangelical thrust of 1–2 Kings: wisdom cannot save Israel; the temple cannot save Israel; kings cannot save Israel. Prophets provide life for those who hear and believe their words, but ultimately not even the prophetic movement prevents Israel's destruction.

According to Exod. 12:12, the final plague at Passover is not only a challenge to Pharaoh, but a judgment on the gods of Egypt: "I will strike down all the firstborn in the land of Egypt, both man and beast; and against all the gods of Egypt I will execute judgments—I am Yahweh." During Elijah's ministry, Yahweh does the same, asserting his supremacy to the idols of Israel and the gods of Sidon. "Elijah" means "Yah is my God" (אל יהו), and Elijah's ministry gives repeated reinforcements of this: Yahweh is Lord, and there is no other. The very first verse of 1 Kgs. 17 points to this. Baal is the Canaanites' counterpart to Zeus, the sky god responsible for the clouds, weather, and fertility. But Elijah announces at the beginning of his ministry that Baal is not controlling the weather. Instead, Elijah himself claims to control the weather: "There shall be neither dew nor rain these years except by my word" (17:1). Baal is nothing: rather, Yahweh the raingiver works through his prophet.

When Elijah crosses the Jordan to wilderness, Yahweh's power does not cease. Yahweh is Lord of the wilderness as well as the garden, and he provides for his prophet, preserving the carrier of the word of God in a dry and thirsty land. During a drought, Elijah drinks from a wadi (a seasonal stream) for days and eats the food brought by ravens. Yahweh makes a "garden" in the midst of the wilderness, as he had done for Israel centuries before.

When the water runs out at Cherith, Yahweh sends his prophet to Zarephath, in the region of Sidon, Jezebel's territory, Baal's territory. There too Yahweh proves himself Lord. According to Deut. 32:21–22, when Israel provokes Yahweh with idols, he will provoke them by paying attention to another nation: "They have made me jealous with what is not God; / they have provoked me to anger [כעסוני בהבל יהם] with their idols. / So I will make them jealous with those who are not a people; / I will provoke them to anger with a foolish nation." Just as Yahweh's law instructs Israel to carry out justice eye-for-eye, tooth-for-tooth, burn-for-burn, so he carries out his judgments against Israel "jealousy-for-jealousy." Israel provokes Yahweh to jealousy (להכעים את־יהוה אלהי ישראל בהבל יהם) (1 Kgs. 16:26), so he provokes them to jealousy. Israel looks on other gods with favor, so Yahweh looks for other nations to favor. Yahweh sends Elijah off to a Gentile widow, though, as Jesus said, there were many widows in Israel at the time (Luke 4:25). With all Israel remade in the image of its harlot queen (2 Kgs. 9:22, 30), Yahweh seeks out a poor widow-bride among the Gentiles (1 Kgs. 17:13–24).

Wherever Elijah goes, life breaks out, abundantly, since he is the bearer of the word and presence of the life-giving creator. By providing food for the widow of Zarephath, a Canaanite counterpart to Jezebel, Yahweh shows his superiority to Baal, who, after all, is unable to provide a bit of bread for a Sidonian widow and her household. In the midst of drought and famine, Elijah's arrival makes her house a place of uninterrupted provision. When she honors the prophet by giving him her first cake of bread, Yahweh gives her a prophet's reward (Matt. 10:41), replenishing her oil and flour. In the midst of Baal's territory, Yahweh provides bread for his prophet and for the widow who supports him. In faith, the woman puts bread upon the waters and receives an abundant return.

The greatest test is the last. After Elijah saves the widow and her house from starvation, after Elijah brings new life to the house, suddenly death invades the house. The widow blames Elijah, and we can hear the disappointment and dismay in her accusing question: "I thought you were coming to save me and my son, but you've come to kill. I thought you came as a mediator of life, but you come instead with death." This complaint raises a climactic challenge. Yahweh crosses into the wilderness and gives life; he gives life in Baal's territory. But can he cross the boundary to rescue a boy from Sheol? Yahweh is the lord of life: but is he the lord of death? Again, the answer is yes. Elijah brings the widow's accusation to Yahweh and then prays that the Lord will revive the boy. Yahweh listens to Elijah's voice and restores the boy's soul to his body. Yahweh is not only superior to Baal, the Canaanite god of fertility and life, but also greater than Mot, the Canaanite god of the underworld, snatching the dead boy from the grave (Provan 1995, 132).

The widow thinks that her sins are an obstacle to Yahweh: "What do I have to do with you, O man of God?" she complains; "you have come to me to bring my guilt to remembrance and to put my son to death!" (1 Kgs. 17:18). Even sin is not impenetrable barrier, for Yahweh breaks through sin and demonstrates his forgiveness to the widow by raising her son from the dead, by giving new life, resurrection life, in her house.

Through his prophet, Yahweh demonstrates his lordship, his boundary-bursting power. He shows his power over the wilderness, over enemy territory, over the grave. And in this he manifests his relentless persistence, his unwavering commitment to preserve his prophet and to save Israel. Elijah goes to the wilderness, and Yahweh follows him. Elijah goes to Zarephath, and Yahweh follows him. The widow's son goes to the grave, and Yahweh follows to bring life from death. Yahweh's commitment is not confined to the prophet, but extends to all Israel, for he preserves the prophet for the sake of his people. In the face of Yahweh's persistent loyalty, if Israel fails to respond with trust and love, it is because of its own hard-heartedness, for Israel is left without excuse.

This is the God of Jesus Christ, the God who comes to us in Christ Jesus. Will our God enter the wilderness for us? He has done, in Jesus. Will he cross into the territory of the "prince of this world" for us? He has done, in Jesus. Will he cross the boundary between the living and the dead for us? He has done, in Jesus.

Elijah is superior to Baal too, for he claims that rain and dew awaited *his* permission ("except by *my* word" in 17:1), and at the end of the chapter he gives another demonstration of power. Under the law, corpses are intensely unclean, not only unclean in themselves but "mothers of uncleanness" that transmit uncleanness. Uncleanness is strongly associated with death (Wenham 1979, 176–77), so that anyone who enters a room with a corpse is infected by the death radiating from it (Num. 19:14). That does not happen to Elijah. Elijah touches the body when he carries the boy upstairs, enters the room, and then spreads himself out on the boy. Instead of being infected by death, however, Elijah communicates life. The Pentateuch is full of wonders and signs, but Moses never raises the dead, and, apart from Elisha, no one else does either until the time of Jesus. Elijah and Elisha are uniquely carriers of the life of Yahweh.

Prayer is the conduit for the power of the Spirit to go from Yahweh to Elijah and then to radiate life to widows, children, and ultimately Israel. Through prayer, Elijah receives life and food in order to give life and food. Though not stated in this passage, the drought is a response to Elijah's prayer, as seen in James's interpretation: "Elijah was a man with a nature like ours, and he prayed earnestly that it might not rain; and it did not rain on the earth for three years and six months" (Jas. 5:17). Even before he appears in Kings, Elijah is praying, asking Yahweh to withhold the rain and dew. According to Deuteronomy, when Israel turns from Yahweh and pursues idols, Yahweh will bring all manner of curses (28:15), and among the curses is drought: "The heavens that are over your head shall be bronze, and the earth that is under you iron. Yahweh will make the rain of your land powder and dust; from heaven it will come down until you are destroyed" (28:23–24). Elijah knows the covenant and understands God's curses; he observes the idolatries of Omri and Ahab, and he prays that God will keep covenant by cursing a disobedient and rebellious people and driving them to repentance. Elijah anticipates Yahweh's plans because he knows Yahweh's character from Scripture (Van't Veer 1980, 53).

Elijah's first prayer is a prayer for judgment, not a prayer for stability and calm or the maintenance of the status quo. For Elijah, the status quo is intolerable. He cannot overlook the fact that Israel, the people of Yahweh, turns to Baal and other false gods, and he does not want Yahweh to overlook that fact either. Such prayers do not spring easily to the minds and lips of modern Christians, but the Psalms are full of petitions for judgment and exhortations to praise when God answers (e.g., Ps. 96:11–13). Prayers for judgment do not come out of delight in destruction and death, nor does such prayer arise from a harsh and vindictive spirit. When God judges, he enters a disordered world, a world where nothing is as it should be, to reorder it and set things right. When we pray for judgment, we are simply praying that God will set things right, that he not be satisfied with things as they are, that he keep his promise to establish peace and right in the creation.

James also writes that the "effectual fervent prayer of a *righteous* man avails much" (Jas. 5:16), and he cites Elijah as the example.[4] Elijah is a man of powerful prayer because he is a righteous man: Yahweh commands, and Elijah obeys. The writer of 1–2 Kings reinforces this point by the way he records Elijah's obedience, using a "command-compliance" structure (Davis 2002, 223). Yahweh says, "Go away . . . and turn eastward, and hide yourself by the brook Cherith, which is east of the Jordan" (1 Kgs. 17:3). Elijah's obedience is described in almost identical language: "So he went and did according to the word of Yahweh, for he went and lived by the brook Cherith, which is east of the Jordan" (17:5). Then the Lord says, "Arise, go to Zarephath, which belongs to Sidon, and stay there; behold I have commanded a widow there to provide for you" (17:9). Elijah's obedience is again recorded in almost identical language: "So he arose and went to Zarephath, and when he came to the gate of the city, behold, a widow" (17:10). Elijah's obedience is letter perfect, and as a result his prayers are effective. Conversely, "he who turns his ear from listening to the law, / even his prayer is an abomination" (Prov. 28:9). When anyone closes his or her ears to God's word, God responds by closing his ears. Prayer is a dialogue, a matter of mutual speaking and mutual hearing. Prayer is inherently an act of trust, evoked by confidence in the word of God and by hope that God can and will do something in response to our prayers. Anyone with the boldness to ask God to listen to his or her words and petitions should do God the courtesy of first listening to his.

Elijah's righteousness is manifested in his strict and exact obedience to the word of Yahweh. That rhythm is established early in the passage, but at the end of the passage is an astonishing reversal. Elijah speaks to Yahweh, "Let the child's life return to him" (1 Kgs. 17:21). Then the punch line: "Yahweh heard the voice of Elijah, and the life of the child returned to him and he revived" (17:22). When Yahweh says X, Elijah does X. Now, when Elijah says Y, Yahweh does Y. The command-compliance pattern is reversed, for the Lord's answer to Elijah's prayer is stated in the same words as Elijah's prayer. There can be only one way to put this in the context: Yahweh heeds the voice of

4. Fervency should not be ignored. The rhetoric of Elijah's prayer in 1 Kgs. 17:20 is noteworthy. The widow comes with an accusation against Elijah, and ultimately against God, and when Elijah prays, he takes up her accusation: "O Yahweh my God, have you brought calamity to the widow with whom I am staying, by causing her son to die?" Elijah does not refrain from expressing his anguish and the bitterness. There is no pious softening as he takes up the widow's complaint as his own. God does not need to be protected from our fury, rage, and disappointment, as if they can be hidden away from his sight. Saints express their anguish and frustration openly. They express their rage at sin and its effects and their dismay that God has not yet acted to correct it. "How long, O Lord?" is a characteristic prayer of the Psalms.

Elijah; Elijah commands, and Yahweh responds. When Joshua calls on Yahweh to make the sun stand in the sky, we are told "there was no day like it before it or after it, when Yahweh listened to the voice of a man" (Josh. 10:14). But here is a day like it, for the Lord listens to the voice of Elijah (Davis 2002, 223; Walsh 1996, 235).

Yahweh is the boundary-transgressing, infinite, boundless God. He never retreats, never suffers a setback, is never frustrated. Nothing can hold him or hold him back. Drought cannot limit him; in fact, he sends the drought. Death cannot keep him away. He is the lord of life and of death and demonstrates his power over life and death in the resurrection of Jesus. And he promises to put his infinite resources at the disposal of those who pray in righteousness and faith. He is our helper, ready and waiting to receive "instructions" through the effectual fervent prayers of righteous believers.

1 KINGS 18:1–46

First Kings 18 conflates two narratives from Exodus (Cohn 1982, 340–41). On the one hand, this covenant-renewal event runs parallel to the covenant making of Exod. 20–24 (Roberts 2000, 636–38). Like Moses at Sinai, Elijah sets up an altar of twelve stones (1 Kgs. 18:30–32; Exod. 24:4). In both events, sacrifices are offered and a covenant meal is celebrated (1 Kgs. 18:41; Exod. 24:9–11). In both events, Yahweh manifests his glory in fire and Israel confesses Yahweh as Lord and king (1 Kgs. 18:39; Exod. 24:7). On the other hand, this covenant renewal takes place after the covenant has been broken and in this respect resembles the events of Exod. 32. When Israel worships the golden calf at Sinai, Moses calls the faithful to execute the idolaters (Exod. 32:25–29), as Elijah commands Israel to destroy the prophets of Baal (1 Kgs. 18:40). After Moses destroyed the calf, he ascends Sinai alone to plead with God to renew the broken covenant (Exod. 33–34), and Elijah goes to Sinai to plead with God to judge Israel (1 Kgs. 19). The incident at Carmel cleanses the land of Baal prophets and reestablishes the kingdom of Ahab on a Yahwist basis (Roberts 2000).

One of the petitions of Solomon's prayer at the temple dedication deals with the curse of drought (8:35–36). During the days of Ahab, the northern kingdom turns from the Lord, and as a result Yahweh shuts the heavens for three years, a lengthy drought. In the "third year" (18:1), Yahweh tells Elijah to end his exile in Zarephath and return to the land. With Elijah, the word of Yahweh, with all its potency for blessing, also returns to Israel. In fact, Elijah returns so that the Lord will send rain. Elijah's return initiates a third-year "resurrection" of Israel, a foreshadowing of the third day when the Father raises the true Israel from the dead.

Yet something is amiss. Solomon's prayer is premised on Israel's repentance: when "they pray toward this place and confess your name and turn from their sin"—*then* Yahweh is supposed to take notice. But Ahab is not repentant. Whatever Ahab believes when Elijah first prophesies the drought, he comes to see that Elijah is responsible, but even this acknowledgement does not go very far. When the prophet meets the king, Ahab immediately accuses Elijah of being the "troubler of Israel" (עכר ישראל) (18:17), a charge that Elijah simply turns back on Ahab (18:18). The phrase originated during the conquest, when Achan became a troubler of Israel by stealing Yahweh's holy plunder from Jericho (Josh. 6:18; 7:25; 1 Chr. 2:7: עכר עוכר ישראל). Because of Achan's sin, Israel is defeated in battle with Ai and gains the victory only after executing Achan. A troubler brings evil on Israel by displeasing Yahweh. Elijah causes turmoil, but the one who brings the Lord's wrath is Ahab, not Elijah. Though Ahab recognizes that the Lord brings the drought and the resulting famine, he blames Elijah (and implicitly Yahweh) rather than humbling himself and turning from his idols.[1]

Ahab's idolatry is compounded by persecution. Jezebel kills prophets of Yahweh, forcing the rest into hiding (1 Kgs. 18:4), where they are cared for by Obadiah, a faithful worshiper of Yahweh who protects and supplies the prophets of Yahweh. When Elijah first meets him, Obadiah is looking for water, another satirical jab at Baal, who is supposed to supply water to his worshipers. Even Obadiah is more effective than Baal, because he provides water to prophets of Yahweh. Prophets may be hiding in caves and in Gentile territory, but even there Yahweh provides food.

As "mayor of the palace" Obadiah holds a high position in Israel, with responsibility for Ahab's palace, estates, and livestock. Both Elijah and Obadiah (whose name, עבדיהו, means "servant of Yah") are faithful servants of Yahweh, the God of Israel, but radically differ in their position and mode of service. Elijah confronts Ahab from outside the court, while Obadiah works for the preservation of the prophets—and hence the preservation of the word of Yahweh—from within Ahab's court, subverting the official policies of the court even while acting as chief steward. Not every faithful believer is called to be an

---

1. Throughout Scripture, enemies of God accuse the righteous of being troublers. Pharaoh accuses Abraham of wrongdoing when Abraham is in Egypt (Gen. 12), and Laban accuses Jacob (Gen. 31). Israel accuses Moses of provoking Pharaoh (Exod. 5:20–21), and Jesus is considered a "troubler" of Israel who leads the people astray. Accusing the righteous is a favorite ploy of Satan, whose name means "accuser." Elijah is not intimidated by the accusation, nor does he respond with a pseudo-humble: "You've got a point there, Ahab. We're both partly to blame." He simply turns the charge back and refuses to consider Ahab's accusation. Of course, everyone sins, and Christians must be quick to hear a rebuke when it comes, but often what comes disguised as an angelic rebuke is really a satanic accusation designed to render us impotent by dissolving energy in guilt. That must be resisted—and must be resisted from the vantage of the gospel: who can bring a charge against God's elect? it is God who justifies; who is the one who condemns? The accuser of believers has been cast down, so those who are in Christ do not have to fear the accusations of the accuser. We entrust ourselves to the God who judges justly, the God who will vindicate those who trust in him and are able to resist the paralyzing scapegoating of those who are enemies of the gospel.

Elijah. Many are called to the tricky work of remaining faithful in a faithless context, to the business of serving Elijah and Yahweh as "master" (18:7) and serving Ahab as "master" (18:8).[2] Obadiah's position is not merely tricky; it is dangerous. A false shepherd, Ahab tolerates Jezebel "cutting off" (בהכרית אִיזֶבֶל אֵת נְבִיאֵי יְהוָה) prophets (18:4), but is reluctant to "cut off" any of his cattle (וְלוֹא נַכְרִית מֵהַבְּהֵמָה) (18:5). Jezebel the Baal worshiper is willing to tolerate golden calves and other forms of idolatrous worship, but she cannot tolerate the intolerance of the Yahweh worshipers.

All this intensifies the question: Why is Elijah back anyway? What has happened to the covenant? Is Yahweh breaking his own rules? Is he ignoring Israel's sin? How can the holy God turn to Israel when Israel has not turned to him (Van't Veer 1980, 154)? Despite the slander that the God of Israel is harsh and impulsive, the history of the northern kingdom repeatedly reveals him as the opposite, indulgent nearly to the point of irresponsibility (see the introduction to this commentary). The man of God from Judah announces that a Davidic scion named Josiah will destroy Jeroboam I's shrine, which caused Israel to sin, but Josiah is not the next king in Judah, nor the next nor the next. We read chapter after chapter waiting like Jonah for the fire from heaven that will consume Bethel, but it does not come. In 1 Kgs. 19, Yahweh tells Elijah that Ahab's house will be destroyed by Hazael, Jehu, and Elisha; Elisha appears briefly late in that chapter, but does nothing to arrest idolatry, and Hazael and Jehu do not appear for another dozen chapters. The Arameans besiege Samaria (1 Kgs. 20), and we think finally that Yahweh is making some headway, but Ahab is victorious in two battles. Nor is this pattern confined to the Omride dynasty: Manasseh seals the fate of the southern kingdom (2 Kgs. 21:10–15), yet in the following generation Josiah leads the greatest of Judah's reformations. In the light of 1 Kgs. 8, the history of the Omride dynasty highlights with particular force the Lord's apparent toleration of evil. For Scripture, the question is not, as it is for moderns, How can we square our belief in an omnipotent God with our experience of evil? The question is, Why does Yahweh show so much kindness to the wicked?

As posed by what Jürgen Moltmann calls "protest atheism," the problem of evil is usually framed as a contradiction within theism, particularly biblical theism (1974, 221). Evil things happen, and God is either good but impotent to stop evil or omnipotent but malign, such that evil expresses some aspect of his character. Since Augustine's polemics against the Manichees, this dilemma has been answered by emphasizing the negativity of evil. Evil has, in Milbank's words, no "ontological purchase," but is instead strictly a negation of being and a privation of good (1990b, 432). At least in some formulations, however, the conclusion that evil is nonexistent has been pressed into a form of dualism

---

2. This is not to say that Obadiah's handling of his position is flawless. Faithful though he is, Obadiah is fearful about announcing Elijah. Elijah forces Obadiah to take a side more publicly, just as he later leads Israel as a whole to stop "limping on two divided opinions" (18:21).

that is difficult to square with Scripture's claims about God's comprehensive lordship.

Biblically, the existence of natural evil cannot be separated from the reality of sin and God as judge of all the earth. As Thomas Aquinas insists, in bringing natural disasters of various sorts God is not doing evil because he is punishing evil. He addresses the objection that such punishment goes contrary to the good, since in punishing God withdraws some good (e.g., health, happiness, wealth) from the person being punished. Thomas replies that "punishment is contrary to a particular good," yet the removal of particular goods is consistent with the nature of God as supreme good, since "the addition of other, sometimes better, goods takes away particular goods." A higher good might thus displace a particular good. Thomas uses the example of the higher good of God's established order of justice, saying that this might "take away the good of a particular nature as a punishment" (Thomas Aquinas 2003, 141–48). Though he does not elaborate, this enables Thomas to address the problem of hell and eternal punishment; hell is a matter of God putting a good in place of a good, not a matter of God putting an evil in place of good. The good in this case is the good of divine justice; and that good of divine justice trumps the good of a particular sinner's happiness.

When moral evils are considered—how can immorality coexist with the goodness of God?—the problem of evil is more biblically formulated as a problem of prevenient grace. Also originating with Augustine, this notion emphasizes that God's grace and work always goes before, *prevenire*, human response. Scripture assumes that God exists and that he is the supreme and wholly righteous judge. If injustice exists, it does not count as evidence against the existence of God, but instead provokes laments and prayers for justice to be done. From this angle, what looks like a "problem of evil" is really the question of why God shows mercy to people who have shown no inclination to repent. Why does God preserve flagrantly wicked people, and why does he allow them to prosper? When the problem of evil is put in this context, we discover that many biblical passages directly address the problem (Ps. 37; 73). With its recurring emphasis on the patience of Yahweh, 1–2 Kings is one of the key biblical narratives on this question.

When Ahab arrives, Elijah proposes a contest on Mount Carmel, in the north of Israel toward the Mediterranean Sea. Elijah takes charge of the whole contest, and Ahab complies with Elijah's every instruction (1 Kgs. 18:19–20). After he calls Elijah a "troubler," Ahab disappears from the narrative until 18:41, and after 18:17 Ahab never speaks again. Ahab, like Baal his god (18:29), falls silent. The prophets of Baal also submissively, even comically, follow Elijah's orders (Walsh 1996, 249). He tells them to choose an ox, prepare it, and call on Baal, and they do (18:25–26). Even when he mockingly instructs them to cry out more loudly; they follow his instructions (18:27–28). They continue their antics throughout the day, but the day of Baal is nearly over. At evening, a new day begins, the day of Yahweh.

Yahweh shows mercy to demonstrate that he is God. This is a common theme in the prophets, who claim that Yahweh forgives Israel, restores it, brings it back to the land, for the sake of his own name. Repentance is a gift of God, and if God gives a gift of repentance it is because he has already decided to show mercy to his people. In explaining why he does not destroy Israel when they rebel against him, Yahweh says through Ezekiel: "I acted for the sake of my name, that it should not be profaned in the sight of the nations among whom they lived, in whose sight I made myself known to them by bringing them out of the land of Egypt" (20:9; cf. 20:14, 22). Israel's continuing existence does not ultimately depend on Israel's faithfulness, but on Yahweh. He displays his glory, the glory of his name, before the nations, and he saves Israel, sends renewal and resurrection to Israel, time and again, for the sake of his name. Yahweh, as Elijah confesses, "turns the heart" (1 Kgs. 18:37). Israel cannot turn to Yahweh unless he turns to them first. When Israel begins to pray toward Jerusalem, confess their sins, and turn away from them, they realize that God is always already there first.

Elijah tells the people to "draw near" (18:30), an invitation to join him in worshiping Yahweh (Walsh 1996, 250). The altar represents the nation, with its twelve stones (18:31), and it represents the nation as a well-watered mountain, a land flowing with milk and honey, drenched with twelve jars of water from above (18:33–34). The fire that comes from heaven symbolizes the judgment that falls on the nation, a judgment that consumes water, as the drought has done (Jordan 1988a, 235–36). This incident is also reminiscent of other events when Yahweh initiates worship with fire from his presence (Lev. 9:22–24; 1 Chr. 21:26–27; 2 Chr. 7:1). Carmel is not only the place of Yahweh's victory, but Yahweh designates it as his "house," where he is to be worshiped. The people fall to worship Yahweh (1 Kgs. 18:39) and slaughter the false prophets, renewing their commitment to follow Yahweh as God of Israel. Yahweh's fire falls on the altar, not on the people, so that Yahweh's judgment falls on a substitute Israel in order to deliver Israel itself. Judgment is always a prelude to blessing, the renewal of rain and dew: after fire falls from heaven, the Lord sends rain. Elijah had prayed for the drought, and now he crouches and prays intensely for an end to the drought (18:42). Elisha later "crouches" (the same Hebrew verb) over a boy to raise him from the dead (2 Kgs. 4:34), and Elijah spreads himself on the earth as if to raise the land from the dead (1 Kgs. 17:21).

Elijah "ran before" Ahab to Jezreel (18:46). A runner before a king is a herald and a king's servant, and Elijah returns to Jezreel to announce that the blessing of Yahweh has returned to the land and to proclaim the return of the king to one of his chief cities. He is "before Ahab" in the sense that he is "before Yahweh" (17:1), a servant to the king. Yet, in another sense, Elijah is "in front of" the king, leading the way. The covenant renewal at Carmel restores the proper order of king and prophet, with the king following the man of God (Cohn 1982, 341). Israel's renewal demands that Ahab receive the word of Yahweh, conduct his reign under the guidance of Elijah, and allow Elijah to stand before him as chief advisor and prophet. At the end of this chapter, that seems a live possibility, with Elijah "running before" Ahab into the city of Jezreel.

As Roberts (2000; cf. Walsh 1996, 285–86) points out, the instruction to Ahab to "eat and drink" on top of Carmel (18:41) is the climax of the covenant renewal, corresponding to the meal of the elders on Sinai during the covenant making there (Exod. 24:9–11). One imagines that Ahab does not feel much like eating. With the corpses of the prophets turning the Kishon to blood, Elijah tells him to eat and drink at the top of Carmel. And Ahab, who conforms to every command of Elijah, silently, perhaps grimly, complies. At the center of the chapter is a contrast between Obadiah and Jezebel: Jezebel kills prophets of Yahweh, cutting them off, while Obadiah saves them in caves. Jezebel supplies food and drink for four hundred prophets of Asherah at her table, while Obadiah faithfully supplies bread and water for the hidden prophets. But now the king himself sits at a table spread by the prophet, ruling a people who have confessed that Yahweh is God. Yahweh's unasked intervention into the Omride dynasty appears to work: Israel is back in covenant with its Lord.

In the end, the covenant renewal with Ahab is stillborn, but Yahweh's mercy in the third year points to his greater demonstration of righteousness and mercy in Jesus. At Carmel, Yahweh manifests the glory of his name and vindicates himself over against Baal by sending fire that destroys an altar that represents the nation of Israel. And in the fullness of time, when Israel has again turned from Yahweh to its own ways, distorting and twisting his good law for the sake of their traditions, God intervenes again, prior to any turning from Israel.

Carmel anticipates another mountain, a mountain outside Jerusalem, where the fire of God's judgment falls on a substitute Israel, when Jesus, the altar of God, is crucified to save his people. At Carmel, in the third year, Yahweh sends rain that renews the land; and in Jerusalem, on the third day, he raises Jesus from the dead to renew the world. At Carmel, the judgment of God is followed by rain; and at Jerusalem, the one who baptized by fire on the cross ascends to baptize his disciples with the Holy Spirit, pouring out the Spirit like showers from heaven. He does all this to demonstrate his righteousness in the present time, to shame the gods of the nations, to show the nations that he is the Lord and that there is no other.

1 KINGS 19:1–21

Yahweh wins a decisive victory over Baal at Carmel, and the people who bowed to golden calves and kissed the Baals fall on their faces to declare, "Yahweh is God! Yahweh is God!" Yahweh's victory over Baal is so public that the people obey Elijah's command to slaughter the prophets of Baal, none of whom return from Carmel. When the rain comes, Elijah runs ahead of Ahab to Jezreel, announcing the return of the rain and the return of the king. It seems possible that Ahab will follow Elijah as his lead prophet, that Elijah will shape the future of Israel from a position of prominence. The covenant renewed, Israel is back on the right track.

It is not to be. Wisdom does not save Israel from division, and this covenant renewal will not save the dynasty of Ahab from disaster. Ahab goes home and tells Jezebel all that Elijah has done. Elijah's work is comprehensive, as the repetition of the word "all" in 1 Kgs. 19:1 indicates. Ahab holds Elijah responsible for everything—for Baal's defeat, for the slaughter of Baal prophets. Ahab's report, perhaps by design, incites Jezebel against the prophet. Jezebel, after all, is the chief architect of the anti-Yahweh policies of Ahab's court, cutting off the prophets of Yahweh (18:4). Ahab submits to Elijah's every command on Carmel—gathering prophets, setting up the contest, eating and drinking, returning to Jezreel ahead of the rainstorm. Jezebel, however, instantly and decisively sends a messenger to Elijah warning him that she intends to make him like one of the prophets of Baal whose corpses are sent down the wadi Kishon.

Just when Elijah enjoys a moment of success, his enemies pick a fight. And this is not the last time. Just when it appears that a true prophet has arisen in Israel, just when many suspect that Jesus is *the* prophet, the Jewish leaders conspire with the Romans to crucify him: and we thought this one would bring redemption to Israel (Luke 24:21). Just when the gospel is making headway among Gentiles, the Judaizing heresy arises to drive Paul to distraction. Why do the church's enemies have to pick a fight just when things get rolling?

The answer is, they *don't* (Van't Veer 1980, 320). The church does. Jesus does not come to bring peace but a sword, to set brother against brother, mother against daughter, father against son. Following its master, the church likewise provokes the hostility, hatred, and resentment of the world at every turn. This is not the result of some flaw in the church's ministry, but the opposite. When the church is faithful, it announces judgment of this world (John 12:31), the universal corruption and disorder of humanity (Rom. 1:18–32), the overthrow of the prince of this world. We do not need Nietzsche to tell us that we are dominated by lies and violence, motivated by pride, envy, lust, wrath, and vengefulness; we do not need Foucault to teach us that the world languishes under the dominion of the dark powers, principalities, and wickedness in high places. We proclaim Christ crucified, and Jesus says that in his death the judgment of the world was passed. We have the Spirit, who is given for sin, righteousness, and judgment (John 16:1–11). Inherent in the gospel is the condemnation of this world, and when we preach such a gospel, we cannot help but start a fight.

Marcion and his host of modern disciples teach that while condemnation is characteristic of the Old Testament, in the New Testament condemnation yields to affirmation and inclusion. The reality is very nearly the opposite. As Van't Veer points out, the old covenant is characterized by a confinement of battle:

> We could say that the Lord attacked the powers of darkness, the kingdom of satan on earth [in the old covenant], within the boundaries of Canaan. The land of rest was also the land of struggle, the land where the Kingdom of the Lord did battle with the powers of satan. There the blows rained down as the two powers confronted each other in the full light of the complete antithesis between them. There the light was revealed to combat the darkness. The chariots of the Lord of hosts were mobilized and arranged in ranks to charge at the forces of the evil one. The Seed of the woman struggled against the seed of the serpent, waiting for and working toward the hour of full revelation when the battle would spill across the borders of the "promised land" to the ends of the earth because of a victory in principle. (Van't Veer 1980, 341)

When he moves to Zarephath, Elijah does not carry on a battle with Baal: "We should not say that Elijah was wrong in this regard. He was simply acting in accordance with the Old Testament dispensation, in which the struggle of the Seed of the woman and the seed of the serpent was carried on within the borders of Canaan." After Pentecost, however, "the church's battle entered a new phase. Paul could not flee the battle or call a certain area neutral or write off some territory as under enemy control. Wherever he went, he had to unleash the battle" (Van't Veer 1980, 349). Jezebel's actions are not unexpected, and they are not really actions. They are reactions. Elijah is the aggressor, and so is the church, if we do not forget ourselves. The church does mean to do harm to unbelief, injustice, and wickedness. We mean to cast down every vain imagination and every thought that exalts itself against Christ Jesus (2 Cor. 10:1–5), to proclaim the gospel until all knees bow and every tongue confesses Jesus is the Christ.

Van't Veer's comments lend nuance and depth to Wright's suggestion that under the old-covenant order God collects and concentrates sin and uncleanness in Israel, funneling it through the holy nation, so that it can come to rest on the Messiah, who will bear it away (Wright 1993, 151–53). Van't Veer also helpfully characterizes the paradoxical character of Israel's specialness: Israel is the object of Yahweh's favor above all other nations, but precisely for that reason Yahweh is at war with Israel's sin and rebellion in a way that he is not at war with the rebellion and sin of humanity as a whole. Holiness brings both privilege and danger. Israel often seems worse than other nations, so much more stiff-necked and bone-headed, but that is a distortion. Yahweh chooses Israel to wage a battle to the death with sin, death, and Satan and, having triumphed, raises Israel from the dead.

Elijah hopes his ministry will turn the house of Ahab, and Israel, back to Yahweh, but he sees his hopes come to nothing. He leaves the land and heads south, first to Beersheba and then to Sinai. It is often said that Elijah flees from Jezebel out of fear, and some translations actually say "he was afraid, and rose, and ran for his life" (1 Kgs. 19:3). Many preachers see this passage as a reassuring story emphasizing Elijah's human flaws and weakness. Fearful of Jezebel, he flees the land, whines and complains, even going so far as to exaggerate his isolation as a prophet.

Davis vigorously and convincingly challenges this line of interpretation on several fronts (2002, chap. 24). First Kings 19:3 does not say that Elijah "fears" but that he "sees" (וירא), and the word for "flee" is simply a Hebrew word for "go" or "walk" (וילך). Prophets are "eyes of Yahweh" who "walk" to and fro on the earth, collecting "evidence" to present before the Lord (Zech. 4:10). Eyes are organs of discernment and judgment in Scripture (Gen. 1; Ps. 11). As a prophet, Elijah sees Jezebel's plan and also perceives that Jezebel and not Ahab is really in charge of royal policy. As in 1 Kgs. 17, Elijah's withdrawal is a judgment on Israel. Beersheba, furthermore, is at the southern edge of Judah, and Sinai is another two hundred miles beyond Beersheba. Elijah's movements do not indicate flight, but a journey to a specific destination, a return to the mountain where Yahweh first cut covenant with Israel.

At the same time, we should not minimize Elijah's frustration and sense of failure. At Carmel, he announces to the prophets of Baal, "I alone am left a prophet of Yahweh" (18:22). After fire fell from heaven, it seems that this is no longer the case. Elijah appears to win the majority of Israel to his side, but now he sees that nothing changes. Twice, at Sinai, he states: "I alone am left" (19:10, 14). It looks like the one prophet has expanded into a multitude; but Elijah realizes that he is alone again. Elijah wishes to die, but this is not simple despair. He realizes that he is no more effective than his prophetic fathers in calling Israel back to the covenant. Israel's renewal is not going to take place, at least not the way that Elijah envisions. As a prophet, Elijah is bound to bring an accusation against Israel. Like Jonah, he is reluctant to do this, and like Jonah Elijah would rather die than stand against Israel. He has "great sorry and unceasing grief in his heart" concerning his fellow Israelites (Rom. 9:1–5). He is a Moses, desiring to die for the sake of Israel (as the apostle Paul was as well). At the broom tree in the wilderness he is refreshed. He lies down (a symbolic death), but the angel raises him up and feeds him (a symbolic resurrection). Refreshed by water and bread baked on "live coals" (עֻגַת רְצָפִים) (1 Kgs. 19:6; cf. Isa. 6:6),[1] he continues to his destination, Sinai. Under the broom tree, Elijah is restored to the prophetic calling he is tempted to renounce (Nelson 1987, 123).[2]

Elijah is again moving through the history of Israel. Having confronted the Pharaoh-like Ahab and his "court magicians," the prophets of Baal, he wins a great victory by humbling the gods of Ahab. Under threat from Jezebel, he leaves the land and is fed miraculously in the wilderness on his way to Sinai. In his earlier journey into the wilderness, he was undergoing prophetic training, as Moses does before the exodus. After Carmel, Elijah acts as a representative of Israel, returning to the place where the covenant between Yahweh and Israel was first formed, to inform Yahweh that Israel broke covenant.

When Elijah arrives at Sinai, Yahweh asks him to "state his purpose" (מַה־לְּךָ פֹּה אֵלִיָּהוּ) (1 Kgs. 19:9). Elijah is not at Sinai to vent, but to exercise the privilege of the prophet. Israel's prophets are essentially members of Yahweh's council, "officers of the court" of the judge of heaven and earth. According to Jeremiah, false prophets have not "stood in the council of Yahweh, / that he should see and hear his word." But "if they had stood in my council, / then they would have announced my words to my people, / and would have turned them back from their evil way / and from the evil of their deeds" (Jer. 23:18, 22; cf. Heschel 1955, 1.21–22). Prophets stand in the court of Yahweh to listen to the sentences passed and to offer briefs on behalf of the people. Elijah is convinced that things are beyond repair, and he presents evidence for the prosecution. Yahweh tells him to "stand before Yahweh" (וְעָמַדְתָּ בָהָר לִפְנֵי יְהוָה), assuming his prophetic position and role (1 Kgs. 19:11). Yahweh comes roaring to him in wind, earthquake, fire, and voice—all associated in Scripture with Yahweh's advent (2 Sam. 22:11; Ps. 11:6; 104:3; Isa. 29:6). But

---

1. These two passages are the only places in Scripture where the word for "live coals" is used.

2. Why does this happen twice? Perhaps as representative of Israel Elijah is raised up from the ground in order to eat, as Israel does at Carmel. The scene shows that there is going to be a second resurrection for Israel, as there is for Elijah. After an even more severe judgment on Israel, the remnant of Israel will be saved.

1 Kgs. 19 emphasizes that Yahweh is more fundamentally associated with his word than with any other phenomena.[3]

Elijah insists that he has been jealous (קַנֹּא קִנֵּאתִי) for Yahweh (19:14), just as Yahweh is for Israel. Yet, Israel turns from Yahweh's covenant, altars, and prophets. Unlike Moses, who also sees Yahweh's glory on Sinai and covers his face with a veil (Exod. 33:17–34:9; 34:29–35; cf. 1 Kgs. 19:13), Elijah does not intercede for Israel, but instead formally accuses Israel (19:10, 14). Elijah is right. Israel forsook the covenant of Yahweh when it turned to golden calves and Baals. Israel tore down Yahweh's altars, including the one on Carmel that Elijah healed. Israel killed the prophets of Yahweh, urged on by Jezebel. There are other prophets, hiding in caves, but Elijah is the only prophet actively opposing Ahab and Jezebel. Elijah is not exaggerating his isolation or the condition of Israel. Even if commentators do not, Yahweh agrees with Elijah's assessment of Israel's condition. This is the strongest evidence that Elijah is not "losing it": Yahweh does not rebuke Elijah for his loss of confidence, but concurs with Elijah's accusation and gives him three tasks to overthrow Ahab's house (Davis 2002, 266): Elijah is to anoint Hazael (a Gentile) and Jehu (an Israelite) as the two swords of Yahweh and Elisha as a prophet.

The parallels with Moses in Exod. 33–34 highlight another dimension of this incident. Moses speaks to God after a first covenant is breached, symbolized by the shattered tablets, and he persuades Yahweh to show mercy and renew the covenant. Yahweh does, issuing a second set of tablets along with a promise to accompany Israel to the promised land. As a new Moses, Elijah is also the mediator of a new covenant. Yahweh no longer intends to call the house of Ahab back from the brink, but to take down the house of Ahab as he took down the house of Jeroboam I and Baasha. Ahab's house has a chance for renewal at Carmel, but loses that chance when Jezebel turns against Elijah. Now the renewal of Israel will begin with the community within Israel, centered not on the king or the temple but on the prophet. Yet, even while Yahweh turns his particular attention to the Israel within Israel, he remains the God of all Israel, showing mercy and judging.

Likewise, Jesus comes healing the sick, casting out demons, stilling storms, doing many wonderful works, but those wonders have no appreciable effect on first-century Israel. Herod and Pilate are not persuaded, and, though surrounded by dazzling signs on all sides, the Pharisees ask for a sign. Jesus says that the only sign will be the sign of Jonah, a sign of death and resurrection and also a sign of the prophet leaving for Gentile lands. Signs do not convince Ahab and Jezebel either, and the sign given to them is a sign of death and resurrection, Elijah's own symbolic death and resurrection under the broom

3. Yahweh's appearance along with wind, earthquake, and fire also pictures what Yahweh will do with Israel. He is going to shake Israel down, but after he will speak quietly to his people, like a husband wooing back his wayward bride (Hos. 2:14–20).

tree in the wilderness. But in the midst of that judgment, the Lord does not forget his people.

Elijah first calls Elisha, as Moses designates Joshua as his successor. Elisha is plowing with the twelfth of twelve pairs of oxen, a picture of his later "yoking" and "guiding" of Israel. As a plowman, Elisha prepares the ground for planting the seeds of a new Israel. Given his place in Israel's history, he is a plowman who beats his plow to a sword. Elisha does go back to his parents, but he accepts the prophetic call, since he burns the yoke (Provan 1995, 149–50). He becomes an apprentice to Elijah, in order to become like his master. Elijah "passes by" Elisha, as Yahweh passes by him on Sinai (1 Kgs. 19:11), and throws the mantle of prophetic office over Elisha's shoulders. This investiture with a prophetic mantle, the mantle that Elijah wears as he stands in official capacity before Yahweh, serves as Elisha's anointing. The mantle covers Elijah when he hears that Yahweh is unsheathing his triple sword against Israel. Now that mantle is placed on Elisha, who will bear—who will *be*—one of the swords.

Paul quotes 1 Kgs. 19 in Rom. 11:2–4, a passage addressing the question of God's righteousness in the history of Israel: if God was faithful to his promises, as Paul insists he is, why does Israel, who received the promises, not enjoy their fulfillment? In answer, Paul first points to his own experience: a son of Abraham and a Benjamite, he is a follower of Jesus and thus included in the consummation of the covenant. In this context, the surface meaning of the quotation from 1 Kgs. 19 is clear: just as the Lord keeps some Israelites faithful during the days of Elijah, when most in Israel follow the Baals, so the Lord calls some of the seed of Abraham in the days of Paul, when many in Israel reject Jesus. In both cases, a community of renewal gathers around a wonder-working prophet.

But there is another level to the connection as well. Elijah states that he is alone a prophet of Yahweh, but Yahweh promises to raise up three "swords" against Israel and to preserve seven thousand who never bow to Baal. In Paul's day, Israel faces a similar future: a looming judgment hangs over the temple, the coming Roman attack on Jerusalem that Jesus predicted at length (Matt. 24; Mark 13; Luke 21; cf. Wright 1996a, chap. 8). Just as Jehu comes to destroy Ahab's house and the temple of Baal in Samaria, so the Romans will destroy Israel and topple the temple in Jerusalem. In the midst of this crisis, Paul knows from Old Testament precedent that the Lord will bring a new people, a remnant, out of the ruins of the old, that he will raise a new Israel from the dead.

Paul elsewhere describes himself in terms of the Elijah model. His mysterious trip to Arabia (Gal. 1:17) suggests that Paul follows the route of Elijah (Wright 1996c). Arabia is the location of Sinai (4:25), so that Paul's trip to Arabia could have been a journey to Sinai. Likewise, Paul's postconversion itinerary—Israel to Arabia to Damascus—repeats the itinerary of Elijah in 1 Kgs. 19. Paul discerns that his ministry is like that of Elijah, the first prophet to turn to Gentiles. Paul's anguish over Israel's lack of faith (Rom. 9:1–2) and even his desire that he could die for his siblings (9:3–4) reflect Elijah's anguish over Israel's failure to repent after the events of Mount Carmel. Both Elijah and Paul preserve, or provoke, the faith within Israel by ministering to Gentiles, rather than exclusively within Israel. Elijah goes to Zarephath, a type of the gospel going to the Gentiles, as Jesus says (Luke 4), and Paul sees his mission to the Gentiles as a provocation to jealousy for Jews (Rom. 11:13–14).

If Paul is indeed viewing his own ministry through an Elijah typology (as he does sometimes with Moses; 2 Cor. 3), then the sequence of his argument in Rom. 11 becomes clearer: Paul alone recapitulates Elijah, and the faithful few in the days of the Omrides finds a parallel in the believing Jews of Paul's day. In both cases, further, the lone prophet/apostle is God's means for preserving faith, so that a remnant of Jews will be saved through the judgment. Paul thinks of the remnant in the way described above (see the commentary on 1 Kgs. 17:1–24): through the ministry of the lone prophet, Jesus, and the lone apostle, the remnant that is "all Israel" shall be saved through the devastating final judgment on Jerusalem's temple.

Fully in keeping with the remnant theology of the Old Testament, Paul emphasizes that the preservation of any part of Israel is an act of sheer mercy. He wants to insist on the "I have kept" of Rom. 11:4, which emphasizes God's initiative in preserving Israel. If there is a remnant, it is not because some Jews have been able to remain sufficiently faithful to Torah to win God's favor. The remnant is "according to the election" and is preserved as a sheer act of mercy on God's part. *All* Israel deserves death, but the Lord will preserve a portion for later restoration and incorporation into a new Israel in which there is neither Jew nor Greek.

1 KINGS 20:1–43

Near the middle of *The Anti-Christ*, Nietzsche mocks Ernst Renan's life of Jesus for attempting to convince the world that Jesus is a "hero."[1] Nothing, Nietzsche says, is less evangelical than heroism, for "if anything is unevangelical it is the concept of the hero. Just the opposite of all wrestling, of all feeling-oneself-in-a-struggle, has here become instinct: the incapacity for resistance becomes morality here ('resist not evil!'—the most profound word of the Gospels, their key in a certain sense), blessedness in peace, in gentleness, in not *being able* to be an enemy" (Nietzsche 1982, 600–601 [emphasis original]).

While Nietzsche means this as an attack on Christianity, many Christians agree and see one of the chief virtues of Christianity as its depriving people of the ability to be enemies. Liberal theology means many things, but one of its central themes is the denial of enmity and especially the denial that God has enemies. On this score, however, conservative evangelicals often share much common ground with liberals. Nowhere is this more evident than in hymnody, always a key barometer of theology and piety. For someone raised on nineteenth-century revival hymns, the most surprising thing about the Psalms is the prominence of enemies and the psalmists' militant reaction to them. For many Christians, Nietzsche's description is precisely accurate.

Eliminating the category of "enmity" from social and political theory has been one of the grand projects of modernity. Enmity is essential to politics, Carl Schmitt argues, and liberalism is wrong to attempt to turn the enemy into a mere competitor or interlocutor (Hollerich 2004; Meier 1998). Sociology and anthropology reimagine the enemy as "outsider" or "stranger," as a member of an "out-group," while postmodern philosophy is obsessed with the "other." Put a McDonald's and a Gap in every major Middle Eastern city, and

---

1. The material in the following paragraphs is drawn from Leithart 2005c.

terrorism will drown in a wave of Happy Meals. When liberal modernity does not simply ignore the existence of the enemy, it denies the existence of enmity that cannot be cajoled, coopted, convinced, or smilingly coerced to become an ally. Strangely, it is not just abstract theorists who hope for a world without enemies, but politicians, even in the aftermath of the attacks of September 11, the Madrid and London bombings, and continuing terror throughout the Middle East (Kagan 2004).

To some extent, this theoretical and practical removal of enmity is a product of the gospel and the culture of the gospel that we call Christendom, for the foundation of Christendom is the destruction of ancient enmities. Yet, it simply will not do for Christians to ignore the reality of enmity. Eliminate enemies from the biblical story, and you eliminate most of the biblical story. Certainly, you delete the early chapters of the story. As soon as Yahweh places Adam in the garden and gives him a bride to protect, the conditions are set for enmity. And immediately, there is an enemy at the gate—*the* enemy—seducing and tempting and breathing threats. Enmity arises *before* the fall, and Adam's sin from one angle is his inability to recognize an enemy or, more accurately, his refusal to *be* an enemy.[2]

The closing events of the reign of Ahab raise these issues with particular intensity. The final three chapters of 1 Kings leave off the story of Elijah and record a series of incidents that focus on Ahab's sins. Ahab sins in his policies toward Gentiles (1 Kgs. 20), in his treatment of one of his subjects (1 Kgs. 21), and finally in his response to the word of a prophet of Yahweh (1 Kgs. 22). Ahab's three sins parallel the sins of Saul (1 Sam. 13–15), though in reverse order (Leithart 2003d). As the Philistines amass their armies to fight Israel, Saul is ordered to wait for Samuel at Gilgal, but he becomes impatient and sacrifices before Samuel arrives. When the battle is finally joined, Saul imposes a fast on his soldiers and threatens to execute his son Jonathan when he eats honey during the battle. Finally, Saul spares Agag, an Amalekite king that the Lord has ordered him to destroy. Saul's clemency to Agag is repeated in Ahab's generosity to Ben-hadad; Saul's threat to Jonathan finds a parallel in Ahab's murder of Naboth; Saul's impatience at the altar is similar to Ahab's refusal to listen to the Lord's prophet Micaiah.

2. Scripture recounts that enmity intensifies after the fall, as God himself tells Adam (Gen. 3:15). One cannot read far in the Psalms before encountering David's enemies: "O Lord, how my adversaries have increased; / many are rising up against me" (Ps. 3); "O Lord, lead me in your righteousness / because of my foes; / make your way straight before me" (Ps. 5); "my eye is wasted away with grief; / it has become old because of all my adversaries" (Ps. 6); "save and deliver me from all those who pursue me / lest he tear my soul like a lion" (Ps. 7); "when my enemies turn back, / they stumble and perish before you" (Ps. 9). And there are still 140 psalms to go. Nor is enmity a harsh Old Testament notion; the New Testament speaks of enemies of the cross and enemies of Christ and enemies of the church (Phil. 3:18; Rom. 11:28), and no Old Testament passage is quoted more often in the New Testament than Ps. 110, which promises that Christ's enemies will be subdued beneath his feet.

To see the full scope of this sequence, we need to look even further back in history, to the early chapters of Genesis. Genesis 1–6 records three falls: (1) Adam sins at the tree in the garden and is cast out of the garden; (2) Cain sins against his brother Abel and is cast out of the land; and (3) the sons of God sin by intermarrying with the daughters of men, and as a result Yahweh sends a flood that destroys the entire earth. Genesis 1–6 records a fall in the sanctuary garden, a result of a sin against God; a fall in the field, as one brother attacks another; and a fall in the world, as sons of God get into bed with the daughters of men. Genesis 1–6 lays out the three realms in which human life takes place: sanctuary, the place of worship, where we deal with God directly; the land, the place of work and relationships, where we deal with our siblings; and the world, the place of mission and witness, where we deal with unbelievers.

During the monarchy in Israel, the kings are called to faithfulness in these zones of life. They are to preserve sound worship, rooting out idolatry and maintaining the temple of Yahweh; to protect and not oppress their siblings; and to bear faithful witness in the world and fight Yahweh's battles against his enemies. Saul fails in every area, and Ahab does as well. Ahab's dynasty, like Saul's, is doomed as a result. Ahab enters into covenant with idolaters at the beginning of his reign, and as soon as he climbs into bed with idolaters (literally!) his dynasty is doomed.

Ahab's first sin is his failure to be a resolute enemy to the Arameans. On Sinai, Yahweh tells Elijah that the Arameans will bring a sword against Ahab's house (1 Kgs. 19). Hazael of Aram will come at the house of Ahab with a sword, and whoever escapes from his hand will be left for Jehu and Elisha. First Kings 20 opens obligingly with an Aramean siege of Samaria, the first time in 1–2 Kings that Gentiles penetrate Israelite territory and besiege an Israelite city (1 Kgs. 16:15, 17). It is not the last: this initial siege of Samaria foreshadows the later sieges carried out by Assyria (2 Kgs. 17) and Babylon (2 Kgs. 24–25). As Shishak's invasion gives Judah a small taste of exile (1 Kgs. 14:25–28), so Aram does in Israel. Exile looms over the divided kingdom throughout its history.

Yet, Ahab successfully breaks the siege and wins a second battle at Aphek, both with help from prophets.[3] Because of the siege, Ahab initially agrees to the terms that Ben-hadad proposes (20:1–3), thinking it better to become Ben-hadad's servant than to allow Samaria to be destroyed, thereby displaying wisdom that the people of Jerusalem will fail to show when threatened by Nebuchadnezzar (Jer. 27). Sensing an advantage, Ben-hadad presses for more concessions and demands the right to enter Ahab's palace to take away

---

3. A historical note: the Arameans are from Damascus to the east of Israel. During this period of history, Assyria is expanding, pushing the Arameans westward toward Israel. Ben-hadad leads an anti-Assyrian alliance of thirty-two kings and attempts to bring Ahab into that alliance as well. One of Solomon's adversaries is Rezon, who reigns over the Arameans in Damascus (11:23–25). Ahab is a counterfeit Solomon, and like Solomon he faces an internal adversary (Jehu) and an external one (Aram).

everything that Ahab desires ("all the desire of *your* eyes") (1 Kgs. 20:6). Ahab resists and gains the support of the elders (20:8). In the midst of a tense and deteriorating diplomatic situation, a prophet comes to Ahab, bringing word that Yahweh promises to give Ahab the victory not for Ahab's sake but to demonstrate to Ahab, once again (1 Kgs. 18), that he is Yahweh. Just as Yahweh sends plagues on Pharaoh so that he would "know that I am Yahweh" (Exod. 7:5, 17; 8:22; 14:4), so Yahweh delivers Ahab in order to reveal his character. Elijah is previously the only prophet to have any direct contact with Ahab, and he always comes with a word of judgment. For the first time in Ahab's career, a prophet comes with good news. If Ahab persists in his idolatries after this, he will be flouting Yahweh's kindness.

Yahweh instructs Ahab to send the inexperienced "lads" into battle first and to send them in broad daylight (1 Kgs. 20:14–16). Overconfident, Ben-hadad is already celebrating the victory with a drinking party in his tents (20:16), acting like one who is ready to take off his armor rather than one who is putting it on. After Ahab's victory, another prophet gives Ahab instructions about how to respond to a future attack from the Arameans (20:22). Apparently Ahab follows this advice: in the first battle, the Arameans get as far as Samaria, but the second battle is fought at the border town of Aphek (20:30).

As the prophet predicts, the Arameans return the following year for a second battle. They have made a theological assessment of their earlier defeat: Yahweh is a god of mountains, but on the plain the gods of Aram will be superior (20:23).[4] Yahweh again sends a prophet with good news for Ahab, with an oracle very similar to that of the earlier prophet (20:13, 22, 28). In the second Aramean war, like the first, Yahweh delivers Israel "so that you will know that I am Yahweh" (20:28). Ahab wins and shows clemency to Ben-hadad, accepting him as a "brother" rather than a "servant" (20:32–33).

With Ahab's victory in the battle of Aphek, the initial situation at the beginning of the account is neatly reversed. At the beginning of the story, Ben-hadad is the aggressor and dominant party, imposing conditions on Ahab; at the end of the story, Ahab is in the dominant position. At the beginning, Ben-hadad claims ownership of Ahab's possessions; at the end, Ben-hadad makes concessions by letting Ahab set up markets or claim streets in Damascus. At the beginning, Ben-hadad provokes trouble by demanding the chance to come through Samaria and seize whatever pleases Ahab, showing no mercy; at the end, Ahab uses his dominant position to show clemency to Ben-hadad. If the chapter ended at 20:34, we would have a story of unexpected mercy to Ahab and unexpected mercy shown by Ahab, a comic episode in Ahab's reign.

4. The Arameans also believe that it was a mistake to go to war with an alliance of thirty-two kings. By replacing the kings with "commanders," Ben-hadad centralizes the military command (20:24). Ben-hadad's servants want him personally to muster the army and oversee the next campaign (20:25).

Again (see 1 Kgs. 18), the story raises questions about evil. How exactly is Yahweh's reputation enhanced when he apparently winks at the Baal worship that he condemns? Does Yahweh take Baal worship seriously? Is *Yahweh* himself incapable of being an enemy? Is he in the end, despite his rages and his wraths and his indignations, the indulgent grandpappy of our imaginations and hopes?

One of Scripture's central answers to the question of evil is that the wicked will not prosper forever. They might flourish and appear invincible and invulnerable for a time, but sometime, whether now or later, they will fade. "Do not fret because of evildoers," David says in Psalm 37, "For they will wither quickly like the grass, / and fade like the green herb." The psalm is fundamentally an exhortation to trust God, do good, cultivate faithfulness, and delight in the Lord, confident that we will eventually see the wicked perish and the enemies of God vanish like smoke. Yahweh shows mercy to Ahab and to Israel, stretching out his hands to a disobedient people, but when Ahab spurns that mercy, hardens himself, and persistently refuses to turn, Yahweh brings him down. It may not be soon, but it will happen. The wicked will not flourish forever.

For Christians in a new covenant, the hope that God will deal with sin and evil once for all is not theoretical. As Paul says in Rom. 8:3, Israel's Torah is neutralized because of "flesh," and so God has taken things into his own hands. Sending his Son in the likeness of sinful flesh, he has condemned sin in flesh. In Jesus, God has displayed his righteousness, which includes his determination to establish righteousness and rid the world of sin. To paraphrase Hebrews, we do not yet see evil expelled from the creation, but we do see Jesus. And so, the Lord endures with much patience vessels formed for wrath in order that he might make known the riches of his glory upon vessels of mercy, which he prepared beforehand for glory (9:19–24).

First Kings 20 makes it clear that the wicked do not prosper forever, for 20:34 is not the end of the story, and the sequel contains the whole point of the passage, a point that becomes clear from reflection on the narrative structure. The two battles with the Arameans follow a similar sequence:

Aramean attack (20:1–12)	Aramean attack (20:26–27)
prophet visits Ahab (20:13–14)	man of God visits Ahab (20:28)
Ahab wins battle (20:15–21)	Ahab wins battle (20:29–30)
prophet advises Ahab (20:22)	—
Ben-hadad's servants advise him (20:23–25a)	Ben-hadad's servants advise him (20:31)
Ben-hadad takes advice (20:25b)	Ben-hadad takes advice (20:32–34)

After the second battle, the rhythm of the text leaves us expecting another prophet to appear, perhaps offering further advice about how to protect against another Aramean advance. No prophet appears.

When he does, he is out of narrative sequence, and his message to Ahab is wholly unlike the favorable prophetic messages earlier in the story. An anonymous prophet carries out a prophetic drama, reenacting the story of Ahab and

Ben-hadad (20:35–43). Another man refuses to strike him, as Ahab refuses to strike Ben-hadad. As a result, a lion kills him, just as a lion kills the disobedient man of God from Judah (13:24). The prophet tells the king an allegory of the story of Ahab and Ben-hadad, and just when Ahab thinks he has caught the prophet in self-condemnation, the prophet throws off the disguise and catches the conscience of the king.

Ahab is condemned for not devoting Ben-hadad to destruction (20:42). The Hebrew term for "devote to destruction" (םרח) is used for the war of complete destruction that Joshua carries out against the Canaanites. According to this form of warfare, everything that breathes is to be put to death (Deut. 20:16–18). In other wars, however, Israel is to put to death all the men of whatever city opposed them (20:10–15). How is Ahab to know that he is supposed to fight holy war? There are several clues. Ben-hadad apparently intends to reduce Samaria to rubble (1 Kgs. 20:10), and in responding to this threat, Ahab should meet utter destruction with a force of utter destruction. Further, the battle of Aphek is a reenactment of the battle of Jericho. The two armies wait seven days before engaging, and then the wall of Aphek falls and crushes 27,000 Arameans. Most important, Israel wins the victories over the Arameans purely through the Lord's strength, as Yahweh gives the enormous Aramean army into the hand of Ahab and brings the wall down on the remnants of the army. Yahweh even gives Ahab the battle strategy, as the commanding king of Israel's hosts. Ben-hadad is not Ahab's prisoner but Yahweh's. "Devoted to destruction" essentially means "reserved for Yahweh," and Ahab should know from everything about the battle that the decision whether Ben-hadad lived or died is not his to make. Ahab once again proves himself an Achan, a "troubler in Israel" (18:17).

In the prophet's parable, the man who places the captive in the prophet's hands says, "If for any reason this man is missing, then your life shall be for his life, or else you shall pay a talent of silver" (20:39). The arrangement is not simply life-for-life; there was a possibility for ransom. But when the prophet announces Ahab's sentence (20:42), he does not mention this alternative, but says simply, "Your life shall go for his life, and your people for his people." Perhaps Ahab has gone so far that there is no choice but life for life. But there is another, subtler explanation. The prophet's story holds out hope for atonement, and Ahab could seize that hope in response to the parable: "Ahh. But what about the talent of silver? Can't I atone for the wrong?" Instead of playing the Syro-Phoenician woman and seizing the opening, Ahab responds with rage. Hardened and resentful, seething in anger, he slouches silently back to Samaria. Like Jeroboam I's wife (1 Kgs. 14), Ahab forgets that every word from God is an act of grace, an invitation to conversation because it is an invitation to conversion.

Ajax and Hector fight to a standoff on the windy plains of Troy and then remove their armor and exchange gifts to formalize a friendship. Plutarch's treatise "How to Profit by One's Enemy" breathes a similar spirit, though in a more philosophical idiom. Classical enmity is functional, strategic, temporary, and superficial. For ancient heroes, enmity always plays out under a canopy of basic agreement; battles are fought under the egis of a code of honor to which both sides adhere, but there is no battle over the code. The Bible teaches an enmity that goes to the bone. For the Christian there can be no compromise with the enemy, but only battle until victory. Can one imagine Moses combating Pharaoh through nine plagues and then calling it all off and moving back into Pharaoh's palace? Can anyone imagine David and Goliath fighting to a draw and then going off to share a pint? We might as well imagine Jesus dining with the devil after his temptations in the wilderness. Pagans are happy to incorporate any new god into the pantheon, including Jesus; but Paul asks, What harmony has Christ with Belial? Far from deleting enmity from history, Christianity immeasurably and fundamentally deepens it.

1 KINGS 21:1-29

Americans, if they believe in idolatry at all, believe it is a victimless sin. Though it is debatable that the framers of the American Constitution envisioned a secular state, the First Amendment has come to be understood as a protection of all religious belief, though not necessarily a protection of religious behavior (e.g., polygamy is not a protected religious behavior). According to contemporary interpretations of the First Amendment, it makes no social and political difference what people believe. They can worship a thousand gods or none; they can worship Yahweh or Allah or Jesus; and it has absolutely no public consequences. All can live in harmony and peace despite our religious differences, because the sacred canopy overarching all our particular religious commitments is a commitment to the American system. Particular religions are subordinated to the American civil religion, a religion to which all Americans adhere. Whatever we are ethnically or religiously, we are all hyphenated Americans: Christian-Americans or Buddhist-Americans or Muslim-Americans or atheist-Americans, but always Americans. This is what O'Donovan had in mind when he suggests, shockingly to many American Christians, that the First Amendment "can usefully be taken as the symbolic end of Christendom," since, whatever the intentions of the framers, it "ended up promoting a concept of the state's role from which Christology was excluded, that of a state freed from all responsibility to recognize God's self-disclosure in history" (1996, 244–45).

Indifference to idolatry has its roots in the early modern period. According to a common telling of the story, Europeans discovered that theology was bloodily divisive and concluded that the only way to restore comparative harmony was to expunge theology from the public square, forcing theological decision and debate into the recesses of the conscience or, at best, safely behind the walls of the church (Pannenberg 1989, 12–15). William

Cavanagh vigorously and persuasively challenges this account of secularization, arguing that the wars of religion did not move religion into a private space but instead invented the modern concept of religion (2002, 15–42). Besides, all efforts to establish social harmony on the foundation of theologically neutral concepts of nature and human nature are doomed to failure. To found a constitution on the premise that human beings are something *other* than the image of God is not to found a constitution on neutrality. It is, so Christians must testify, to found a constitution on falsehood.

Scripture does not treat idolatry as morally or politically indifferent. What and how we worship shapes the kind of persons we become. After describing false gods as speechless, blind, deaf, immobile, and powerless, Psalm 115 says that "those who make them will become like them, / everyone who trusts in them" (115:8). Idolaters are as dumb, blind, deaf, and impotent as the gods they worship. On the other hand, as the Gospels demonstrate, those who turn to Jesus in faith are healed of all such diseases. Worshipers of the living God live.

Israel's prophets focus a great deal of attention and passion on the connection between idolatry or false worship and social injustice (Isa. 1:10–17; Amos 3:14), and this prophetic insight comes to a climax in Paul's lengthy indictment of human "ungodliness and unrighteousness" in Rom. 1:18–32. This harrowing descent begins when those who "know God" refuse to "honor him as God or give thanks" (1:21) and exchange "the glory of the incorruptible God for an image in the form of corruptible man and of birds and of four-footed animals and crawling creatures" (1:23). God judges idolaters by giving them over to the consequences of their idolatry, which leads from sexual perversions (1:26–27) into a social chaos of envy, murder, dissension, slander, rebellion against authority, and cruelty (1:28–32).[1]

Ahab's career follows this trajectory. Ahab is introduced as the most overtly idolatrous king that Israel suffered, but Ahab's resistance to God does not stay in a safe "religious" arena. It manifests itself first in his ungodly alliance with Ben-hadad of Syria (1 Kgs. 20) and then in oppression of a fellow Israelite (1 Kgs. 21). Ahab is a David, seizing what is dear to his neighbor and arranging for his neighbor's death (2 Sam. 11–12); with Jezebel, he is a Cain, attacking a "brother" in Israel; incited by Jezebel, he is Adam, who takes forbidden fruit, the fruit of another's vineyard.

---

1. On the surface, Paul directs this polemic against Gentiles, but in the course of this litany of human evil he alludes to several events of Israel's history (compare Rom. 1:23 with Deut. 4:16–18), and the narrative line of Rom. 1 serves well as a dispiriting summary of Israel's history. Rhetorically, this is very clever: Jewish readers would cheer along with nearly everything that Paul says against the Gentiles, but as soon as they are cheering along, Paul levels the same indictment against them (Rom. 2:1–2, 17–29). Paul is a prophet indeed, in the tradition of Nathan: "You are the man."

From one perspective, the narratives of Elijah (1 Kgs. 17–2 Kgs. 2) form a unit, internally organized by a roughly chiastic structure:[2]

A Elijah appears suddenly and leaves the land (1 Kgs. 17)
   B fire from heaven in a contest of gods (1 Kgs. 18)
      C Elijah complains to Yahweh on Horeb and is assured that Ahab's house will perish (1 Kgs. 19)
         D Ahab spares the Gentile king Ben-hadad (1 Kgs. 20)
         D′ Ahab kills the faithful Israelite Naboth (1 Kgs. 21)
      C′ Ahab is killed after being warned by a lone prophet (1 Kgs. 22)
   B′ fire from heaven in a contest of gods (2 Kgs. 1)
A′ Elijah suddenly departs on the east side of the Jordan (2 Kgs. 2)

The two central chapters are structurally similar: both tell stories that resolve neatly, only to be disrupted by the disturbing intervention of a prophet. Ahab's actions in the two chapters summarize his apostasy: he loves Gentiles and their gods while hating faithful Israelites and their God. He fails to carry out holy war against Ben Hadad, but prosecutes it instead against Naboth and his house (2 Kgs. 9:26). He does not know how to fight enemies, and, to say the same thing, he does not know how to protect friends.

Israel is a vineyard (Ps. 80; Isa. 5), and Naboth, the owner of the vineyard next to Ahab's palace, is a paradigmatic Israelite, the tender of the Lord's vine, an Israelite who clings to the Lord's gift. When the king wants to purchase his vineyard, he objects that the land is an inheritance and, according to the Levitical regulations, inalienable (Lev. 25). Naboth's objection is theological: it would be "profanation to Yahweh" (חלילה לי מיהוה) (1 Kgs. 21:3) if he were to sell his vineyard for mere convenience. According to the laws of Lev. 25, since the land belongs to Yahweh, Israelites may lease it for a period of time but return it to the original owner's family in the year of Jubilee. Naboth has the right to give up his property, but the presumption of the Jubilee legislation is that Israelites would part with land only if they were too poor to do anything else.

The only other place where the Old Testament uses the phrase "vegetable garden" (לגן־ירק) is Deut. 11:10, referring to the land of Egypt. Symbolically, Ahab's intention is to turn the vineyard of Israel into an Egyptian vegetable patch, and this is consistent with his entire policy of "re-Canaanitization" of Israel. Ahab wants to "drive out" Naboth and "take possession" (1 Kgs. 21:19, 26), as Israel once did to the Canaanites (Gen. 15:7; Num. 13:30; Josh. 18:3;

2. This structure should not be seen as contradictory of competitive to the structure given in the commentary on 1 Kgs. 17:1–24. Though I am unable to demonstrate it here, texts are as structurally complex as a musical composition, which can be organized by many structures (melodic, harmonic, rhythmic) simultaneously.

Judg. 2:6). Like the crowds that follow Moses from Egypt, Ahab wants to return to slavery and idolatry (Provan 1995, 157–58; Nelson 1987, 141).

When Naboth refuses, Ahab crumples, but while Ahab pouts on his bed, Jezebel intervenes. She writes letters, as David does to Joab (2 Sam. 11:14–22), arranging for false accusations, a kangaroo trial, and a judicial murder of Naboth and his house. Ahab knows that Jezebel persecutes prophets of Yahweh and that she will not sit while her will is thwarted. Ahab's self-pitying passivity is perhaps an implicit plea for Jezebel to do something to make his hurt go away (Walsh 1996, 321). Whatever his intentions, Ahab is responsible for Jezebel's plot. When Elijah confronts Ahab, he addresses him with the question, "Have you murdered and also taken possession?" (1 Kgs. 21:19). Ahab perhaps hopes for some degree of deniability, but Yahweh and Elijah do not leave that opening. Ahab murders Naboth just as surely as David murders Uriah, just as surely as Adam is responsible for the first sin despite being "incited by his wife."

Ahab is weak, perhaps deliberately so, but he is not the only weak man in Israel. Jezebel writes letters to the nobles and elders of the city of Jezreel, and her instructions are followed to the letter. Jezebel writes, "Proclaim a fast" (21:9); so they "proclaimed a fast" (21:12). She writes, "Seat Naboth at the head of the people" (21:9); so they "seated Naboth at the head of the people" (21:12). She writes, "Seat two sons of Belial before him" (21:10); so "the two sons of Belial came in and sat before him" (21:13). She writes, "Let them testify against him" (21:10); so the two sons of Belial "testified against him, even Naboth" (21:13). She even provides the charges, "Say, he cursed God and the king" (21:10, 13). Jezebel writes that the men of Jezreel should "take him out and stone him to death" (21:10); so "they took him outside the city and stoned him to death with stones" (21:13). The author uses a "command-compliance" pattern usually reserved for Yahweh's commands to his prophets. When Yahweh speaks to Elijah, the prophet obeys, and his obedience is described in exactly the same words as the commandments. Elijah obeys to the letter—and so do the elders and nobles of Jezreel. As it is written, so it is done.

Naboth is victim of a conspiracy that encompasses the leading citizens of the city of Jezreel. It is naïve to think that every event is the result of some nefarious, centuries-long conspiracy stretching from the Masons of Solomon's temple through the Knights Templar to the Illuminati and the Trilateral Commission. It would be equally naïve to think that the wicked never plot against the righteous, never conspire, never breathe together in a plot. Naboth is hardly the last faithful man victimized by a plot. The vicious idolatry promoted with force by Ahab and Jezebel corrupts and cows all the people of Jezreel. For the writer of 1–2 Kings, idolatry is anything but politically indifferent.

Naboth's blood is spilled on the outskirts of the city of Jezreel, and it is done very cleanly, very stylishly. Ahab has his vineyard, and he has done nothing to get it. Though the letters to the nobles and elders go out over his seal, he can always shrug and blame his uncontrollable wife. By the account in 1 Kgs. 21, he is in bed all the while (21:4, 16), a passive king like David (1:1–4) if not a sick one. All the people who know of the plot are part of the plot and can be blamed if they reveal it. Humanly speaking, the case is closed, and there is no way to break it open.

Ahab and Jezebel, however, miss the most important factor in the situation: there is a God from whom no secrets are hid, a God before whom all the thoughts and intentions of the heart are open and revealed. Yahweh breaks the case open and sends Elijah to meet Ahab in the vineyard of Naboth, which Ahab claims as his own (21:17–18). Elijah is told to "arise, go down to meet King Ahab," a command reminiscent of Yahweh's commission to Moses to confront Pharaoh. Ahab kills an innocent in Israel, as Pharaoh once did, and his kingdom, like Pharaoh's, is to be overthrown. Elijah brings the most severe and far-reaching prophecy yet. Because of Ahab's sin, his dynasty is doomed to extinction, as the dynasties of Jeroboam I and Baasha are (21:21–24).[3]

In response, Ahab removes his royal robes, dons sackcloth, fasts, sleeps in sackcloth, and goes about despondent (21:27). He refuses food when he cannot get the vineyard, and he refuses food because of the doom pronounced over his house. Yahweh responds to the outward signs of humility, as he does in the case of Nineveh (Jonah 3). Still, the only thing that Ahab can hope for at this point is a delay, not a cancellation of the sentence. The Lord says he will not bring judgment in Ahab's time, but it will come.[4] Ahab gets a reprieve, but his dynasty is still doomed. Naboth's blood will not go unavenged. The same will happen later to Hezekiah (2 Kgs. 20:16–21) and Josiah (22:18–20).

The story is an allegory: the vineyard is Israel, and idolatrous Ahab seeks to turn the vineyard of Israel back to Egypt. Naboth represents the faithful within Israel holding onto the promise to Abraham and the inheritance given by Yahweh. That allegory becomes even sharper when we recognize the pun on Naboth's name (נבות), which is close to the Hebrew word for "prophets" (נביאים). Earlier in Kings, Jezebel cuts off the prophets of Yahweh (1 Kgs. 18:4), and now Ahab murders Naboth, whose name marks him as a representative of the persecuted prophets. The story of Naboth's vineyard becomes, in Jesus's telling of the parable of the vineyard, an allegory of the whole history of Israel (Matt. 21:33–46), the nation that persecutes the prophets, the master's servants sent to collect rent.

Throughout the centuries, the blood of the righteous has been spilled on the earth: the blood of Abel and the blood of countless innocents who died during the violent times before the flood; the blood of the nameless infants

---

3. There appears to be a difficulty in 21:19. The text says that dogs will lick Ahab's blood in the same location as they licked up Naboth's, but the next chapter shows that Ahab dies in Samaria and that his blood is spilled there (22:38). Yet, a number of members of Ahab's house are killed in Jezreel—Joram, Ahaziah, and Jezebel (2 Kgs. 9). They are all of Ahab's blood, which the dogs lap up. The Lord's judgment is eye for eye, evil for evil (1 Kgs. 21:20–21), blood for blood, lick for lick.

4. In this, Ahab's story foreshadows the later history of the Davidic kingdom. Josiah's much more thorough repentance does nothing more than buy Judah a little time.

of Israel slaughtered by Pharaoh and the blood of the innocents shed during the reign of Manasseh; the blood of the prophets sent to Ahab and Jezebel and the blood of the infants surrounding Bethlehem slaughtered by Herod; the blood of Stephen and James and Peter and Paul; the blood of Thecla and Polycarp and Lawrence and Ignatius and Agnes and Hippolytus. They have been crucified, skinned, torn in pieces, fed to lions.

From all appearances, these martyrs are forgotten forever. There are no war-crimes tribunals; there are few monuments, few memorials, few memories. Hundreds and thousands remain forgotten, nameless, faceless. By one estimate, seventy million martyrs have been killed in the history of the church, as many as forty-five million in the past century. They have been killed in Russia and in Nazi Germany, in Turkey and in Algeria, in Nigeria and Sudan and Pakistan. As many as 160,000 Christians have been killed every year since 1990 (Colson 2002). Who even knows? Their blood has soaked into the ground and is silent forever.

That is what Ahab and Jezebel think, and that is what all the cruel powers who prey on the innocent have always thought—and hoped. As Girard argues in book after book, all religions and cultures outside of Christianity are premised on this perverse hope that blood is only blood, the hope that innocent blood can be silenced. When imitative desires fracture a society into a war of all against all, harmony is restored by uniting all energies and hostilities against a scapegoat. The scapegoat does not cause the descent into social anarchy, but suffers as if he or she had and restores social order (Girard 1986; 2001; Boersma 2004, 133–51). In all these systems, the gods underwrite the powers, the scapegoating majority, instead of defending the scapegoat. Girard argues that the Bible is unique in proclaiming the innocence of scapegoats and in revealing a God who hears the cry of innocent blood.

The innocent scapegoat is not some peripheral issue in Scripture but its central message: the gospel is the story of a man whose enemies conspire against him, a man falsely accused of blasphemy, a man taken outside the city to endure an unjust execution (Heb. 13:10–13). Naboth's body, like the flesh of a purification offering, is taken outside the camp to be destroyed (Lev. 4:11–12, 20–21), foreshadowing the greater purification offered by Jesus. In one sense the blood spilled from the cross speaks a word of mercy for the world, a better word than the blood of Abel (Heb. 12:24). Yet, the Lord remains an avenger of blood even after the cross (Rev. 17–19), and the blood of martyrs cries out for vengeance against the persecutors of Christ, his bride, and his gospel. That cry will be heard; that blood will be avenged.

1 KINGS 22:1–40

Ahab's life ends in a battle with the Arameans, but the narrative of Ahab's death includes another, deeper battle—the battle between true and false prophecy, a battle first initiated in 1 Kgs. 13. At the heart of 1–2 Kings, the author's deepest concern is highlighted: the crux of Israel's history is not its political fortunes or the various battles that the kings fight, but the contest of true and false prophecy. Those who hear the prophet and keep Yahweh's word live; those who refuse to hear are destroyed. And because Israel as a whole refuses the word of Yahweh's prophets, it is speeding toward exile.

Ahab's life ends the way it begins, with Ahab ignoring Yahweh's prophet, yet he cannot escape the prophet's word by ignoring the prophecy or by attempting to subvert it. Despite his efforts to elude his fate, Ahab's death fulfills many words of Yahweh, and this chapter gathers together much of the life of Ahab into a single climactic story. He is confronted by prophets, as he is throughout his reign (1 Kgs. 17:1); he fights Arameans, as he has before (1 Kgs. 20); his building projects are mentioned, as they are at the beginning of the account of his reign (16:32–34). In 1 Kgs. 20, an unnamed prophet confronts Ahab because he spared the Aramean king Ben-hadad. After Ahab murders Naboth and takes possession of his vineyard, Elijah announces the doom of his house. Finally, Micaiah specifically predicts that Ahab will fall in battle with the Arameans.

Three prophets, three warnings, three witnesses. These prophecies are a sign of Yahweh's continuing mercy to Ahab. Ahab cannot plead ignorance and therefore cannot plead innocence. Yahweh warns, and Ahab becomes sullen and angry. Yahweh warns again, and Ahab goes through the motions of repentance. Yahweh warns again, and Ahab defiantly goes to battle, disguising himself to escape the doom that Micaiah spoke. He gets three chances; but then comes strike three, in the *third* year (22:1), and the game is over.

Ahab plans to attack Ramoth-gilead, a border town just across the Jordan from the northern kingdom controlled by Arameans. Given its location, Ramoth-gilead is an important defensive position against invaders from the east. Apparently, Ramoth-gilead is also on a trade route, so that Aram's control of the city gives access to income of various duties and fees. Ahab specifically complains that the Arameans did not keep their end of the bargain made in the previous battle with Israel, whose terms require the surrender of Ramoth-gilead (20:34).

For several chapters, 1 Kings concentrates on the northern kingdom under Ahab. Judah is virtually forgotten, and Jehoshaphat of Judah is introduced here as a subordinate of Ahab. His name means "Yah judges," and its repetition throughout the story (thirteen times in 22:1–32) reminds the reader repeatedly of the prophecies against Ahab. At the end of the chapter, the author informs us that Jehoshaphat is a righteous man and a reformer, though he is wrong to ally with Ahab (22:41–50). Earlier chapters concerning Ahab's reign suggest that he intends to restore Canaanite worship and culture in Israel. With Jehoshaphat's appearance, the narrator gives the first hint of the wider ambition of Ahab and Jezebel to establish a unified kingdom over Israel, devoted to Baal and ruled by the descendants of Ahab.

Jehoshaphat is inordinately eager to help (22:4), and his speech suggests that he is a "twin" to his northern counterpart. This does not bode well for Judah, as will become apparent when Jehu is anointed to destroy the house of Ahab. Jehoshaphat is clearly more faithful than Ahab, since he asks for a prophet of Yahweh (22:5, 7), yet even before he knows where the campaign is going or whether Yahweh approves, he devotes his kingdom to Ahab's use.

Ahab first brings out four hundred prophets who all agree that the "Lord" will give Ramoth-gilead to Ahab (עלה ויתן אדני ביד המלך) (22:6). The scene resembles Elijah's confrontation with Ahab on Mount Carmel (1 Kgs. 18) (Provan 1995, 162; Walsh 1996, 345). In both cases, one faithful prophet confronts four hundred false prophets. But this situation is significantly different. These prophets, unlike the prophets at Carmel, claim to have some access to the word of Yahweh. Zedekiah (whose name means "Yah is righteous"), one of the court prophets, puts on a set of horns and enacts his prediction of victory (22:11), claiming to speak in the name of Yahweh: "Thus says Yahweh" (כה־אמר יהוה). His prophecy is probably drawn from Deut. 33:13–17, where Moses blesses the tribes of Ephraim and Manasseh, the two dominant tribes in the north: "His glory is like the firstling of his bullock, / and his horns are like the horns of a bull; / with them he shall push the people together / to the ends of the earth; / and they are the ten thousands of Ephraim / and they are the thousands of Manasseh" (Davis 2002, 322–23). Yahweh makes promises to the tribes of Joseph through Moses, and since Ahab rules the kingdom of Joseph, Zedekiah reasons, he can be confident of victory. Zedekiah clearly claims inspiration from Yahweh: when he slaps Micaiah, Zedekiah wonders how the Spirit of Yahweh (רוח־יהוה) slips out of his fingers and gets to Micaiah

(1 Kgs. 22:24). The other prophets join in, agreeing that "Yahweh will deliver it into the king's hand" (22:12, 15).[1] The situation of Micaiah and the false prophets thus foreshadows the final days of the kingdom of Judah, for by the time of Jeremiah most false prophets claim to speak in the Lord's name (Jer. 28), and the same is true in Jesus's day. Satan's efforts to foment open idolatry fail, so he comes disguised as a Yahwist. Mephistopheles clothed in black and reeking of sulfur is *so* obvious, and a disguise as an angel of light provides an elegant change of style. When the dragon fails to kill the bride directly, he calls up surrogate beasts from sea and land for assistance (Rev. 12–13).

At Carmel, it is easy to identify a false prophet. One simply has to look for the prophets crying out to Baal and gashing themselves with stones. Things are more complicated at the gate of Samaria. Micaiah claims to speak in the name of Yahweh; so does Zedekiah. Micaiah says, "Thus says Yahweh," but so does Zedekiah. According to Torah, the true prophet is ultimately revealed by the outcome; if he is a true prophet, then what he prophesies will happen (Deut. 13:1–11), and in this story, Micaiah is shown to be the true prophet because Ahab dies in battle. But Ahab and Jehoshaphat have to make a decision before they know the outcome. How can they know which advice to follow? How can they tell a wolf cleverly disguised in sheep's clothing from a sheep?

Jehoshaphat apparently discerns that something is wrong. When he hears all four hundred prophets in agreement, all agreeing that *Yahweh* promises success, he still wants to hear a prophet of Yahweh (1 Kgs. 22:7). Jehoshaphat is probably spiritually attuned enough to know that the word of God does not come with the message, "Everything is perfectly okay. You're okay just the way you are." As Barth says, dogmatics is the science that tests the church's proclamation by the standard of the word of God, and if dogmaticians emerge from their study to announce "all is well; steady as she goes," they have made a mistake in calculations.[2] Or, to put it in the blunt terms that Long uses, "God is not nice" (2004). He does not exist to underwrite our projects, to ensure

1. Perhaps these are prophets from the shrine of Bethel, who claim to be worshiping the God of the exodus.

2. More fully, Barth 1939–69, 1.1.323: "Repeated exposition, in harmony with the intentions of the theologians named, will, of course, be indispensable for dogmatics at every step. But dogmatics is not meant to be exhausted in exposition. Its scientific quality consists not so much in confirming as rather in disturbing Church proclamation as it meets it in its concrete forms to date, and above all in the present concrete form of the day; in putting it at variance with itself as it truly belongs to itself, in driving it outside of itself and beyond. . . . Dogmatics becomes unscientific when it becomes easy-going. . . . There is absolutely no need for it to be merely the so-called 'stiff' dogmatics of the old style (frequently Catholic style) which in this sense must be termed unscientific. Just the same may and must be said of the most fluid, active, and pious modern dogmatics so far as its critical nerve is perhaps dead, so far as for its Church environment it signifies nothing but a pleasant certification that everything is in order and may continue as before. So long as the Church on earth is the Church of sinners and her proclamation therefore involved in the hardest problems, we shall be able to say with all definiteness that a dogmatics which assumes this attitude and has this result is in the wrong."

that our pursuit of money and fame and American empire goes smoothly. He is the "judge of all the earth," whose word is an instrument for bringing all our projects, intentions, and aims, especially the most pious of them, under scrutiny and judgment.

It is always a temptation to prefer a smooth, self-affirming word over a confronting word, and that temptation has been institutionalized, systematized in many contemporary churches. The word "sin" is avoided as needlessly offensive, especially to wealthy church members. Churches advertise their welcoming, nonjudgmental atmosphere, not so subtly (and viciously) implying that there are harsh judgmental churches out there and we all know which ones they are. American churches mirror consumer culture, offering a range of choices so that everyone can settle back into a Muzak spirituality, confident that they will not be confronted by any demands for radical change. But the word of Yahweh does not affirm us in our plans. It challenges our plans, confronts them, undoes them.

Jehoshaphat has another reason for discomfort with the court prophets of Ahab. The Hebrew of 22:6 says that "the Lord will give into the hand of the king." But the prophets do not say what is going to be given (Ramoth-gilead? a person?) or about which king they are talking. The prophecy could mean "Yahweh will deliver the city into the hand of Ahab," or it could mean "Yahweh will deliver Ahab into the hand of the king of Aram." As Herman Melville, who was haunted by this passage, understood, the prophets' word is a lying word because it is ambiguous. For prophets, ambiguity lends a great deal of job security. If Ahab goes to Ramoth-gilead and wins, the prophets can say, "Like we said: the Lord will give Ramoth-gilead into the hand of King Ahab." If Ahab goes up and fails, they can say, "We told you so: the Lord will give Ahab into the hand of the king of Aram." A prophecy that cannot be disproved cannot come from a true prophet (Davis 2002, chap. 28). Yahweh's word is discriminating, not only because it cuts to the heart but because it says *this* and not *that*.

Pressed by Jehoshaphat, Ahab reluctantly brings Micaiah, whose name means "who is like Yah?" to the gate to stand before the kings (22:10). Gates are places of judgment, and threshing is often an image of judgment, since it involves separation of wheat and chaff. Micaiah has been in another court and sees another king whose judgments transcend any decisions of Ahab and Jehoshaphat (22:19).[3] Micaiah at first agrees with the court prophets, using

---

3. The parallel structure of the passage reinforces the connection of the earthly thrones with a heavenly throne, the court at Samaria with the heavenly court (modified from Davis 2002, 318):

22:5–14	22:15–28
inquiry	inquiry
answer	answer
dissatisfaction of king: Jehoshaphat	dissatisfaction of king: Ahab
Micaiah mentioned	Micaiah's prophecy

their own equivocal phrasing (22:12, 15). Ahab recognizes that Micaiah is lying, but when the other four hundred prophets say *exactly the same thing*, Ahab, with unconscious but profound irony, believes it.

How does Ahab know that Micaiah is lying? It is entirely plausible, as many commentators suggest, that Micaiah speaks with a sarcastic tone. The text, however, does not mention this, and it does give another reason for Ahab's insight: Micaiah has ironically employed the words of the court prophet before (22:16). On his way to the court, Micaiah tells the messenger, with an oath, that he can speak only what Yahweh puts in his mouth (22:14). Unlike the messenger, unlike Ahab, Micaiah is a true prophet who knows that the word of Yahweh is not his to control, but his first words are a false prophecy. Micaiah plays the part of one of the lying prophets (22:22), but as he says later, this misleading prophecy *is* the word of Yahweh, the word of Yahweh designed to lure Ahab to his death.

Micaiah's true prophecy consists of two parts. The first describes Israel scattered on the mountains without a king-shepherd (22:17), as Israel will again be at the time of Jesus, when the Ahab-like Herod sits enthroned as king of the Jews (Matt. 9:36). The second vision is a scene from the heavenly court, where Yahweh reveals his plan to send a deceiving spirit to the prophets of Ahab, so that he will be enticed to his death (1 Kgs. 22:19–23).

Everything happens as Micaiah predicts. Ahab's plan to escape Micaiah's prophecy highlights again that the two kings are interchangeable. Ahab takes off his royal robes to enter the battle disguised as a common soldier, while Jehoshaphat dresses like a king (22:30). Ahab appears brave, but his real intention is to protect himself (22:31). Like Saul (1 Sam. 28:8; cf. 1 Kgs. 14:1–16), Ahab puts on a disguise, and his plan involves a voluntary "defrocking." Ahab's plan seems to be working when the Arameans begin chasing Jehoshaphat, but Ahab's plans cannot overcome Yahweh's. Like Saul (1 Sam. 31:3), tormented by an evil spirit, Ahab is killed with arrows.

Micaiah's vision of Yahweh asking for a volunteer to entice (פתה) Ahab is one of the most puzzling passages in the Bible and difficult on many levels. The least problematic aspect of this incident is that Yahweh is seeking help from surrogates, though the quaintness of the scene almost seems more at home in Goethe than in the Bible. The more troubling problem is the moral one: how can the God who is truth, whose word is truth, send out a lying spirit to inspire people to lie to Ahab? Is Yahweh ultimately just another trickster God, unreliable and deceptive?

One popular option is to distance Yahweh from the actual deception by claiming that the spirit who volunteers is the devil or some demon (1 Kgs. 22:21).[4] This does not relieve the difficulty of the passage very much and is

| throne scene: Samaria | throne scene: heaven |
| pressure on prophet | imprisonment of prophet |

4. Augustine 1983, 376: "God therefore doth use evil angels not only to punish evil men, as in the case of all those concerning whom the Psalm doth speak, as in the case of king Achab,

impossible to sustain exegetically. Nowhere else in the Old Testament is Satan called a "spirit," and, contrary to most translations, it is not "a spirit" that comes forth to offer his services but "*the* spirit" (הרוח), suggesting that Yahweh is sending out his own Spirit as a haze over the prophets of Ahab.[5]

Another method for distancing Yahweh from the deception distinguishes between permission and command. In his treatment of the question of whether God causes sin in *De malo*, Thomas Aquinas raises a possible objection from 1 Kgs. 22 and Yahweh's command to Hosea to commit adultery. Thomas responds: "We should not understand the statement 'Go forth and do so' by way of command but by way of permission, just like the statement to Judas, 'What you do, do quickly.'" Thomas claims that "God's command causes what would otherwise be a sin not to be a sin," and cites Bernard to the effect that "God can dispense in regard to the commandments of the second tablet, commandments whereby human beings are directly regulated regarding their neighbor, since the good of one's neighbor is a particular good. But God cannot dispense in regard to the commandments of the first table, commandments whereby human beings are regulated regarding God, who cannot turn others away from his very self, since he cannot deny his very self" (Thomas Aquinas 2003, 146).

Dismissing the distinction between God's permission and God's doing as an "evasion," Calvin insists that God *does* as he pleases, including in his dealings with Ahab: "Whatever men or Satan himself may instigate, God nevertheless holds the key, so that he turns their efforts to carry out his judgments. God wills that the false King Ahab be deceived; the devil offers his services to this end; he is sent, with a definite command, to be a lying spirit in the mouth of all the prophets." This cannot be reduced to a bare permission: "It would be ridiculous for the Judge only to permit what he wills to be done, and not also to decree it and to command its execution by his ministers" (Calvin 1960, 1.18.1). Calvin's suggestion that the volunteer deceiver is the devil cannot be sustained; but Calvin is right to insist that Yahweh *wills* to deceive Ahab. Yahweh does not merely step aside to permit the spirit to deceive Ahab, but actively solicits a volunteer and orders him to follow through with his plan. The deception of Ahab is an expression of God's purpose, not a mere allowance.

These exegetical points simply intensify the question: What kind of God is this that puts misleading prophesies into the mouths of the court prophets

whom a spirit of lying by the will of God did beguile, in order that he might fall in war." Thomas Aquinas quotes the passage in answering the question whether humans are assailed by demons (1920, part I Q. 114 art. 1).

5. This is perhaps what Zedekiah means when he says that Micaiah steals the Spirit of Yahweh from him (22:24). He may be saying, "How did you get the Spirit to prophesy?"—implying, of course, that Zedekiah mocks Micaiah's claim to have the Spirit of Yahweh. It is also possible that he was sarcastically picking up on Micaiah's own statement: "You say the Spirit has come as a deceiving Spirit. How then are you prophesying lies? How did you end up being filled with *my* deceiving Spirit, the Spirit of Yahweh?" (Davis 2002, 328n10).

of Israel? How is this consistent with the New Testament's affirmations that "it is impossible for God to lie" (Heb. 6:18) and that "in him is no variation or shifting shadow" (Jas. 1:17)?

As Davis points out, there is ultimately no deception here or, more accurately, the deception is completely telegraphed (2002, 327). Yahweh's Spirit inspires the prophets to mislead and lure Ahab to his death, but then Yahweh sends Micaiah to *tell* Ahab he is being lured to his death. Yahweh sets a trap for Ahab, but politely shows Ahab the trap before he springs it. Yet, Ahab blindly goes to Ramoth-gilead, confident that he can cheat death and escape the word of Yahweh. Further and more basically, this passage makes it abundantly clear that Yahweh is not a great marshmallow in the sky. He is not a God who plays softball. Nor is he the god of the philosophers, a gorgeous but impotent force in heaven. He is a warrior who fights to win, and deception is part of his art of holy war. Elsewhere, Yahweh encourages his people to use deceptive military tactics (e.g., Josh. 7), and on more than one occasion he deploys an "evil spirit" to set traps for his enemies (Judg. 9:23; 1 Sam. 16:14; 18:10; 19:9; Ezek. 14:9).

Many of the church fathers gesture toward the insight that God is a trickster when they develop atonement theories that suggest the cross is a divine trap laid for Satan. Recent work on the historical Jesus confirms the patristic insight into God's shrewdness without adopting the "bait theory." Jesus's challenging parables, his provocative prophetic actions, his counterintuitive images and exhortations, his shrewdness in debate—all this testifies that Jesus is the incarnation of the God who lured Ahab to the battlefield of Ramoth-gilead.

He is straight with the straight, merciful to the humble, but cunning with the wicked (וְעִם־עִקֵּשׁ תִּתְפַּתָּל) (Ps. 18:25–26), the God who catches the wicked in their own devices, who leads his enemies into the very traps that they set for the righteous. This is a God to be loved. But he is also a God to be feared. One should be grateful to be and remain in his good graces, for it is a fearful thing to fall into the hands of this God. Yahweh is the ultimate trickster that outfoxes all human attempts to escape him. Yahweh is not only cunning. He is transcendently, infinitely cunning. The conclusion that God employs deception against deceivers should not lead to distrust or anxiety. There is a simple way to avoid falling into the traps of the infinitely cunning God: humbly trust him, for he is merciful to the merciful, and to the pure he is pure.

1 KINGS 22:41–2 KINGS 1:18

Strikingly, 2 Kings begins, as does 1 Kings, with a sick king, confined to bed. Both David and Ahaziah receive prophets on their deathbeds, but the results are quite different. Though Elijah is fully capable of raising the dead (1 Kgs. 17:17–24), Ahaziah seeks help elsewhere. Instead of raising the king from his deathbed, Elijah predicts that he will die there.

This is not Elijah's first prophecy against the descendants of Ahab. Earlier, Elijah delivered a prophecy that announced the end of the Omride dynasty, the utter destruction of Ahab's house. Because Ahab repents, Yahweh relents and says that Ahab's family will not be destroyed in his lifetime but in the lifetime of his son (21:29). Ahaziah is that son and looks as if he is ripe for judgment. He walks in the ways of his father Ahab and in the ways of his mother, serving Baals and provoking Yahweh to anger (22:53). When he falls and injures himself, Ahaziah sends messengers to the Baal of Ekron, a specific example of his devotion to the gods of his mother and father.

The narrator brings the wickedness of Ahaziah into more pronounced relief by contrast with the brief account of the reign of Jehoshaphat (22:41–50).[1] Jehoshaphat is not a perfect king by any means. He is criticized for making

---

1. The break between 1 Kings and 2 Kings is nonsensical, since it comes in the middle of the account of the reign of Ahaziah. To understand what is happening in 2 Kgs. 1, we need to see it as a continuation of the account begun at the end of 1 Kings. The passage is structured as follows (modified from Cohn 2000, 5):

    A Ahaziah's reign and sickness (1 Kgs. 22:51–2 Kgs. 1:2a)
        B Ahaziah sends messengers meet Elijah (1:2b)
            C Yahweh's messenger sends Elijah (1:3–4)
                D report of Elijah's words to the king (1:5–8)
        B′ Ahaziah sends soldiers to get Elijah (1:9–14)
            C′ Yahweh's messenger sends Elijah to the king (1:15–16)
    A′ Ahaziah's death and end of his reign (1:17–18)

peace with the king of Israel, his son marries the daughter of Ahab and Je-zebel (2 Kgs. 8:25–26), and he fails to remove the high places of the land, a constant failing of even good kings in Judah. He has ships, as Solomon did, at Ezion-geber, the northernmost point of the Gulf of Aqaba (1 Kgs. 9:26), and he attempts to revive the trade with Ophir, again a throwback to the halcyon days of Solomon when gold poured into the kingdom in abundance (9:28). Yet Jehoshaphat is no Solomon (Provan 1995, 167–68). His ships wreck, and he ultimately refuses to revive the trade efforts with Ahaziah. Despite these failures, the judgment on Jehoshaphat's reign is generally positive, in that he "walked in all the way of Asa his father; he did not turn aside from it, doing right in the sight of Yahweh" (22:43). He continues Asa's liturgical reforms, removing the remaining cult prostitutes that Asa failed to expel (22:46). He apparently controls Edomite territory, and a deputy of Jehoshaphat sits on the throne of Edom, ruling as a deputy of the king of Judah (22:47).[2]

In contrast to the righteous and comparatively successful Jehoshaphat, Ahaziah is a wicked failure, an assessment signified by the opening verse of 2 Kings: "Moab rebelled against Israel after the death of Ahab." Though the story of the Moabite rebellion is not told until 2 Kgs. 3, this verse is not out of place at the beginning of 2 Kings. Moab lies just to the east of the Jordan River. Mentioned only briefly thus far in Kings (see 1 Kgs. 11:7), it was a client state of Israel during the days of David and Solomon. David, who had family connections with Moab (Ruth 4), incorporated Moab into Israel (2 Sam. 8:2, 12), and between David and Ahaziah, Israel ruled Moab. With Ahab's death, Moab rebels (וַיִּפְשַׁע), pulling out of Israel's orbit. While Jehoshaphat controls Gentiles, Ahaziah loses control over Gentiles. Because of the idolatries of the family of Ahab, the Lord diminishes the power of Israel's king. In this respect as in others, Ahab's life and legacy mimic Solomon's: after Solomon dies, his son reigns over a truncated kingdom, and Ahaziah does as well. The kingdom is as sick as the king, and the dynasty is dying.

Everything is in place for the collapse of the Omride dynasty and the end of the family of Ahab. The trajectory of 2 Kgs. 1 leads us to expect a final end, but it leaves us unsatisfied, with the house of Ahab still standing (Provan 1995, 169). In this, the house of Ahab is like the house of Jeroboam I. The man of God from Judah prophesies the end of the house of Jeroboam (1 Kgs. 13), and in the following story we learn about the sickness of his son Abijah, who dies before the dynasty ends. Like Jeroboam's son, Ahab's son dies peace-fully with the dynasty still intact, but the dynasty falls during the reign of a second son.

In Genesis, older sons (Ishmael, Esau, Reuben) repeatedly prove unfaith-ful and are removed in favor of a younger son (Isaac, Jacob, Joseph/Judah). This pattern points to the overarching structure of biblical history, where the

2. First Kings 22:47 does not explicitly state that the deputy was Jehoshaphat's but that is implied in the context.

"older" son Adam is replaced by the younger "last Adam." In 1–2 Kings, the pattern has a different twist. An older son is removed, but instead of being replaced by a faithful younger son, the younger son receives the full weight of judgment. With Ahab's family as with Jeroboam's, the pattern is this: fathers sin and doom their dynasties to extinction; an older son lives and dies without incident, and the judgment falls on a younger son.

This pattern too is played out on a large scale in the history of Israel. Israel and Judah are siblings, corulers of the two kingdoms, and in some respects at least Israel is the older (Ezek. 23). Israel turns to idols, and the prophets continuously predict the doom of the northern kingdom. The northern kingdom does fall, but the full weight of Yahweh's punishment falls on Judah, which follows the example of its older sibling. And the same pattern recurs in the fulfillment of Israel's history in the gospel. Adam is the father of all humans, and God threatens that if he eats from the tree he will surely die. He eats, is cut off from the garden, and eventually dies. For all we can tell, Adam, like Abijah ben Jeroboam and Ahaziah ben Ahab, dies peacefully in his bed, and the curse of death does not fall initially on his first son, Cain, but on the second, Abel. In a larger perspective, Adam's younger son is the last Adam, Jesus, who takes the full weight of the curse against Adam. Jesus is the last Adam, receiving the punishment of father Adam's sins. Jesus is the younger brother of Genesis, who takes the place of his older brother at Yahweh's right hand. Jesus is also the younger brother of 1–2 Kings who bears the sins of the older. Jesus is Judah, suffering for Israel.

Ahab's house intensifies the wickedness of the house of Jeroboam. Jeroboam sets up golden calves and worships them, but when his son gets sick, he sends his wife to visit a prophet of Yahweh (1 Kgs. 14). The house of Ahab worships Baal, and when Ahaziah gets sick, he does not seek out a prophet of the Lord, but the Baal of the Philistine city of Ekron (2 Kgs. 1:3). As noted above (see the commentary on 1 Kgs. 16:15–34), the name Baal-zebub (בעל זבוב) means "Baal of the flies" and is probably a deliberate corruption of the name Baal-zebul, which means "Baal the prince" or "exalted Baal." The writer shows little deference to the pieties of the worshipers of Baal, mocking the names of their gods. This is not a unique instance (18:27) and suggests that the writers of Scripture do not share our modern knee-jerk respect for false and bloodthirsty gods. Long ago, Israel conquered Philistia, and Yahweh shames their gods, but Ahaziah consults with the gods of the Philistines. Ahaziah is like the generation of the exodus that longs to return to Egypt and its defeated gods. Elijah judges Ahaziah's consultation in Ekron as a sign of unbelief, and three times poses the question: "Is there no God in Israel that you are sending to inquire of Baal-zebub, the god of Ekron?" (2 Kgs. 1:3, 6, 16).

With its emphasis on consultation (1:2, 3, 6, 16), 2 Kgs. 1 provides a useful diagnostic test for practical atheism. A person's and culture's basic religious commitments are evident in their "oracular" practices. Obviously, Christians who consult horoscopes, drop in for a weekly palm readings, or dabble with tarot cards possess a faith that is less than skin deep, but consultation with Baal-zebub can also take more respectable forms. Modern society relies heavily on experts, especially scientific elites who claim to be able to offer truth in a world dominated by opinion. Despite the purported shift to postmodernity, contemporary American culture is in this sense still deeply modern. In at least some of its main forms, the Enlightenment project is built on the belief that science is useful for undermining traditional superstitions and prejudices and that such knowledge should be spread universally. Yet, at the same time, this scientific truth is actually discovered by various experts, who alone have the training and insight to assess the truth of various claims. There are times for expertise. One would not want an amateur performing a quadruple bypass, but the post-Enlightenment reliance on experts is often a form of practical idolatry, a version of consulting Baal-zebub instead of Yahweh. Elijah could well challenge churches that rely on Freud for counseling, on Marx or Weber for their sociology and politics, on Madison Avenue for their evangelistic planning with the question, "Is there no God in Israel, that you go to inquire of Baal-zebub of Ekron?" (Gay 1998).

Yahweh does not allow Ahaziah to carry out his plan. Ahaziah sends messengers (מַלְאָכִים) to consult with Baal (1:2), but the "messenger of Yahweh" (מַלְאַךְ יְהוָה) sends Elijah to intercept Ahaziah's messengers (1:3). As elsewhere in 1–2 Kings, the prophet's ministry runs "perpendicular" to the activities of kings. Like his father, Ahaziah is a Saul, since Saul too consults with a false oracle and is interrupted by a true prophet (1 Sam. 28). Like Samuel at Endor, Elijah speaks one last time to a king from the house of Ahab. As elsewhere in 1–2 Kings, too, the writer contrasts Elijah to the false gods. Elijah is more powerful than the Baal of Ekron, a point that the writer emphasizes by using a literary technique that he also uses in 1 Kgs. 21. Second Kings 1:3 records the message of the angel of Yahweh, but in the middle of the speech the scene changes and Elijah himself takes up the message. Yahweh's word is identified with Elijah's word, and Yahweh's word prevails over the word of Ahaziah. The narrator underscores the contrast of Elijah and Baal by the description of the prophet in 1:8. Ahaziah sends messengers off to consult with Baal-zebub, but his messengers meet a "baal of hair" (בַּעַל שֵׂעָר)—right title, wrong god—Elijah. The "baal of hair" can raise the sick from his death bed; Baal-zebub of Ekron is impotent.

Putting aside his desire to consult the Philistine Baal, Ahaziah sends three sets of fifty soldiers to capture Elijah, the Israelite Baal. Again Elijah proves himself to be the bearer of the power of God, more powerful than Ahaziah or his gods. Like Yahweh himself, Elijah sits on a mountain. When the captains call on Elijah as a "man of God" (אִישׁ הָאֱלֹהִים), Elijah sends the "fire of God" (אֵשׁ־אֱלֹהִים) to consume the first two sets of soldiers. Elijah was a man like us (Jas. 5), but through fervent righteous prayer he is capable of sending fireballs from heaven. The pun on "man" (אִישׁ, 'îsh) and "fire" (אֵשׁ, 'ēsh) points to Elijah himself being the "fire of God" sent from heaven to consume Israel with his burning words (Jer. 1:10). There is a comical futility in Ahaziah's cartoonish insistence on sending troops to apprehend Elijah: "Fifty men were burned alive the first time? Let's send fifty more and *demand* that Elijah come quickly. That'll do the trick." Idolatry, as Paul emphasizes, blinds idolaters. Not only do they seek out gods that are no gods, but they also keep going back and back and back.

The passage repeats "go up" and "go down" several times. The angel of Yahweh sends Elijah to "ascend" to call the messengers/angels of Ahaziah (2 Kgs. 1:3), and Elijah's message is that Ahaziah will never "come down" from the bed where he "ascends" (1:4). Elijah's oracle, including the "come down" and "go up," is repeated in 1:6 and 1:16, and in between two captains with their fifty soldiers "go up" to the hill of Elijah (1:9) to command him to "come down" (1:9, 11). Instead of Elijah, fire "comes down," as Elijah predicts (1:10, 12). The third captain "goes up" (1:13), and because of his humility, Yahweh tells Elijah to "go down" to the king (1:15). All this is precipitated by Ahaziah's "fall" from an upper chamber (1:2).

Frequently in Scripture, the wicked are pictured as being destroyed by a kind of gravitational pull—they fall into traps and go down to the pit. This chapter reverses that symbolism. Though Ahaziah falls from a height (as did his father's dynasty) at the beginning of the story, he dies in a "high place," ironically reversing the initial cause of his injury. Elijah is high up, exalted like Yahweh on a mountain, but he comes down to deliver a message. This hints at the character of Elijah's prophetic ministry. A prophet has "gone up" to the presence of God, and therefore can "come down" to deliver Yahweh's word. Elijah's ministry will end with an ascension, a going up that is not followed by a coming down (2:11). Even then, Elisha receives Elijah's mantle and a double portion of Elijah's spirit, so that in a sense Elijah "comes down" in Elisha to carry on the work. Ascending and descending are the movements of a true prophet, a true "messenger/angel" who climbs up and down a ladder to heaven.

Elijah's ups and downs in this story not only symbolize his own authority as a prophet, but also suggest the character of the God he serves. Yahweh is high and lifted up, exalted above the heavens, but he also comes down, and in this he shows his superiority to all idols. God is not only higher than all the gods of the nations; he is lower than all other gods, descending deeper into the darkness than Tartarus or Hades can imagine. He does not simply throw fireballs from the safety of heaven, but draws near, gets in our face, confronts kings with annoying prophets who interrupt their lives and plans. Yahweh refuses politely to recuse himself from human affairs. For many people, this is unbecoming to a god. Any decent, sophisticated god will remain where he belongs, in blissful heavenly repose, and have the decency not to meddle with our checkbooks, our marriages, our use of natural resources, our treatment of the poor. He will express no opinion on these subjects. But the God of Israel refuses to stay put. The God of Elijah, the God of Abraham and Isaac and Jacob, the Father of Jesus Christ, is the God who comes down in the man of

God and in the fire of God, in word and judgment, in flesh, in bread and in wine. Ascension is a demonstration of divine power; but so is, even more, incarnation.

Though the name Baal-zebub occurs only in 2 Kgs. 1 in the entire Old Testament (Cohn 2000, 5), it appears as a title for Satan in the Gospels, when the leaders of Israel accuse Jesus of casting out demons by Beelzebub, the prince of demons (Matt. 10:25; 12:22–28; Mark 3:23–29; Luke 11:17–20). Ahaziah consults Baal-zebub because he is sick, and Jesus is accused of being in league with Baal-zebub after healing a demon-possessed man (Matt. 12:22). The Pharisees who challenge Jesus in effect claim the high prophetic ground of Elijah, charging Jesus with the sin of Ahaziah, the king who consorts with idols. Jesus is, in their thinking, the upstart blasphemer with a new teaching in Israel. "Is there no God in Israel," the Pharisees say, "that you should be casting out demons in the name of Beelzebub?" But that Jesus chases demons from the possessed shows that there is a God in Israel, a God who "comes down" as fire from heaven to bring in his kingdom (12:28).[3] Standing before the Pharisees is a prophet greater than the "baal of hair," who like Elijah is stronger than the strong man.

3. Thanks to Pesher Group member Peter Roise for this insight.

2 KINGS 2:1–25

Starting with Moses, Jesus teaches his disciples that all the Old Testament Scriptures are about the sufferings and glory of Christ (Luke 24:27). That hermeneutical rule is more obviously applicable to some passages than to others, but there is no problem applying it to 2 Kgs. 2. Elijah is a type of John the Baptist (Matt. 11:14; Mark 9:9–13; Luke 1:17), and the transition from Elijah to Elisha foreshadows the succession from John to Jesus. Like John, Elijah is a lone voice in the wilderness, but Elisha is surrounded by disciples. Jesus's ministry is a ministry of life-giving miracles—cleansing lepers (Mark 1:40–45), raising dead sons and restoring them to their mothers (Luke 7:11–17), relieving distress. Similarly, Elisha raises the dead (2 Kgs. 4:18–37), provides a meal for one hundred men from twenty loaves of barley bread (4:42–44), cleanses a leper (2 Kgs. 5). On the surface of things, Elisha is a type of Jesus.

But the typology works another way as well: Elijah is a type of Jesus himself, and Elisha of the disciples who continued Jesus's ministry after his ascension. Elisha first appears plowing a field, but he leaves home and family (1 Kgs. 19:19–21) like the disciples of Jesus who leave their fishing boats and tax booths to follow him. At the beginning of 2 Kgs. 2, Elisha doggedly follows his master, refusing to stay behind, until Elijah is taken from him in a whirlwind. Because he follows Elijah, Elisha becomes like his master, and after Elijah departs he immediately begins to replicate his ministry. Having received the promised double portion of Elijah's spirit, Elisha is a "reincarnation" (or "reanimation") of Elijah, as the church is the body of Christ in the Spirit of Jesus. The sons of the prophets recognize the family resemblance between Elisha and his predecessor, just as the Jews perceive the courage of Peter and the apostles and remember they have been with Jesus (Acts 4:13).

From this angle, the Elijah-Elisha narrative directly foreshadows the sequence of the biography of Jesus (Brodie 1999, chap. 5). The Gospels begin with the ministry of the Elijah-like John, who confronts the ambivalent King Herod and his bloodthirsty queen and calls Israel to repentance (Mark 1:1–8; 6:14–29). John baptizes Jesus as his successor (Mark 1:9–11), as Elijah calls Elisha (1 Kgs. 19:19–21); and Jesus receives the Spirit as he is baptized, as Elisha receives the spirit of Elijah. Jesus announces the destruction of Jerusalem's temple (Mark 13), and Elisha anoints the temple-destroyer, Jehu (2 Kgs. 9:1–10). Jesus comes eating and drinking (Luke 7:34), and Elisha's ministry is like Jesus's above all in giving central attention to the gift of food and drink. He heals the deadly waters at Jericho (2 Kgs. 2:19–22), provides healthy food for the sons of the prophets (4:38–41), multiplies loaves to feed a multitude (4:42–44), feeds Aramean soldiers who come to capture him (6:20–23), and provides food for besieged Samaria (7:1, 18–20). The Gospels end at an empty tomb, and Elisha's story ends with his life-giving grave (13:20–21).[1]

The story of 2 Kgs. 2 reaches backward as well. Throughout his ministry, Elijah is a new Moses, and Elisha his Joshua. Ahab is Pharaoh, and once his son dies (Passover), Elijah and Elisha leave the land whose gods are defeated and whose prince is dead (exodus). Elijah departs on the far side of the Jordan, as Moses does, while Elisha returns to carry on a conquest, significantly starting at Jericho. The christological typology is thus multilayered: Moses is Elijah is John; Joshua is Elisha is Jesus. Yet also, Moses is Elijah is Jesus, and Joshua is Elisha is the church.

The difficulty of this passage is not to discover its typological dimensions but to understand the events and motivations at the literal level of the narrative. Elijah, for starters, takes an unusual route out of the land. Several places are known as "Gilgal" in ancient Israel, but the most famous of these is close to the Jordan, east of Jericho (Josh. 4:19–24). From there, Elijah travels some fifteen miles west to Bethel and then back to Jericho, near the Jordan. Gilgal, Bethel, and Jericho are associated with Israel's original arrival in the land. Israel camps at Gilgal when it first enters the land, and there the Israelite men are circumcised and Israel celebrates the first Passover in the land (5:1–12). Bethel is associated with the city of Ai and was destroyed along with Ai during the conquest (8:9, 12, 17), and Jericho, of course, is the site of the great battle where the walls tumble down. Each of these cities, in short, is associated with Joshua's conquest. Under the idolatrous Omride dynasty, Israel moves, as it were, backward in time, as the Omride kings promote the worship of Canaanite gods, particularly Baal. With his departing itinerary Elijah demonstrates this reversal, preenacting the exile of Israel and Judah on the far side of the Jordan. Like the exile later in Israel's history, however, this reversal of the conquest sets the stage for a new conquest.

1. As Brodie points out, the Gospels match the Elijah-Elisha narratives not only in content but in form. These chapters of 1–2 Kings are approximately the same length as Mark, and both the Gospels and the Elijah-Elisha narratives are divided into relatively self-contained pericopes (1999, 88–89).

The strategy of Elisha's "conquest" of the land is foreshadowed at the end of 2 Kgs. 2: first he heals the waters of Jericho (2:19–22) and then curses the mocking "boys" of Bethel (2:23–25). Elisha's entire ministry (mainly 2 Kgs. 4–8) follows the same order. First he works to form communities of "sons of the prophets." He assists an indebted widow (4:1–7), gives a child to the Shunammite woman and raises him from the dead (4:8–37), offers food to the sons of the prophets (4:38–44), tells the Aramean Naaman how to be cleansed (2 Kgs. 5), and recovers an ax head from the Jordan (6:1–7). Once the community of the faithful within Israel is flourishing, Elisha gives assistance to King Jehoram in battles with the Arameans (6:8–7:20). The double-sidedness of Elisha's ministry is critical: he does not minister to the prophetic communities in such a way as to neglect or forget the concerns of all Israel. Even while he mediates life to the prophetic communities and those associated with them, his work always manifests a deep concern for the entire people of God.

Only after this ministry of mercy to the prophetic communities and to the rulers of Israel is completed does Elisha carry out his commission of anointing Hazael of Aram (8:7–15) and Jehu (9:1–10) to take vengeance against the house of Ahab. When Jehu's vengeance falls, there is a church full of living faith so that some persist through the judgment and are reunited with the faithful of Judah late in Judah's history (see the commentary on 2 Kgs. 18:1–20:21 and 22:1–23:30). Though Elisha does not appear in 2 Kgs. 9–12, his work is not completed until Jehu and Joash have purged the land of the house of Ahab and the remnants of Baal. It is perfectly fitting that Elisha reappears again after the story of Joash for his final prophecies and miracles (13:14–21). Joash's renewal of the temple marks the completion of Elisha's (ultimately incomplete) "conquest" of Canaan, just as Solomon's construction of the temple completed Joshua's conquest. Strikingly, though, by the time of Jehu, the prophetic communities disappear from the narrative of 1–2 Kings. Successful as Elisha is in ministering the life of Yahweh, his ministry does not save even his own prophetic communities from suffering, as all Israel, faithful and unfaithful, suffers in the judgment of exile. Yet, Elisha's ministry lays the foundation for a new house to be built by the remnant on the far side of exile.

At Bethel and Jericho, Elijah and Elisha meet groups called "sons of the prophets" (2:3, 5). The very existence of the sons of the prophets is a surprise. Three times Elijah describes himself as a lone prophet (1 Kgs. 18:22; 19:10, 14; cf. 1 Kgs. 20), though Yahweh promises at Sinai to preserve seven thousand that will not genuflect to Baal. But as Elijah prepares to leave, prophets pop up at various places. In 1 Kings, the plural "prophets" is used frequently of false prophets (18:19, 22, 25; 22:6, 10, 12, 13; cf. 18:4; 20:35), but after 2 Kgs. 2 the plural is used almost exclusively for true prophets, the "sons of the prophets" gathered with Elisha (the exceptions are 3:13 and 10:19). Elijah is a potent "father" of the sons of the prophets (2:12), and Yahweh raises up faithful communities in the northern kingdom, a "renewal church" movement within the mainline Church of the Golden Calf. One bold and uncompromising prophet—an Elijah, a Luther, a Karol Wojtyla—does not remain alone, but his courage elicits courage from others. Soon, the faithful who have been in hiding emerge from their catacombs into the open light of day, Lutheran churches dot the landscape, renewal movements break out in mainline churches, Solidarity challenges despots, and African bishops, toughened by persecution, begin planting churches in the northern hemisphere. Importantly, the sons of the prophets establish themselves at the centers of Israel's idolatry—Bethel (1 Kgs. 12) and Jericho (1 Kgs. 16). Jeroboam I's golden calves are at Bethel, and Jericho is never supposed to be rebuilt, but once Jericho is back on the map, the Lord sends sons of the prophets to establish a church in the very heart of the rebellion.

Elijah's behavior is as odd as his itinerary. Three times he tells Elisha to stay behind—at Gilgal, at Bethel, at Jericho—and each time Elisha refuses, taking an oath that he will remain with his master. Elisha knows from the first encounter with Elijah that he is destined to receive the mantle of prophetic leadership (19:19–21), and for Elisha following his master to the end is necessary if he is going to receive the spirit of Elijah that will enable him to continue Elijah's ministry.

Elijah and Elisha leave the northern kingdom, which has become an Egypt, in an exodus through the Jordan. While Moses used a staff to divide the waters (Exod. 14:16), Elijah uses a folded mantle, the mantle that he wore on Sinai when Yahweh appeared to him (1 Kgs. 19:13). Normally, of course, Elijah wears the mantle, which symbolizes not only that he is a prophet but that he is a human "staff," an incarnate "rod of judgment." Wrapped in Elijah's mantle, Elisha becomes the instrument for carrying out the judgment promised at Sinai (19:15–18), the human rod that will strike the land. As they cross, Elisha asks for a "double portion" or "double mouth" (פִּי־שְׁנַיִם) of Elijah's spirit, the portion of the firstborn (Deut. 21:17) that marks Elisha as the preeminent "son of the prophet."[2] He asks for twice as much spirit as Elijah possesses, and according to Jewish tradition, Elisha does twice as many miracles as Elijah (sixteen to eight by one count). Jesus likewise promises his disciples that they will do "greater things" when the Spirit comes.[3]

With Elijah gone, the question has to be asked again: is there a God in Israel? When the man of God sends the fire of God on Ahaziah's men, he demonstrates that he, not the king of Israel, is the human "god" in Israel (2 Kgs.

2. Though a younger son, Joseph receives a "double portion" of land because his two sons, Ephraim and Manasseh, each receive a share of the land. Joseph is thus treated as oldest son, and this is the patriarchal background for seeing Ephraim (the northern kingdom) as the older in relation to Judah.

3. In 1 Kgs. 3, Solomon asks Yahweh for wisdom. The request of Elisha is different in important respects: he asks Elijah, not Yahweh directly, suggesting that Elijah as a prophet is a channel for Yahweh's spirit; and Elisha asks for the spirit, rather than for wisdom. To reiterate an earlier point, Israel's renewal does not depend on royal wisdom or political success, but on the work of Yahweh's Spirit in his prophet.

1). After Elijah goes into heaven, Elisha returns to the Jordan and asks the fifty sons of the prophets who watch him leave, "Where is Yahweh, the God of Elijah?" Does Elijah's departure imply Yahweh's departure, as it has in the past (see the commentary on 1 Kgs. 17:1–24)? Elisha's initial miracles answer that question and show that Yahweh is even more powerfully at work now that Elijah has gone away. Elisha divides the waters with his mantle, as Elijah had done (2 Kgs. 2:14). Instead of destroying Jericho, as Joshua had done, he heals the waters and the land (2:19–22). The land is "unfruitful" or "barren," causing "miscarriages" or "abortions" (2:19), and Elisha uses salt, symbolic of seed, to heal the land and make it fertile. Elijah, father of the prophets, gives birth to a prolific "son," and by repeating the work of Elijah, Elisha establishes himself as the new "father" of the sons of the prophets (13:14). Elisha shows that there is a God in Israel, and Elisha is his prophet. What Elisha says and does, Yahweh says and does. So too, Jesus goes away, but does not leave his church alone, but sends his Spirit so that the church can continue to embody God's presence in the world.

In 2:3 and 2:5, the sons of prophets inform Elisha that "Yahweh will take your master from over your head today" (הידעת כי היום יהוה לקח את־אדניך מעל ראשך). Elijah is Elisha's protector, guide, and "head," and Elisha is about to lose that leadership. As Elisha's head, Elijah enters heaven, while Elisha continues the work of his master in Israel, just as the church's head is enthroned victorious in heaven as it suffers, serves, and overcomes on earth (Eph. 1:20–23).

This repeated statement from the sons of the prophets helps to explain the story at the end of 2 Kgs. 2, one of the most controversial passages in Scripture. The phrase "little boys" (נערים קטנים) in 2:23 can mean "young men"[4] or "subordinates." Bethel is the site of Jeroboam I's golden calf shrine, and the context suggests that these are not children, but "Levites" of the idolatrous shrine.[5] Elisha's curse is an act of warfare, a Joshua-like attack on a center of idolatry. This is reinforced by the chiastic structure of the chapter:

A   removing the head (2:1–6)
  B   fifty men (2:7)
    C   cross Jordan: Elijah divides waters (2:8)
      D   Elisha requests spirit (2:9–10)
        E   chariot separates them (2:11a)
          F   Elijah by whirlwind into heaven (2:11b)
        E'   Elisha sees, calls to chariot, tears clothes (2:12)
      D'   mantle (2:13)

4. Remember Rehoboam's "boys" in 1 Kgs. 12.

5. The new-conquest context makes it possible that the "boys" are children of ten–twelve years. Under Joshua, Israel is commanded to slaughter not only fighting men, but women and children, at several cities (Deut. 20:10–18).

C′ divides water (2:14)
  B′ fifty men (2:15–18)
A′ bald head (2:23–25)

The young men mock Elisha because his "hairy head," his "baal of hair" (1:8), is taken from him. Perhaps he literally shaves his head in mourning over Elijah's departure, but it is also possible that they are mocking Elisha because they assume he is unprotected without Elijah. Their taunt to Elisha to "ascend" also points back to Elijah: "You know where you can go, Elisha!" Elisha again demonstrates that he bears the spirit of Elijah, which is the Spirit of Yahweh, for he can call out bears from the forest as readily as Elijah can call out fire from heaven to consume the soldiers of Ahaziah (Davis 2005, 39), as readily as Yahweh can unleash lions against disobedient prophets (1 Kgs. 13:20–25; cf. Lev. 26:22).

At the structural center of the passage is Elijah's departure. The horses and chariots of fire are the Lord's glory that is his own chariot (Kline 1986), and Elijah, a human "god," ascends like Moses into the glory. Specifically, he is taken up by the windstorm, often the specific empirical marker of the presence of God (1 Kgs. 19:11; cf. Job 38:1). Elisha calls Elijah his "father" and also calls him (in the Hebrew text) the "chariot of Israel and its horseman" (2 Kgs. 2:12). Elijah does not simply ride Yahweh's chariot, but *is* Yahweh's chariot, the prophet who bears God's presence and serves as the true protector of the land. Elisha confesses that the true power, the true defense of Israel does not lie with the kings or with his horses and chariots but with his master Elijah.[6] For the original exilic readers, the message is that the apparent failure of the Davidic dynasty does not leave Israel without protection. Today, Jesus, the ascended prophet, is the chariot and the horseman of his people; or, the body of Christ, filled with his Spirit, is the mobile throne and warhorse of the living God.

The story of Elijah's departure into heaven follows the sequence of a sacrificial rite (Lev. 1). By their mutual journey around the land, Elijah and Elisha form a unit, a "two of them" (2 Kgs. 2:7). They cross the Jordan, as parts of a sacrificial animal will be washed before being placed on the altar. Fire descends from heaven, dividing them in two, one ascending in fire to God, as the altar portions of the animal ascend in smoke to heaven. In the ascension (or "wholly burnt") offering, the skin of the sacrificial animal is given to the priest, and the mantle-skin of Elijah, the hairy garment of the "baal of hair," is left for Elisha. Through this human "sacrifice," Elisha becomes a successor to Elijah, and a new phase of prophetic history begins. In this sense too the story is a type of the sacrifice of Jesus, who is washed in the Jordan, gives himself over to be cut in two, ascends into a cloud, and leaves his Spirit and his mantle with his disciples.

6. This title for the prophet is connected to the Deuteronomic command that Israel's kings should not multiply horses and chariots (Deut 17:16). Israel has no need for royal horses and chariots, since it has sufficient protection in the prophetic chariot of Yahweh.

Sacrifices are completed in celebration, in a meal, and following the "sacrificial" departure of Elijah, Elisha embarks on a ministry of feasting. Already in 2 Kgs. 2 Elisha is characterized by what he eats. When Jesus promises that his Father will not deny the Spirit to those who ask, he uses food metaphors: a father will not deny bread and fish to his children, so the heavenly Father will not deny the Spirit (Luke 11:11–13). Elijah's response to Elisha's request for the spirit also uses a food image. As noted above, in the Hebrew Elisha asks for "two mouths of your spirit" or "a double mouthful of the Spirit" (2 Kgs. 2:9). For both Elisha and Jesus, the Spirit is food, and Elisha can provide abundant food because his mouth is filled with the Spirit. Following on the sacrifice of Jesus, our Father offers bread and wine, a token that he will not deny the Spirit to those who seek him. And more than a token: through this meal, we eat and drink spiritual food (1 Cor. 10:1–4), as we feed on the Son through the Spirit. "Open your mouth wide, and I will fill it," says the Lord, and the greater Elijah who has ascended into heaven fills us with a double mouthful of his Spirit.

2 KINGS 3:1-27

The story of Israel's war with Moab has a familiar feel to it. It is an exodus story: the journal of Jehoram and Jehoshaphat follows Israel's itinerary as they approach the promised land, moving to the south through Edom and then coming up to Moab before crossing the river into the land (2 Kgs. 3:8, 24; Num. 20:14–21; Deut. 1:1–5). As the kings travel through the wilderness of Edom, they run out of water (2 Kgs. 3:9), and a prophet promises water and victory (3:14–19). The Lord miraculously provides water for them (3:20), as he does when Israel comes out of Egypt (Exod. 17:1–7). The water is the death of the Moabites (2 Kgs. 3:21–26), like the waters of the Red Sea that simultaneously deliver Israel and destroy Egypt (Exod. 14). When the water comes, it looks like blood (2 Kgs. 3:23), reminiscent of the water that actually turns to blood in Egypt (Exod. 7:14–19). There is even a "song of Moses" (Exod. 15) in the harp that accompanies Elisha's prophecy (2 Kgs. 3:15).

It is also a holy war story: when Joshua invades the land, Yahweh miraculously gives Jericho into his hand (Josh. 6), disturbs natural phenomena to give Joshua victory over an alliance of kings led by Adoni-zedek of Jerusalem (Josh. 10), and provides Joshua with battle plans to defeat the city of Ai/Bethel (Josh. 7). Specifically, the battle with Moab is like the battle at Jericho in several particulars: it involves a seven-day period (2 Kgs. 3:9; Josh. 6:1–5), and in the end Israel gathers at the walls of an enemy city (2 Kgs. 3:27; Josh. 6:20–21). During the period of the judges, further, Yahweh intervenes to deliver Israel from opponents with much larger armies, when Israel is in desperate straits. He raises up Ehud to kill the Moabite king Eglon (Judg. 3), gives victory to Deborah and Barak against Jabin of Hazor and his commander, Sisera (Judg. 4), and enables Gideon to defeat the Midianites with a handful of men (Judg. 7). Samson is a one-man army, possessed of the Spirit of Yahweh to win victories over impossible odds (Judg. 13–16). Here in 2 Kings, Yahweh traps the

Moabites, luring them unsuspecting into the wilderness, where Israel falls on them and panics them.

The war against Moab is a familiar story, and it should end with Israel gaining total victory over the rebellious Mesha, with Israel reducing Moab to its prior status as a vassal state in Israel, with Yahweh vindicating himself against the gods of the Gentiles. So Elisha prophesies, it seems: "You shall strike every fortified city and every choice city; and fell every good tree and stop all springs of water, and mar every good piece of land with stones" (2 Kgs. 3:19). This is a story of Israel facing crisis and escaping by the skin of its teeth, winning at the last moment and against all odds—all by the faithful mercy of Yahweh.

If the story ended at 3:26, it would be comfortably, reassuringly familiar. But it goes on for another verse, and that verse deconstructs the story and disturbs our complacency, as the writer of Kings does habitually. We think we are reading another story about the crafty covenant Lord trapping his enemies, but when we reach 3:27, we realize we are reading a story about a doubly crafty God who traps Israel at the very moment he appears to be trapping Moab. M. Night Shyamalan would be proud: the surprise ending transforms the story from an exodus into a satire of exodus, from a story of Israel's holy war to a parody of holy war, a story of Gentile victory over Israel.

What actually happens at the wall of the Moabite capital of Kir-hareseth? According to 3:27, King Mesha of Moab offers his firstborn son and heir on the wall as an "ascension" offering. Apparently as a result of that offering, "great wrath" breaks out against Israel so intense that Israel is forced to leave Moabite territory. Commentators offer several explanations. One is that the "great wrath" is not divine wrath but human wrath. When the Moabites see their king sacrificing the crown prince on the wall of the city, they are infuriated at Israel and fight so desperately and energetically that Israel has to withdraw. Psychologically plausible as this may be, the word used for "wrath" normally refers to God's wrath, not to human wrath (Davis 2005, 48). Even if this scenario were true, human wrath cannot stand against God's wrath. If Yahweh intends to give victory to Israel, he would have done so, no matter how excited the Moabites get.

Perhaps the wrath is that of the Moabite God Chemosh (Nelson 1987, 168). Inactive during most of the battle, he responds once the king offers a suitable sacrifice and fights for Moab. This is the view of Mesha himself, who records his wars with Israel on a tablet known as the Moabite stone: "As for Omri, king of Israel, he humbled Moab many years . . . , for Chemosh was angry at his land. And his son followed him and he also said, 'I will humble Moab.' In my time he spoke (thus), but I have triumphed over him and over his house, while Israel hath perished for ever! (Now) Omri had occupied the land of Medeba, and (Israel) had dwelt there in his time and half the time of his son (Ahab), forty years; but Chemosh dwelt there in my time" (Pritchard 1969, 320). But this explanation cannot stand as the final word in 1–2 Kings. Baal is decisively defeated at Carmel (1 Kgs. 18), and Baal-ekron does not have the power to heal anyone (2 Kgs. 1); and for the author of 1–2 Kings Chemosh is no more powerful than Baal. Whatever reality lies behind Chemosh, it is under Yahweh's control.

The other explanation is that "great wrath" comes from Yahweh. This explanation has its problems, since the wrath appears to be a response to Mesha's human sacrifice, yet, on balance, it is the best explanation. Why would Yahweh be angry with Israel? It is questionable, first of all, whether Moab should have been part of Israel in the first place. In Deut. 2:9, Moses tells Israel: "Do not harass Moab, or provoke them to war, for I will not give you any of their land as a possession, because I have given Ar to the sons of Lot as a possession." Possibly, this applies only to the time of Moses, but it raises questions about the legitimacy of holding Moab as a client state. Moab and Ammon are, after all, cousins to Israel, however scandalous their origins (Gen. 19:30–38). The Omrides, moreover, impose a terrific tribute on the Moabites: one hundred thousand lambs and the wool of one hundred thousand rams (2 Kgs. 3:4), a sign that the Omrides are illegitimately oppressing Gentiles incorporated into Israel (Exod. 22:21).

Israel, finally, directly violates the Mosaic laws of war during their Moabite campaign. Deuteronomy 20:19–20 forbids Israel from making war against the trees of an enemy land, yet when Israel invades Moab, each "threw a stone on every piece of good land," and they "stopped up all the springs and felled all the good trees" (2 Kgs. 3:25). Israel is at times instructed to engage in holy war, but that is not the normal practice of war for Israel, and even in holy war Israel does not destroy the natural products of the land. When Jehoram fights Moab, however, Israel makes war against land, springs, and trees, not only against the Moabites themselves. Yahweh's "great wrath" burns against Israel because they conduct their war in flagrant disregard of his laws.

All these explanations run up against the reticence of the text itself. Great wrath—but whose? And why would great wrath come against Israel after a human sacrifice? What we can say with confidence is that Yahweh is a God who sets traps, not only for Gentile Moabites but for Israelites. He is an equal-opportunity trapper. Yahweh lures Moab into false assurance of victory with the combination of water and sunrise, but he is simultaneously luring Jehoram into false confidence in a battle that ultimately turns against him.

Ironically, Jehoram predicts this. A whiner like his father, Jehoram crumples as soon as he faces an obstacle to his plan and complains that "Yahweh has called these three kings to give them into the hand of Moab" (3:10). Jehoram is a Calvinist of sorts, who recognizes that the blessed Lord gives and takes away. But his sort of Calvinism is the faith of neither Calvin nor the Scriptures. Faith is not simply belief that God has the power to triumph over all things or the belief that God in control. Even devils believe that and tremble. A true believer believes not only in God's will, but in God's *good* will (Nelson 1987, 165). Faith is the confidence that God does all he does *for our good*. Scripture does not teach a naked sovereignty. Scripture teaches that God is sovereign, triumphant, infinite, omnipotent *good*; he is sovereign, triumphant, infinite, omnipotent *love*. Faith like Jehoram's might seem honoring to God because it acknowledges God's sovereign rule, but it is ultimately an insult to God because it denies God's goodness. Anyone who believes in the way that Jehoram believes will get just what he or she expects.

Once we read the end of the story, hints and clues about the final outcome begin to emerge earlier in the story. It is like watching *Sixth Sense* a second time. Some of the clues become evident when we consider the echoes between this event and the battle with the Arameans that ends 1 Kings (Provan 1995, 183–84). In that earlier account, Jehoshaphat of Judah cooperates with Ahab and states his cooperation in exactly the same words he speaks to Jehoram: "I am as you are, my people as your people, my horses as your horses" (1 Kgs. 22:4; 2 Kgs. 3:7). Before that earlier battle, Jehoshaphat asks Ahab to provide a prophet of Yahweh to consult (1 Kgs. 22:7), and when the three kings get stranded in the wilderness, Jehoshaphat again asks for a prophet of Yahweh (2 Kgs. 3:11).

When Jehoshaphat asks for a prophet in the Aramean war, Ahab summons Micaiah, who tells Ahab that Yahweh is luring him to his destruction, and that background hints that Elisha's prophecy may somehow be misleading, a trap for Jehoram. Elisha's prophecy is not false (Westbrook 2005); everything he predicts happens as he predicts. He says that "that valley shall be filled with water" (3:17), and in the morning "water came by way of Edom, and the country was filled with water" (3:20). He says that Yahweh will "give the Moabites into your hand" (3:18), and Yahweh lures the Moabites out to the three kings for slaughter. He says that Israel will "strike every fortified city and every choice city" (3:19), and they "struck the cities" (3:25), including Kir-hareseth. He says that they will sow the land with stones, stop up the springs, and knock down every good tree (3:19), and that is precisely what they do (3:25).

Yet, Elisha's prophecy is ambiguous in at least one respect: does Elisha *command* Jehoram and Jehoshaphat to destroy the good trees of the land and to stop up the water supply? His prophecy is open to that reading, but this would imply that Elisha instructs the kings to violate the Torah's rules of warfare, which is unlikely. Elisha's prediction is a prediction and nothing more. Further, Elisha's prophecy is certainly incomplete. Yahweh gives Moab into the hand of Israel, as Elisha predicts, but Elisha does not finish the story, and that incompleteness, like the prophecies of the false prophets in 1 Kgs. 22, sets a trap for Jehoram.

The other set of clues has to do with King Mesha of Moab himself. This is the story of an exodus and a conquest, but in the end it is not a reenactment of *Israel's* exodus. It is *Moab's* exodus, an exodus led by a Moabite "Moses," Mesha (the two names pun in Hebrew, and "Mesha" [מישׁע] is, like "Joshua," built on the verb "save"). Heavily oppressed like Israel in Egypt, Moab rebels, with Mesha leading his people out of Israel/Egypt. Even the horrific slaughter of his firstborn son on the wall of Kir-hareseth is part of an exodus typology, an infernal Passover that delivers Mesha while wrath burns against his enemies. This is also Mesha's holy war. In biblical holy war stories, Israel is normally outnumbered and Yahweh intervenes to rescue them from certain defeat. Here, Moab is the underdog, yet they win the battle because Yahweh takes their side.

Two exodus stories intersect in the chapter: the exodus of Israel and the exodus of Moab. Two holy war stories are being told simultaneously: the holy war that Israel wages against Moab and the holy war that Moab wages against Israel. In the end, Moab's exodus is successful, and Israel's is not. This fits the internal typology of 1–2 Kings: Ahab is a perverse Solomon, and just as Israel divides in the days of Solomon's son, so the northern kingdom divides in the days of Ahab's son (compare 2 Kgs. 3:5 with 1 Kgs. 12:19).

Yahweh occasionally gives the Omride kings victories, in spite of their rebellion, but so long as Israel tolerates idols it is not successful militarily over the long run.[1] Yahweh makes war against his enemies with infinite power and infinite cunning, and he is perfectly willing to direct his shrewd energies to trap his own people when they turn from him.

This unnerving story reveals something of God's ways with humanity in general. What is God up to in history or in the specific history of our individual lives? That is often difficult to answer, and frequently, just when we think we have a sense of what God is doing, he turns things inside out and upside down and does something else. He is a living God, and that means he is the God of surprise endings. He does this not because he takes malicious delight in toying with us, nor does he trap us to guffaw over the resulting pratfalls. The God of surprises is wholly righteous, wholly good, wholly just, wholly love, wholly light without a shadow of turning. He is faithful with the faithful, but the faithful throughout the centuries testify that God is a God of surprises. God surprises us because we have only the slightest grasp of what is actually going on in history or in our lives. God surprises us because he is doing far, far more than we can imagine, and his plans are far, far bigger than we can perceive. God surprises us with roadblocks and obstacles because he wants us to grow up from complaining, sentimental childish Jehorams into mature adults, into the image of Jesus, who learns obedience by what he suffers.

We have no control over our ends, whether the end of our lives or the end of any particular storyline of our lives. We cannot number our days. When we recognize this, we might respond with fear and anxiety at the feeling of utter helplessness, bottomless *dependence*. But recognizing that we are not in control of our ends only produces anxiety when we assume that we *should* be in control. In Scripture, recognizing that we are not in control is a source of joy because it is combined with the confidence that someone is in control,

---

1. In fact, the only reason that Yahweh pays any heed to Jehoram is because Jehoshaphat the Davidic king is close by (2 Kgs. 3:14) (emphasized by Davis 2005, 48). As in exile, Israel has hope only if it is joined with Judah.

someone who is far wiser than we. Recognizing our utter dependence removes the heavy yoke and leaves us buoyant, lighter than air. This is the wisdom of Ecclesiastes, the wisdom that freely confesses that the world is vapor—and then proceeds to eat and drink and make love (Eccl. 9:7–9). Recognizing that we cannot control our endings is just the reverse side of our basic Christian confession that *God* controls our endings. Our helplessness is inherent in the basic confession that God is God and we are not. The meaning of our life story depends on what happens tomorrow, what happens at the omega-point of our lives, and we do not know what will happen tomorrow. But there is a God in heaven who knows and controls every alpha and every omega, a God who *is* alpha and omega.

Second Kings 3 does not leave us with an arbitrary God, but it certainly does not reveal a tame God. This story leaves us precisely where the whole of Scripture leaves us: utterly dependent upon the God who is sovereign love and sovereign good. This odd and mystifying story urges us to take this one stance in life: trust him, remembering that the greatest surprise ending is the double surprise of the gospel—the shocking horror of the Son of the King crucified outside the walls by his own "fathers" and the wild joy of a risen Lord.

2 KINGS 4:1–44

At the Feast of the Assumption in 1993, Pope John Paul II spoke to young Catholics at Cherry Creek State Park near Denver, Colorado. He took John 10:10 as his theme, noting that "young people from every corner of the world, *in ardent prayer* you have opened your hearts to the truth of Christ's promise of new Life." This new life, he continued, is not for the young people alone. Young Catholics have "become more conscious of your *vocation and mission* in the Church and in the world." Their commitment to the abundant life of Jesus means that young Catholics are inevitably engaged in struggle, for "this marvelous world—so loved by the Father that he sent his only Son for its salvation (cf. Jn. 3:17)—is the theater of a never ending battle being waged for *our dignity and identity as free, spiritual beings*." He compared this battle to "the apocalyptic combat described in the First Reading of this Mass. Death battles against Life: *a 'culture of death' seeks to impose itself on our desire to live, and live to the full*." All who prefer darkness for light will reap the consequences: "Their harvest is injustice, discrimination, exploitation, deceit, violence. In every age, a measure of their apparent success is the *death of the Innocents*." Though a perennial challenge to the church, the culture of death in the twentieth century "assumed a social and institutional form of legality to justify the most horrible crimes against humanity: genocide, 'final solutions,' 'ethnic cleansings' and the massive taking of lives of human beings even before they are born, or before they reach the natural point of death."[1]

Like many of the late pope's sermons, this one stimulated Protestants as much as Catholics, and "culture of death" has rightly become a catchphrase for antiabortion and antieuthanasia forces. To speak of a culture of death is to

---

1. See "Homily of Pope John Paul II at Cherry Creek State Park, Denver, Colorado, on the Feast of the Assumption, 1993," at www.columbia.edu/cu/augustine/arch/jp2/denver17.html (emphasis original).

conjure memories of Roe v. Wade, of Terry Shiavo being starved to death, of the macabre trade in organs that operates clandestinely in our society. One of the most memorable recent illustrations of the culture of death comes from Weigel, who asks in *The Cube and the Cathedral*, "What are we to make of the Swedish company Promessa, which advertises a service in which cremation is replaced with human composting, the dead being immersed and frozen in liquid nitrogen before being smashed to smithereens by ultrasound waves and then freeze-dried and used for fertilizer?" (Weigel 2005, 21).

To concentrate attention on these appalling symptoms, however, may distract us from seeing how deeply the culture of death permeates modern society and culture, arising from and forming our basic perceptions and modes of thought. Even some of the most treasured of modern values serve as cornerstones of the necropolis of modern society. We boast, for example, that we define personhood in terms of freedom to make decisions. Any human being who is no longer free and autonomous, any human being who is wholly dependent on others, is increasingly bereft of rights. Instead of consuming resources that might be used for the living, the weak and frail should simply get out of the way. Euthanasia is the perfectly logical extension of our basic definition of personhood, which is often touted as key to modern freedom and prosperity.

For centuries, furthermore, we have believed that the most certain way to knowledge is through scientific analysis. Anatomy was, along with geometry, one of the model sciences of early modernity, and sciences modeled on anatomy treat the world as a corpse, as "dead matter" that we can probe and pierce and take apart. The world is a machine, and we can remove the pieces to see how it works. Control of life is instinctive to moderns, but it too displays a love of death. English theologian Pickstock points to the modern mania for mathesis, for attempting to "map" reality, reducing the flux and flurry of time to a controllable space. This "pseudo-eternity" treats things "which are only preservable and manageable as finite, and therefore as 'dead'" (1998, 104).

Even the modern effort to expunge every *memento mori* from pubic life is not so much a banishment of death as an effort to kill and fix time: "Modernity less seeks to banish death, than to prise death and life apart in order to preserve life immune from death in pure sterility. For in seeking *only* life, in the form of a pseudo-eternal permanence, the 'modern' gesture is secretly doomed to necrophilia, love of what has to die, can only die. . . . If death and life are seen as discrete and opposed, then existence itself is turned into a closed object—which is to say, given over to death" (Pickstock 1998, 104). Our virtues, as much as our vices, prop up the culture of death.

Ultimately, as 1–2 Kings shows, the culture of death is a culture of idolatry, the idol that Pascal called the "god of the philosophers." His inactivity and reticence suited him perfectly to fill the position vacated by the collapse of Christendom. The god of modern politics and science is at best a "watchmaker God" who set the world in motion, then settled back on his throne—now an easy chair—to see how things would go. He does not have a jealous bone in his body and is rather flattered to hear his name invoked periodically for this or that crusade. Long before Nietzsche, the god of the philosophers had been rendered effectively inert, which was his chief charm and leading qualification for the post of cultural deity.

During the time of the Omrides, Israel is living in a culture of death, a result of the Omride devotion to dead idols, and death permeates the daily lives of the people of Israel. Yahweh had given Israel a living, fruitful land, flowing with milk and honey and watered by rain from heaven, but idols make the land deadly. When the Shunammite's son goes out from the maternal indoors to the paternal fields, he immediately dies of a head wound (2 Kgs. 4:18–19). Israel suffers famine (4:38), and when the sons of the prophets gather what little fruit there is from the vines of Israel, it is poisonous. Stew made from the fruit of the land is "death in the pot" (4:39–40).[2]

The people of the land become deadly as well. The anonymous widow at the beginning of 2 Kgs. 4 faces creditors forcing her to sell her sons into debt servitude. Slavery is sometimes required in ancient Israel as a mechanism for making restitution for property crimes, and an Israelite might also enter slavery to pay off a debt (Lev. 25:39–43). Though the widow pursues a legitimate legal option, her creditors act unjustly. Yahweh himself protects orphans and widows, and Israel is to follow his lead (Exod. 22:22; Deut. 10:18–19), not leaving the vulnerable as easy prey for ruthless bankers. The Torah provides specific guidance on debt relief. Creditors are required to cancel debt in the seventh year (Deut. 15:1), granting a Sabbath of rest, rather than pressing the case against widows and orphans, and Israel's kings are particularly charged to protect widows and orphans from this kind of oppression (Ps. 72:1–4). Ahab is not this sort of king: in the one business deal that Ahab makes he murders to get what he wants, and his sons come from the same mold, so that oppressed widows are forced to turn to prophets rather than the king's court for justice. As in the first century, predatory creditors devour widows' houses (Matt. 23), depriving them of livelihood and of life, in order to ensure their own profits, while the leaders either cooperate with or wink at this oppression. With its kings useless and as good as dead, Israel is plagued with poisonous food, when there is food at all, and economic and social death stalks the land.[3]

2. Significantly, this takes place at Gilgal (4:38), the place where Israel first eats the produce of the land during the conquest of Joshua (Josh. 5:10–11). Under the Omrides, there is an ironic reversal of this conquest theme, since the prophet leaves the land to receive food. Thanks to Pesher Group member Brent Harken for this suggestion.

3. The method that Elisha uses to deliver the widow is significant in a number of ways. It requires faith on her part: an expectation of plenty in the midst of dearth is a mark of genuine faith. Further, it demonstrates the inexhaustible resources available to those who trust Yahweh and his prophet. The story thus serves to illustrate the difference between a biblical economics, which assumes the infinite resources of the creator, and a modern economics with its presumption of scarcity.

Elisha comes as a life giver to an Israel bereft of its husband,[4] and in a number of ways, his ministry continues Elijah's. Like his master, he helps a widow in desperate circumstances (2 Kgs. 4:1–7; 1 Kgs. 17:8–16) and raises a child from the dead (2 Kgs. 4:29–37; 1 Kgs. 17:17–24). In several respects, Elisha's miracles are reminiscent of the incident on Mount Carmel (compare 1 Kgs. 18:26, 29 with 2 Kgs. 4:31; 1 Kgs. 18:42 with 2 Kgs. 4:34–35), and in 2 Kgs. 5, Elisha assists a Gentile citizen of an enemy nation, as Elijah assists the widow of Zarephath. But Elisha's ministry is not simply a repetition of Elijah's. Elijah is the lone Moses confronting the Pharaoh-like Ahab, without even an Aaron to assist him. What Elijah does singly, Elisha does in a community or with that archetypal bumbling sidekick, Gehazi. Elijah's ministry focuses on calling Ahab to repentance, but once the fate of Ahab's house is sealed (1 Kgs. 21:17–24), Elisha concentrates on building a living community of faith within Israel, a living community within the corpse of Omride Israel. When Elisha speaks to the kings of Israel, he normally brings good news (2 Kgs. 3:13–20; 6:8–10; 7:1). Elijah conducts much of his ministry through dramatic public confrontations with Ahab and Baal; Elisha works largely behind closed doors.

The difference is symbolized geographically. Elijah spends much of his life on the far side of the Jordan, at the wadi Cherith and Zarephath (1 Kgs. 17), then at Sinai (1 Kgs. 19), and again when he is taken to heaven (2 Kgs. 2). As noted above (see the commentary on 1 Kgs. 17:1–24), his absence is theologically important, a sign that Yahweh sends the word of Yahweh into exile with the prophet and deprives the people of his word. Elisha spends most of his ministry in the land. He is apparently traveling with the king during the Moabite war (2 Kgs. 3:11) and is in Damascus to consult with Hazael (8:7–15), but otherwise his miracles are all done within the boundaries of Israel. Even when he performs a miracle for a Gentile, Naaman, he does it from Israel using the Israelite river rather than the rivers of Damascus (2 Kgs. 5). Elijah is only briefly in Jezreel (1 Kgs. 18:46–19:3; 21:17–24), but Elisha is in Samaria to meet Naaman (2 Kgs. 5:3, 9) and during the Aramean siege (2 Kgs. 6–7). The difference is dramatically evident when we consider similar miracles. Elijah multiplies the food of a widow of Zarephath, but Elisha multiplies oil for a widow of the sons of the prophets and bread for a gathering of prophets. Elijah raises the Gentile widow's child; Elisha, the miracle-child of a Shunammite woman. Elijah announces the judgment to come and enacts that judgment in his frequent departures from the land; with the doom of the

---

4. Early in 1–2 Kings, women appeal to kings and receive what they need (Bathsheba and David in 1 Kgs. 1; prostitutes and Solomon in 1 Kgs. 3). For most of 1–2 Kings, however, women find no relief from kings (2 Kgs. 6:24–31), but the women who consult with prophets receive life and food and justice (1 Kgs. 17; 2 Kgs. 4), and Jehoram provides justice for the Shunammite only under the influence of a prophetic tale (8:1–6). Jehoram is the last king in 1–2 Kings shown in scenes of this type. But then, there are no more prophet-with-women scenes after Elisha leaves the scene either, though there is a neat twist in 2 Kgs. 22: a king-before-prophetess scene.

house of Ahab echoing all around him, Elisha nurtures the seed of a renewed Israel within Israel.

Elisha's miracles, like those of Jesus after him, are not only δυνάμεις, but σημεῖα, signs as well as acts of power. Jesus turns water to wine at a wedding as a sign that he has come as the bridegroom to give life to the world. He cleanses lepers as a sign that he comes to restore people to fellowship with God, to make them fit to enter God's presence. He heals the lame and the blind and the deaf to fulfill prophecies of Isaiah concerning the return from exile (Isa. 35).[5] Likewise, Elisha's miracles reveal that his ministry is that of a "kinsman-redeemer," a גֹּאֵל. In the Old Testament, the kinsman-redeemer is responsible to redeem a near relative from debt and slavery (Lev. 25:47–55), a duty that Elisha fulfills in his dealings with the widow and her two sons (2 Kgs. 4:1–7). A kinsman-redeemer provides an heir to a brother who dies without children (Deut. 25:5–10), and Elisha accomplishes this for the Shunammite twice over.[6] Kinsman-redeemers purchase property back when poor relatives are forced to sell (Lev. 25), and in 2 Kgs. 8:1–6 Elisha indirectly recovers property for the Shunammite, who is forced to leave the land during seven years of famine. By fulfilling these duties, Elisha announces in action that he has come to proclaim liberty to captives, to announce the favorable year of Yahweh, to bring a Jubilee of freedom and life into the culture of death that dominates Omride Israel. For the original exilic readers of 1–2 Kings, the message is clear: while the kings sow death, there is life to be found, redemption from slavery and debt, restoration to the promised land, the gift of children, abundant life in all respects—these blessings will come to those who stay close to the prophets.

Centuries before, when Israel was in slavery under Pharaoh, Yahweh himself came as a near kinsman to deliver it from slavery, restore it to life, and give it property. Yahweh first confronted Pharaoh by emphasizing his kin-relationship with Israel: "Israel is my son, my firstborn. So I said to you, 'Let my son go, that he may serve me'" (Exod. 4:22–23). During the Omride dynasty, Yahweh again comes as kinsman-redeemer, but in this case, he operates through Elisha. Elisha forms a culture of life within the culture of death because he is very nearly an "incarnation" of Yahweh, the life giver, animated by the Spirit of Yahweh and Elijah. His ministry foreshadows the later work of Yahweh, who promises through various prophets that he will again come near to exilic Israel as its kinsman-redeemer once again to ransom it from slavery in Babylon (e.g., Isa. 43).

The Shunammite recognizes that Elisha is holy (2 Kgs. 4:9), sanctified by Yahweh's Spirit. Throughout Elisha's ministry, the presence of Yahweh

---

5. For a discussion of Jesus's ministry as a "return from exile," see especially Wright 1996a.

6. That Elisha plays the part of the kinsman-redeemer is underscored by allusions to the story of Ruth. When the boy dies, the Shunammite holds the child on her knees until he dies (Ruth 4:16) and then runs to Elisha to express her "bitterness" (1:20). Elisha is "Boaz" to the Shunammite, who is both Naomi and Ruth, a representation of Israel.

moves around the country with him, serving as the "chariot" of Yahweh. Like Jesus later, Elisha heads a counter-temple movement (Wright 1996a) and acts as a traveling temple, a human "tabernacle" that bears the life-giving glory of Yahweh. Elisha supplies everything that united Israel seeks from the temple—the water of life and cleansing, food, access to the presence of God. Like the temple in Jerusalem, Elisha is Israel's garden of Eden, its holy mountain, the embodiment of Yahweh within Israel. Elisha is the house of prayer for all nations. As noted above (see the commentary on 1 Kgs. 6:1–38; 7:13–51), the temple is a well-watered place with a large bronze sea and ten "chariots" carrying water to the corners of the earth. Cut off from the temple (12:25–33), the northern kingdom is also cut off from the life-giving waters of the temple's ministry. Yahweh does not abandon Israel to desolation, however, but provides water to the sons of the prophets through the human "temple" Elisha. Through Elisha, water at Jericho is purified (2 Kgs. 2:19–22); through Elisha's word, water comes from nowhere to sustain the armies and animals of the three kings (3:20); Elisha directs Naaman to the water of cleansing (2 Kgs. 5), makes iron float (6:1–7), and directs Jehoram to give water to Aramean soldiers (6:22–23). Tertullian says (1964, 21 §4.9), "*Nunquam sine aqua Christus*"—Christ is never without water, and the same can already be said of Elisha. He is a son of his heavenly Father, the creator who divides water from water and walks upon the sea.

All this explains why the Shunammite sets up a little "temple" for Elisha in the "upper room," the small-scale holy mountain, where she places a bed, table, chair, and "menorah" (מטה ושלחן וכסא ומנורה) (4:10), the same furniture as in the Jerusalem temple (table = showbread; chair/throne = ark; bed = altar). This is also why Elisha speaks to the woman through his "priest," Gehazi (4:12–13), why the Shunammite visits the prophet on Sabbaths and new moons (4:23),[7] and why sons of the prophets bring him their firstfruits (4:42). What Israel normally expects at the temple is available from Elisha; what Israelites would expect to do at the temple they do in the presence of Elisha. He is a "protoincarnation," so much so that his title "man of God" might almost be rendered as "God-man."

To all appearances, the human temple of the prophetic community in the north is pathetically small, a shoestring operation by comparison with the impressive bustling temple complex of Jerusalem or Samaria. While the faithful of Jerusalem can point to the temple and palace as concrete evidence of Yahweh's covenant and favor, the faithful of Israel can point only to a sparsely furnished upper room inhabited by an itinerant miracle worker with a receding hairline.

---

7. Keil claims that the prophets organized around Elisha provide an alternative to the Levitical priesthood: "The pious in Israel were accustomed to meet together at the prophets' houses for worship and edification, on those days which were appointed in the law . . . for the worship of God; . . . in the kingdom of the ten tribes not only were the Sabbath and new moons kept, as is evidence from Amos viii.5 also, but the prophets supplied the pious in that kingdom with a substitute for the missing Levitical priesthood" (Keil 1965, 311n1).

Yet, Yahweh is with Israel through Elisha just as certainly and just as effectively as he is with Judah through his temple and king. Renewal movements always look pathetic, meeting in basements or catacombs, crowding into living rooms to croak out their psalms, while mainline congregations luxuriate to the strains of Tallis in ever roomier stain-glassed cathedrals. Elisha's ministry culminates in the destruction of Samaria's Baal temple (2 Kgs. 10) and the renewal of the Jerusalem temple under Joash (2 Kgs. 11–12). In a sense, the prophets of Israel always aim at the restoration of the temple of Yahweh in Jerusalem, the single sanctuary for the one people of God, which will be reestablished after the exile that reunites Israel and Judah. After the dynasty of Ahab is destroyed and Elisha dies, the narrator turns his attention back to Judah and its reforming kings. In the interim, in a divided Israel, as in a divided church, the prophet serves as a temple site. And the glory of Yahweh is always there where a bedraggled band of two or three gather around word and table in the name of Jesus, the greatest of the prophets and the living temple.

There are a number of verbal links between 2 Kgs. 4:42–44 and the festivals of firstfruits in Lev. 23. Leviticus 23:14 prohibits Israel from eating bread or roasted grain or "new growth" until the first sheaf is offered to Yahweh at the sanctuary, while 2 Kgs. 4:42 refers to the man's gift of "barley" and "new growth" (כרמל). A man brings "the bread of the firstfruits" (לחם בכורים) to Elisha (4:42), a phrase elsewhere found only in Lev. 23's prescriptions for the day of Pentecost (23:20). In narrative time (if not in actual time), these stories of Elisha's miraculous feasts follow the story of the woman of Shunem, whose son is born to her "at the time of living" (2 Kgs. 4:16). That temporal marker, apparently a reference to the rebirth of the earth during spring, along with the resurrection motif of the story, links the story with Passover. Thus, the chapter follows the festival sequence of Lev. 23, beginning with Passover, and moving to first sheaf and Pentecost, in preparation for the "ingathering" of the Gentile Naaman in the following chapter.[8]

Elisha's provision of a son to the Shunammite illustrates that he radiates the life and glory of Yahweh. In return for her kindness (her "trembling") (2 Kgs. 4:13), Elisha promises the woman that she will have a son despite the age of her husband (4:14–15). The doorway setting, the phrase "at this time next year," and the woman's protest are all reminiscent of Sarah (Gen. 18) (Cohn 2000, 29). Like Sarah, the woman represents unfruitful Israel, who cannot bear seed, being as good as dead. When 2 Kgs. 4 is compared to Gen. 18, it is clear that Elisha stands in the narrative location of the angel of Yahweh, because

---

8. The Hebrew word translated "new growth" here is כרמל, the same as the name of the mountain of Elijah (1 Kgs. 18) and Elisha (2 Kgs. 2:25; 4:25). Elisha is thus associated with the new growth and the first sheaf that begins to peek out of the dry ground of Israel. He is the bringer of a new "Pentecost" to Israel. See also Isa. 32:15, where the gift of the Spirit poured out from heaven transforms the wilderness into a fertile field and the fertile field into a forest ("fertile field" translates Hebrew כרמל).

he is the angel-messenger of Yahweh.[9] When the boy dies, Elisha sends his servant, but like Jesus's disciples, Gehazi is unable to perform the necessary miracle, and his lack of success is described in the same terms as the failure of Baal in 1 Kgs. 18:29. The prophet's staff is not sufficient; only when Elisha himself, the prophet clothed in the mantle of Elijah, lies on the boy does he come back to life. Instead of becoming unclean by his contact with the boy's body (Num. 19), Elisha's body communicates life to the boy's dead flesh (2 Kgs. 4:34), making his nostrils breathe and sneeze as Yahweh does to the nostrils of Adam. Similarly, only when poisonous stew is brought to Elisha does it give life, and only when loaves are brought to Elisha are they multiplied to feed many. Where Elisha is, there is life because there is Yahweh.

Yahweh comes near again as a kinsman-redeemer, becoming our brother in the person of his Son, to announce the greater Jubilee (Luke 4; cf. Isa. 61). For both Elisha and Jesus, redemption relieves material as well as spiritual need. In a world where economic relationships are destroyed by greed and injustice and meanness, God in Christ has established an economics of life among his people. In a hungry world, God in Christ has given us true, life-giving bread. Within the culture of death, God is shaping a culture of life for those whom the Father has joined to his risen Son by his Spirit.

9. Commentators, missing the incarnational character of Elisha's person and ministry, assume that Elisha promises something that he cannot deliver or even usurps the place of Yahweh in giving life. It is taken as a sign of Elisha's arrogance. This objection works only if Jesus is arrogant.

2 KINGS 5:1–27

Many treatises on baptism have been written in the course of two millennia of church history, but most have devoted inexcusably little attention to the Old Testament background (Leithart 2005b). Circumcision obviously has pride of place among the initiation rites of Israel, but washings and baptisms are common (Lev. 15:5–8, 10–11, 16–18; Num. 19:11–22). From the perspective of the apostles, the great "water events" of the Old Testament are baptisms. Through the cleansing judgment of the flood, the world is recreated (1 Pet. 3:18–22); Israel is saved from Pharaoh to serve Yahweh through the baptismal waters of the Red Sea (1 Cor. 10:1–4); and the patristic writers who see Israel's crossing of the Jordan in a similar light are certainly maintaining apostolic modes of interpretation.

The story of Naaman is the richest Old Testament story of baptism and anticipates Christian baptism in a number of specific ways. For starters, it is an important typological witness because the subject of baptism is a Gentile, an Aramean general. Naaman is not the first Gentile convert in Scripture. At each major juncture of Israel's history, a Gentile appears as a "sponsor" of the covenant people.[1] Abraham encounters the Gentile priest and king Melchizedek as he returns from battle (Gen. 14:17–20); the throng that leaves Egypt in the exodus is a "mixed multitude" that consists of both Hebrews and Egyptians (Exod. 12:38); and Jethro, a Gentile, assists Moses in setting up a representative system of government for Israel (18:13–27). Rahab the Canaanite harlot converts during the conquest (Josh. 2:1–21), and Ruth the Moabite converts during the period of the judges (Ruth 1). David has contact with a number of Gentiles who share his faith in Yahweh, and Hiram of Tyre assists Solomon in building the temple (1 Kgs. 5). During the exile, a number of Gentile kings

---

1. I borrow this phrase from James B. Jordan.

acknowledge Yahweh as a powerful God, even if they do not become exclusive monotheists (Dan. 4; 6). From the beginning, Yahweh intends for all the families of the earth to be blessed in Abraham's seed (Gen. 12:1–3). This promise of Gentile inclusion is brought to its climax in the new covenant, but even in the old covenant the grace of God extends far beyond the bounds of Israel. During the period of Elisha's ministry, Naaman is the leading Gentile figure.

The story of Naaman's conversion is one of the most detailed and one of the most sociologically and psychologically rich conversion stories in the Bible. Almost for the first time, the Bible depicts the change of mind and heart, as well as the change of status, that occurs when a sinner turns to the God of Israel. Naaman's conversion involves a change of status that makes him acceptable before God. Second Kings 5:1 introduces him in exalted terms: he is a captain of the hosts, a great man, highly honored, decorated with many victories, a man of substance. But the verse concludes with a crashingly bathetic, and in Hebrew very blunt, qualifier: a leper (גבור חיל מצרע). Naaman is the perfect "natural man," but having achieved all that a hero could achieve, he still finds himself excluded from life.

Old Testament leprosy is not Hanson's Disease, the modern form of leprosy that causes limbs to rot and fall off (Wenham 1979, 194–97). Instead, it is closer to psoriasis, and its symptoms included flaking skin, discoloration of bodily hair, and exposure of the flesh through the skin (Lev. 13). It is not so much a physical as a symbolic disability, a condition that excludes the leper from the presence of God. When Naaman first arrives to see Elisha, Elisha speaks to him through his intermediary, Gehazi, another indication that Elisha's house is the "temple site" to which the unclean cannot draw near. After Naaman is cleansed, Elisha permits him to come "before" him, into his presence (2 Kgs. 5:15). As in the story of the Shunammite, the "doorway" (5:9) is again a symbol of birth (as in Gen. 18), foreshadowing Naaman's rebirth. Turning to Yahweh makes him acceptable to God, able to come into the presence of Elisha to speak with the prophet of the Lord. Though dead in leprosy, Naaman is made alive together with Christ.

Naaman's "dipping" in the Jordan is the effective ritual sign of this change of status. Just as the washings of the Levitical system cleanse from various forms of defilement, so Naaman is cleansed and brought near through washing. Because he is a Gentile, Naaman's baptism is a particularly apt sign of Christian baptism, which marks out a new community of worshipers in which the distinction of Jew and Gentile is utterly dissolved (Gal. 3:26–29). Naaman shows an admirable grasp of the implications of his baptism. Having been baptized, he realizes that he is exclusively devoted to Yahweh and promises to worship no other gods (2 Kgs. 5:17). As Thomas Aquinas puts it, baptism is a "deputation" that confers the right and the obligation to participate in the cultus Dei (1920, part III Q. 63 arts. 1, 6).

Naaman converts from pride to humility. He shows some initial humility by accepting the suggestion of a servant girl from Israel, but, typical of his class, he assumes that real power is confined to royal courts. The little girl suggests that he consult the "prophet who is in Samaria" (5:3), but the letter that Naaman secures from the king of Aram asks the king of Israel to provide the cure (5:6). The king of Israel knows that only God cures lepers, but he, like his brother (2 Kgs. 1), forgets that there is a God in Israel who can heal and that this God works through his prophet. In its initial stages, the story undermines the wisdom of the wise, the power of the powerful. Naaman is impotent to heal himself, as is his king. Israel's king is no help either. Once again, the narrator contrasts the impotence of kings to the power of Yahweh's prophet.

Naaman's experience not only challenges his social attitudes and his assumptions about power, but his personal pride. Naaman comes to Elisha with an entourage (5:9) designed to impress the prophet, but Elisha refuses to see him. Enraged at Elisha's apparent snub, Naaman is especially offended that Elisha does not show proper respect for a man of his status (in Hebrew "to me" is the first phrase in Naaman's complaint in 5:11). Naaman is a "great man" and expects "great things" to be done for him (5:13) (Cohn 2000, 37). He wants Elisha to come and "stand" before him (יצא יצוא ועמד) as his servant (5:11), but Elisha is a servant of Yahweh not of Naaman (5:16).[2] Naaman eventually takes his servants' advice, and his flesh "turns" to the flesh of a newborn. He realizes that he must humble himself as a little boy, and stand before Elisha (ויעמד לפניו) if he is going to be healed (5:15). Unless he "goes down" into the water, he will not be healed.

Like Naaman, some Christians doubt what the New Testament says about the power of baptismal water. When he finishes his Pentecost sermon, Peter tells the Jews how to respond to his message: "Repent, and let each of you be baptized in the name of Jesus Christ," he says, "for the forgiveness of sins, and you shall receive the gift of the Holy Spirit" (Acts 2:38). Through baptism we have died and been buried with Christ so that we can walk in newness of life (Rom. 6:1–11); through baptism the Spirit joins Jews and Greeks into one body (1 Cor. 12:12–13); baptism clothes us in Christ (Gal. 3:26–29); in baptism we have been circumcised with a circumcision without hands (Col. 2:11–12), a circumcision that removes the flesh; baptism now saves us, Peter says (1 Pet. 3:21); and Paul talks about baptism as a "washing of regeneration and renewal of the Holy Spirit" (Titus 3:5). How can water do such wonders? Because baptism is not simply water, but water and word, water and promise. God does wonders, but he promises to do wonders through water. To say that water can cleanse leprosy, wash away sins, or renew life is an insult to intelligence. Water is just too simple, not to mention too physical

---

2. As Provan (1995, 195) points out, the specific wording of the exchange in 5:10–13 is important. Elisha promises that the leprosy will be healed (5:10), but Naaman hears only that the waters of the Jordan will "cleanse" him (5:12). Naaman's servants (like the little girl at the beginning) are more insightful than he. They not only highlight the simplicity of Elisha's instructions, but also correct Naaman's hearing. They in effect ask, "Hasn't the prophet said a great thing? Has the prophet talked only of cleansing? Didn't he also talk of healing?"

and tangible. But that is exactly the point. Baptism is an insult to the wisdom of the world: through the foolishness of water God has chosen to save those who believe. Baptism is a stumbling block for the powerful, who want to do something impressive or at least have something impressive done to them. God says, trust me, let me wash you up, and you can become a temple of the Spirit and sit at my table in my kingdom. He says, become as a little child, and believe what I say about baptism. As Jordan (1998) says, all baptism is infant baptism.

Though converted, Naaman does not become a Jew, and though he stands before Elisha and before Yahweh as his servant, he returns to the service of Aram's king. Most remarkably, he asks pardon from Elisha for continuing to go with his master into the house of Rimmon (= Hadad), and Elisha gives permission to continue to fulfill this part of his service to the king of Aram. Elisha's apparent indifference to idolatry is a puzzle. Naaman is a Gentile, and Elisha would likely not have given the same permission to a Jew. Further, Naaman does not consider bowing in the temple of Rimmon morally indifferent; he asks for pardon, not merely permission. Even with these qualifications and explanations, Elisha's response is remarkable and shows something of God's gentleness in dealing with believers in tricky moral and political circumstances. Elisha does not expect Naaman to abandon the world or withdraw into a ghetto where he can escape moral dilemmas and difficulties. As Paul says, "let each one remain with God in that condition in which he was called" (1 Cor. 7:20). If one can leave that condition, one should; but there is no sin in remaining in the condition in which one was called. There are clearly times when converts must be exhorted to find a new place: a converted prostitute should not be urged to offer her services "to the glory of God." But many Christians are zealots, insisting on far more "purity" than do Paul or Elisha—not to mention God.

The conversion story ends in 2 Kgs. 5:19, and the chapter is only two-thirds over.[3] The sequel highlights the themes of service and access, a theme underscored by verbal repetitions throughout the chapter (Provan 1995, 195–96). Naaman stands "before" the king of Aram (5:1), and this sets up parallels with Naaman's maidservant, who stands "before" his wife (5:2), and with Gehazi, who stands "before" Elisha (5:25). Naaman moves from a position "before" the king of Aram to a position "before" Elisha (5:15), while Gehazi moves the other direction. Gehazi begins as Elisha's associate, but at the end of the story,

---

3. This is a frequent device in Scripture, particularly in the parables of Jesus. Jesus tells a story that seems to be finished, but then the story goes on, and the appendix contains the point of the whole story. In the parable of the prodigal, for instance, Jesus tells a tale of wandering and return, but then goes on with the appendix concerning the older son. That might seem a digression from the point, but in fact it is the point. Jesus tells that parable while sitting at table with Pharisees who are criticizing Jesus's table companions, who are criticizing Jesus for eating and drinking with returned exiles. Jesus tells a parable that includes a character who complains about his father's celebration of his son's return.

he goes out from "before" Elisha (5:27) and never returns to service to the human temple. The Gentile Naaman replaces Gehazi as the one who stood before the prophet as his true servant. Gehazi is introduced in 5:20 as the "boy" (נער אל ישע) of Elisha, linking him with Naaman, whose flesh is turned into the "flesh of a little boy" (כבשר נער קטן) (5:14), and with the "little girl" (נערה קטנה) (5:2) at the beginning of the story (Kim 2005).

As Cohn points out, these "servants" are contrasted in various ways:

> Whereas the "young maiden" (na'arāh qĕtannâ) wanted to help Naaman, Gehazi, the "young man" (na'ar) aims to exploit him. And while Naaman was concerned to support his lord with his "hand" ('al-yādî, v. 18), it is from that very hand that Gehazi wants to steal. . . . The centering of the phrase, "and he leans on my hand," above (v. 18) focuses the contrast between Naaman, who asks advance pardon for showing loyalty to his lord, and Gehazi, who excuses himself in advance for his treachery and criticizes his lord. With the derogatory epithet, "this Aramean," Gehazi impugns the man who has declared his faith in YHWH and who is about to act on it. (Cohn 2000, 40)

Naaman is not merely a Gentile, but an *Aramean* military hero, and during this period of Israel's history the Arameans are the greatest military threat to Israel (1 Kgs. 20; 22; 2 Kgs. 6–7). For Elisha to assist an Aramean general is like a colonial pastor assisting a British general during the American War of Independence and also analogous to Jesus's ministry to Roman centurions. In offering this aid, Elisha fulfills the Song of Moses (Deut. 32), where Yahweh threatens to respond to Israel's provocations by a provocation of his own. When Israel turns from its Lord to other gods, the Lord will turn from Israel to other nations (Leithart 2003a). With Naaman, the Lord makes good on that threat. Like Daniel later, the prophet Elisha gives aid and comfort to the enemy of Israel.

In the Song of Moses, Yahweh extends mercy to Gentiles as part of rejecting Israel, and Gehazi represents an Israel rejected in favor of the Gentiles. Elisha charges Gehazi with "taking" not "receiving" (Brueggemann 2000, 339), and Elisha expands the charge into a larger condemnation of all taking, reminiscent of 1 Sam. 8. Gehazi's greed is on a par with the worst excesses of the kings of Israel. He commits fraud against a stranger and is made a stranger as a result. He sins against a Gentile and is put in the place of a Gentile.

Israelites first read this story while in exile, and it instructs them how they are to conduct themselves among the Gentiles. They are to serve Gentiles, directing them, as the little slave-girl does, to Yahweh as the source of cleansing and life. They must not be zealous nationalists who refuse help to the uncircumcised. If they strive to be super-Israel, they will end up not-Israel. To Israel as to Gehazi, the Lord also says: if you lust after Gentile wealth and power, then you will find yourselves going all the way, inheriting also Gentile exclusion and uncleanness.

The temptation to seek the goods of the Gentiles is still intense, but when the church lusts for Gentile wealth and power, it also receives Gentile diseases. Sider writes:

> The findings in numerous national polls conducted by highly respected pollsters like The Gallup Organization and The Barna Group are simply shocking. "Gallup and Barna," laments evangelical theologian Michael Horton, "hand us survey after survey demonstrating that evangelical Christians are as likely to embrace lifestyles every bit as hedonistic, materialistic, self-centered, and sexually immoral as the world in general." Divorce is more common among "born-again" Christians than in the general American population. Only 6 percent of evangelicals tithe. White evangelicals are the most likely people to object to neighbors of another race. Josh McDowell has pointed out that the sexual promiscuity of evangelical youth is only a little less outrageous than that of their nonevangelical peers. (Sider 2005)

The moral of the story of Gehazi is that the Lord judges our lusts by giving us what we lust for. Those who leave houses and family for the sake of Christ receive a hundredfold return (Mark 10:29–30). A similar return is offered to those who leave the kingdom for the world: Christians who seek the world and its righteousness will get everything they desire, and all the world's pathologies will be added unto them.

Gehazi's is a cautionary tale, but ultimately 2 Kgs. 5 points to the mechanism by which the Lord will bring salvation to the Gentiles. The exchange between Naaman and Gehazi points to the blessed exchange of the cross, where the one who knows no sin is made sin for us, where Jesus the Jew takes on the leprosy of the world and is excluded from the presence of God, so that Gentiles and Jews might be washed and brought near in him.

2 KINGS 6:1–23

Marcion's is a theology of discontinuity, between law and gospel, between the God of justice and the God of goodness (or, perhaps, between a good and evil god), between soul and body, between Old and New Testaments (Pelikan 1971, 71–81). Fittingly, his most important book, now lost, is titled *Antitheses*. For a theology of discontinuity, Marcionism has had remarkable staying power. Though an ancient heresy, it comes into its own particularly in modern theology. Marcionism infects sacramental theology (Leithart 2005b), and Jones (2003) writes of the "present-day Gnosticization of Biblical Studies," which began in the nineteenth century and continues in the work of John Dominic Crossan and others. Harnack's sympathy for Marcionism is evident in his description of Marcion's Paulinism in his *History of Dogma* (1895–1900, 1.266–81). On the other side of the theological spectrum, solidly conservative dispensationalist theologians assume a strict separation of Old and New Testaments, of Israel and the church, and in its extreme forms dispensationalism even restricts the New Testament books that remain relevant to the Christian church. In Marcion, liberal and hyperconservative theologians find a strange mutual bedfellow.

Ethical discontinuity between Moses and Jesus is among the most important discontinuities advanced by Marcion. Marcion finds some ethical value in the moral law (Pelikan 1971, 77), but is offended by various aspects of the Mosaic system and the entire tone of Old Testament ethics, which to his mind stand in stark contrast to the love ethic of Jesus. In refuting him, Tertullian defends the justice of Moses at length. The *lex talionis* is not, he argues, "a permission to mutual injury," but the opposite, "a provision for restraining violence." Food laws are not irrational, but teach continence in all things: "When . . . the law took somewhat away from men's food, by pronouncing unclean certain animals which were once blessed, you should understand this to be a measure for encouraging continence, and recognise in it is a bridle imposed on that appetite that, while eating angels' food, craved after the cucumbers and melons of the Egyptians" (Tertullian n.d., 2.18). The details of Torah are not beneath God, but encourage Israel to recognize God in the "common transactions of life" (2.19). The law's ultimate meaning is revealed in the coming of the Christ, but even in its literal meaning and historical function within Israel, it is intended to "bind a man to God." Contrary to Marcion (not to mention his modern progeny), the prophets are not attacking Torah, but are sent "to help forward this beneficent, not onerous, purpose of the law" (2.19).

Marcion's influence in contemporary theology is perhaps most particularly seen in ethics, where, under the often beneficial influence of Anabaptist traditions, the ethics of the Sermon on the Mount, interpreted in contrast to the ethics of the Old Testament, are the touchstone of Christian ethics. Even decisively non-Anabaptist realists largely accept the Anabaptist reading of Jesus. From the story of the woman taken in adultery (John 8), Niebuhr draws the insight that "we are to forgive those who wrong society not only because God forgives, but because we know that in the sight of God we also are sinners." Yet, this insight of Jesus will subvert the power of punishment, without which social order cannot be maintained. Thus, it is "impossible to construct a socio-moral policy from this religio-moral insight of Jesus', as, for instance, Tolstoi attempted in his objection to jails and other forms of social punishment." In fact, the effort to draw out a social ethic from the ethics of Jesus blunts his most important insights: "When, for instance, liberal Christianity defines the doctrine of non-resistance, so that it becomes merely an injunction against violence in conflict, it ceases to provide a perspective from which the sinful element in all resistance, conflict, and coercion may be discovered." Instead of contrition it produces self-righteousness (Niebuhr 1963, 29). Niebuhr's interpretation of Jesus is itself highly questionable (Wright 1996a; Worth 1997). Torah unarguably includes a social and political ethic, and for Niebuhr's argument to work he must assume a quasi-Marcionite separation of old and new.

Both of the incidents in 2 Kgs. 6:1-23 are, in different ways, refutations of this Marcionite position, in that both demonstrate the deep humanity and mercy embodied in Torah. The story of the floating ax head (6:1-7) seems trivial and pointless, something that might appear in the hagiographical biography of a minor medieval saint. It lacks the oomph of raising a dead child or curing leprosy. Yet, further reflection reveals some depth to the story. The ax head is lost during a construction project undertaken by the sons of the prophets, and their house building fits into the exodus-conquest motifs that thread through the Elijah-Elisha narratives. Israel comes from Egypt with spoils to build the tabernacle, and similarly the sons of the prophets, liberated from the Omride kingdom, build a house, an alternative to the various houses and shrines that the Omrides built. From caves, they have moved to chapels, if not yet cathedrals.

One of the sons of the prophets loses his "iron" (6:5) and becomes distressed because the iron is "asked" (6:5). According to the law a borrower is responsible to restore damaged property (Exod. 22:14–15). Iron is a rare commodity in ancient Israel, so that losing an ax head will lead to significant debt. If he cannot pay, the debtor might have to enter "debt slavery" until he can restore the cost of the borrowed item. (The creditor, of course, can also forgive the debt.) The law thus encourages lending, without requiring an inhuman indifference to property and goods from the lender. The law reaches into the crannies of life not only, as Tertullian says, to remind Israel of Yahweh's thoroughgoing lordship, but also to inculcate an ethic of care that respects the rights of the victims of loss and crime.

From this perspective, Elisha's miracle is no trivial demonstration of power. In recovering the ax head, he delivers the man from indebtedness and potentially slavery, as he delivers the widow (2 Kgs. 4:1–7). He is again acting as a kinsman-redeemer, restoring life and property to those who follow him. Elisha's instruction to "take it up" (6:7) echoes his instruction to the Shunammite woman to "take up" her son (4:36), suggesting that by saving the ax head Elisha gives the man new life. His reversal of the laws of gravity reverses the laws of death and destruction, the tragic plot of loss (Dillard 1999, 121–26). Elisha heals and delivers by throwing salt into a spring (2:19–22) and meal into a pot (4:38–41), and these repeat the miraculous healing of the waters at Marah (Exod. 15). That Elisha accomplishes this miracle through a stick of wood would have interested Origen, turning the miracle into a sign not only of Easter but of Good Friday.

The miracle also symbolizes the future of Israel. The ax head sinks into the water and returns, like Jonah the prophet. In Jonah, submersion and return is an image of Israel's exile in the sea of Gentiles and its return to the land (Leithart 2000a, 179–86), and the ax head passing through the Jordan further strengthens the association with Israel's exile and return. For the original exilic readers of 1–2 Kings, this narrative demonstrates again that clinging to the prophet and his word is the way of return—both the way of repentance and the way of restoration to the land. When Israel is sent to slavery to pay off its debt of sin, it hopes for a new exodus that will restore it to the land, in a cosmic Jubilee.[1]

It is significant, further, that this resurrection image takes place in water, through submersion and return. In the previous chapter, Naaman goes down into the same water and comes back cleansed from his leprosy, reborn with flesh "like the flesh of a little child" (2 Kgs. 5:14), and the ax head sinks into the waters of the Jordan and is restored, saving the prophet from a debt. This event is thus not only a pointer to the great reversal of the return from exile, but also to the great reversal accomplished in Jesus's baptism, for Jesus goes

---

1. Death-by-flying-ax is a biblical paradigm of manslaughter (Deut. 19:4–10). A manslayer is allowed to flee to a city of refuge, where he stands trial and is either admitted to the safe haven of the city or cast out to face the blood-avenger (Num. 35:9–34). The allusion to this law here suggests that the sons of the prophets are creating a "city of refuge," an oasis of life and health in the midst of the land cursed by the Omride kings.

down into the waters of Jordan to receive the Holy Spirit, the Spirit that em-
powers him to preach the gospel to the poor, heal the lame, open the eyes of
the blind. Through Christian baptism, we participate in the resurrection of
Jesus. As Paul says, we are buried with him in baptism, "so that we too might
walk in newness of life" (Rom. 6:4). As the baptized person passes through
the waters, he or she is joined into the fellowship of Christ, shares in his body,
shares in the Spirit that inhabits and animates the body, and participates in
the resurrection power of Jesus.

The second incident in 2 Kgs. 6 shows even more clearly the connection
between Elisha's ethics and those of Jesus. Ahab's descendants, like Ahab, fight
against Aram (1 Kgs. 20; 22). Apart from Elisha, the characters in this story are
not named; the kings are simply "kings," a literary device that lends a parabolic
feel to the story. Like the previous story, it suggests that Israel and its kings are
successful and safe if they rely on prophets and prophetic power rather than
on their own resources. If they acknowledge the prophet as "father" (2 Kgs.
6:21), all will go well.

Sight plays a key role in the story. The king of Aram tells his men to "see"
(6:13), Elisha prays twice for Yahweh to open eyes (6:17, 20), and the Aramean
soldiers, like the men of Sodom (Gen. 19), are bedazzled (2 Kgs. 6:18). In
the course of the story, the sight/blindness dynamic explores the reversals that
follow in the wake of the prophet's ministry. Elisha's spiritually blind attendant
learns to see, while the Arameans who have been sent to see Elisha are blinded.
Yahweh darkens understanding and opens the eyes of the blind, and he delegates
this power to his prophet. Wielding this power, Elisha is more in charge of the
Arameans than is their own king. Not only is the prophet superior to Israel's
king; he is superior the king of the Gentiles. These reversals prepare for the
more striking reversal later in the story, the reversal from war to peace when
Elisha offers his POWs food and drink and sends them home.

Elisha's relations with the Arameans and with the king of Israel are curious.
He baptizes an Aramean general into the kingdom (2 Kgs. 5) and then spreads
a royal banquet before an invading Aramean army (2 Kgs. 6). Yet, he also assists
Jehoram in each of his battles. He prophesies deliverance during the war with
Moab (2 Kgs. 3), provides intelligence about Aramean bands (6:8–14), and
predicts that the famine of Samaria will end (7:1). In sharp contrast, Ahab and
Jezebel never consult Elijah, even when Jehoshaphat asks for a prophet of Yahweh
before the battle at Ramoth-gilead (1 Kgs. 22). Elisha functions as Jehoram's
chief prophet, though Jehoram himself is hardly a faithful disciple.

Unlike premodern Christians, modern Christians are often functional em-
piricists, who instinctively believe that only visible things are real. At best, we
are deists: of course, there is God up there somewhere, but he is a long way
off. We do not think we have to press through a crowd of angels every time we
move; we do not think that a small angelic deployment runs ahead of us into
danger; we do not think, as the poet Francis Thompson does, that we disturb
an angel every time we turn a stone; we do not think, to quote Thompson

again, that Jacob's ladder is pitched between heaven and Charing Cross. But the Bible and Christian tradition are united in the insistence that angels are real and active. The Lord Jesus appears to his people in the Old Testament as the "angel of Yahweh," and the psalmist promises that God sets his angels as guardians around us, lest we dash our foot against a stone (Ps. 91:11–13). Angels are mediators of the law (Gal. 3:19), join in our worship on a heavenly Zion and are observers of our witness (1 Cor. 11:10), minister to Jesus after his temptation in the wilderness (Matt. 4:11), and serve as God's ministers (Ps. 103:20). Humans are made for a while lower than angels, but we are destined to judge angels (1 Cor. 6:3). Yet, they are servants of God and humans, constantly active in God's world.

We are, in short, Elisha's servants. When we face dangers and troubles, we often despair and fear because we are seeing only with the eyes of flesh. Paul says that "we walk by faith, not by sight," but we frequently do the opposite. If we hope to see the fiery chariots that surround us, we need to have our sight cleansed and our sins forgiven. We must come to Jesus with the prayer of Bartimaeus: "Lord, that I may receive my sight."

In addition to "sight," the passage includes several plays on the notion of "guarding" (2 Kgs. 6:9, 10, 17). The king of Israel leaves the borders so porous that Aramean bands saunter through unopposed. Accompanied by the horses and chariots of Yahweh, Elisha is the true guardian of the land. The phrase "horses and chariots of fire" (סוסים ורכב אש) (6:17) is elsewhere used only in 2:11, where it refers to the cloud of glory that whisks Elijah to heaven. Elisha is at the center of this angelic host, a "man of God" who shares in the glory and power of God himself. Elisha bears Yahweh's glory and presence, a human, mobile glory cloud and tabernacle of Yahweh. The king of Aram sends the strength of his glory (וחיל כבד) to seize the prophet (6:14), but the prophet surrounded by the כבד of Yahweh is a Samson who can break through a nighttime siege without effort (Judg. 16:2).

Instead of capturing Elisha, the Aramean troops are captured by Elisha and led back to the capital city of Samaria. The king of Israel, impotent as he is in the face of the Aramean threat, is eager to shoot the fish once they are safely in the barrel, his eagerness captured in a series of quick Hebrew phrases. Perhaps he hopes to make up for Ahab's failure to destroy the Arameans in an earlier war (1 Kgs. 20). Elisha's refusal suggests that even in normal war the king will not kill captured prisoners. The prisoners do not belong to the king of Israel and cannot be disposed of as he sees fit. They are Elisha's prisoners and, more basically, prisoners of Yahweh. Instead of destroying them, Elisha extends the hospitality of God to them on the high place that is Samaria. The reference to Dothan (2 Kgs. 6:13) suggests a connection between Elisha and Joseph, the "seer" of Egypt.[2] Jacob sends Joseph with food for his brothers, but Joseph initially does not find them at Shechem (Gen 37:13–15). A man

2. The only other reference to Dothan in the Hebrew Bible is Gen. 37:17.

tells him that Joseph should search for them in Dothan instead (37:17), and it is at Dothan that his brothers strip him of his robe and sell him into slavery. In 2 Kgs. 6, the Aramean king sends his men to find Elisha, having been told, "Behold, he is in Dothan" (6:13). Elisha escapes the troops of Arameans sent to capture him and instead takes them to Samaria, where he orders Jehoram to feed them. In the next chapter, Elisha again provides food for a king who is trying to kill him—food during a severe famine.

Elisha is a new Joseph: attacked by his fellow Israelites (as well as by Gentiles), he responds by giving bread and water to his persecutors and in so doing heaps coals of fire on their heads (Rom. 12:19–21). Elijah provides bread to the widow of Zarephath who honors him, and early in his ministry Elisha does the same. But now Elisha offers bread to those who oppose him. He was a son of his heavenly Father, who sends rain on the just and the unjust and feeds friend and enemy.

Elisha is surrounded by the hosts of heaven and has no need to fight with the sword. Instead, he fights the Arameans with generosity and overcomes their hostility with an abundance of hospitality—a "great feast." That is what Paul says as well: if your enemy is hungry, feed him; if he is thirsty, give him something to drink (Rom 12:19–21). That is what Christians commit themselves to at the Lord's table, because that is what is taking place at this table. While we were yet sinners, Christ, the bread of life, gave himself for us. While we were enemies, we were reconciled to God through the death of his Son (5:10). God calls his enemies and spreads a "great feast" before us, and to the church he says: go and do likewise.

Most basically, then, this is a gospel passage, a sign that, Marcion notwithstanding, the God of Israel is the God of Jesus. The God of Elisha reverses the laws governing buoyancy for the benefit of the sons of the prophets, and he reverses the power relations between Aram and Elisha and between Aram and Israel through prayer. He can make the blind see and dazzle into blindness those who can see. This is the God who performs the great reversal of raising the dead—raising Israel from the death of exile on the far side of the Jordan and raising the true Israel, Jesus from the grave. The floating ax head is the sign of Jonah, which is the sign of Jesus.

At his baptism, Jesus is filled with the Spirit (Luke 3:21–22). As any Jew will know, a battle is sure to follow. Like Othniel (Judg. 3:10), Gideon (6:34), Jephthah (11:29), Samson (13:25; 14:6; 15:14), and Saul (1 Sam. 11:6), Jesus receives the Spirit to prepare him for war. Filled with the Spirit, Jesus proves himself the "stronger man" by triumphing over Satan and demons (Luke 4:1–13, 33–36, 41). Depend on it: when the Spirit comes, somebody's gonna get hurt.

Once Jesus triumphs over the "ruler of this world" in the wilderness, he begins a victory tour around Galilee, proclaiming release to those under Satan's rule, and eventually "ascends" to Jerusalem, the city that kills prophets. The passage from Isaiah that he reads in the Nazareth synagogue summarizes his entire ministry, just as the quotation in Luke 3:4–6 is a summary of John's ministry. The phrase "acceptable year of the Lord" (4:19) refers to the Jubilee year, the "year of release" (Lev. 25:10). According to Lev. 25, Israel has a Jubilee year every fifty years. During this mega-Sabbath year, land sold during the previous fifty years reverts to its original owner, and slaves are freed. Isaiah refers to this legal institution to describe Israel's return from Babylonian exile: the land of Israel will be restored to its original owners (Israel), and the Jews held captive in Babylon will be liberated (Isa. 61:4–11). In the favorable year, the Lord liberates those "downtrodden" by the Herods and Pilates, and, more important, those in bondage to Satan and under the dominion of the curse are released. Jesus restores the land, the whole earth, to those who become disciples of the anointed Son who inherits the nations (Ps. 2). Jesus's message of release depends on his prior victory over Satan.

Throughout his ministry, especially as recorded by Luke, Jesus is throwing down the high and mighty and proud and lifting up the humble poor, enacting his mother's song throughout his ministry (Luke 1). Fittingly, Luke also most fully describes Jesus's meals and table talk. Seven meals are explicitly mentioned (5:29; 7:36; 9:16; 11:37; 14:1; 22:14; 24:30), and an eighth takes place at a roadside inn between Jerusalem and Emmaus, on the eighth day, the day after the Sabbath, the beginning of a new week (24:30) (LaVerdiere 1994). For Luke, Jesus's meals are not merely occasions of fellowship and teaching (especially Luke 14) but of conscious and provocative confrontation with the Pharisees and other Jewish leaders. Pharisaism is, in the description of Neusner, a "table-fellowship sect" that "required keeping everywhere the laws of ritual purity that normally apply only in the Jerusalem Temple, so Pharisees ate their private meals in the same condition of ritual purity as did the priests of the holy cult" (1979, 67). Their program for the redemption of Israel is centered on maintaining the purity of Israel by maintaining the purity of Israel's meals. The table has become a "microcosm of Israel's intended historical structure, as well as a model of Israel's destiny" (Borg 1998, 95).

When Jesus comes eating and drinking with outcasts—publicans and sinners—he challenges the Pharisaical program for Israel's renewal. As Borg explains:

> To say, and to express in action, that the Kingdom of God included these meant to his opponents that he had rejected their understanding of Israel's holiness as separation, both as present practice and as final destiny. In short, to the extent that Jesus was a public figure, his action was perceived as a serious challenge to the internal movement of reform which was intended to make Israel a holy community, a kingdom of priests, in the sense in which those expressions were then used. (Borg 1998, 99)

Instead of maintaining a scrupulously pure table by excluding the unclean and sinners, Jesus welcomes the outcasts in order to heal them. Long before he enters the temple at the end of his long march to Jerusalem, Jesus is practiced at overturning tables.

As noted in the last chapter, Torah itself enjoins mercy and compassion to enemies and to the marginal, and the so-called prophetic critique of Israel is motivated by Torah rather than a critique of Torah. Jesus is certainly in line with prophetic tradition, but Moses was the paradigmatic prophet. The book of Kings is in line with that pentateuchal and prophetic challenge to exclusiveness and self-righteousness within Israel, and 2 Kgs. 6 is as radical a parable of reversal as anything in Jesus's teaching. Like Jesus's parables, it is social and religious satire (Nelson 1987, 187, 191).

This story of the Aramean siege of Samaria parallels the story of the Aramean war in the previous section in a number of ways (Nelson 1987, 188). Both open with a king concerned about the state of his kingdom—the Aramean king worries about moles in his court, the Israelite king observing the barbarism of Samaria during a siege. Both kings blame Elisha for the problems they face, and both kings send soldiers to capture or kill Elisha. In both cases, Elisha

provides food—a banquet for his Aramean captives and plunder from the
Aramean camp. While the king of Israel can do nothing but tear his clothes at
famine-induced cannibalism, Elisha prophesies deliverance for Samaria. This
episode is also structurally parallel to the Moabite rebellion in 2 Kgs. 3. In both
stories, a siege is broken; in both, Elisha prophesies, specifically about provi-
sions for Israel. In 2 Kgs. 3, the Moabite king sacrifices his son on the wall of
Kir-hareseth; and in 2 Kgs. 7 a woman tells the king about killing and eating
a child on the wall of Samaria. In both chapters, further, Yahweh is revealed
as a trickster, a God who is shrewd with the shrewd. He tricks the Moabites
into thinking that the three kings have slaughtered each other (3:21–24), and
he tricks the Arameans in the opposite way, by chasing them away from their
camp so that Israel can plunder them (7:6–7). The two chapters are chiastically linked (Leithart and Jordan 1995) and are neatly inverted: in one, an
army leaves a city expecting to find an empty camp and is surprised to find
an army; in the second, lepers leave a city expecting to find a full camp and
are surprised to find an empty camp. In both stories, too, Elisha's prophesies
miraculous provision—of water (3:17) and food (7:1).

The break at 2 Kgs. 7 is understandable,[1] but ultimately, however, the chapter
division is infelicitous. Elisha is sitting with the elders in his house in 6:32,

---

1. Second Kings 7 is clearly marked off by a chiastically structured inclusio:
    A at this time (7:1)
      B seah of fine flour at a shekel
        C and a double-seah of barley at a shekel
          D in the gate of Samaria
        C′ double-seah of barley at a shekel (7:18)
      B′ and a seah of fine flour at a shekel
    A′ at this time tomorrow
          D′ in the gate of Samaria
Second Kings 7:2 and 7:19 match just as neatly:
    A answered the officer (7:2)
      B which to the king he leaned on his hand
        C to the man of God
          D and he said
            E look! Yahweh making windows in the heavens
              F could this thing/word be?
    A′ answered the officer (7:19)
        C′ to the man of God
          D′ and he said
            E′ now look! Yahweh making windows in the heavens
              F′ could this word/thing be?
Within this frame, the chapter as a whole is concentrically arranged:
    A Elisha predicts, officer doubts (7:1–2)
      B leprous men discover the camp (7:3–8)
        C lepers return and report (7:9–11)
          D king suspicious, suspicions overcome (7:12–13)
        C′ messengers sent out (7:14–15a)
      B′ messengers return (7:15b)
    A′ fulfillment of prediction (7:16–20)

and he is still there in 7:1 when the messenger from the king of Israel arrives at the door; and the oracle in 7:1 is Elisha's response to the question of 6:33. There is, to be sure, a gap in the story in that 7:2 introduces a character that was not previously mentioned and implies that Elisha delivers his oracle to the king himself (6:32; cf. 7:17). Yet, the king's arrival at Elisha's house is never explicitly mentioned, perhaps a sign of his utter subordination to Elisha, which is consistent with the narrative's emphasis on the king's impotence. When they come before a prophet, kings have no right to make a grand entrance. (Notice the parallel of 2 Kgs. 6:32 and 1 Kgs. 14:6.)

Bringing the latter part of 2 Kgs. 6 into play highlights the contrast between the king of Israel and the prophet of Israel, as well as the differences between cannibal women who eat their own sons and the generous lepers who share their spoils. The account of the siege of Samaria, however, is part of a larger structure that extends to 8:6:

A king's impotence: woman's appeal; king wants to kill Elisha (6:24–31)
   B Elisha's prophecy (6:32–7:2)
      C four lepers discover the camp: plunder it (7:3–8: if we die, we die)
         D lepers bring good news (7:9–10)
      C′ five horses discover camp: Samaritans plunder the camp (7:11–16a: if they die, they die)
   B′ Elisha's prophecy fulfilled (7:16b–20)
A′ king redeems the Shunammite because of Elisha (8:1–6)

The king of Israel is the primary character at the beginning and end of the sequence, and the two scenes are similar in many details: both deal with famine, both portray a woman crying out to the king for redress of a grievance, both refer to children, and in both Elisha is mentioned but does not appear. Yet, the king's response in the two cases is strikingly different. The king tears his garments in frustration and anger when confronted with the story of cannibalism, but gives justice to the Shunammite. In 8:1–6, the king is again favorable to Elisha, listening to stories of his exploits and redressing the Shunammite's distress based on her relation with the prophet. In place of the official of 7:1–2, Gehazi the leper appears, standing before the king as Naaman the leper stands before his king. By the time of the events of 2 Kgs. 8, Gehazi has fully taken over the role of Naaman the king's servant, and the king of Israel apparently learns something about the value of lepers. The king of Israel learns that there is a prophet in Israel who gives bread to the hungry, land to the dispossessed, life to the dead.

Second Kings 6:23 tells us that Arameans stopped invading Israel, but in 6:24 we read of Arameans besieging Samaria. Perhaps 6:23 simply means that the Arameans stopped invading with marauding bands. Instead of continuing inconclusive guerilla warfare, they pull out all the stops and begin a total war. In any case, this siege anticipates the later sieges that bring Israel's habitation of the land to an end (Lam. 2:20; 4:10),[2] as Yahweh tightens the noose. There is, however, another explanation for the apparent discrepancy. Given the concentric structure outlined above, it seems likely that the famine of Samaria in 2 Kgs. 6:25 is the same as the seven-year famine mentioned in 8:1.[3] Second Kings 7 describes the conclusion of the famine (cf. 1 Kgs. 18; and see the commentary on 2 Kgs. 8:1–29), as the Lord transforms mourning to dancing and famine to feasting in the sabbatical year. On this reconstruction, the famine is not a result of a siege, but is the occasion for Ben-hadad to renew his invasion of Israel.[4] Thus, there is an interruption of hostilities, perhaps for as many as six years, before Ben-hadad besieges the city. This reconstruction also helps to explain why Jehoram considers Elisha responsible for the siege and seeks to kill him (6:32–33): Elisha announces that Yahweh has called for famine (8:1; cf. 1 Kgs. 18:10). In the last war with Aram, Jehoram obeyed Elisha and called him "father" (2 Kgs. 6:21), but after several years of famine and a siege to top it off, he blames Elisha and seeks to make him a scapegoat. Like his father, he believes that prophets are troublers in Israel.

The siege leads to famine so severe that unclean donkey heads and dove dung become rare treats (6:25; cf. 18:27). The woman on the wall cries out to the king for "salvation" (הושיעה אדני המלך) (6:26), and in the context, salvation means both redress of an injustice and provision of food (6:27). The king does not know where salvation is to be found, forgetting that there is a prophet in Israel whose name means "my God saves." As Yahweh had threatened (Deut. 28:52–57), Israel's disobedience has led to siege and cannibalism, particularly cannibalism of children, cannibalism of the future. The woman's story is chilling, and her request more so. She does not present a case against her murderous friend, but instead asks the king to approve yet another murder of yet another child. She is Israel herself, the mother who devours her own children and boils her kids in mother's milk (Deut. 14:21), in contrast to the faithful in Israel, symbolized by the Shunammite, whose son is raised from the dead and who inherits the land. When Israel appeals to a king, there is no help; but the Israel that seeks help from Yahweh's prophet, or a king under the influence of a prophet, lives. Unlike Solomon, Jehoram lacks wisdom to pass

2. The reasoning of the lepers anticipates the counsel of Jeremiah during the Babylonian siege: better to surrender and take our chances with Aram than to starve to death in the city (2 Kgs. 7:4).

3. Breck (1994) argues that chiastic structures function "helically" and can be read A-A, B-B, C-C, D, and so on. Read in this way, the report of famine in 6:24–31 is filled out in 8:1–6:

    A there was a famine in Samaria
    A' indeed, it lasted seven years

4. Thanks to Pesher Group charter member Peter Roise for this suggestion.

wise judgment in an impossible situation.[5] He can only tear his robe (2 Kgs. 6:30; cf. 5:7) and threaten to strike Elisha with a head wound (אִם־יַעֲמֹד רֹאשׁ אֱלִישָׁע) (6:31). He is too late, for Elisha's head, Elijah, is already indestructible in the heavens (see the commentary on 2 Kgs. 2:1–25).

As Jesus says, there are lepers in Israel, but only the Gentile Naaman is cleansed, an inversion of Israel's expectation that foreshadows the greater reversal accomplished through Jesus. Second Kings 6 records yet another reversal: within Israel lepers excluded from the city, rather than the official who stands in the gate, discover and announce the "gospel" of the city's deliverance and rebirth (7:9). Lepers feast while those in high places get trampled. While the king huddles within the walls of his fortress, four lepers lead a comical "attack" on the Aramean camp; confronted with cannibalism in his capital, Jehoram can only tear his clothes and threaten the prophet, but the four excluded lepers provide abundant food for the city. The world is turned upside down, as lepers save a city they cannot even enter.[6] So too, Jesus says that the subjects of the kingdom are cast out, and watch, noses pressed to the window pane, as many from east and west feast with Abraham, Isaac, and Jacob (Matt. 8:11–12).

Like Passover and the later deliverance of Jerusalem (2 Kgs. 18), salvation comes to Samaria at night. While people sleep, the sleepless Lord of heaven goes out with horses and chariots and, like an angel of death, frightens the Arameans (7:6). After Passover, on the evening of a new day (7:7), the lepers plunder "Egypt." Initially, the lepers act like Achan or Gehazi, taking plunder only for themselves and hiding it away (7:8), but they eventually think better and share the wealth. As with Zacchaeus the tax collector, salvation comes to the homes of outcasts who give their wealth to feed the hungry.

Salvation for Samaria is not an elevation to a sphere where economics no longer matters. Yahweh saves Israel by giving it abundance in the land and a rescue in history. He is lord of the market and can pull the rug out from under the supply-demand curve as easily as he can bring a shortage that drives prices out of sight. Economic life is not governed by impersonal forces of scarcity, but

---

5. Like the incident in 1 Kgs. 3:16–28, this brief passage resonates with tantalizing typological hints. One child is taken, and another left, in a kind of Passover. The inverted Passover allusion is strengthened by the women, grotesquely, specifying that the first child is "boiled" (2 Kgs. 6:29; cf. Exod. 12:9). The women engage in a macabre eucharist, feeding on the son. The hidden child protected by his mother looks ahead to the heroics of Jehosheba, who hides Joash in the temple when another cannibal mother, Athaliah, is killing the royal seed.

6. Provan (1995, 202–3) points to two entertaining puns in the story of the siege of Samaria in 2 Kgs. 6–7. The first puns on "lepers" (מְצֹרָעִים) (7:3) and "Egypt" (מִצְרַיִם) (7:6): the Arameans become frightened by the sound of an army, thinking that Egyptians are attacking, but there is nothing but lepers, scrounging for food. God makes the Arameans panic at the dropping of a leaf. The word for "windows" (אֲרֻבּוֹת) (7:2) also puns on "four" (אַרְבָּעָה) (7:3). The skeptical royal official does not believe that Elisha's prophecy could come true even if Yahweh drops grain through the windows of heaven, but ultimately four lepers bring the good news that there is food in abundance. The four lepers are the windows of heaven through which Yahweh delivers bread to his people.

by a God of infinite resources, who can indeed open the windows of heaven. The salvation brought by Jesus the greater Elisha is equally a restoration of abundant life on earth and in history, as well as a promise of eternal life in a new heavens and new earth. Not only economically, but socially, 2 Kgs. 6 is a preview of the gospel. All cultures draw lines between who is inside and who is outside and between different classes of people within the culture. Cultures lift some high and consider others low. The gospel confounds the boundaries of all worldly cultures, precisely because it confounds the line between creator and creature in the incarnation. In the salvation of Samaria, we see a foreshadowing of the great confounding event of the incarnation and the upending of the world that begins with the coming of the kingdom, the strange kingdom that welcomes humble, generous lepers and excludes the proud.

When the lepers return to the city, they bring "good news" (7:9), using a word (שׂרה) elsewhere employed to describe the good news of Israel's redemption, the gospel of the coming Messiah. Here as elsewhere, the good news is good news of victory, the victory of the God of Passover and exodus, the God who employs things that are not to overcome things that are (Ellul 1972, 61). Here as elsewhere, it is good news about Yahweh intervening to change the specific circumstances of life, not to provide a heavenly rescue from the difficulties of life (Brueggemann 2000, 360). Here as elsewhere, the gospel is the good news of food, the fulfillment of a prophetic promise of a table spread in the presence of enemies. Here as in the New Testament and throughout the history of the church, the good news is given to outcasts on the margins, so that salvation arises not in Jerusalem but outside the walls, in Nazareth of Galilee.

2 KINGS 8:1-29

In her delectable first novel, *Housekeeping*, Marilynne Robinson's narrator Ruth observes that absence is an intense form of presence. As long as friends and family are physically empirically *here*, they are localized and circumscribed. Absent, memory discovers them in every nook and cranny—a beloved wife is always in the kitchen and the bedroom and curling up in her favorite chair and fixing her hair all at once and all the time. But of course Robinson says it better: "Sylvie [Ruth's aunt] did not want to lose me. She did not want me to grow gigantic and multiple, so that I seemed to fill the whole house, and she did not wish me to turn subtle and miscible, so that I could pass through the membranes that separate dream and dream. She did not wish to remember me. She much preferred my simple, ordinary presence, silent and ungainly though I might be . . . if she lost me, I would become extraordinary by my vanishing" (1980, 195). Of course, there is more to Christ's real absence/real presence than this, but there is at least this. This is why it is good for him to go away, and how his going away enables him to fill all things.

At the beginning of 2 Kgs. 8, the memory of an absent prophet proves politically powerful, even salvific. This chapter concludes the storyline of the Shunammite woman. Earlier, through Elisha's word, she gives birth to a son and has seen her son restored from death (2 Kgs. 6). That "Passover" event is followed by an exodus and return. She leaves the land because of famine,[1] as Israel does in the days of Jacob, and she remains for seven years in exile among the Philistines, as Israel remains for four generations in Egypt. When she returns after exile, she receives her land.

---

1. As noted in the commentary on 2 Kgs. 6:24–7:20, this is apparently the same famine as in 2 Kgs. 6–7, and the relief provided by the Aramean retreat permits the Shunammite woman to return.

Elisha serves again as her kinsman-redeemer. Grown gigantic by his absence, his reputation alone is enough to influence the king. The Shunammite's return to the land is a "Jubilee" (Lev. 25), a restoration to ancestral property. Beyond Jubilee, the king restores all the produce of the land that she lost during her exile. Her seven years of exile not only allude backward to the exodus, but also point ahead to the seventy years of exile in Babylon. Exilic readers can hope that those who comply with the prophetic command and maintain the prophet's memory (2 Kgs. 8:1) will likewise return to the land promised to Abraham. In her previous appearances, the Shunammite has been identified as a "great woman" (אשה גדולה) (4:8), but now she is identified as a beneficiary of a prophetic miracle, the "woman whose son Elisha restored to life" (האשה אשר־החיה את־בנה) (8:1, 5). Her fame is not dependent on wealth and status but arises, like Israel's, from Yahweh's favor. In all these respects, the "great woman" of Shunem represents the faithful Israel whose life challenges the death realm of the false Israelite Queen Jezebel.

King Jehoram has a remarkable change of heart. Confronted by another woman pleading for (perverse) justice (6:24–31), the king of Israel can only tear his clothing, protesting that only Yahweh can answer the woman's needs (6:27). In 2 Kgs. 8, by contrast, the king acts with divine largesse, restoring the woman to her land. He eagerly listens to tales of Elisha's ministry, the prophet that he earlier is eager to kill. No doubt the end of the siege of Samaria provokes this response. Brueggemann interestingly suggests that the woman's land reverts to the king during her exile (2000, 369), and if this is the case Jehoram is a reverse Ahab, who unlike his father (1 Kgs. 21) freely returns seized property.[2]

Yet, the sequence of events in 2 Kgs. 8 is jarring. Apparently deeply impressed with the power of Elisha following the deliverance of Samaria, Jehoram performs the one genuinely royal act of his recorded reign. For the first time since Solomon (1 Kgs. 3:16–28), a woman appeals to a king and receives justice. For the first time during the Omride dynasty, a king voluntarily, rather than reluctantly, responds to a prophet. Jehoram dispenses justice under the influence of Elisha's ministry and reputation. Yet, the very next story introduces the long-delayed Hazael (1 Kgs. 19:17), Yahweh's Gentile avenger against the house of Ahab. Just when the dynasty of Ahab reaches its peak, its one brief

2. The effect of Gehazi's recitation of Elisha's "great deeds" (8:4) on the Shunammite's situation is cleverly rendered by the textual intertwining of past and present. Woodenly translated, 8:5 reads:

    A recounting [how] he restored to life the dead
        B behold, the woman whom he restored to life her son
            C crying out for her house and her field
        B′ and Gehazi said, "My master, king, this is the woman and son
    A′ whom Elisha restored to life"

The woman materializes in the middle of Gehazi's story, so that the king's action becomes an extension of the story already in progress.

moment of piety and justice, it is destroyed. The dissonance is evident when we take a broader view as well. Jehoram is the *best* of the Omrides (2 Kgs. 3:2), and he proves (occasionally) responsive to Elisha (3:13–20; 6:20–23) and permits the communities of prophets to flourish instead of forcing them into caves. He is not Stalin but Gorbachev, and yet it is during his reign that Yahweh unleashes his wrath against the house of Ahab. Why now?

For starters, the Lord is faithful to his word as delivered through his prophet. Elijah announces that the destruction of the house of Ahab will happen during the reign of Ahab's son (1 Kgs. 21:27–29), and that word is fulfilled. Jehoram, moreover, only partially reverses the policies of his parents. Jehoram is not so reliable a king as a surface reading might suggest. He confesses that the Lord brings disaster on Israel (2 Kgs. 3:10; 6:27), but he almost never turns to the only possible source of help—Elisha (as Jehoash later does in 13:14–19). Jehoshaphat, not Jehoram, seeks a prophet of Yahweh when the kings are in the wilderness without water (3:11), and Jehoram does not think to send Naaman to the prophet when the Aramean comes seeking cleansing (2 Kgs. 5). Instead of humbly turning toward the human "temple" Elisha to intercede during the famine in Samaria, he sends a delegation to kill him (6:31).

However jarring, this is not a unique sequence of events in 1–2 Kings. The northern kingdom experiences a time of political renewal (if not spiritual renewal) prior to the Assyrian invasions (2 Kgs. 13:22–25; 14:23–27), and Judah falls shortly after the reformation of Josiah. Yahweh's judgments do not fall on Israel during the darkest days of persecution and idolatry, but instead when day seems just beginning to dawn. Likewise, the judgment of God falls on Jesus during the week after a multitude welcomes him to Jerusalem as king.

Jehoram's threat to kill Elisha is particularly important for understanding the sequence of events in 2 Kgs. 6–8, which roughly matches the sequence of events in 1 Kgs. 18–19:

Elijah ends a drought (1 Kgs. 18)	Elisha ends a famine (2 Kgs. 7)
Jezebel swears to kill Elijah (1 Kgs. 19:2)	Jehoram swears to kill Elisha (2 Kgs. 6:31)
Elijah goes to Sinai (1 Kgs. 19:3–8)	Elisha goes to Damascus (2 Kgs. 8:7)
Elijah to anoint Hazael and Jehu (1 Kgs. 19:17)	Elisha anoints Hazael and Jehu (2 Kgs. 8:13; 9:1–3)

From these parallels, it appears that the decisive last straw for both Ahab and Jehoram is an attack on the "head" of the prophets.

Elisha's reputation as a wonder worker extends beyond Israel, as shown in the story of his visit to Damascus. This is Elisha's first departure from the land since he followed Elijah across the Jordan, and it is a sign of impending judgment on Israel. While in Damascus he follows the instructions of Elijah by telling Hazael that he will be king.[3] As in 2 Kgs. 5, when he assists the Aramean commander Naaman, Elisha (like Jeremiah after him) appears to

---

3. As a historical matter, the plausibility of Elisha visiting Damascus turns on the plausibility of the account in 2 Kgs. 6 of Elisha sparing the Aramean army. A prophet who has shown

be a turncoat, giving aid to Israel's most threatening political enemy. Hazael comes to Elisha at the behest of his master, Ben-hadad, another of the sick kings in 1–2 Kings. Unlike Ahaziah of Israel (2 Kgs. 1), Ben-hadad knows that there is a God in Israel and where to find him. Naaman the Aramean sends for help to the king of Israel, but the Arameans learn from that episode that Israel's power is not in the king's court but among the sons of the prophets, and especially with the "father" of the prophets (9:9). It is a painful reflection of Israel's state that the Aramean king knows better where to seek divine help than do most of Israel's own kings.

Prophets are political actors from the beginning of Israel's monarchy, but Israel's prophets do not interfere with Gentile politics during the days of Saul, David, or Solomon. Elijah has contact with Gentiles, but never assists or contacts Gentile rulers. Elisha is the first Israelite prophet to anoint a Gentile king, and this initiates several centuries of prophetic ministry toward the Gentiles. Israel's fall leads Yahweh in search of other nations to bless through his prophets. Israel's fall means riches for the world (Rom. 11), as the Lord raises up a succession of empires as guardians for his people (see the commentary on 2 Kgs. 23:31–25:30).

Yahweh mentions Hazael as an instrument of vengeance against the house of Ahab during his encounter with Elijah at Mount Sinai (1 Kgs. 19). Over ten chapters intervene between the first and second references to Hazael. From 1 Kgs. 19, readers expect Hazael much sooner and expect in the meantime that fire from heaven will already be falling on Ahab's house. This reminder of the prophecy of 1 Kgs. 19 also raises an important question about Elisha's ministry, for Elisha too is described by Yahweh as an instrument of wrath, clearing the debris that Jehu leaves behind. Yahweh's statements about Elisha leave the reader expecting Elisha's ministry to be destructive. Instead, apart from the unfortunate "boys" of Bethel (2 Kgs. 2:23–25), Elisha feeds the hungry, raises the dead, assists widows in distress, delivers orphans from slavery. How is Elisha's a ministry of judgment? Where, Jonah might ask, are the fireworks? Why this delay of the parousia?[4]

Elisha's ministry of life is precisely the ministry of judgment that Yahweh describes. Elisha, after all, is a force of destabilization. By giving life and freedom to the faithful poor, the loyal sons of the prophets, he upsets the natural hierarchy of the northern kingdom. By engaging in a ministry of life, he condemns to death those who refuse to follow his word. Elisha's ministry of "putting to death" is in fact carried out on a larger scale than Hazael's or Jehu's, for Elisha's does not bother with cutting individual enemies in two. His ministry

such clemency, and has saved the lives of an Aramean unit, would certainly be free to show his face in Damascus.
    4. In historical terms, it is likely that the Arameans lose more than a little confidence in their king following the humiliation of the army "defeated" by a great feast in Samaria (6:15–23) and scattered by bumps in the night (7:6–7). Clearly, Ben-hadad's kingdom, and not just his person, is weakening, and Hazael seizes the opportunity to take the throne.

cuts the Israelite nation in two—dividing sons from fathers, daughters from mothers, princes from prophets—and cutting a thing in two is a sure way to kill it. Like Jesus's, Elisha's ministry of healing and redemption is a sword that divides the nation of Israel. As noted in the introduction to this commentary, Yahweh sets about repairing the breach between Israel and Judah through the paradoxical method of dividing Israel.

Again, this has intriguing ecclesiological implications. Within many mainline churches, renewal movements are seeking to turn the denomination back to orthodoxy and faithfulness. They are ministries of life, but those renewal movements are also instruments of judgment against the whole church. When a renewal movement begins in the Methodist or Presbyterian church, the denomination is internally divided. Resources, personnel, and energy required to keep the denomination running are depleted and redirected, as resources and personnel that would be devoted to denominational programs are diverted to the programs and plans of the renewal movement. Renewal movements often drain a denomination of its best and brightest leaders and its most vibrant churches. Renewal of the mainline follows the same process as all renewals: the path of renewal is not moral reformation, but slaughter and transfiguration, division and reunion, death and resurrection.

Yahweh pronounces judgment, and then delays, and this delay has two purposes: it gives time for the sins of the Amorite-like house of Ahab to become ripe (1 Kgs. 21:26; cf. Gen. 15:16), and it gives time for Elisha to form a community that will serve as a seedbed for the renewal of Israel. We have the same sequence in the New Testament: Jesus declares that the temple and Jerusalem are doomed (Matt. 24), but there is a generation delay during which the Jews who kill Jesus persecute his apostles (Acts 7) and during which the Lord gathers some within Israel seeking escape from the wrath to come.[5]

Elisha apparently instructs Hazael to lie to his master (2 Kgs. 8:10). Most versions translate his words to this effect: "Tell him he shall live, but I know that he shall die." The Hebrew is more ambiguous: אמר־לא חיה תחיה והראני יהוה כי־מות ימות, which might be translated, "Say, 'not living you shall live,' and Yahweh shows me that dying he shall die." If "not" negates the whole phrase, then Elisha instructs Hazael to tell his king he will surely *not* live. In Hebrew, the negative sounds just like the prepositional phrase "to him" (both words are pronounced "lo"), and Hazael chooses to hear Elisha's words as an instruction to life: "Say *to him*, 'Living you shall live.'" Hazael reports to Ben-hadad that he will recover: אמר לי חיה תחיה ("he said to me, 'Living you

5. More broadly, we can perhaps draw the conclusion that the Lord permits wicked regimes to persist in order to give his church time to recover from persecution. Today's Russia, for example, is ruled by former Soviet apparatchiks even though the Soviet regime has fallen. The blood of hundreds of thousands of Christians martyred during the Soviet years remains unavenged, and yet the regime remains largely unchanged. Where is the God of justice? Perhaps the Lord is giving time for the Russian church to become strong enough to persist through an even more drastic collapse, an even more thoroughgoing judgment.

shall live'") (8:14). Perhaps this is another example of Elisha predicting what will happen without endorsing it (3:16–19), because he knows that Hazael will kill Ben-hadad and then carry out a war of utter destruction against Israel (8:12). Even though Elisha understands that Israel deserves judgment, like Jesus, Elisha weeps over the prospect (Matt. 23:37–38). A true prophet prophesies to those he loves.

The last part of 2 Kgs. 8 turns attention to the southern kingdom, catching up with the kings following Jehoshaphat. Jehoshaphat cooperates with Ahab on more than one occasion, and his reign sets the pattern for this period of Israel-Judah relations. Jehoshaphat is the head of an "ecumenical" movement, cooperating with Ahab's plan to reunite the two nations. Once Judah and Israel attain this level of cobelligerency, Judah begins to adopt some of the liturgical practices of the northern kingdom, and Jehoshaphat goes so far as to let his son marry Ahab's daughter (8:18). Israel and Judah are becoming indistinguishable, so much so that even the names of the kings are the same. There is a Joram in Judah and in Israel, and an Ahaziah in Israel and in Judah, with the result that Jehu's zeal to destroy the Omride dynasty also threatens David's house.

The only episode recorded from Joram of Judah's reign is the revolt of Edom. All the details are familiar: Edom revolts (פשע אדום) (8:20), and Joram goes to suppress the revolt. During the battle, Joram is surrounded by the Edomite army on the field and attempts to break through the Edomites at night. Though he is able to break free of the Edomites and their chariots, his soldiers run home in defeat. This sequence of events is a reenactment of the revolt of Moab from the northern kingdom (2 Kgs. 3). Not only Edom, but Libnah revolts as well (תפשע לבנה) (8:22). Libnah is near the Philistine border, and the loss of this city is a deep cut into the southern kingdom. David's descendants are not only losing outlying areas, lands that have been conquered by David and ruled by Solomon, but towns within Judah. When Judah mimics the harlotry of her older sister Israel (Ezek. 23), Yahweh chips away portions of Judah, as he does to Israel during the Omride dynasty.

Influenced by his family, Ahaziah, Joram's successor, continues his policy of cooperation with Ahab. Like his grandfather, Jehoshaphat, he cooperates in wars with the son of Ahab, fighting against the Arameans at Ramoth-gilead (2 Kgs. 8:28), the city where Ahab died. Joram is also wounded at Ramoth-gilead, and he retreats to Jezreel, an ominous retreat that leaves Joram of Israel in the very town where Ahab stole the vineyard of Naboth, perhaps in the very palace adjoining the vineyard. He retreats to the very place where the dogs will lick the blood of Ahab (1 Kgs. 21:19), and the blood of Ahab courses through his veins. Ahaziah of Israel joins him in Jezreel. Everyone gathers in one place, like characters in the concluding chapter of an Agatha Christie novel, so that when the bomb drops it will have maximum effect.

The text includes yet another ominous note. Ahaziah of Judah begins to reign in the twelfth year of Joram of Israel (2 Kgs. 8:25), and we know already from 3:1 that this is the final year of Joram's reign. We also learn that Ahaziah reigns only one year (8:26). For the attentive reader, the text signals that this will be a fateful year, witnessing the deaths of kings in both north and south. We know that Joram, like Ahaziah of Israel (2 Kgs. 1), will not rise from his sick bed, but will die in Jezreel, and we expect that the dogs of Yahweh are ready to lick the blood of the house of Ahab.

2 KINGS 9:1–10:36

In what is surely the funniest book of New Testament theology ever written, Schweitzer details how the modern "quest of the historical Jesus" repeatedly discovered, much to its surprise, a Jesus who happily confirms and conforms to its own cultural prejudices: "Each successive epoch of theology founds its own thoughts in Jesus; that was, indeed, the only way in which it could make Him live" (1952, 4). Rationalists embarked on massive historical research and discover a rationalist Jesus; moralists, a teacher of morals; revolutionaries, a political agitator. Most popular of all is the image of Jesus as the "pale Galilean," gentle Jesus meek and mild, a dewy-eyed wandering wraith of a flower-child *avant la lettre*. Renan's *Vie de Jesus* presents this Jesus, but this christological vision comes into its own especially in the "beautiful soul" of German romanticism and Hegel (Hart 2003, 64–65) and is popular not only in theology and philosophy, but in countless popular paintings and icons.

As Hart points out, Nietzsche understands that his arguments against Christianity are more esthetic than logical, a matter of distaste for the Christ of Christian faith. Strangely, Nietzsche is making common ground with orthodoxy here, for Christianity has long understood that it cannot offer any more fundamental argument for the faith than the form of Christ himself, nothing more basic than the narrative of the gospel (Hart 2003, 116–17). Nietzsche recognizes this and vehemently expresses his distaste for Jesus, but—again occupying common ground with orthodoxy—it is the idol Jesus of German romanticism that he detests.

Nietzsche finds it difficult to fit Jesus into his story of will to power and *ressentiment*. Jesus renounces power, but not out of resentment. What to do with him? Nietzsche makes two key moves, first cutting off Jesus from the church by asserting his utter uniqueness and then arguing that Jesus was decadent and life denying to begin with. Nietzsche's account of Jesus depends heavily on the biblical scholarship of his time, but he is more forthright than most scholars that he is pursuing an imaginative construct of Jesus, rather than what he considers an inaccessible historical Jesus. He attempts to describe the psychology of Jesus, but he does so without much real attention to the Gospels' account of Jesus. With the Gospels no more than a palimpsest, Nietzsche is free to paste together what fragments he likes to make a Jesus useful for his own purposes (Hart 2003, 116–19).

For Nietzsche, the Jesus of the Gospels has no capacity for enmity and therefore cannot be a hero. Instead, he "lived in a sweet delirium, in which a life of eternal love seemed present in each moment, in which all men appeared as equal, the children of God; an inner world of his own creation, one to which he fled principally on account of his excessive sensitivity to touch and abrasion, his morbid dread of reality's sting; his was a child's evangel, an exhortation to simple faith, a devotion to an inner light and an immunity to all concrete realities" (Hart 2003, 119). This Jesus is not Jewish; he is not an apocalyptic prophet; he is not one to drive money changers from the temple. All such sharpness and edginess is a Jewish falsification of the gospel. Nietzsche's Jesus floats through life in a kind of angelic retreat from the world. Nietzsche in fact finds nothing in the Gospels except what is given by liberal Protestantism, and he even repeats the tired liberal Protestant gesture of divorcing Jesus from Paul. Jesus was the first and only Christian, but Paul restores Jewish resentment to Christianity in his interpretation of the cross, in an effort to assert his sacerdotal control of the masses.

That Nietzsche should misread Christ is not surprising, but the ease with which a similar Christology infects the church is alarming. The slightest typological sensitivity should be sufficient to inoculate the church against such sentimental vanities. Second Kings 9–10, where Jehu is depicted as a type of the coming Messiah, provides an important corrective. Second Kings 9 fulfills part of the prophecy first made in 1 Kgs. 19, where Yahweh instructed Elijah to anoint three horseman of the Omride apocalypse: Elisha, Hazael, and Jehu. As noted in the previous chapter, Elisha's ministry is largely concerned with carving out a zone of milk and honey within a land flowing with death and blood, but the prophet's ministry of life is a judgment against the house of Ahab as Yahweh subdivides Israel. Now, Yahweh begins to complete his threat against the house of Ahab. Jehu is aptly named: יהוא means "he is Yah," and he is the son of Jehoshaphat, which means "Yah judges" (2 Kgs. 9:2). It is likely that "Jehu" is a contraction of a longer name designed to emphasize the identity between the actions of God and of his human avenger.[1]

---

1. When he first appears, Jehu is with Joram "guarding Ramoth-gilead" (שמר ברמת גלעד) from the Arameans (2 Kgs. 9:1, 14; cf. 1 Kgs. 22). Apparently, Ramoth-gilead is again in Israel's hands. Ahab dies in battle at Ramoth-gilead, and the plot against his sons begins when Jehu is anointed at Ramoth-gilead.

Jehu's work of vengeance begins in secret, just as much of Elisha's ministry takes place indoors (Elisha heals behind closed doors, remains in a room when others come for help, knows what the king of Aram says in his bedroom). The scene of Jehu entering a house (2 Kgs. 9:6) is reminiscent of the doorway scenes earlier in 1–2 Kings (1 Kgs. 17:19; 2 Kgs. 4:33), and as in those earlier scenes the doorway is an image of birth. Jehu is anointed behind closed doors (9:6–10), but what is whispered in secret is soon proclaimed in the open. Jehu comes out of the house in an "advent," foreshadowing Jesus's arrival in Jerusalem, his challenge to the Ahab-like Herod, and his condemnation of the temple of Jerusalem, no better than a house of Baal. The prophet who comes to Jehu is a "madman" (המשגע) (9:11), but he transfers his madness to Jehu (כי בשגעון ינהג) (9:20).[2] Zeal for the house of Yahweh eats him up (10:16; cf. Ps. 69:9; John 2:17). Like Elijah, Jehu is zealous (2 Kgs. 10:16) for the honor of the God whose name is zealous (Exod. 34:14).

In 1–2 Kings, three main kings are anointed: Solomon the temple builder, Joash of Judah the first great temple reformer, and Jehu the temple destroyer. Jehu is the only king in the history of the north to be anointed (2 Kgs. 9:6) (Wiseman 1993, 218–19), the only "Messiah" among the kings of the north. All three foreshadow the coming Anointed One who, like Jehu, will avenge the blood of the prophets (9:7; cf. Matt. 23:29–36). Further, nowhere else in the Hebrew Bible do subjects lay down a carpet of garments for a king (2 Kgs. 9:13), a scene that will not be reenacted until Jesus's entry into Jerusalem on Palm Sunday (Matt. 21:7–8). Jehu is a figure of Christ, and this suggests too that deliverance from the Omrides is salvation for those faithful Israelites gathered around the life-giving holy man, Elisha. As a "Christ," Jehu is similar to the kings of the Davidic line who destroy idols, but also, more ominously, to Saul (the phrase "flask of oil" [פך־השמן] in 2 Kgs. 9:3 is used elsewhere only at 1 Sam. 10:1) (Wiseman 1993, 219). The allusion to Saul suggests that Jehu's dynasty will not last long.

Jehu's work of destruction is an act of vengeance (2 Kgs. 9:7). Through Jehu, Yahweh avenges the blood of his prophets who perish at the hands of Jezebel. Vengeance is often seen as inherently evil, but according to Paul Christians refuse to take vengeance not because it is evil but because vengeance is God's work (Rom. 12:19). When Christians refrain from vengeance, they "leave room for the wrath of God," as well as for the "governing authorities" empowered as "avengers who bring wrath" (13:4). In taking vengeance, Jehu fills a role analogous to that of Elisha. Elisha fulfills the duties of a kinsman-redeemer by delivering from death and debt, while Jehu plays kinsman-redeemer by avenging the blood of Yahweh's kin, the prophets (Num. 35).

2. The young prophet's flight (9:3) enacts the later flight of Jehoram and Ahaziah before the determined Jehu (9:23, 27). What prophets say sculpts history; what prophets *do* also drives history forward.

Jehu carries out the threat and promise of Deut. 32:43: "Rejoice, O nations, with his people; / for he will avenge the blood of his servants, / and will render vengeance on his adversaries, / and will atone for his land and his people." This text goes beyond talk about vengeance to suggest that Yahweh's vengeance against his adversaries "atones" or "covers" the sins of the land and people of Israel. There are several indications that Jehu's vengeance has an atoning effect. Like a priest, Jehu "fills his hand" (וְיֵהוּא מִלֵּא יָדוֹ) to carry out the sacrifice (2 Kgs. 9:24; cf. 2 Sam. 21), and "fill the hand" is the Hebrew phrase translated "ordain" in Exod. 29 and Lev. 8–9. Jezebel's death is also described in sacrificial terms. She is both the instigator and the symbol of Israel's idolatrous harlotries (2 Kgs. 9:22), and when Jehu arrives, she decides (playfully, perhaps) to play the part, painting her eyes and adorning her head as if to welcome a John (9:30). She calls Jehu "Zimri," alluding to another general who led a coup but lasted only a week on the throne (1 Kgs. 16:8–20). Jehu finds some allies among Jezebel's attendants, who throw her down. She is a feast for dogs, like the harlot of Revelation (19:1–2, 19–21), and is reduced to refuse (2 Kgs. 9:37). Her blood "sprinkles" the wall (וַיִּז מִדָּמָהּ אֶל־הַקִּיר) (9:33), a verb normally used for sprinkling atoning blood on the altar. Having offered his "peace" sacrifice, Jehu goes to eat and drink, celebrating the "supper of the Lamb" now that the harlot is destroyed (Rev. 19:6–10).[3] Jezebel feeds Baal prophets at her table and refuses the food offered by Elijah and Elisha, and so she becomes food for dogs; drunk with the blood of Yahweh's prophets, her blood becomes drink for beasts (Appler 1999). The whole sequence of Jezebel's death follows the order of a sacrificial rite.

Like father, like son: sons who live like Ahab die like Ahab. Joram is killed with an arrow (2 Kgs. 9:24; cf. 1 Kgs. 22:34–35), Ahaziah is wounded and dies in Megiddo (2 Kgs. 9:27). Ahaziah's death also anticipates the later death of Josiah at Megiddo (23:29). The blood of vengeance is shed in the same place as the blood of Naboth (9:25), the innocent Abel whose blood cries from the ground. Jehu is aware of Elijah's prophecy and sees himself as the fulfillment (9:26), just as the first-century assault on Jerusalem fulfills the prophecies of Jesus and avenges the blood of the prophets (Matt. 23:34–36).

These anticipations of the judgment of the harlot in Rev. 18–20 fit with the eschatological resonances of Jehu's actions. Nelson (1987, 200) notes that the story of Jehu's coup includes seven acts of destruction, culminating in the destruction of the temple of Baal:

1. Joram (involves deception)
2. Ahaziah

---

3. This section closes with a reference to the beginning of Ahaziah's reign. It seems misplaced, but this is a bit of black humor, since the narrator tells the story of his death before getting around to telling us that he becomes king: he is *so* doomed. Jehoram has no death notice at all. The last we hear of him, his corpse is being tossed unceremoniously onto the field of Naboth to rot.

3. Jezebel (peace, queen mother)
4. seventy sons of Ahab (involves deception)
5. forty-two brothers of Ahaziah (peace, queen mother)
6. all remaining loyalists in Samaria
7. temple and worshipers of Baal (involves deception)[4]

The sevenfold pattern connects Jehu's work with creation and specifically with Sabbath. Jehu does not come in peace. The question "is it peace?" runs as a leitmotif through the passage (2 Kgs. 9:11, 17–19, 22) and is answered in the negative, but ultimately Jehu brings bring peace and rest through atoning vengeance. Like Gideon (Judg. 8:30), Ahab has seventy sons, a number associated with the Gentile nations (Gen. 10) and at times with Israel as the new human race (Exod. 1:5). The destruction of Ahab's house thus anticipates the eschatological judgment of the world and the judgment passed against all nations in the cross of Jesus (John 12:31). Further, the sequence of slaughter charted above alternates between Judah and Israel: Joram of Israel, Ahaziah of Judah, Jezebel, relatives of Joram, relatives of Ahaziah, and allies of Joram in Samaria. This alternation sets up an expectation of some eighth event in Judah to correspond to the destruction of the house of Baal. Nothing happens during the time of Jehu, but the structure leaves the reader anticipating the destruction of the house of Yahweh in Jerusalem, which has been ignored or plundered by the Davidic kings.

After killing the kings and the queen mother, Jehu controls Ahab's "second city," Jezreel, but to solidify his rule he needs to conquer Samaria. Jehu's conquest is carried out through letters. Writing is often associated with deception in Samuel and Kings (2 Sam. 11–12; 1 Kgs. 21). Like the early modern novels that warn against the perils of novel reading (*Don Quixote*, *Northanger Abbey*), the text of 1–2 Kings cautions against texts. On the surface, the first letter invites the leaders of Samaria to elect a successor to Ahab and defend the capital from Jehu. They take the letter as a threat, aware that they cannot stand against the "meshuga," the madman gripped by divine frenzy. They offer themselves instead as Jehu's servants (2 Kgs. 10:5). The second letter tests their loyalty, beginning with the conditional "if [or, since] you are on my side" (10:6). In Hebrew and in English, "head" can mean either the spheroid at the top of the neck or a leader. Jehu plays on the ambiguity, instructing the elders to bring the "heads" of the men to Jezreel. This might be taken as an invitation to parley, but it might also be taken as an instruction to decapitate Ahab's sons. Jehu retains deniability: "I didn't mean *literal* heads," we can hear him protesting on the evening news. By taking "head" literally, the leaders of

---

4. Walsh (2001, 43–45) notes a cyclical pattern of death that extends into 2 Kgs. 11:

Joram of Israel (9:14–26)	seventy sons of Ahab (10:1–11)	Jehu (10:29–36)
Ahaziah of Judah (9:27–29)	forty-two brothers of Ahaz (10:12–17)	seed of Ahaziah (11:1–3)
Jezebel (9:30–37)	Baal worshipers (10:18–28)	Athaliah (11:4–20)

Samaria remove a considerable obstacle to Jehu's power and demonstrate at the same time that they are Jehu's followers. After they kill seventy of Ahab's house, there is no going back to the house of Ahab.

Jehu has two contrasting encounters on the road to Samaria. Ahaziah's relatives are traveling to pay respects to the king and queen mother (10:13), and Jehu kills them because, though they are from the house of David, they are also members of the house of Ahab. When judgment falls on Ahab's house, it engulfs David's as well. Jehu also meets Jehonadab son of Rechab, otherwise unmentioned in 1–2 Kings. Jeremiah uses the Rechabites as an object lesson for Judah, since the Rechabites follow the Nazirite-like discipline established by their ancestor Jehonadab (Jer. 35). According to the genealogy of 1 Chr. 2, Jehonadab descended from the Kenizzite Caleb and thus is a Gentile presence with Jehu. His father's name, Rechab, puns on the word "chariot" (רכב). While the brothers of Ahaziah oppose Jehu, who is Yahweh's agent, Jehonadab the half-Gentile fights with Jehu, and the son of a chariot gets into his chariot.

When Jehu gets to the capital city of Samaria, he quickly embarks on plans to destroy the temple of Baal. Jehu sets a trap for the worshipers of Baal, no doubt violating the free-exercise clause and demeaning Baal worship through subterfuge. Jehu carries out the same *herem* warfare, the war of utter destruction, against Baal worshipers that he prosecutes against Ahab's house. He follows the example of Joshua by tearing down all the idol shrines in the land, turning the great temple of Baal into a toilet.

The word "right" or "upright" occurs several times in the chapter (2 Kgs. 10:9, 15), culminating in Yahweh's declaration that Jehu is upright in his sight (10:30) (Provan 1995, 216, 218). At every turn, Jehu's actions fulfill the word of Yahweh (9:36–37; 10:10–11, 30), but the last reference is jarring: bloody Jehu fulfills all that is on Yahweh's "heart." This gives a new twist to the idea that David is "a man after God's own heart" and shows that vengeance against the wicked, especially against the wicked who attack Yahweh's prophets, is very dear to Israel's God (Matt. 21:33–46). Further, Jehu accomplishes "all that was in my heart" *through deception*. As in his other dealings with the twisted house of Ahab, Yahweh is twisted with the twisted, the infinitely cunning God.

As zealous as Jehu is in eradicating the worship of Baal, he tolerates the golden calf shrines at Dan and Bethel (2 Kgs. 10:31), and in response Yahweh continues to slice off pieces of Israel, reversing the conquest and settlement of Israel by reducing its boundaries (10:32–33). Yet, Jehu is commended as no other king in the northern kingdom is commended, as one who "did well" and did "what was right in my eyes" (10:30). Jehu compares favorably to David, and because of his faithfulness is promised a dynasty (10:30). He is the great "Christ" figure of the northern kingdom. He is the only king of Israel to reverse the trend toward idolatry, and his zeal provides a model for the great reforming kings of Judah—Joash, Hezekiah, and Josiah.

And beyond: for Jesus too makes his way over a carpet of garments to Jerusalem and immediately goes into the temple to preenact its coming destruction

(Wright 1996a, 490–93). Jesus comes to Jerusalem as an avenger, mad with zeal to defend the honor of his Father against those who defile his Father's house. Jesus is the greater Jehu, for the Jesus of the Gospels and of Revelation is not Jesus meek and mild, not the sweet "beautiful soul" of nineteenth-century fantasy; but rather, the apocalyptic lamb who burns with perfect holy wrath.

2 KINGS 11:1–12:21

In the northern kingdom, the renewal movement led by Elijah and Elisha comes to a climax in the destructive zeal of Jehu, who destroys Ahab's house. Because of the intermarriage between David and Omri, however, Judah needs its own Jehu. Queen Athaliah, who takes the throne in Judah, comes from the house of Ahab, and she has all the political finesse of her mother Jezebel—or Stalin—killing potential rivals as soon as she takes power (2 Kgs. 11:1; cf. 1 Kgs. 18:3–4). She is the antimother who destroys rather than nurtures the royal seed. She is Israel itself, the cannibal-mother who devours her own children and boils kids in mother's milk (cf. 2 Kgs. 6:24–31). Her reign is unprecedented in the southern kingdom, as a ruler outside the line of David sits on David's throne for the first and only time in this history, and the author signals the irregularity by avoiding the standard formulas to open and close her reign (Provan 1995, 222), as if Athaliah were an intrusion into the history of Judah who never reigns at all.

In contrast to the murderous mother Athaliah, Jehosheba ("Yah swears") is a true mother in Israel who defies her own mother, Athaliah (8:18, 25–26; 11:2). She hates her mother for the sake of David's seed and like many women in Scripture uses deception to protect the seed, turning the serpent's subtlety against him (Exod. 2:2; Josh. 2). A new character, Jehoiada, is introduced in 2 Kgs. 11:4, but only in 11:9 is he identified as a priest. He is the first significant priest to appear in 1–2 Kings since the time of Solomon and plays a creative role normally reserved for prophets.[1]

---

1. My student Jenny Jo points out that the "bedroom" scenes in 1–2 Kings frequently include a man, a woman, and a prophet: David, Bathsheba, Nathan; Jeroboam I's son Abijah, Jeroboam I's wife, Ahijah; Ahab, Jezebel, Elijah. In this bedroom scene, the life-giving prophetic role is filled by a life-giving priest.

Priests have taken such a heavy beating in modern philosophy, theology, and sociology that one is tempted to accept a TKO as the better part of valor.[2] Kant's main target in *Religion within the Limits of Reason Alone* was "priest-craft," the "oldest of all fictions" and the source of perverse "ecclesiastical faith" that views religion as a matter of dogma and rites and overwhelms the pure, enlightened religion of ethics (Kant 1960, 15). Though Nietzsche's attack on Christianity was broader, it focused on the dishonesty and nihilism of priests, who were rehabilitated in a Christian context through the teaching and missionary efforts of Paul (Nietzsche 1988, 50, 85–86, 121, 134). Kantian and Nietzschean strands are intertwined in Weber (see Milbank 1990b, 83–92, 94), whose opposition of charismatic prophecy and routinized priestly religion is very much to the detriment of the latter. Modern Old Testament scholarship rests on a similar evaluation of priests and priestly ministry, as post-Reformation anti-Catholic animus is projected back onto ancient Israel. Though occluded in the Old Testament text, the *real* history of Israel's priesthood is one of bitter strife between various self-interested priestly families and between temple priests jealous of their privileges and country Levites struggling for their piece of the sacrificial pie, yet these same priests who dominated and oppressed both Levites and laypeople meekly acquiesced to every liturgical whim of the Davidic kings. As Chesterton said in another connection, any institution displaying so contradictory a set of vices is not just wrong but wrong in a very strange way (1986, 294).

Not least of the problems with this account is the sandy textual foundation on which it is built. Though there are corrupt priests in Israel, some of the most important prophets were priests (Jeremiah, Ezekiel, probably Isaiah), and there were false prophets without number at least from the time of Ahab. Though he performs no miracles, Jehoiada is a man of faith and action as impressive in his way as is Elijah or Elisha. In Judah, where the temple still functions after a fashion, priests rather than prophets remain important. Even so sober a scholar as de Vaux somehow knows that the Zadokite clan of priests that rose to prominence during the early monarchy was "a conservative-minded family, with little liking for innovation which might change their way of life" (1961, 375). Leaving aside the banality of this characterization—who *isn't* resistant to change?—and the pejorative use of "conservative," the more serious problem is that the texts that de Vaux cites (1 Kgs. 15:12–13; 2 Kgs. 18:3–4; 23) simply do not support his conclusion: first, except for the last text, they do not even mention priests; and, second, even assuming that priests are somehow implied, all of these texts describe large-scale programs of liturgical *reform*, hardly what one expects from a "conservative-minded family." True enough, these reforms were directed against idolatry and the worship of the high places, those outback shrines scattered over the land through much of Israel's history. Thus, de

2. The following paragraphs overlap with my more extended discussion in Leithart 2003c, chap. 2.

Vaux would argue, the reforms did not touch the privileges and position of the Zadokites who operated the central sanctuary. Yet if they did not realize that closing down the high places would "change their way of life," one would have to add "short-sighted" to de Vaux's already fulsome description of the Zadokites' limitations.

Similarly, de Vaux's evidence for strife between the Zadokites and the descendents of Abiathar rests mainly on the prophecy against Eli, the priest of Shiloh in the early chapters of 1 Samuel, and some passages from Jeremiah (1961, 375–76). In each case, however, the prophecies are directed against priests guilty of egregious liturgical abuses. To say that the Abiatharites used these charges as pious garb for what amounted to a power play simply unveils de Vaux's implicit assumption that Israel's priests were astonishingly cynical, even to the point of manipulating Torah to gain an advantage over the competition. No doubt there were power struggles among Israel's priests, as there are among Old Testament scholars, but one must, in charity, firmly eschew the suspicion that either profession was or is wholly devoid of virtue.

Kant's ethical religion is in large measure nothing more than a philosophically consistent form of pietism, but for both Kant and Nietzsche priesthood is a peculiarly Jewish institution, and Judaism, as a purely "external" religion, was inimical both to Kant's faith of pure reason and to Nietzsche's celebration of the natural. Paul, the villain of Nietzsche's story, is, after all, a Pharisee. The same animosity toward priestly Judaism is fundamental to critical biblical scholarship as well. Priests, according to this account, are mean and miserly, that is to say, they are the prototypical Jews of anti-Semitic mythology. Wellhausen, whose *Prolegomena to the History of Israel* dominated Old Testament scholarship for more than a century, claims that the Mosaic theocracy of the Pentateuch, which, he argues, was the source for Judaism, deteriorated from the spontaneous and childlike natural religion of early Israel, "estranged from the heart" so that worship was transformed into "a pedagogic instrument of discipline" (1885, 121–67, quotations from 425). Surely Wellhausen and scholars of similar persuasion, by laying hostility to Jewish legalism and ritualism as a cornerstone of modern biblical scholarship, bear some responsibility for planting the seeds that bore their horrible fruit in the Holocaust (Blenkinsopp 1992, 12).

Important as these considerations are for relations of Christians and Jews, they are equally important for the church's conception of itself and the religion that it believes, confesses, proclaims, and practices, for modern theology and biblical scholarship are constituted by the assumption that Christianity is not just different from Judaism, but a different *kind* of religion from that of priest-ridden Israel. Judaism was, for Kant, not a religion at all, but only a "union of a number of people who, since they belonged to a particular stock, formed themselves into a commonwealth under purely political laws, and not into a church" (Kant 1960, 116). A Judaism with "purely political laws"? The mind boggles. Kant's valuation of Judaism depends on his prior assumption that "pure religion" is private and internal, a matter of good will, regardless of how that will is expressed in action or in habit or in community; using a net constructed on this enlightened pattern, it is hardly a surprise that Kant can catch no fish from ancient Israelite religion. And, it unfortunately still needs to be said, Kant's assumption is one that neither Jesus nor Paul would have embraced.

For the author of 1–2 Kings, Jehoiada is a heroic priest, and heroic precisely because he does not grasp for power but helps to reestablish legitimate royal power. Like Jehu, Jehoiada displays shrewdness in organizing the coup. Jehoiada's instructions about the coronation are obscure (2 Kgs. 11:5–9), but the effect is to bring both the temple of Yahweh and the house of Baal (literally called the "house of destruction" in 11:6) under guard during the day of Joash's appearance and coronation. The restoration of David's house requires a new covenant, a complex three-dimensional covenant between the king, the people, and Yahweh (11:17). Further, the old regime is purged through an act of avenging atonement similar to the slaughter perpetrated by Jehu. Athaliah is killed at the horse gate (11:15–16), as her mother was trampled under Jehu's horse, and the institutions of Baal worship that she promotes are eliminated (11:18). Following the covenant cutting on the temple mount, reminiscent of the covenant at Sinai, the renewed people flow out from the temple to purge the land, as Israel streamed across the Jordan to overthrow the shrines and images of the Canaanites. Only after this wholesale iconoclasm, in obedience to the instructions of Deut. 12, does Joash take the throne (2 Kgs. 11:19), and only then do Jerusalem and Judah enter into joy (11:20).

Jehoiada's overthrow of Athaliah completes the destruction of the house of Ahab, and 2 Kgs. 11–12 runs in parallel sequence to 2 Kgs. 9–10:

2 Kings 9–10	2 Kings 11–12
Jehu's secretive coronation (9:1–10)	Joash's secretive coronation (11:4–8)
trumpets announce new king (9:13)	trumpets announce new king (11:14)
shouts of "Jehu is king" (9:13)	shouts of "long live the king" (11:12)
a king cries "treason" (9:23)	a queen cries "treason" (11:14)
Jehu has Jezebel killed (9:30–37)	Jehoiada has Athaliah killed (11:15)
house of Baal destroyed (10:18–28)	house of Baal destroyed (11:18)

Yet, the similarities bring out important contrasts between the two units. Jehu kills all the royal seed in the house of Ahab, but the Lord preserves Joash when Athaliah attempts to kill all the Davidic princes. As often in 1–2 Kings, Yahweh bestows special care and protection on the house of David, his chosen.

Unlike Jehu, whose work is wholly destructive, Joash not only destroys a temple but restores one, the temple in Jerusalem (2 Kgs. 12:4–16). This is a tale of two houses as well as two mothers: the palace is a house of destruction so long as the queen is a Baal worshiper, but life and safety are found in Yahweh's temple. Under Jehoiada's guidance, Joash becomes the first of the great reforming figures of Judah (but see 1 Kgs. 15:9–15), leading a resurrection of the Davidic monarchy after the bloody interregnum of Athaliah. His reign is thus not only a return of political legitimacy, but involves a restoration of pure worship in Judah.

That restoration has been long in coming. After reading the opening chapters of 1–2 Kings, one expects that attention to the temple will be a critical factor throughout the history of Judah. Between 1 Kgs. 15:18 and 2 Kgs. 11:3, however, the temple is not so much as mentioned, and no king pays the least attention to it. After this long hiatus in the story of the temple, the narrator makes it a major theme in the closing half of 2 Kings. This absence of the temple is partly a function of the narrator's attention to the northern kingdom and the ministries of the prophets Elijah and Elisha, but it also displays that the kings of Judah ignored the temple and its ministry. In Judah, the king is responsible to build and maintain Yahweh's house, while priests perform the daily services. Few kings perform this task, preferring instead to plunder the temple for treasure. After Joash, the temple makes a comeback. Hezekiah prays in the temple (2 Kgs. 19:1, 14–19) and Josiah restores the temple (22:3–7). Wicked kings are evaluated in terms of their treatment of Yahweh's house (16:10–18; 21:7–9). When Nebuchadnezzar breaks into Jerusalem, he demolishes the temple and its furnishings (24:13–17).

In restoring the temple, Joash plays the role of a new Moses ("his nurse" in 11:2 is מֵינִקְתּוֹ; cf. Exod. 2:7, 9). Like Moses, he is hidden away and delivered from the murderous plots of a ruler so that he can later lead Judah out in an "exodus" in the seventh year, leading to Sabbath rest. His coronation is a Jubilee, announcing a year of rest and restoration and bringing peace to the city (2 Kgs. 11:20). Like Moses, Joash leads Israel in a restoration of true worship at the sanctuary of God. Joash is also a new Solomon (Nelson 1987, 212): both have a contested coronation, both reign for forty years, both work on the temple, and both coronations are described in similar terms (1 Kgs. 1:38–40; 2 Kgs. 11:9–12). The parallel with Solomon gives additional depth to the designation of Joash as the "king's son" (11:4, 12), which both highlights his legitimacy as an heir of David's throne and suggests that Joash, like Solomon (2 Sam. 7), is a son of the high king, Yahweh. Joash, after all, is raised in the temple, his father's house, and he is surrounded by temple guards during his coronation (2 Kgs. 11:8), as King Yahweh is surrounded by myriads of angels.[3] In keeping with this Solomon typology, the temple remains central throughout these chapters. Joash is hidden in the temple (11:3), and the coronation takes place in the temple (11:17–18), with Joash standing beside the "standing-pillar" (a pun in Hebrew: עֹמֵד עַל־הָעַמּוּד) (11:14), a sign of Joash's role as a "pillar" of the house of Israel (23:3).

Joash comes to the throne in the seventh year, at the age of seven (11:21), the repetition of the sabbatical number hinting that he, like his great predecessor Solomon, will rule a people at rest. Like Solomon, Joash works on the

---

3. The soldiers function like priests who "do guard duty" around Yahweh's royal son (11:7–8) (cf. Milgrom 1970).

temple, his determination evident in the appearance of the word "house" in nearly every verse. The list of craftworkers hired to do temple repairs (2 Kgs. 12:11–12) is similar to the list of Solomon's workers (1 Kgs. 5:13–18; 6:7). Joash and Solomon are both criticized for tolerating "high places" (1 Kgs. 3:2; 2 Kgs. 12:3). Joash not only points back to Solomon but ahead to Josiah and further to the great temple rebuilding efforts of the postexilic community. In the end, Joash's iconoclasm is not sufficiently complete to satisfy Yahweh.

Besides, Joash is no Solomon, or, more precisely, he follows Solomon both in his attention to the temple and in his eventual defection from Yahweh. Joash keeps the ways of Yahweh only so long as Jehoiada guides him (12:2; cf. 2 Chr. 24:2), and while Solomon's wisdom is displayed in his smooth administration of the temple building project, Joash has difficulty getting the priests to do their work (2 Kgs. 12:7). The text gives a great deal of attention to the sources of funding for the temple repair: "silver" (used fourteen times in this chapter), money raised from "sacred things" (12:4), everything donated to the priesthood and temple, including money used to redeem firstborn animals (Exod. 13:1–16), the "levy" that Moses imposed (2 Chr. 24:6; Exod. 30:11–16), donated property and persons (Lev. 27), and freewill offerings (Exod. 35:22, 29; 1 Chr. 29:1–9).[4] Yet, Joash gathers very little. He makes nothing of gold and silver (2 Kgs. 12:13) and thus fails to restore the temple to its pristine glory. The priests are incompetent (12:6–7), and Joash has to search for men to carry out the work (12:15). Something more than mismanagement and incompetence is apparently to blame. Second Kings 12:7 can be translated (woodenly), "Now take no silver from your assessors, because for the breaches of the house you did not give it" (אל־תקחו־כסף מאת מכריכם כי־ל בדק הבית תתנהו). Like many Davidic kings, the priests misuse, perhaps pillage, Yahweh's silver, a serious sacrilege, and one that makes Joash's later plundering of the temple all the more ironic (12:17–18). They are like Hophni and Phinehas, the sons of the priest Eli, who stole the Lord's and the people's portions of the sacrifices and aroused Yahweh's anger against the sanctuary at Shiloh (1 Sam. 2). Jehoiada's system of collecting silver in a locked box is a response to the priests' mismanagement and theft.[5] Joash's workers who take over the project are so faithful they do not have to give an account of their spending. The story of 2 Kgs. 12 thus sharply contrasts grasping priests with faithful workers, anticipating Jesus's dealings with the greedy Jewish leaders of his day.[6]

---

4. The emphasis on gathering material suggests parallels with Moses (who assembles the materials for the tabernacle in Exod. 25) and David (who gathers the raw materials for the temple in 1 Chr. 28:11–19), as well as Solomon.

5. Contrary to the liturgical usages in some churches, this is not a normal way to collect money, but one designed to prevent greedy priests from dipping their fingers in the pie.

6. Priests continue to be funded (12:16) through the income from guilt offerings (אשם) and sin offerings (חטאות) (Lev. 5:14–19; 6:24–30). The latter is unusual, since the Torah makes no provision for a monetary sin offering. Milgrom (1991, 287–88) suggests that this money is collected from the sale of animals (Deut. 14:24–26).

The most striking contrast between Joash and Solomon appears in 2 Kgs. 12:17–18. Solomon prayed that Yahweh would deliver when his people pray toward the temple (1 Kgs. 8), but when threatened by the Arameans, Joash seeks relief by plundering the temple rather than praying toward it. Ironically, Joash plunders the very temple he has spent his reign repairing, a vivid foreshadowing of the later Babylon plundering of the temple. Second Chronicles 24 fills in the picture, showing a Joash who becomes a paranoid Solomon, an Ahab, a Herod (24:15–22). According to Chronicles, Joash ends his reign more like an Omride than a descendant of David, as he kills the prophet Zechariah son of Jehoiada.[7] The latter part of Joash's reign becomes so intolerable that his own people conspire against him and overthrow him. Conspiracies marked the early history of the northern kingdom (1 Kgs. 15:27; 16:9, 16), but Joash is the first king of Judah to fall victim to a conspiracy.

The history of the northern kingdom demonstrates the folly of relying on other gods. Again and again, Elijah and Elisha warned kings and people to turn from their idolatries and seek the Lord; again and again they demonstrated the superiority of Yahweh to all gods, who are no gods. But as the history of 1–2 Kings turns from the northern prophets to give detailed attention to the last of the Davidic kings, the narrator has an equally important, but more subtle point to make. By the time that Judah is facing the Babylonians, it had developed an insane trust in the physical presence of the temple (Jer. 7:4), as if an empty shell of cedar and gold could deliver them from Nebuchadnezzar. Had the people of Judah paid attention to their own history, it would have been clear that they had no grounds for such trust. False worship at the temple of Yahweh is no more potent than the most sincere worship at Bethel or Dan. Joash's purging of the temple did not save even him from later plundering it, and the removal of idols from the house of Yahweh was not sufficient to remove idols from the hearts of the people of God.

Deeper magic was needed, and the prophets assured Israel that the Lord would provide that magic. Israel and Judah would suffer the death of exile, but on the far side of death lay the promise of a new covenant, a covenant that promised purgation of graven images not from the temple but from human heart by the power of the invading Spirit (Ezek. 36:24–27). Temples of stone were no more to be trusted than images of stone; fleshly Israel turned the temple of stone, even the one made after the pattern of the heavenly sanctuary, into yet another idol. The deeper magic required a temple in flesh, a living temple, living in the flesh of Jesus and in the flesh of the church, which is the temple of the Spirit of the living God. When the Lord sends Nebuchadnezzar in his anger to destroy the temple, he is, as he did in the exodus (compare Exod. 12:12 with Josh. 24:14–15), destroying one of Judah's most cherished idols.

---

7. The tragedy is deepened when we consider that Joash and Zechariah had known each other from childhood.

2 KINGS 13:1–25

The Omride dynasty has a long-lasting impact on both the northern and southern kingdoms. Though the two kingdoms are not ruled by a single dynasty, they become twin prostitutes, as Ezek. 23 describes it. As noted above, the twinning of north and south is brought out providentially in the repetition of royal names in the north and south, and through much of 1–2 Kings these parallels emphasize the south's apostasy. Insofar as the south becomes a mirror image of the idolatrous north, Judah is doomed. In 2 Kgs. 13, the mirroring goes the other way round: Yahweh's faithfulness to David's house is magnified by his faithfulness to Israel for the sake of Abraham (13:22–25).

An exodus/conquest typology runs under the surface of 2 Kgs. 13, linking this passage also to incidents in the book of Judges. Judges records a recurring pattern: Israel worships idols, and Yahweh becomes jealously angry; he gives them into the hands of a foreign king, and they cry for help; so Yahweh sends a savior and delivers them, turning them to true worship until the judge dies and the cycle begins again (Judg. 2:6–23). The pattern of Judges is grounded in the foundational exodus pattern: Israel is delivered from Egypt when Yahweh responds to the cries of his people, remembers his covenant, and raises Moses to save. Second Kings 13:1–3 contains several verbal allusions to the exodus: "going out" is a standard term for the exodus itself (ויצאו מתחת יד־ארם) (2 Kgs. 13:5; cf. Gen. 15:14; Exod. 12:41); "savior" translates מושיע (2 Kgs. 13:5),[1] a pun on the name Moses (משה); "tents" is not literal, but reminds us of the wilderness camp of Israel following the exodus; the basis for Yahweh's deliverance is the covenant with the patriarchs (2 Kgs. 13:22–25; Exod. 2:24–25); and the word for "oppression" (לחץ) in 2 Kgs. 13:4 is used in Exod. 3:9 (Davis 2005, 189).

1. Various suggestions are offered for the identity of the savior, but in the immediate context the best answer is Elisha—whose name includes the verb "save" (Hobbs 1985, 167–68).

Beyond these direct verbal echoes, the pattern of exodus is evident. According to 2 Kgs. 13:4, Jehoahaz "became ill" (ויחל יהואחז). The phrase is translated in the New American Standard Bible as "entreated the favor" but it is the normal word in 1–2 Kings for illness (2 Kgs. 1:2). Yahweh "hears" Jehoahaz, even though the text never indicates that Jehoahaz says anything. Apparently, Yahweh responds to Jehoahaz's illness itself and perhaps to the pain caused by it. Yahweh not only "hears" the sickness of the king, but "sees" the oppression of the nation (13:4), just as he saw that Egypt was oppressing Israel (Exod. 3:9). The combination of "hearing" and "seeing" also connects with the temple dedication passage in 1 Kgs. 8–9, where Yahweh promises to attend to the prayers offered toward the temple. The conquest typology is evident in Jehoahaz recovering cities from Aram.

This chapter provides our last glimpse of Elisha. Oddly, the reign of Jehoash is summarized in 2 Kgs. 13:10–13, but in 13:14, after he is buried, he visits Elisha (Cohn 2000, 87), narratively returning to life in a way that anticipates the actual resurrection in 13:20–21. This disturbance in the text's order is yet another indication that the work of prophets cannot be reduced to the chronicled history of Israel, but burst the bounds of time, change, and death. Jehoash honors Elisha as "father" and "chariots and horsemen" (13:14), the same title that Elisha gives to the departing Elijah (2:12). The king acknowledges the prophet as the true source of Israel's military power and its security, the one on whom Yahweh "rides" through the land and who protects a people without sufficient horses and chariots.

Elisha, for his part, assures Jehoash of victory, using two connected signs. The first identifies the arrow as the arrow of victory, aimed at Aram to the east (13:17). It promises victory at Aphek, reversing Israel's defeat there (1 Sam. 4) and completing Ahab's abortive victory (1 Kgs. 20; cf. 2 Kgs. 13:25). Having identified the arrows as the arrows of victory, Elisha instructs Jehoash to pound the arrows on the ground, the dusty "land" of Aram. Israel is reduced to dust (13:7), but Jehoash has the opportunity to reverse the process and grind Aram to powder. Instead of pursuing total victory, Jehoash (like Ahab) stops short. His victory will be inconclusive; like Ahab (1 Kgs. 20), he lacks the zeal to be an enemy to the enemies of Israel. The word "hand" is used repeatedly in the chapter: several times it describes the power of Aram (13:3, 5, 25), but 13:16 uses the word four times to refer to the hand of Jehoash. It is through *his* hand that Israel will be saved, but only so long as his hand is guided by the hand of the prophet.

Throughout his ministry Elisha is a source of life, and he remains a source of life after his death, raising the dead from the grave in the spring of the year (13:20–21), the time of rebirth, during a time when marauding bands of Moabites are harassing Israel. Mesha's revolt is successful (2 Kgs. 3), not only establishing an independent Moab but providing Moab with the power to turn the tables on Israel and invade across the Jordan. Moab's invasions from the east foreshadow the situation just before the exile of Judah (24:2), and the context here suggests that the prophet's grave is a symbol of exile (as in 1 Kgs. 13; cf. Ezek. 37), a parallel reinforced by the use of the verb "throw" in 2 Kgs. 17:20 and 24:20 to describe the exile (Fretheim 1999, 84). Though marauding bands assault Israel and though Judah is thrown into the grave with Israel, there is still hope for resurrection, but only through contact with the prophets who bear the word and presence of God. Even though the prophets die, Israel can be saved by clinging to the prophetic word. If Israel heeds the words of the prophets, even death will not be the end.

Paul is an accurate reader of Israel's history. Israel's law and Israel's kings are incapable of saving it, for however much it might have delighted in the law in the inner self it remains incapable of doing what it desired. In the end, there is only judgment. But what Torah cannot do, weakened as it is through flesh, God does in Jesus, fulfilling his promises to Abraham, Isaac, and Jacob and demonstrating his power and righteousness (Rom. 1:16–17; 8:1–4). The book of Kings has the same concern. The preservation of the northern kingdom under the dynasty of Jehu does not arise from its faithfulness to Torah, for it has been deeply unfaithful. Nor can Jehu's house rely on a promise to David, for the northern kingdom has long since renounced any portion in David. To account for its preservation and (relative) prosperity in the midst of apostasy, the narrator reaches back beyond David and beyond Moses to promises made to the patriarchs (2 Kgs. 13:22–25). Torah, coming four centuries after these promises, does not nullify the promises, just as the failures of Judah do not nullify the promise to David. Even when Torah is abandoned wholesale, the covenant Lord remains faithful to his promises and does not cast Israel aside. Even in the midst of apostasy, Yahweh is determined to keep his word. For those who trust him, the sentence of death is not final, and the grave will one day give up its dead.

This chapter gives us considerable insight into the situation of post-Reformation Christendom. The book of Kings as a whole makes it clear that there is good and bad union, good and bad division. The Omride dynasty, particularly under Ahab, attempts to reunite Israel and Judah as a Baalist people ruled by an Omride king. It almost works, as Jehoshaphat foolishly allows his son to marry the daughter of Ahab, leaving Athaliah in charge of Judah after Jehu wipes out the Omrides in the north (including the Davidic king Ahaziah). There are hints too (see the commentary on 2 Kgs. 14:1–29) that the dynasty of Jehu gains the upper hand over Judah and reunites the kingdom after a fashion for a couple of generations. There are faithful unions as well: as we shall see below, both Hezekiah and Josiah gather people from Israel and Judah to celebrate Passover, reuniting Israel at the temple.

Yet, the most interesting and relevant portions of 1–2 Kings are those having to do with the status of each nation during the period of the divided kingdom, for the narrator makes it clear that Israel and Judah, together and separately, remain the people of God throughout the period of idolatry, political upheaval, and division. The prophet Shemaiah instructs Rehoboam not to attack his "brothers" in the north (1 Kgs. 12:24), and even after the Omrides had led Israel into Baal worship and filled the land with the blood of prophets, Yahweh continued to consider Israel his people (2 Kgs. 13:22–25; 14:25–26). At the very least, 2 Kings assumes an actual division within the people of God. It is not as if Israel ceased to be the covenant people of God when it separated from the Davidic kingdom, or as if Yahweh rejected Judah when it ignored the temple and worshiped at high places. Judah could not smugly conclude that it alone was the holy nation, the people of Abraham, or that God had written off the idolatrous rebels to the north. Protestants often soften the reality of ecclesiastical division by suggesting that the church is not really divided. The church is intact—among Protestants—while something more or less church-like, but something that is *not* the church, exists in Roman Catholicism and Orthodoxy. Even after Vatican II, Catholics sometimes view Protestants, *mutatis mutandis*, in a similar way. The book of Kings does not leave this comforting option, but shows that it is possible for an officially idolatrous nation to be the covenant people of God. The book of Kings raises the disturbing possibility that Christ himself might be divided (1 Cor. 1:13).

This is an ecclesiology *sola gratia*. As before, Yahweh intervenes to save Israel without any show of repentance from the king or the people. Jehoahaz is an evil king (2 Kgs. 13:2) and the people continue to worship golden calves, and as a result his military power is drastically reduced (13:7). Israel is dust on the threshing floor, an image that evokes the curse of Gen. 3:14, where death is described as a return to dust, as well as the various descriptions of the wicked who are like chaff in the wind (Ps. 1). Yet, Yahweh sends a savior who raises Israel from the dust, purely out of his pity for Israel's oppression. Israel remains, supported only by the grace of God. Israel's history becomes thus a figure of *sola gratia*, and we may hope that the church's division and reunion is likewise destined to be a fulfillment of that figure, which has been figured by Jesus.

Yet, this chapter also provides a more sobering view of Israel's history. For a third of his long story, the narrator of 1–2 Kings focuses on the ministries of Elijah and Elisha (1 Kgs. 17–2 Kgs. 13). These prophets carry out successful ministries of renewal, calling Israel back to worship of Yahweh, forming communities of sons of the prophets, anointing Jehu to destroy the house of Ahab, and ministering life to many. Even in his death, Elisha continues to minister life, but after 2 Kgs. 13 Elisha is gone, and his memory vanishes instantly (in contrast to 2 Kgs. 8). Nor is there any mention of the "sons of the prophets" after one of them anoints Jehu (9:1). Elijah provides food for a widow and raises her son from the dead; he leads Israel to renew covenant on Carmel; he accuses Israel before the Lord; he ascends in a whirlwind to heaven. Elisha, acting in the power of the spirit of Elijah, gives food and drink, raises a boy from the dead, cleanses a leper, played the kinsman-redeemer to the faithful within Israel. And what was the long-term result of this burst of miraculous activity? Almost nil. After a long and wild ride with the prophets, the narrator turns back to the dry-as-dust chronicle, chanting out the irreversible march toward the now-inevitable disaster of exile.

In fact, prophetic ministry almost disappears from the later history of the monarchy. We know from the prophetic books of the Old Testament that the later monarchy witnessed a boom in prophetic activity, but little of this is evident in 2 Kings. The narrator makes generic references to the prophets ignored by the people and kings (17:13; 24:2), and only a handful of prophets are named: Jonah is mentioned in passing (14:25), Isaiah delivers prophecies to Hezekiah (2 Kgs. 18–20) but plays a supporting role to the king, and Josiah consults with Huldah the prophetess after he finds the book of the law in the temple (22:14–20). But as Israel and Judah slouch toward exile, the prophets withdraw from the stage.

Prophetic ministry is yet another of the failed mechanisms for the fulfillment of the promise to Abraham and ends up on the ash heap along with the temple, kingly wisdom, and Torah. The prophets came closest of all, because they were living temples who radiated the life of Yahweh. Elisha gave life from the grave, but—and this is critical—his bones *remained* there. Clinging to the prophet is the way of life, but what happens to that life when the prophet dies and stays dead? Israel will not be saved by any ordinary prophet or by any extraordinary one. Israel needs a prophet who would give life on the other side of the grave by triumphing, once for all, over the grave.

2 KINGS 14:1–29

According to Prov. 1:6, the book of Proverbs is written to give wisdom so as to "understand a proverb and a figure, / the words of the wise and their riddles." The four terms used designate four types of wisdom sayings, and of these the "proverb" (מָשָׁל) is particularly important. In contemporary English usage, a proverb is a pithy summary of common sense or experience, but the Hebrew word has a much more extensive usage. Ezekiel 17 records a parable about an eagle that snips off the top of a cedar tree in order to plant it in other soil, and the parable is introduced as a חִידָה ("riddle") and as a מָשָׁל ("proverb"). Ezekiel 24:3 uses מָשָׁל to describe an allegory in which the besieged city is depicted as a boiling pot full of flesh. מָשָׁל, in short, can mean not only "proverb" in our modern sense, but also "parable" and even "allegory," narrative forms that are indistinguishable in the Hebrew Bible.

Second Kings 14 includes a מָשָׁל told by Jehoash king of Israel (14:9–10), and the chapter as a whole, as well as many other sections of 1–2 Kings, functions as a parable and allegory, designed first of all for the instruction of the original exilic readers and more generally for the instruction of future generations of Israel and of the new Israel. The author of 1–2 Kings opens his mouth with "dark sayings" (Ps. 78:2) in recounting things of old. In characterizing 1–2 Kings as parable, I do not mean to raise doubts about its historical accuracy, but to suggest that the author is concerned to record the past in a parabolic fashion that would be edifying for future readers.

Chronology provides one illustration of the parabolic character of 1–2 Kings. Providing a coherent chronology of the divided kingdom based on the numbers provided by 1–2 Kings has proven a monumental scholarly endeavor. Thiele, who produced the most complete treatment of the chronology of 1–2 Kings, laments that the book's chronological details resist harmonization (1983, 35–36), but his own work has not been universally convincing (Jordan

1990c). The project of harmonizing the data of 1–2 Kings can, like efforts to harmonize the Gospels, obscure the literary and theological significance of particular text. In the Gospels, divergent accounts offer clues to the evangelists' theological agendas, and confusing data in the chronology of 1–2 Kings plays a similar role. A historical/chronological solution to these difficulties is certainly possible, and striving to account for the data is commendable, since it takes seriously the evident historical interests of the author. But this should not obscure the point that the chronology is confusing and gapped because the history is confusing and gapped. The times are out of joint, and, suitably, so is the chronology offered by the text.

Second Kings 14 offers several examples of this parabolic or allegorical style. As Israel begins to wind to a close, for example, history begins to repeat itself. After the reign of Solomon, the kingdom was divided in two, Jeroboam I established a separate kingdom, Rehoboam planned an attack but refrained because of a prophet, and Shishak of Egypt plundered the temple. As noted in the commentary on 2 Kgs. 11:1–12:21, Joash was a new Solomon, which, if the pattern holds, makes his son Amaziah a new Rehoboam. The pattern holds: like Solomon's son (1 Kgs. 12:21–24), Amaziah goes to fight in the north and a prophet intervenes, but unlike Rehoboam, Amaziah refuses to hear the prophet and is defeated by the northern King Jehoash. In retaliation, Jehoash plunders the temple and breaks down the walls of the city of Jerusalem (2 Kgs. 14:13–14), as Shishak did during the reign of Rehoboam (1 Kgs. 14:25–28). Idolatrous Judah ultimately returns to where it began.

The parallels between beginning and end are not confined to Judah. By the end of the chapter, another Jeroboam is in Israel, and the following chapters point to a providential chronological and historical symmetry between the beginning of the northern kingdom and its closing decades:

A   Jeroboam I
  B   seven kings
    C   seventh king: Ahab
      D   Jehu (destroys Ahab's house)
A′ Jeroboam II
  B′ seven kings
    C′ seventh king: Hoshea
      D′ Assyrian invasion

The reign of Jeroboam II begins the countdown to the end of Israel, as the reign of Jeroboam I initiates the separate history of Israel.

The parabolic character of 2 Kgs. 14, though, is most evident in the account of the war between Israel and Judah that takes up the major portion of the chapter. Amaziah is a good king, but he is good as Joash was good and not as David was good (14:3). The comparison with Joash not only points to his failure in connection with high places (14:4; cf. 12:3), but also to the undignified and unrighteous end of his reign (14:17–22). Second Kings 14:5–6 illustrates the righteousness of Amaziah, who follows Torah in taking vengeance against the men who conspire against his father and not against their sons (Deut. 24:16). Like David (2 Sam. 8:13–14), he fights and defeats Edomites and Arameans. Yet Amaziah, unlike David, becomes proud and acts foolishly.

According to Deut. 28:7, those who keep covenant can expect victory in battle. Amaziah does right (2 Kgs. 14:3), while Jehoash does evil (13:11), yet when the two face each other in battle, evil defeats righteousness. Amaziah is a wise king who fears Yahweh, yet Jehoash is the one who tells a wisdom parable and gives sound counsel to his southern counterpart, warning that those who exalt themselves are debased (14:10). This chapter shows the same complexity of rewards and punishments that we find in other wisdom literature, most notably in Job and Ecclesiastes. Jesus was not the first to deny a one-to-one relation between righteousness and success (John 9:1–3). This is a constant theme of Scripture, and certainly by this point in 1–2 Kings, a reader will realize that God is not mechanical or predictable. Throughout the narrative, Yahweh has shown that he is free to show mercy where he pleases. He spares Ahab's kingdom for a generation when Ahab repents, he extends life to Gentiles through the prophets Elijah and Elisha, he preserves and saves Israel despite its persistent idolatries. History does not falsify the promises of Deut. 28, but it does show the free sovereignty of Yahweh, especially his freedom to show mercy.

"Let's face each other" (נתראה פנים) (2 Kgs. 14:8) could be a challenge to battle or an invitation to conference. In either case, it includes an implicit claim to equality. Equals stand face to face, while a subordinate always keeps his or her face low before a superior. In his parable, Jehoash denies the symmetry by comparing himself and his kingdom to the mighty, immovable cedar and Amaziah to a useless, dangerous, cursed (Gen. 3:17) thornbush. Amaziah can no more "face" Jehoash than a thornbush can face a cedar. Jehoash is likely alluding to Judg. 9, implying that Amaziah is an Abimelech, violent and doomed.

The reference to marriage in the parable (תנה־את־בתך לבני לאשה) (2 Kgs. 14:9) is surprising. Perhaps the king's "daughter" is his capital city or his land. If so, Amaziah challenges Jehoash to a combat that will determine the "husband" who will "marry" the land. Amaziah makes a Rehoboam-like bid to reunite the kingdom by force. Jehoash's parable introduces a third party, a beast of the field from Lebanon (14:9). In Hebrew animal symbolism, domesticated animals (oxen, sheep, goats) are analogous to Israel, the people "domesticated" at Yahweh's house and available for sacrifice. Beasts of the field, whether predators or not, represent Gentiles who are not near the house of God. Jehoash thus warns that Gentiles will soon come to trample the thornbush of Judah.

Amaziah pays no heed and proudly continues his preparations for battle. Amaziah fights for honor in a war for which he is ill prepared and from which he can gain little. The two kings "face" each other (14:11), but this leads to a "loss of face" for Amaziah, and the result is an exile for Judah, anticipating the exile of Judah in Babylon. King Amaziah is captured by Jehoash, as Jehoiachin will later be captured by Nebuchadnezzar, and Jehoash continues to the capital to do in part what Nebuchadnezzar will later do more fully—breaking down the wall, plundering the temple and palace, and taking hostages back to Samaria. This proleptic exile of Judah is fittingly carried out by Israel, ironically enough, since it was by following the example of Israel that Judah turned from the way of Yahweh in the first place.

Second Kings 14:15–16 seems out of place.[1] Jehoash's death is recounted twice (13:13; 14:15–16), and the second death notice is placed so that it appears to close the reign of Amaziah rather than that of Jehoash (14:1–2). Perhaps this highlights the contrast between the two kings; Jehoash, who counsels against war, is buried peacefully with the other kings, while violent Amaziah dies a victim of conspiracy. The placement of the death notice also indicates that Amaziah remains subordinate to Jehoash throughout the rest of his reign. There is, after all, no hint that Amaziah returns from his "exile," in spite of his living on for fifteen years after Jehoash dies (14:17). Yet, he is in Jerusalem at his death (14:19). The best resolution to this data is that Amaziah remains a vassal to Jehoash after the battle of Beth-shemesh. His bid to face Amaziah ends with him bowing his face to his rival, the tall cedar of Israel. For more than half his reign, Amaziah is under the hand of Israel.

The conclusion that the kingdom is reunited under Jehu's dynasty is supported by several details in the reign of Jeroboam II. According to 14:25, the borders of Israel extend from Hamath in the north to the Sea of the Arabah in the south, and this southern boundary is far into Judah's territory. Besides, the description of Israel extending from Hamath to Arabah echoes the ideal boundaries of the original united kingdom (1 Kgs. 8:65). Further, 2 Kgs. 14:28 might be translated, "he recovered Damascus and Hamath to Judah in Israel" (הֵשִׁיב אֶת־דַּמֶּשֶׂק וְאֶת־חֲמָת לִיהוּדָה בְּיִשְׂרָאֵל), a difficult verse that hints that Jeroboam II recovers territory for Judah, which is considered a subdivision of Israel ("in Israel"). It is a neat irony that the second Jeroboam presides over a (semi)united kingdom. The text subtly indicates that Amaziah's hope for reuniting the kingdom is realized, but with Amaziah's opponent Jehoash and his son in charge. As at the end of 1–2 Kings, the narrator dates the time of Judah with reference to kings other than Judah's own, in this case, by the time of Jehoash. In another symbolic use of chronology, the narrator indicates that Judah loses control of its history. At the same time, this conclusion reinforces the tropological import of the narrative. It is not merely that Amaziah is abased when he exalts himself; with divinely precise poetic justice, he is abased before the very same king against whom he exalted himself.

As in the reign of Jehoahaz (13:22–25), the revival of Israel's fortunes under Jeroboam II does not result from any fundamental change in the religious orientation of the northern kingdom. Jeroboam II continues the sins of his

---

1. The following paragraphs follow the argument of Provan 1995, 236–38.

namesake (14:24), and during his reign Jonah the prophet heads to Nineveh to preserve that city so the Assyrians can later destroy Israel (14:25; Jonah 1, 3). Israel's fortunes are restored, once again, solely because of Yahweh's infinite compassion. But he will not overlook apostasy forever.

Davis suggests that 2 Kgs. 13–14 is organized concentrically, tracing the revival of the northern kingdom and the dynasty of Jehu from its brush with dusty death to its restoration under Jeroboam II (2005, 214):

A Jehoahaz's reign: Israel weak (13:1–7)
   B double obituaries (13:8–13)
      C Elisha's death (13:14–21)
      C′ successes of Jehoash (13:22–14:14)
   B′ double obituaries (14:15–22)
A′ Jeroboam II's restoration of Israel (14:23–29)

This arrangement highlights the effect of the prophet's death. Elisha's dead bones give life to the corpse thrown into his grave, and as soon as Elisha dies Israel's fortunes begin to change. Ultimately, this points to a wisdom deeper than that communicated in 1–2 Kings, the wisdom that comes with the gospel, for Israel will someday be renewed by the death, and the resurrection, of a greater prophet.

2 KINGS 15:1–16:20

Assyria pops up from nowhere in the narrative, threatening to turn Israel into a tributary power (2 Kgs. 15:19), and like the prophets is a manifestation of the hidden working of Yahweh (1 Kgs. 17:1). From 2 Kgs. 15:19 to the end of the book, Assyria is mentioned forty-eight times (twelve times four), taking the place of Aram as the principal threat to the northern kingdom (Arameans are mentioned briefly in 24:2, but essentially disappear after 2 Kgs. 16). Babylon initially comes into the story in connection with the Assyrian conquest (17:24), but takes on a high profile in 2 Kgs. 24–25, where it is mentioned twenty-six times, with an additional eight references to "Chaldeans." Egypt, which disappears from the text after the early history of the divided kingdom, returns as a tempting ally for Israel and Judah as it struggles against the rising empires to the east (17:4).[1] With these explicit references to imperial powers comes the vocabulary of servitude (17:3; 24:1), capture (17:6; 18:10; 25:6), imprisonment (17:4; 25:27, 29), tribute (17:3–4), and rebellion (18:7, 20; 24:1, 20).

Kings in this imperial situation are assessed as much by their response to the Gentile rulers whom Yahweh raises up as by their response to Yahweh. Israel's kings respond with traditional political efforts, bribing or resisting as opportunity allows. Menahem buys off Pul to protect Israel (15:19–20), but during the reign of Pekah the Assyrians return to cut a large swath of Israel's territory in the north and to capture Israelites for exile (15:29). Hoshea, who overthrows Pekah (15:30), then rebels against the Assyrians by forming an

---

1. All told, Egypt is mentioned forty times in 1–2 Kings, no doubt a significant number. Of these, twenty-five references appear in 1 Kgs. 1–14, and the remainder in 2 Kgs. 17–25. Intriguingly, Egypt is mentioned twelve times in connection with the exodus (1 Kgs. 6:1; 8:9, 16, 21, 51, 53; 9:9; 12:28; 2 Kgs. 17:7 [twice], 36; 21:15), the last of which is virtually a threat that the exodus of the twelve tribes will be reversed because of the sins of Manasseh.

alliance with Egypt (17:4), and this conspiracy provokes Assyria's punitive destruction of Samaria in 722 BC.[2]

Contemporary political debates about empire have inspired historians to produce revisionist accounts of American history. Conservative Bacevich (2004) critiques American imperialism and militarism, and similarly Anderson and Clayton (2005) suggest that empire is not a new phenomenon in American life but the very essence of America's history of expansion. Theologians have also entered the discussion, and theological evaluations of empire are almost uniformly negative. Cavanaugh's suspicion of the nation-state extends further to empire, and he describes globalization as a form of "false catholicity" (2002). O'Donovan discovers a "developing critique of empire" at the time of Israel's exile, a critique rooted in the story of the tower of Babel (Gen. 11):

> The rule of Yhwh was conceived internationally; it secured the relations of the nations and directed them towards peace. But at the international level there was to be no unitary mediator. Israel never entertained the apologia for empire which we find developing in patristic and medieval sources, that the rule of a single world-power represented and mediated the universal rule of Yhwh as high-god. Yhwh's world order was plurally constituted. World-empire was a bestial deformation. It was in the providential disposition of events that Yhwh's rule was seen; and it was mediated only through the authority of prophets and the prophetic people. (O'Donovan 1996, 72)

O'Donovan suggests that the Bible endorses an international order of law rather than of government (1996, 72).

O'Donovan's polarization of "unitary world empire" and a plurality of apparently independent nations is historically naïve, in that most modern nations, including O'Donovan's own, are products of imperial conquest of one sort or another. Scottish and Irish nationalists hardly consider Britain an example of plural government; Italy is the creation of Mazzini and Garibaldi; and the revisionist imperialist histories of the United States, however ideologically driven, capture important features of American political history. On what grounds, then, does O'Donovan consider Britain legitimate but a larger world empire illegitimate? The notion that international order can be governed by law rather than by institutional structures is also naïve. As O'Donovan knows, law requires

---

2. Through several chapters, the author of 1–2 Kings emphasizes Yahweh's faithfulness and mercy to the northern kingdom. He sends prophets to the Omride kings and gives Jehu four generations. Once Yahweh starts moving against the dynasty of Jehu, however, he moves rapidly. Jeroboam II reigns forty-one years over a large territory (2 Kgs. 14:23), but his reign is followed by a succession of comparatively brief reigns: Zechariah (six months; 15:8), Shallum (one month; 15:13), Menahem (ten years; 15:17), Pekahiah (two years; 15:23). Pekah's twenty-year reign (15:27) breaks the pattern, but the time between Jeroboam II and Pekah is a bit over a decade, and during that time there are four kings. The chronology of the period is full of difficulties, a sign, as noted in the previous chapter, that the times are out of joint. Within a lifetime, Israel falls from the comparative glories of a united kingdom under Jeroboam II into the pit of exile.

enforcement, and, more theologically, the notion of a government of laws, not humans, sits oddly as a Christian vision of personalism in government.

For its part, Scripture nowhere condemns empire as such. Israel does not seek world domination, but Moabites, Philistines, Edomites, and Hittites would not have viewed Israel as a nonimperial power. Solomon rules from the Euphrates to the Sea, in fulfillment of Yahweh's promises to Abraham, and this minor empire is the result of his father's violent conquests in the Transjordan. As Judah's monarchy is overthrown, Daniel sees in vision a sequence of empires established by Yahweh to govern the world until the coming of the Son of Man (Dan. 2; 7), and Nebuchadnezzar, Cyrus, and Darius are presented as pious Gentiles who favor wise Jews like Daniel. Jeremiah describes Nebuchadnezzar as a new Adam to whom Yahweh has given humans and beasts on the face of the earth (Jer. 27:5–6), and even though Paul's announcement of the lordship of Christ contained a challenge to the claims of the Roman emperors, he shrewdly deployed his rights as a Roman citizen, traveled on Roman roads, and cheerfully went on a missionary journey to Rome at imperial expense.

Of course, we cannot simply apply these proimperial texts to the current American or, more broadly, capitalist, global empire. We have no Jeremiah to inform us that the American president is the new Adam for the twenty-first century, nor a Daniel to tell us which ruler is the head of gold and which the feet of iron. Yet, these biblical texts undermine a theological assault on empire as such, and they point at least to the *possibility* that the Father of Jesus has established a global American empire as a political means for advancing his purposes.

At the same time, O'Donovan is correct to suggest that the Bible does critique empire and the idolatrous hubris that often drives imperialism, and Cavanaugh is correct that a secular global order is the whorish replica of the Catholic church. Isaiah reminds the Assyrians that they conquer only as the instrument of Yahweh's wrath, warning them not to be a boasting ax (Isa. 10), and Yahweh assures Habakkuk that the Chaldeans will not get away with their harsh treatment of Judah (Hab. 2–3). Babel is certainly not the model for the kingdom of God, but its parody.

The book of Kings is fairly neutral toward empire as such, but the events of 2 Kgs. 15–16 show the temptations that attend the rise of empire, as the narrator reveals how Israel's political and liturgical instability is intensified by pressure from the emerging Assyrian Empire. Assyria's presence to the east destabilizes the northern kingdom, as various kings scramble either to bribe Assyria or to organize doomed anti-Assyrian coalitions. In the south, Assyrian expansion is the occasion for liturgical innovations as well as political upheaval.[3] During the reign of wicked Ahaz, Judah moves closer to Israelite

3. The consensus opinion today is that Assyria does not impose religious uniformity on the peoples it conquers. According to this view, the Assyrian alliance is the occasion for Ahaz's innovations in worship, but he is not forced to adopt pagan worship (Davis 2005, 231–32).

and Gentile idolatry, as Ahaz blindly jumps onboard the ship of Israel (16:3) just as it begins to sink.

The effects of Assyrian expansion are evident in the rapid pace and tumultuous events of the narrative. For superficial readers, 1–2 Kings appears to be nothing more than an endless series of brief and boring accounts, but only two sections employ this sort of rapid-fire chronicle style: 1 Kgs. 15–16 and 2 Kgs. 14–16. These sections share several features besides style. In both sections, the rapid-fire style matches the rapid pace of events, as kings rise and reign and fall in quick succession, both sequences begin with a Jeroboam, and each, as noted in the commentary on 2 Kgs. 14:1–29, summarizes the reigns of seven kings before there is a significant break in the narrative. Both sections also record a plethora of conspiracies, coups, and palace revolutions. Few kings die peacefully, and few are buried in the capital city:

1 Kings 15–16	2 Kings 14–16
Nadab overthrown by Baasha	Zechariah overthrown by Shallum
Elah overthrown by Zimri	Shallum overthrown by Menahem
Zimri overthrown by Omri	Pekahiah overthrown by Pekah
(Ahab's house overthrown by Jehu)	Pekah overthrown by Hoshea

In the center of these two sequences are accounts of the Omrides and successors of Jehu, the only genuine dynasties in the north. Israel's history thus has a generally concentric structure:

A   Jeroboam I plus six more kings; rapid change leads to Ahab
  B   Ahab's family
  B′ Jehu and his dynasty
A′ Jeroboam II plus six more kings; rapid change leads to exile

Second Kings 15:32–16:20 recounts the reigns of two kings from Judah, something of an intrusion into a section mainly concerned with Israel, but this too has its parallel in 1 Kgs. 14–16. In the midst of the account of the history of Israel between Jeroboam I and Ahab in 1 Kgs. 15–16, the writer includes a lengthy account of the reign of Asa (15:9–24), just as in the matching section of 2 Kings he includes the reign of Ahaz. Though Asa is a reforming king and Ahaz an idolater, in certain respects their reigns are similar: both are threatened by Israel, and both seek help from a Gentile power by paying them money pilfered from the temple (1 Kgs. 15:16–22; 2 Kgs. 16:5–9). Asa encourages Aram's first attacks on Israel, and Ahaz directly pays Assyria to attack the northern kingdom. The threat of imperial conquest intensifies the hostility of Israel and Judah, tempting siblings to plot against each other, using Gentiles as their mercenaries.

Second Kings 16:18 contradicts this, however, as it emphasizes that Ahaz introduced various liturgical changes "because of the king of Assyria."

Second Kings 16 is organized chiastically:

A formulaic introduction (16:1–4)
  B threat to Jerusalem and bribe of Tiglath-pileser (16:5–9)
    C state visit to Damascus (16:10–11: altar)
      D Ahaz ministers at the altar (16:12–14)
    C′ continuing worship at the altar (16:15–16)
  B′ tribute to Tiglath-pileser and plunder of temple (16:17–18)
A′ summary (16:19–20)

By centering on Ahaz's interest in the altar of Damascus, the narrator underscores one dimension of the typology of this passage. First Kings shows Solomon and Jeroboam I at altars (1 Kgs. 8; 12:32–33; cf. Davis 2005, 232), and when Ahaz stands before the altar from Damascus, he is another Jeroboam, setting up an alternative worship to that of Solomon's temple. Judah again repeats the history of Israel and is suitably doomed as a result.

The evaluation of Ahaz is more severe than for any king of Judah other than Manasseh. He follows the ways of Israel's kings rather than David. Ahaziah of Judah does the same (2 Kgs. 8:27), but he has the "excuse" of being part of Ahab's family. Ahaz has no such excuse. He goes beyond imitating Israel and begins pursuing the customs of the nations that Israel originally displaced (16:3). The phrase "passing through the fire" is often taken as a reference to human sacrifice, a perverse anticipation of the cross of Jesus (Ezek. 16:20–21). "Abomination" (תעבות) (2 Kgs. 16:3) is specifically a liturgical abuse that defiles the land and causes it to expel the inhabitants (Jordan 1991). The writer emphasizes that worship is conducted "under every green tree" (16:4; cf. 1 Kgs. 14:23). Literally, shrines are located under shrines, and the phrase suggests a (false) Edenic setting for worship. Under Solomon, Judah and Israel rejoice under their vines and fig trees, but under Ahaz, Judah reverts to a Canaanite situation, with idolatrous shrines sprinkled throughout the land. When Judah begins worshiping like Canaanites, can exile be far off?

Israel and Aram, allied against Assyria, threaten Ahaz from the north (Isa. 7), and Pekah is able to capture a town of Judah (2 Kgs. 16:6), driving the inhabitants into a miniexile. Instead of turning in prayer to the temple, Ahaz plunders it as well as the palace and declares himself a covenant vassal, a "son and servant," of Assyria (16:7), in order to get help from Tiglath-pileser. Assyria attacks from the north and takes Damascus and the Arameans into exile. The pressure of empire leads both Israel and Judah into compromising alliances with Gentiles: Israel allies with Aram, its traditional enemy, while Judah allies with the power of the moment, Assyria. The sons of God "marry" the daughters of men (Gen. 6:1–4), and soon a flood of Gentiles will sweep both Judah and Israel into exile (Gen. 6–9).

Ahaz visits Tiglath-pileser at Damascus, perhaps to seal their alliance, and there Ahaz's alliance with Gentile imperialists goes beyond the political (2 Kgs.

16:10). He spies an attractive altar and sends the blueprints back to Jerusalem. The word for "model" is תבנית, used elsewhere to describe the heavenly prototypes for Israel's sanctuaries (Exod. 25:9, 40). In place of the heavenly תבנית, Ahaz follows a Gentile model. Ahaz puts himself in the place of Yahweh or Yahweh's prophet, instructing his priest[4] like a sacred architect to do "according to all King Ahaz sent from Damascus" (2 Kgs. 16:11), a perversion of the demand to do "according to all that Yahweh had commanded" (Exod. 40:16). The establishment of regular sacrifice at the altar parodies the initiation of Israel's tabernacle worship (Exod. 29; Lev. 8–9), and like Solomon at Yahweh's temple, Ahaz dedicates his new sanctuary with sacrifice (2 Kgs. 16:12–13). Meanwhile, Yahweh's altar, made in conformity to the heavenly pattern is put to the side (16:15), used only for consultations (Deut. 18:9–13).

Ahaz sends regular tribute to Assyria, but can only afford it by dismantling the temple. Yet he dismantles and rearranges the temple far more than is necessary to stay in the good graces of Assyria. Though he sends no bronze to Assyria, he removes a number of bronze items from the temple (Davis 2005, 233–34), and this implies that he changes the temple décor simply to innovate. He takes down the bronze sea from the backs of the twelve bulls and dismantles the water chariots (1 Kgs. 7:27–39), symbolically interrupting the flow of water from the temple to the nations. He cuts off the cherubim-adorned panels, as the Babylonians will later cut apart the monumental pillars, Jachin and Boaz. Removing the cherubim symbolically removes the guardians and protectors of the Lord's house: in his zeal to buy protection or favor from Assyria, Ahaz ironically makes himself more vulnerable than ever. Ahaz removes the covered walk and the special temple entry for the king (2 Kgs. 16:18), a sign of a diminished prominence for the Davidic king and a symbol of the severence between Yaweh and Israel's king. Israel, called to be the nation of twelve bulls that holds up the firmament, the nation where Yahweh places a sea of life-giving heavenly water, the nation that bears the sea of Gentiles on its back, is becoming just one more nation among others. The more it resembles the Gentiles, the less reason it has for continuing to exist. By the time the Babylonians arrive, there is not much left to take. Judah has already stripped itself of nearly every visible sign that it is Yahweh's chosen.

That Ahaz does not need the bronze as tribute money perhaps suggests that he is self-conscious about the symbolism of the changes he makes. An early liberal, he finds the temple arrangements pompous, embodying as they do the implicit claim to Israel's uniqueness and centrality among the nations. Even if Tiglath-pileser did not instruct Ahaz to make these changes, they are carried out under the pressure of empire. Empires are, among other things, political and transportation frameworks for trade, and trade is a means for cross-cultural contact. So long as one lives in the same village for a lifetime and has contact with only members of one's own tribe, one's beliefs and practices seem as natural

---

4. Again we have a rare appearance of a priest (cf. 2 Kgs. 11), but Uriah is no Jehoiada.

as one's skin color. As empires push together peoples of various beliefs and practices, one is confronted with what Peter Berger (1979) calls the "heretical imperative," the need to choose, and the recognition that beliefs and practices are chosen rather than imposed can weaken the assurance of those beliefs and practices. For a cultivated international player like Ahaz, who has met the emperor and seen Damascus, no small outpost in a multinational empire can plausibly claim to be the *umbilicus mundi* (cf. Provan 1995, 246). This is one of the temptations of modern empire, that Christian confession will be diluted into opinion as it jostles in the marketplace with other confessions. Religious pluralism is a fact, yet it is crucial to see that this does not inevitably weaken the church's boldness in witness. Early Christians could see the luxuriant proliferation of religious options on every street corner in the Roman Empire, yet they did not shrink from proclaiming Jesus as *the* way and *the* king.

The account of Ahaz raises another challenge to contemporary Christian practice. For a variety of reasons, Christian worship in many contemporary churches has adopted liturgical styles from the worlds of entertainment or advertising. When success depends on copying the latest methods, the church's apparently staid traditionalism, its claim to be the object of God's special favor, its claims to be the Eden of God, the holy mountain, the house of the living God, can look quaint if not downright proud. Better to adjust our worship and our language to the dominant cultural power, it is thought, than to keep up the arrogant pretense that we enjoy a special status. In adapting itself to the world, the church is departing from the pattern or model that should govern its worship. Only when the church follows the תבנית of heavenly worship does water flow from the temple to the world. If the church adopts the תבנית of Damascus, then the nations are on their own, and no water will flow to renew the parched land. Soon such a church will cease to have any purpose for being; ultimately, it will no longer be.

2 KINGS 17:1–41

Nothing in Christian theology is more important, Protestants often declare, than to distinguish rightly between law and gospel. Though this distinction has often been deployed in antinomian fashion that separates grace from any concern for moral order, this is, with regard to Luther as much as the Swiss Reformers, a deep misreading. Far from renouncing moral order and the law's work in shaping of human action, Luther, Yeago argues, insists that "the bestowal of God's grace through the gospel is . . . the only true formation of the human heart, that which alone sets the heart truly in order" (1998, 164).

For Luther, distinguishing between the prelapsarian and the postlapsarian functions of the law is crucial. In Luther's own words, "when Adam had been created in such a way that he was, so to speak, drunk with joy towards God, and rejoiced also in all other creatures, then there was created a new tree for the distinction of good and evil, so that Adam might have a definite sign of worship and reverence toward God" (quoted in Yeago, 1998, 176). Thus, for Luther the commandment is given to Adam so that "Adam's love for God" could "take form in an historically concrete way of life," as the "concrete social practice of worship." After Adam's fall, the function and meaning of the law changes because Adam changes. The subject presupposed by the original commandment in the garden, "the subject that is drunk with joy towards God," is no longer there, and in his place is a person "who has withdrawn from God, who believes the devil's lies about God and therefore flees and avoids God" (1998, 177). Yet, when God renews a sinner by the Spirit, he restores him or her to something like Adam's relation to law. Understood spiritually, all commandments must be referred to the first, the demand to have no gods before God (1998, 176–77).

For graced human beings, the law comes as a call to faith. For Luther, "it is in a certain sense a misunderstanding of the divine commands to say that they demand particular behaviors; it is more accurate to say that they *demand* a heart that fears, loves, and trusts God, and that they *offer* such a heart the concrete form of life appropriate to it" (Yeago 1998, 181). This does not make the concrete commandments optional, for one cannot truly love and fear God and ignore his word. Rather, "every commandment implicitly but also intrinsically calls for a particular sort of *person*, a particular mode of human existence within which the specific behaviors also called for can play their proper role" (1998, 181). The law is not fulfilled apart from the commitment of the heart: Luther says, "His law also calls for the ground of the heart and cannot be satisfied with works," and this is a demand that we cannot fulfill (1998, 181–82 [emphasis original]). This means, Luther says, that "it calls for Christ, and presses us towards him, so that we first become different people through his grace in faith, and become like him, and then do genuine good works" (1998, 183). The law announces, "You must have Christ and the Spirit," which means, Yeago argues, that "the law calls for faith, since faith is precisely the New Testament name for the bonding of our lives with Christ and the Spirit" (1998, 184).[1]

Understood in this fashion, Luther's theology of the law is profoundly consistent with the evangelical theology of 1–2 Kings. Contrary to some readings of the Old Testament, Torah is not in conflict with faith. As 2 Kgs. 17 makes clear, the law is simply a call to faith, and the northern kingdom is packed away into exile because it "did not believe in Yahweh their God" (17:14). The chapter's overwhelming emphasis on Israel's violation of the first commandment shows that loyalty to God is always the crucial, and in some sense the sole, demand for Israel (17:12). As Fretheim notes, "the language of 'forsaking' the covenant is oriented, almost exclusively, in terms of the first commandment,"[2] and he suggests that the Sinaitic and Davidic covenants are two phases of a single covenant seen from different perspectives: "From the divine side, the focus is on promise; from the human side the focus is on the first commandment, or, in other language, on faith and trust in God alone. Thus, the only 'condition' of the latter is finally faith and trust" (1983, 22–23). Provided this is understood as Luther understood it—that the specifics of the law are specifications of the life of faith—Fretheim's assessment reflects the concerns of 1–2 Kings. Like the generation of the exodus, Israel

1. Yeago suggests that this bond of faith with Christ and the Spirit is what Luther means by justification: "For Luther, the forensic relationship is secondary to a relationship of *union*, the union of the believer to the person of Christ as a living member of Christ's body, the church." Thus, justification "is just this utter joining-together of Christ and the believer, by virtue of which we live in heaven and Christ is, lives, and works in us. The righteousness by which we are saved is Christ himself, living in us," and the forensic declaration is "dependent on this primary relation of union." Justification by faith involves a death and resurrection, as the old self-reliant self, the old self alienated from Christ, dies and a new self is born, a self shaped by the form of Christ (Yeago 1998, 184–85 [emphasis original]).

2. Fretheim cites Deut. 17:2–3; 29:25–26; 31:16, 20; Josh. 23:16; Judg. 2:20; 1 Kgs. 11:9–11; 2 Kgs. 17:15.

does not rely on Yahweh, does not trust him, but looks for other saviors (Gray 1970, 647).

Though the chapter describes the fall of Samaria, 2 Kgs. 17 emphasizes that both Israel and Judah fail to put their trust in Yahweh. The chapter includes several explicit references to Judah (17:19–23), so that the exile of Israel serves as a cautionary tale for Judah, and the specific sins listed in 17:9–12 and 17:16–18 are not unique to the northern kingdom (Provan 1995, 248). Judah also worships on high places (17:9, 11) and sets up shrines "under every green tree" (17:10; cf. 1 Kgs. 14; 2 Kgs. 16:4). The "two calves" of 17:16 are the calves of Jeroboam I, but 17:17 mentions causing sons and daughters to pass through the fire, a perversion that only a Judahite king practiced (16:3). The same is true of divination (17:17; 16:15) and worshiping the host of heaven (21:5). Israel becomes a harlot and is destroyed (like Jezebel the harlot); Judah is a junior whore and will suffer the same fate. The references to Judah are particularly important since 1–2 Kings includes no comparable passage at the end of Judah's history, which trails off into chronicle (2 Kgs. 24–25). When the history of 1–2 Kings as a whole is considered, Judah cannot be evaluated separately from Israel, and placing the evaluation of both kingdoms at this point in his narrative shows that the narrator wants not only to highlight the parallels between north and south but to show that they headed toward a common fate. Importantly, the announcement that Judah will fall comes prior to the great reforming movements of Hezekiah and Josiah. From the time that Samaria falls to the Assyrians, Judah is doomed as well. As Radner points out, the whole kingdom of Israel—Israel and the remnant that remains after the fall of Samaria in Judah—is destroyed. Reunion comes only through the *common* experience of exile (1998, 36).

The narrator shows that there is an eye-for-eye justice in God's dealings with his people (Provan 1995, 249). Israel never "turns away" from their sin (17:22–23), so Yahweh "turns away" his people (17:23). Israel "rejects" Yahweh's statutes and covenant (17:15), so Yahweh "rejects" it (17:20). Yahweh has the Canaanites "carried away to exile" (17:11), and he does the same with the Israelites who follow Canaanite customs (17:8). Israel cannot complain against the justice of Yahweh and has no grounds for suggesting that he is unfaithful to his covenant. Israel's breach of covenant is evident in the ten violations listed in 17:15–17 (Davis 2005, 243), numerically matching the Ten Words of Moses that summarize the original covenant in which Israel receives the land. The book of Kings is theodicy, justifying God's ways with Israel by showing that Israel and Judah both sinned in the face of Yahweh's persistent mercy and repeated warnings.

The name Hoshea (הושע) means "savior" and is related to the names Joshua and Jesus, and there is a clever providence in Joshua's bringing Israel into the land while Hoshea is king when Israel is removed (and another Joshua later leads Israel after the exile). The account of Hoshea's reign begins in the normal fashion (17:1–6), but never ends. His is an abortive reign, as Israel's history in the land is an aborted history. Hoshea is condemned like the other kings of Israel, but there is a slightly positive note in 17:2. Israel's history does not end with the worst king, but with a comparatively decent king, just as the Omride dynasty ends not with Ahab but with the superior Jehoram. Marginally better though Hoshea is, Yahweh has already determined to destroy Israel, and the introduction of Shalmaneser in 17:3 jarringly contrasts with the hint of decency in 17:2. In this respect, the final days of the northern kingdom again anticipate the final days of the south, for Yahweh sends Judah into exile after and in spite of Josiah.

Hoshea turns traitor against Assyria by trying to form an alliance with Egypt. Trusting in Egypt, or in any power other than Yahweh, is disastrous, a breach of covenant because it is a breach of faith. These events too foreshadow the later exile of Judah: Jehoiakim, like Hoshea, rebels against an overlord (24:1), provoking Nebuchadnezzar to invade. Within this parallel there is an important contrast: Hoshea is taken to exile and disappears from history, while Jehoiachin, who becomes king during Nebuchadnezzar's march toward Jerusalem, is lifted up at the end of 2 Kgs. 25. David will be restored; not so Hoshea, the false savior.

Second Kings 17:7–23 is a straightforward description of Israel's covenant unfaithfulness. Israel violates the Sinai covenant (17:7, 36, 39) and, as noted above, specifically the commandment to worship Yahweh exclusively (17:7). Israel's fall is not merely a result of its unfaithfulness to the covenant in the first instance, but a result of its defiance of Yahweh in the face of his patience and his repeated appeals through the prophets (17:13–14). Israel proves stiff-necked and hardened itself, like Israel in the wilderness and like Pharaoh (see Rom. 9). According to Deut. 10:13–22, constructing the golden calf at Sinai is a specific example of Israel's hard-heartedness, and this is the recurring sin of the northern kingdom. The Israelites worship vanity and become as vain, light, and airy as the gods they serve (2 Kgs. 17:15).

Especially in the times of the judges, Israel resists Gentile tyrants and is delivered, and King Hezekiah also seeks Yahweh and is delivered from an Assyrian siege. Yet, when Hoshea attempts to break free from the tribute imposed by Assyria, it is an act of "conspiracy," a word used elsewhere in Kings to describe the machinations of nobles and illegitimate kings to take power (1 Kgs. 16:20; 2 Kgs. 12:21; 14:19; 15:15). Why is Hoshea judged a conspirator while Gideon and Samson are celebrated as heroes of the faith? The prophecies of Jeremiah, with exhortations to submit to Babylon (Jer. 29), raise the same issue. The answer is that Yahweh moves history to the "times of the Gentiles," and resisting the new Gentile empires is resisting God.

For all its reverence for the ways of the ancestors and for ancient landmarks, the Bible is not finally a conservative document. When Korah resists the "innovative" priestly order of Aaron, he and his family are swallowed alive into Sheol (Num. 16), and when Rehoboam attempts to preserve the united kingdom, a prophet stops him (1 Kgs. 12). Ultimately, this pattern culminates in the church's union of Jew and Gentile, opposed by conservative Judaizers. Yet, the order of the church and the political setting of its ministries periodically undergoes tectonic shifts. Because it features the creator as its chief character, Scripture is a continual record of new things, and those who oppose the work that God is doing prove themselves enemies.

The purposes of God are not, however, elastic, as if Baalism might someday become the new Yahwism, adultery the new form of marital faithfulness, or homosexual activity an acceptable alternative lifestyle. There are continuities that run throughout the history of revelation and the history of the church. God works within history, and thus his work develops over time, with all the attendant fluctuations that entails. But God's work in history has a logic and moves along a trajectory set at creation and, Paul says, before creation (Eph. 1:3–14) toward its culmination in Christ.

Paul's letter to the Galatians is an important text for reflecting on the continuities and discontinuities of redemptive history. On the one hand, Paul argues for a massive discontinuity between Israel and the church, insisting that the coming of Christ decisively undermines the division of Jew and Gentile (Gal. 2:11–16; 3:23–29). At the same time, Paul is at pains to show that this change is precisely in keeping with the purposes of God already expressed to Abraham (3:1–14), so that the "new thing" is inherently a very old thing, a thing older even than the law, which was added as a means for realizing the Abrahamic promise (3:19). From Galatians, one might draw this rule of thumb: any "new thing" in the church that is not simultaneously the realization of some "old thing" represents a false path.

As Nelson notes, the situation after Israel is removed is little different from the situation before (1987, 231–32). Assyria resettles the land with foreigners (2 Kgs. 17:24), who bring their gods with them, and Yahweh sends lions to attack the idolaters (as in 1 Kgs. 13; 20; 2 Kgs. 2). On the assumption that Yahweh is a local deity who must be appeased, the Assyrians bring back an Israelite priest to help. At least the pagan settlers respond to lions, displaying more sensitivity to Yahweh's judgments than Israel ever does (Davis 2005, 248). The lion that eats the man of God from Judah, after all, makes no impression whatever on Jeroboam I or on any of the kings after him, who continue in his "way" (1 Kgs. 13). Israel is expelled from the land for idolatry, and a presumably idolatrous priest is brought back to lead the people in "fearing Yahweh" while they continue to "serve their gods" (2 Kgs. 17:32–33). Second Kings 17:34 shows us the writer's judgment about this syncretism: it is not "fearing Yahweh."

Israel came into the land charged with the duty of purging the land of pagan shrines and establishing Yahweh's worship. In a tragic reversal, the land is back to its preconquest state, full of idolatrous shrines. Even exile does not change the face of the northern kingdom. This is Israel's Good Friday, the dark day of being cast from the face of God (17:18, 20, 23). Israel dies; and there is only a distant rumor of resurrection (17:39). It is like another dark day, when the one true Israelite bears the sins of his people on a Roman cross, when from the darkness, the true Israel cries, "My God, my God! Why have you forsaken me?"

2 KINGS 18:1–20:21

The sequence from 2 Kgs. 17 to 2 Kgs. 18 is similar to the sequence from 1 Kgs. 19 to 1 Kgs. 20. When Elijah appears before Yahweh on Sinai to accuse Israel, Yahweh gives him the tools to destroy the house of Ahab (19:15–18). Among these weapons are the Arameans (19:15, 17), and immediately Ben-hadad lays siege to Samaria (20:1). To all appearances, the judgment that Yahweh passes at Sinai is being fulfilled, yet Yahweh delivers Israel from the Arameans twice (1 Kgs. 20), and Ahab's house does not fall for another generation. Similarly, 2 Kgs. 17 describes the ruin of the northern kingdom, but, as noted in the previous chapter, also details the sins of Judah (17:19). The logic seems impeccable: Judah "walked in the customs that Israel had introduced" (17:19); Israel falls to the Assyrians (17:6); therefore, Judah will fall as well. This impression is strengthened by 18:9–12 again summarizing the case against Israel, just before the narrator begins his account of the Assyrian siege of Jerusalem. It looks as if the prophetic oracles against Jerusalem and Judah are about to be carried out.

As in the case of Ahab, however, Yahweh delays the final blow. In this case, the delay is easier to understand. Ahab shows no signs of repentance, yet Yahweh delivers his capital from the Arameans; Hezekiah, during whose reign the northern kingdom falls, turns away from the idols of his fathers and leads Judah back from the brink (18:4). During his reign, Judah and the Davidic line experience another renewal, as it does under Joash (2 Kgs. 11), for Hezekiah is the polar opposite of his father Ahaz (16:2). The kingdom is reunited in worship for the first time since Jeroboam I, as Hezekiah gathers people from "Beersheba even to Dan" to his Passover (2 Chr. 30:5–6). He is the most David-like king since David (2 Kgs. 18:3; compare 18:7 with 1 Sam. 18:14), ready to battle the boasting and blaspheming Goliath-bully Sennacherib and to subdue Philistia (2 Kgs. 18:8; Provan 1995, 260). He keeps the Mosaic law (18:6), removes the high places (18:4), and, like a new and better Adam, crushes the serpent fetish Nehushtan (18:4). It has been a long time since Judah was ruled by an Adamic king (see the commentary on 1 Kgs. 3:1–28).

Much of the account of his reign focuses on the Assyrian threat. Hezekiah initially pays tribute to Assyria, but then rebels against Assyria, as Jehoiakim later does against Babylon (2 Kgs. 24:1). After the Assyrians finish off the northern kingdom (18:9–12), they turn south to Judah to force Hezekiah back into tributary status. Hezekiah readily confesses his "sin" against Sennacherib (18:14) and promises to pay whatever is demanded. Like earlier kings of Judah, he plunders the temple and the palace, going so far as to remove the remaining gold leaf from the doors and doorposts, gold that he has restored to the temple (18:16). Despite apparent assurances from Hezekiah, Assyria is not satisfied, and Sennacherib sends an army to teach Judah's king a lesson. He lays siege to Jerusalem and calls for negotiations with Hezekiah's officials at the "conduit of the upper pool" in Jerusalem (18:17). It is not an auspicious start, and we suspect that the writer's enthusiasm for Hezekiah's piety may have been exaggerated, and we also suspect that this time Yahweh will not deliver his people from this Gentile threat.

From 18:13, the story of the Assyrian siege of Jerusalem is told in a parallel structure:

A Assyrians arrive at Jerusalem (18:13–16)
    B messengers from Assyria speak to the people (18:17–37)
        C Hezekiah seeks the prophet and prays (19:1–5)
            D Isaiah prophesies (19:6–7)
A′ Assyrians leave (19:8–9a) (break in text)
    B′ Assyrian letter to Jerusalem (19:9b–13)
        C′ Hezekiah responds by entering temple to pray (19:14–19)
            D′ Isaiah prophesies (19:20–34)
A″ Assyrians leave for good (19:35–37)

The narrator attends particularly to the exchanges between Hezekiah's representatives and the Assyrian official known as the Rabshakeh. Shrewdly employing the rhetoric of Israelite faith even while undermining it, the Rabshakeh speaks to the people of Judah at the wall of the city. His two speeches alternate between promises of blessing from the Assyrian king and warnings that Judah should not trust Yahweh or Hezekiah:

A don't trust Egypt (18:19–21)
    B don't trust Yahweh or Hezekiah (18:22)
A′ king of Assyria, not Egypt, will give chariots and horses (18:23–25)
    B′ don't trust Hezekiah or Yahweh (18:29–30)
A″ king of Assyria will take you to a promised land (18:31–32)
    B″ Yahweh cannot protect, any more than other gods (18:33–35)

At a number of points, the Rabshakeh's speech echoes the message of the prophets. He hammers on the question of trust (18:19–21), the key issue in 2 Kgs. 17, emphasizing, as the prophets do, that Egypt is unreliable (18:21; cf. Isa. 30:2–3, 7). He also offers a theological challenge, pointing out that Hezekiah has destroyed places of worship, which provokes Yahweh's displeasure, and implying that neither Hezekiah nor Yahweh can be trusted (2 Kgs. 18:22). Sennacherib, however, offers chariots and horses to Judah (18:23–24), tempting the king to forget that the prophets are the chariots and horsemen of Israel (2:12; 13:14). Besides, Assyria has already conquered the people of Yahweh to the north. His speech ends with the audacious claim that Sennacherib, not Hezekiah, is doing the Lord's will (18:25) and that the Assyrian king will be Israel's shepherd-king, a composite of Moses, Joshua, and Solomon who will lead Judah to green pastures beside the still waters, into a promised land flowing with wine, oil, and honey (18:32). Judah should not seek deliverance from Yahweh, who could no more deliver Judah than the gods of the nations surrounding Judah have been able to withstand the Assyrian advance.

As Brueggemann (2000, 498) points out, the section of the speech mocking Yahweh's power to save is structured to emphasize that Yahweh is only one among many gods:

A   will Yahweh deliver?
   B   has any god delivered?
      C   gods of Hamath and Arpad, etc.
   B′   what gods have delivered?
A′   can Yahweh deliver?

The Rabshakeh's last argument goes too far, issuing a challenge that Yahweh will not leave unanswered and revealing the implicit idolatry of the rest of the speech. The king of Assyria claims to be able to accomplish things that only Yahweh can accomplish, and this in spite of his accomplishing what he does only by Yahweh's permission (19:25–26). Importantly, the Rabshakeh's scholarly argument arises from and culminates in an idolatry of empire. While other peoples have gods to deliver them, Assyria has only the king of Assyria, before whom no gods can stand. The issue of faith is posed sharply: faith in Yahweh and faith in empire are at war. Faith in Yahweh may take the form of submission to empire (as it does in Jeremiah), but Israel can never place its faith in empire or emperor without betraying its true Lord. Despite his "Yahwist" rhetoric, the Rabshakeh is not a Yahwist but an imperial propagandist and a student of comparative religions, standing above and outside particular religious claims in order to assess their relative strengths.

In its origins, the study of comparative religion in the West arose within a Christian context, and many of the early writers in this field emphasized the imperfections of other world religions and attempted to show how those imperfections were realized or corrected in Christianity. In an 1871 volume entitled *Ten Great Religions* (first serialized in *The Atlantic Monthly*), James Freeman Clarke argued that "comparative theology" (tinged with competitive Darwinism) could be used to establish the superiority of Christian faith. A "fair survey of the principal religions of the world" will show that Christianity is superior at every point: "While they are ethnic or local, Christianity is catholic or universal; that, while they are defective, possessing some truths and wanting others, Christianity possesses all; and that, while they are stationary, Christianity is progressive." That Christianity is so perfectly adapted to human nature is an argument for its truth, for "when we see adaptation we naturally infer design" (quoted in Masuzawa 2005, 77–79).

Well meaning as this apologetic effort may have been, from the perspective of the Christian tradition it rests on theological errors. On the surface, it depends on the notion that Christianity is one religion among others and thus depends on a definition of religion that has a fairly brief pedigree in Western history. Milbank criticizes the authors of *The Myth of God Incarnate* for treating Buddhism, Islam, and Hinduisms as species within a particular genus, an approach that subsumes "alien cultural phenomena under categories which comprise Western notions of what constitutes religious thought and practice." To treat the various religions as variations on one phenomenon is a "covert Christianization" (Milbank 1990a, 176–77). Religions are fundamentally incommensurate, and Christianity can be shown superior to other faiths by remaking these other religions into faiths, something they would not be on their own.

Efforts to locate common features among religions, furthermore, invariably fail because there are always exceptions. The narrower the definition of religion, the less apt it is to serve as a description of many different religions; but the larger the definition of religion, the more difficult it is to distinguish from culture. As Milbank notes, "any conception of religion as designating a realm within culture, for example, that of spiritual experience, charismatic power, or ideological legitimation, will tend to reflect merely the construction of religion within Western modernity" (1990a, 177).

Behind this treatment of religion as a genus is an implicit denial of the classic Christian claim that God neither belongs to a genus nor is a genus. According to Thomas Aquinas, God is not a member of any class. His essence is to exist, and this distinguishes him from all other beings: "Species is constituted by specific difference added to genus. Hence the essence of any species possesses something over and above its genus. But existence itself, *ipsum esse*, which is God's essence, does not comprise within itself any factor added to some other factor. Thus, God is not a species of any genus." Since a genus "potentially contains specific differences," it is comprised of act and potency, and since there can be no potency in God, God is not a genus. Further, the essence of a thing—what it is—derives from its genus, but its existence—that it is—is established by specific differences within a genus. Since God's essence is to exist, his existence is not established by any specific differences, he cannot be a genus (Thomas

Aquinas 1993, 16–18). From a Thomist perspective, comparative religion is implicitly idolatrous, assuming as it does an immanent God, a being among other beings, who can be compared to other existing or nonexisting beings. Even before the Rabshakeh begins to challenge the supremacy of Israel's God directly, his argument is already implicitly idolatrous because it assumes that there is a class of divine beings of which Yahweh is one member.

Scripture frequently compares Yahweh to the gods of the nations and employs the generic term "god" for Dagon and Baal as well as for Yahweh (Judg. 10:6; 1 Kgs. 11:2), but the character of these comparisons confirms Thomas Aquinas's point, though of course without his technical philosophical apparatus. The Old Testament confesses the superiority of Yahweh in a way that shows he is God in a quite different sense than the gods of the nations. There is an analogical gap between "God" as applied to Yahweh and "god" as applied to Chemosh or Molech. Yahweh shows that he is greater than all gods by bringing Israel through the waters of the exodus (Exod. 15:11), and David can confess that there is "no one like you among the gods, O Lord" (Ps. 86:8). Quite literally, no one in the skies is "comparable to Yahweh" (89:6). Those who are worshiped as gods by the Gentiles do not really qualify for the title: they are "not-gods" (2 Kgs. 19:18; Jer. 2:11; 5:7; 16:20; Gal. 4:8). Yahweh judges the Rabshakeh's comparison—and would likewise judge much modern comparative religion—as blasphemous.

The remainder of the siege story is one of repentance: like the delegation who hears the Rabshakeh's speech, Hezekiah, who relies on wealth and treasure to save him, tears his robes at the blasphemy of the Rabshakeh (2 Kgs. 19:1) and turns to Yahweh for deliverance. Instead of plundering the temple treasuries, he now uses the temple the way it is designed to be used—as a house of prayer (19:1, 14) (Cohn 2000, 141). Hezekiah also sends for Isaiah, who promises that Yahweh will send panic through the Assyrian camp by a rumor (19:7) and will lure Sennacherib, as he had Ahab (1 Kgs. 22) and the Aramean army (2 Kgs. 7), to destruction. The threats that Hezekiah "hears" will be undone by what Sennacherib will "hear." Sennacherib does hear a report, but instead of returning home sends a letter renewing the threats of his previous speech, warning against trust in Egypt and threatening to carry out a war of utter destruction (19:8–11). Hezekiah again turns to prayer, and this second prayer echoes Solomon's temple dedication prayer in his request that Yahweh will "open his eyes" and "incline his ears" and respond to Assyria's blasphemies (19:16; cf. 1 Kgs. 8:37–40). His main concern is that Yahweh will vindicate his own name (2 Kgs. 19:34).

Isaiah's second prophecy pictures Jerusalem taunting the Assyrians (19:21), returning mockery to Assyria's mockery. Whatever Sennacherib's threats, Isaiah prophesies that Zion will remain a virgin (19:21), unviolated by the Gentile rapist at her gates. Sennacherib raises his eyes and voice to challenge Yahweh, almost claiming to rival Yahweh in his ability to divide the waters of Egypt (19:24) and cut cedars (19:23; cf. Ps. 29). For this pride, he will be thrown down. Yahweh claims that Assyria's power is completely dependent on his (2 Kgs. 19:25) and threatens to capture Assyria and lead Sennacherib away like a beast (19:28). Judah is not grass that withers, but a deeply rooted plant that will grow strong and produce fruit (19:29–31) and will triumph over Assyria without firing a shot. In the distance, Isaiah looks forward to the restoration of the surviving remnant of Judah and Israel, who would return and flourish in the land after the exile.

As Byron noticed, the deliverance of Jerusalem is a Passover event. At night, the angel of death destroys 185,000 Assyrians, driving Sennacherib home to an ignominious end (19:35–37). The Passover that destroys Assyria brings new life for Judah, and the "third year" promise of deliverance (19:29) points to the "third day" resurrection of Jesus. The tree threatened with destruction survives, as Yahweh again shows himself, as he did against Egypt, to be incomparably greater than all gods and all emperors.

The first episode in 2 Kgs. 20 takes place during the Assyrian crisis ("in those days") (20:1), and Hezekiah's sickness actually occurs during the siege.[1] Berodach (sometimes spelled Merodach) sends messengers when he hears of the sickness (20:12), and thus the visit of Babylon is closely connected with the siege as well. We can infer that the Babylonian visit occurs before the siege, since it is unlikely that the Assyrians would have permitted a Babylonian delegation through their siege lines. It is thus likely that Hezekiah shows Babylon his treasures because he intends to call on Babylon for help against Assyria and that the Babylonian visit emboldens Hezekiah to rebel against Sennacherib (18:7). In this, Hezekiah's actions reverse the relations between the Gentiles and Solomon (Nelson 1987, 245). When Sheba comes to visit, Solomon tells and shows her everything. She is impressed and all that she observes reinforces Israel's and Solomon's preeminence. Babylon's visit to Judah is a sign of Hezekiah's subordination to the rising Gentile empire. Hezekiah "hears" the Babylonians (20:13), a misstep for a king who should listen instead to Yahweh's voice.

Sick kings in 1–2 Kings normally die (1 Kgs. 14; 2 Kgs. 1), and their dynasties shortly follow them into the grave. Consultation with a prophet is often part of scenes of the sick king (1 Kgs. 14; 2 Kgs. 8:7–15), but the prophet normally brings bad news. The story of Hezekiah's sickness is similar, but ultimately breaks the rhythm. Isaiah comes without bidding, and, more important,

---

1. Isaiah tells Hezekiah that he has fifteen more years (20:6), and he reigned for twenty-nine years total (18:2), so the sickness and cure must have happened in the fourteenth year of his reign, the same year of the Assyrian siege (18:13). Second Kings 20:6 indicates that Jerusalem is under siege or about to be under siege while Hezekiah is sick (Hobbs 1985, 288–89). This is confirmed by extrabiblical chronological information. Berodach-baladan II's reign is broken into two sections: 721–710 BC and then for six months in 703/2 BC. Hezekiah's solo reign begins around 716 BC, and 701 is the date of the Assyrian siege (Wiseman 1993, 288). Thus, the Babylonian visit occurs a year or so prior to the siege of Jerusalem by Sennacherib, and Isaiah's prophecy about a Babylonian invasion overshadows Judah throughout the Assyrian crisis.

when Isaiah brings a message of death (20:1), Hezekiah does not turn his face to the wall and die. He prays, something that no other sick king does before (20:2–6). Hezekiah has been accused of praying in a self-interested and even self-righteous fashion, but this kind of prayer is common in the Psalms. He calls on Yahweh to remember his faithfulness and to deal kindly with him. Yahweh promises to guard, protect, and heal those who cling to him in hope and faith. Hezekiah does just that and trusts Yahweh to keep his covenant.

In a major reversal of the typical pattern, Hezekiah recovers. Isaiah returns with a promise of fifteen additional years, which matches the promise that the city will be saved in another "third day" resurrection (20:8). Given that Hezekiah faces death, it is surprising to learn that he is suffering from a boil (20:7). Boils are among the plagues of Egypt (Exod. 9:8–12) and among the curses of Deut. 28:27. Hezekiah's boil is a sign that Judah is threatened as Egypt was and that its king is threatened with disfiguring skin disease. He is healed, and Israel is delivered once again from "Egyptian" diseases. Hezekiah is healed with a cake of figs, for instead of pestilence and boils the land will be filled with vineyards and fig trees.[2]

The restoration of the city and the raising of the king above all demonstrate the incomparable power of Yahweh. He is not one among many gods, but the living God, who shows his power preeminently in bringing creation out of nothing and life from the dead. Jerusalem is dead; but behold, it lives. Hezekiah "dies" and rises again. Though Samaria has fallen, Judah survives into another generation. But the oracle of 2 Kgs. 17 is already spoken, and the kingdom of Judah is already doomed to exile.

---

2. If Hezekiah is already healed, why did he need a sign? Given that he has a skin blemish that would prevent him from entering the temple, he needed a sign that he can enter the temple early (on the third day). Normally, he would be able to enter only after an eight-day ritual (Lev. 14). Isaiah promised a sign that represents what happened to Hezekiah. His life was moving toward evening, but the Lord reversed the lengthening shadow and gave him a new life. Yahweh is not bound by time and can speed the clock of cleansing as readily as he can reverse the process of death. The "steps of Ahaz" perhaps refer to his altar, and the sign showed that the kingdom of Judah, entering senescence because of Ahaz's idolatries, had another chance.

2 KINGS 21:1–26

Judah's ultimate end came through forgetfulness, under a king whose name means forgetfulness. The original Manasseh was so named because his birth comforted Joseph in exile, causing him to forget his suffering (Gen. 41:51). Significantly, the name Manasseh is used twelve times in 1–2 Kings, eleven times of the son of Hezekiah whose fifty-five-year reign sealed Judah's doom (2 Kgs. 21:1). He is appropriately named not because he caused Israel to forget its troubles, but because he forgot the Lord, his deliverance of Israel from Egypt, and his commandments (21:7–15).[1] Each time the Bible says that Judah is condemned to exile "because of Manasseh," the original readers would have recognized they are condemned because of forgetfulness: forgetfulness seduced them to do evil (21:9); because of forgetfulness the land became full of innocent blood (21:16); and even after Josiah the Lord did not turn from his wrath "because of all the provocations with which 'forgetfulness' had provoked him" (23:26). Finally, the Lord sent bands of raiders "because of the sins of 'forgetfulness'" (24:2–3). The story of the consequences of forgetfulness was a stimulus to remind exilic Israel never to forget again.

Forgetfulness condemned Judah to exile, but from another angle memory condemned Judah to exile, for Yahweh refused to forget and forgive all its sins of "forgetfulness" (24:4). Salvation is from the human side an act of memory and from the divine side a gracious act of forgetfulness by which the Lord remembers his promise to be gracious and puts our sins out of mind (Ps. 25:7; 79:8). The promise of the new covenant was the promise to reverse the relation of memory and forgetfulness: Israel will remember the Lord, and he will put its sins away and remember them no more (Jer. 31:34; Heb. 8:8–12).

Memory shapes identity both individually and communally, because memory binds together who we were with who we are. Families share collective memories

---

1. Manasseh experiences a demonic "repentance." The Hebrew of 21:3 says that "he turned, he built" (וישב ויבן), using the verb normally used for sinners turning toward Yahweh but here describing Manasseh's turning from the ways of Yahweh and of his father. There are times for building and times for tearing down (Eccl. 3): because of his improper building, Manasseh causes both Jerusalem and the temple to be torn down (2 Kgs. 21:13–14).

around the dinner table, and those memories are a large part of what makes the Smiths different from the Stevensons or the Spencers. Congregations have communal memories, and the catholic church memorializes God's great acts in Christ through liturgy and creed. One of the great evils of the modern church, and particularly in certain branches of Protestants, is its communal amnesia. Protestants can act as if the church began in 1517 and reached its zenith in the 1640s, and Protestant evangelical memory often cannot extend beyond the mid-twentieth century, if that far. But the whole history of the church is our history, and the history recorded in Scripture is an essential part of our history. Paul said to Christians at Corinth that "our fathers" (1 Cor. 10:1–4) were baptized in the Sea, were fed with manna, and rebelled in the wilderness. Jeroboam I and Baasha and Zimri and Omri and Ahab and Jehu are all part of our story, the story of the church. If memory shapes our sense of who we are, it is no accident that the communal amnesia of the modern church produces churches without root or rudder, churches that trim their sails to every wind of doctrine. Forgetfulness is ingratitude, and ingratitude is one of the original sins. Worship is history class, where we are renewed in our communal memory and where we confess our forgetfulness of the Lord and his commandments.

Memory binds our past with our present, but in Scripture memory of the past is never nostalgic, but always evokes confidence for the future. As we reflect on how Yahweh's prophet enters into the history of Ahab, we are encouraged to hope that he will not leave us in our darkness and sin, that he will not allow the lamp of Israel to go out. Throughout his sermons in Deuteronomy, Moses urged Israel to remember Egypt precisely so they would be fearless in facing down their future enemies in Canaan.

In a fascinating book on aging and the brain, Goldberg offers an intriguing angle on this by focusing attention on the phenomenon of "pattern recognition," the "ability to recognize a new object or a new problem as a member of an already familiar class of objects or problems" (2005, 85). With experience, our ability to recognize patterns can increase, and problem solving can actually get easier. Think of the old pastor who cuts through thousands of hours of counseling and magically (prophetically) gets to the heart of a marital problem in a few seconds, and you have a good idea of the phenomenon that Goldberg is talking about. Personal memory thus nurtures wisdom. But Goldberg suggests that pattern recognition is based not only on individual experience and "generic memory," but on cultural memory:

> We humans are spared the hardship of discovering the world from scratch. Instead, we benefit from the incremental effect of knowledge accumulated gradually by society through millennia. This knowledge is stored and communicated through various cultural devices in symbolic form and is transmitted from generation to generation. Access to this knowledge automatically empowers the cognition of every individual member of human society by making it privy to society's cumulative, collective wisdom. If wisdom is defined as the availability of a rich

repertoire of patterns enabling us to recognize new situations and new problems as familiar, then we truly are a wise species. (Goldberg 2005, 88–89)

Jacobs (2004) describes our age as a dark age, and for Jacobs that means an age characterized by collective amnesia. Skills that used to be second nature have been lost; knowledge that used to be common has disappeared; standards of behavior that once constituted the bare minimum of civil conduct are flouted. For the church, the task is monumental: Christians face the task of reevangelizing a world that was already evangelized once, retraining our culture in beliefs that long seemed natural, and restoring practices that were once part of the fabric of Western social life. The author of 1–2 Kings would have recognized the situation, for the age of Manasseh was a similarly dark age, a time of cultural and especially religious amnesia.

As explained in the introduction to this commentary, the God revealed in 1–2 Kings appears irresponsibly indulgent toward his people. He warns, he threatens, he cajoles; still his people sin and sin and sin. Yet he never seems to make good on his warnings. At long last, he judges the northern kingdom of Israel, but the remnant that remains in Judah is equally rebellious against his covenant. With Manasseh, finally, he loses patience and determines to destroy Jerusalem and his temple and to send Judah into exile. Why now?

The internal typologies of 1–2 Kings help to answer that question. The book of Kings is framed by accounts of the united kingdom of Israel. The kingdom is united under Solomon (1 Kgs. 1–11) and reunited to some degree by the dynasty of Jehu and more fully by Hezekiah and his successors (2 Kgs. 18–25). These two framing sections run parallel. First Kings begins with David, who hands his kingdom to Solomon, whose idolatries lead to the division of the kingdom. Hezekiah is a new David, and his successor Manasseh takes the idolatries of Solomon even further. In this scheme, Josiah is an inverted Jeroboam I, reuniting the kingdom that Jeroboam I divides and destroying the calf shrine at Bethel. Manasseh, like Solomon, is a great builder, who "makes" (21:3, 7) and "builds" (21:3) high places (cf. 1 Kgs. 11:7). Second Kings 21:7 alludes specifically to the promise made to Solomon, the first time that Solomon's name has appeared in the narrative since 1 Kgs. 14:26. Solomon's idolatries are punished with a division of the kingdom, but the effects of Manasseh's will be more drastic—exile. When Judah goes into exile, it is not only Judah. All of Israel dies in the death of Judah. As at the end of the northern kingdom, the end of the southern kingdom matches its beginning:

1 Kings 1–12	2 Kings 18–25
David: on a bed; revived	Hezekiah: on a bed; revived
Solomon: builds idolatrous shrines	Manasseh: builds idolatrous shrines
Rehoboam	Amon
Jeroboam I: divides the kingdom; Bethel	Josiah: reunites the kingdom; Bethel

Just as Yahweh judges Solomon's idolatries by dividing the kingdom, so he disciplines Manasseh's intensified idolatry by tossing Judah into the cauldron of exile.

Overlaying this scheme is another set of parallels. Manasseh's sins are explicitly compared to the sins of Ahab (2 Kgs. 21:3), and as a result Yahweh will judge Jerusalem as he judges Ahab's Samaria (21:13). Only Ahab and Manasseh are compared to the Amorites who live in the land before Israel conquers it (2 Kgs. 21:11; 1 Kgs. 21:26). This is not inconsistent with a Solomonic typology for Manasseh, since, as noted in the commentary on 1 Kgs. 16:15–34, the Omri-Ahab sequence is also a variation on the David-Solomon sequence. The reference to Amorites recalls Yahweh's promise to bring Abram's descendants from Egypt into the land in the fourth generation "for the iniquity of the Amorites is not yet complete" (Gen. 15:16). The link with Gen. 15:16 explains why Ahab and Manasseh are the last straws for their respective kingdoms: in their reigns, the "sins of the Amorites" come to maturity, and it is time to reverse the conquest and bring in Gentile "Joshuas" to purge the land of Israelito-Canaanites and their abominations.

Less obvious are the allusions to Jeroboam I, whose sins doom Israel to extinction (2 Kgs. 17:21–23). Like Jeroboam (and Ahab), Manasseh is worse than all the kings before him (21:11; cf. 1 Kgs. 14:9; 16:25, 30; cf. Knoppers 1994, 106). Further, Manasseh's building ends in destruction, just as Jeroboam's construction of the bull shrine ends in ruin (Knoppers 1994, 109). Beyond this, the narrator points to the influence that Manasseh has over the people of Judah. Throughout 1–2 Kings, the narrator reports that the kings of Israel follow the ways of Jeroboam I, who "made Israel sin" (1 Kgs. 14:16; 15:26, 30, 34; 16:2), a phrase used some twenty times in the book. Throughout the whole of 1–2 Kings, however, no king "makes Judah sin" (ויחטא את־יהודה)—until Manasseh (2 Kgs. 21:11, 16). Every dynasty that makes Israel sin is destroyed—Jeroboam's, Omri's, Jehu's—and when Manasseh leads Judah astray, the Davidic dynasty is also judged. Just as Jeroboam's dynasty is not rescued by the comparative goodness of his son Abijah, and just as Ahab's dynasty is not rescued by his repentance, so the reforms of Josiah will not rescue the dynasty of David from the discipline of exile once a Davidic king "makes Judah sin." When a Davidic king, called to shepherd Yahweh's people, turns into an enemy of the people of God, then the dynasty has to die.

Manasseh's reign is uniquely evil in another way as well. Ahab not only pursues idolatry, but kills opposing prophets and faithful Israelites like Naboth (1 Kgs. 21). Manasseh is another Ahab in this respect as well, filling the city with blood (2 Kgs. 21:16), violence that is cited as one of the causes for Judah's exile (24:4). Naboth's blood cries out against Ahab for vengeance and calls up Jehu as the avenging angel. During the reign of Manasseh, blood cries from the ground of Jerusalem, and Nebuchadnezzar hears the cry. The last man in Judah to shed blood during peacetime is Joab (1 Kgs. 2:5), and he too ends badly (2:28–35). Though the text does not explicitly say that Manasseh persecutes prophets, the sequence from 2 Kgs. 21:10–15 to 21:16 leaves that distinct impression. As with the Omride dynasty, Yahweh has enough when a king of Judah assaults his messengers (see the commentary on 2 Kgs. 8:1–29; cf. Matt. 21:33–46). In 2 Kgs. 15, Assyria suddenly appears in the text shortly after we learn of Menahem's vicious assault on Tiphsah and Tirzah (15:16), indicating that Assyria is summoned up as the avenger of innocent blood. So too Babylon: as the blood of the innocent cries from the ground, Yahweh commands the avenger Nebuchadnezzar to scour the land (24:3–4).

The temple itself is no guarantee of Yahweh's favor (even though Yahweh's name in the temple is an assurance of his presence with Israel), but the name "set" there during the time of Solomon (אָשִׂים אֶת־שְׁמִי) is replaced by the image that Manasseh "set" there (וַיָּשֶׂם אֶת־פֶּסֶל) (21:7). Again, Manasseh's idolatries are unique in Judah's history. Solomon builds a shrine to Chemosh on the Mount of Olives opposite the temple (1 Kgs. 11:7) and Ahaz remodels the temple according to his own design (2 Kgs. 16:10–20), but no Davidic king before Manasseh has the audacity to place an idol before the face of Yahweh.[2] Manasseh commits "abominations" (21:2, 11), the Asherah pole in the temple being the chief of them—an abomination to bring desolation, an abomination that will cause the land to spew out the inhabitants.[3]

In the days of Ahab, Yahweh sends prophets to call the king to repentance, and he mercifully does the same during the days of Manasseh (21:10). Like Israel, Judah has a chance to turn and will ultimately be judged for stiff-necked resistance to the prophets. Yahweh threatens to make ears tingle with the news (21:12), a phrase used in 1 Sam. 3:11 of the destruction of Shiloh. As Jeremiah says (Jer. 7; 19:3), Yahweh makes Solomon's temple another Shiloh, a cautionary tale for the nations. Judah does "evil" and so the Lord brings "evil" on it (2 Kgs. 21:12). Because they refuse to "listen" (לֹא שָׁמֵעוּ) (21:9), refuse to hold to their great confessional Shema about the uniqueness of God, they have to listen instead to ear-tingling reports of devastation. Led by King Forgetful, Israel forgets its lord and husband, and so he plans to send a message it will never forget.

---

2. Second Kings 21:3 gives a catalogue of specific sins, moving from the high places, which are distant from the temple (21:5), to the temple itself (21:7). As the abominations draw nearer to Yahweh's face, his anger intensifies. The text progresses from violations of the first commandment, to the second, and to the third. Second Kings 21:4 describes offenses against the "name," and this is repeated in 21:7. Both the second and third commandments have threats attached (Exod. 20:1–7), and those threats will be carried out against Judah.

3. Nelson (1987, 250) points out that this passage turns many of God's promises into threats. Second Kings 21:15 refers to the exodus, but instead of being an assurance of Yahweh's care for Judah it is described as the beginning of apostasy. Yahweh's promise of rest at the end of wandering is reversed, with the threat that Judah will wander again (21:7–8). Yahweh normally protects his inheritance, but now he is willing to abandon it.

2 KINGS 22:1–23:30

Like Joash, Josiah is a boy king, only eight years old when he ascends the throne (2 Kgs. 22:1). In his eighteenth year, again following the example of Joash, he begins to repair the temple, reversing the damage done by Manasseh. These two kings set up a running parallel sequence that covers the final large sections of 2 Kings:

> A Athaliah, daughter of Ahab, kills the royal seed (2 Kgs. 11:1)
> > B Joash's reign (2 Kgs. 11–12)
> > > C quick sequence of kings of Israel and Judah (2 Kgs. 13–16)
> > > > D fall of Samaria (2 Kgs. 17)
> > > > > E revival of Judah under Hezekiah (2 Kgs. 18–20)
> A′ Manasseh, a king like Ahab, promotes idolatry and kills the innocence (2 Kgs. 21)
> > B′ Josiah's reign (2 Kgs. 22–23)
> > > C′ quick succession of kings of Judah (2 Kgs. 24)
> > > > D′ fall of Jerusalem (2 Kgs. 25)
> > > > > E′ elevation of Jehoiachin (2 Kgs. 25:27–30)

These parallel sequences each reproduce, on a small scale, the overall structure of 1–2 Kings (see the introduction to this commentary and Leithart 2005a), displaying the parallels between the kingdom established by Jeroboam I and that established by David as well as demonstrating Yahweh's unending mercy to the house of David, his determination to raise up the tent of David after its collapse.

A key turning point in Josiah's reign is the discovery of the book of the law in the temple by Hilkiah the priest, another Jehoiada (22:8–13). The phrase "book of the Torah" (ספר התורה) (22:8) is similar to the phrase "book of the covenant" (ספר הברית) used in Exod. 24:7 to describe the original Torah revelation at Sinai. Though the contents of the book are not stated, not to mention the title, it is usually believed to be some form of Deuteronomy, largely based on the importance of centralized worship in Josiah's reform (Deut. 12; 2 Kgs. 23:8–9).[1] Josiah mourns when the written Torah is read, demonstrating what Huldah later describes as his "tender" or "fearful" heart (22:19; cf. Deut. 20:3; Isa. 7:4), the most responsive royal heart since the hearing heart of Solomon. Josiah then seeks additional direction from a prophetess, Huldah, a "mother" in Israel who is consulted even though a number of male prophets are active at the time (2 Kgs. 22:13–20).[2] When he sends a delegation of men to a female prophet he recapitulates in reverse Jeroboam I's dispatch of his wife for a consultation with Ahijah (1 Kgs. 14), and both kings receive prophecies of doom and destruction of their respective kingdoms.

Huldah's prophecy is divided into two sections. First, she speaks an oracle against Judah and Jerusalem, insisting that their fate is sealed (2 Kgs. 22:16–17). The curses of the book will be brought against "this place and on its inhabitants" because of their idolatrous provocations. The second section commends Josiah for his response to the warnings of the book and promises that Josiah (like Ahab and Hezekiah) will not see evil in his own day. Just as the Lord eventually lost patience with the dynasty of Omri, with Ahab's house, and with the northern kingdom as a whole, so he now loses patience with Judah.

Josiah does not, however, simply acquiesce in the judgment and coast through his reign in the knowledge that he will be at peace. Knowing that his efforts are doomed, he embarks on the most extensive reform in the history of Judah's monarchy. The process begins with a renewal of the covenant. Like Solomon at the temple dedication (1 Kgs. 8), Josiah gathers a people described as "the men of Judah and the inhabitants of Jerusalem" (2 Kgs. 23:2), a designation used with increasing frequency in the latter part of 2 Kings. It is a new name for Judah, now that the names Judah and Israel no longer pertain. First the king "stood in" (ויעמד המלך) the covenant (23:3), and then the people "took a stand" in the covenant (ויעמר כל־העם בברית). The people of Judah have refused to serve Yahweh for generations, but in renewing covenant they present themselves as attendants who will "stand to serve" their divine king. In ancient Israel, kings are never merely political or governmental in character, but represent the people as heads to the corporate body. By joining with the king, the people make a covenant with Yahweh, just as Jesus makes a way into covenant with the Father that his people enter through him. Standing beside the "standing pillar" (על־העמוד) (23:3), Josiah cuts covenant with Yahweh

---

1. Davis (2005, 319) points out, however, that none of the reforms listed in 23:4–20 are said to be inspired by the book found in the temple.
2. The explanation offered by various rabbis that Josiah thinks Huldah will be more pliable and merciful than a male prophet is quaint but unpersuasive. Huldah is not the least bit pliable.

to be a pillar for the house of Judah, standing at the gate of Yahweh's house like the monumental pillar Boaz and guiding Israel like a pillar of fire.

Once the covenant is renewed, Josiah embarks on a thorough purgation of the land. Though the account of Josiah's reform can give the impression of randomness, there is order to the story. The account of Josiah's reign is chiastically organized:

A opening: Josiah does not turn to right or left (Deuteronomic) (22:1–2)
  B book of the Torah found (22:3–20)
    C renews covenant according to "book of the covenant" (23:1–3)
      D reforms of Josiah (23:4–20)
    C′ Passover according to the "book of the covenant" (23:21–23)
  B′ all the word of the Torah (23:24)
A′ Josiah does law of Moses: turns to Lord with heart, soul, might (Deuteronomic) (23:25)

Josiah's reform is literarily framed by the covenant ceremony (23:1–3) and the Passover (23:21–23), held in the eighteenth year of Josiah's reign, the same year he discovers the book of Torah in the temple. Thus, the passage as a whole moves from the covenant renewal at the temple to the great sabbatical feast of the first month. Josiah reverses the order of Joshua: Joshua begins in Passover (Josh. 5) and then embarks on a conquest to destroy the shines of the Canaanites, while Josiah destroys the shrines of Canaanite-Israel and then celebrates Passover.

Within this frame, there is an overall organization to the reform, radiating out from a purgation of the temple in Jerusalem. Josiah begins at the temple (2 Kgs. 23:4–9), where he brings out idolatrous vessels and does away with priests (23:4–7). He defiles the high places in Judah and relocates the priests of the high places into Jerusalem to serve the refurbished temple (23:8–9). From there, Josiah turns attention to the shrine erected by kings of Judah, as he attempts to undo the idolatries of his predecessors, particularly Solomon, Ahaz, and Manasseh (23:11–13). Josiah then embarks on a reforming circuit through Samaria, the northern kingdom, which focuses on his destruction of the shrine of Jeroboam I at Bethel (23:15–20) (Cohn 2000, 158–60) and runs parallel to his purgation of the south (Knoppers 1994, 201). What Josiah does throughout this account is curiously similar to what Nebuchadnezzar will soon do in Judah: removing vessels from the temple, breaking down shrines, and sending people into "exile."[3] Reform is a kind of judgment.

---

3. The passage is also unified by word repetitions. The verb "burn" (שׂרף) is used six times in the passage, and other words for burning are also used. Three times the verb is used for burnings in Judah and Jerusalem, and three times for the burning of the main shrine of the northern kingdom. This sixfold burning is numerologically significant, since it falls short of the sevenfold burning that would have designated a completion, and thus the passage leaves room for yet more burning, which will come with Nebuchadnezzar. The word for "bones" (עצמות)

Grammatically, Josiah is the sole actor throughout this chapter, the subject of all the verbs, a one-man iconoclast movement, and the passage can be organized around Josiah's "commands" and "commissions" (Davis 2005, 314). In this, Josiah is superior to his predecessor, Joash, whose reforms depend on the guidance and inspiration of Jehoiada. Josiah the king sends (23:1); the king commands (23:4); the king commands the Passover (23:21); he brings out vessels of Baal worship (23:4) and does away with idolatrous priests (23:5); he burns the Asherah, grinds it to powder, and scatters the dust in the Kidron Valley (23:6). Fittingly, 23:4–20 describes twelve of Josiah's actions (Davis 2005, 320), a numerological sign that he is performing a twelvefold purging, reforming all twelve tribes of Israel and renewing the kingdom from Bethel to Beersheba.

Hezekiah is a new David, and Manasseh an idolatrous Solomon. Josiah inverts the first Jeroboam (Nelson 1987, 255) by bringing a final end to Jeroboam's liturgical experiments and reuniting the kingdom around a purified worship of Yahweh, the extent of his reach being marked by the phrase "Geba to Beersheba" (23:8), reminiscent of the earlier "Dan to Beersheba" (1 Kgs. 4:25). Josiah is the only one in Scripture said to fulfill Torah with a whole heart (2 Kgs. 23:25), as required by the Shema (Deut. 6:4–9), and his faithfulness is comparable to that of the greatest heroes of the Old Testament. He, like Hezekiah, walks as David walked (2 Kgs. 23:2); like Joash, he maintains the temple (22:4–7; cf. 12:6–16), but he does not fall as Joash does. He is a Joshua, refusing to turn to the right or left (23:6; cf. Deut. 5:32; 17:20; Josh. 1:7) and reversing the Canaanitization program of Israel's kings and their allies in Judah and completing the conquest. Between Joshua and 2 Kings there are only two Passover celebrations—Joshua's (Josh. 5) and Josiah's (2 Kgs. 23:21–23), and Josiah's is explicitly performed "as it is written in this book of the covenant" (23:21). Josiah is a Moses, who conforms to the law of Moses (23:25), proclaims that law, and destroys golden calves. These comparisons with Moses support the claims about his incomparable righteousness (23:25) (cf. Sweeney 2001, 39). He is a "man of God from Judah" who like the man of God earlier in Israel's history destroys Jeroboam I's altar (1 Kgs. 13:1–5)—though this time it is destroyed for good. He is the climactic eighth king commended as "doing right" in the eyes of Yahweh (Davis 2005, 315), who begins his reign in his *eighth* year (2 Kgs. 22:1), the number of circumcision, renewal, rebirth—the day after the Sabbath and the first day of a new week.

Brueggemann suggests that the reign of Josiah (especially 2 Kgs. 22) marks a transition from a temple-based Judaism to a Torah-based Judaism (2000,

---

is also used six times, and again the distribution of the word is important. Three times the word is used to describe acts of defilement, as Josiah spreads bones to infect idolatrous shrines with death (23:14, 16, 20; cf. Num. 19). The rest of the uses all occur in 2 Kgs. 23:18, where the word refers to the preserved bones of the old prophet of Judah. There are bones of defilement, but also bones that lead to life, and the bones of the man of God are like the bones of Joseph that pledge future exodus (Gen. 50:24–25).

548), yet, as noted in the introduction to this commentary, the Josiah narrative finally moves in a very different direction by showing the powerlessness of Torah. First Kings 1–11, which recounts the reign of the supremely wise Solomon, ends in idolatry and division. Wisdom drops from 1–2 Kings after Solomon's reign, a sign that wisdom is not capable of preserving Israel from division and ultimately dissolution unless it comes as an incarnation of divine wisdom. In a similar way, near the end of 2 Kings, the narrator writes a two-chapter description of the perfect Torah-observant king, Josiah. He is the only king in the history who actually hears Torah and reads it (Knoppers 1994, 134), and like Solomon (1 Kgs. 3:9), he has a "hearing heart" (2 Kgs. 22:10–11, 18–19; 23:25), open to the rebuke of Israel's God and committed to Israel's Shema.

Great as he is, Josiah cannot save Judah from destruction. Like the house of Ahab (1 Kgs. 21:27–29), Judah is doomed despite the repentance of the king, and as with the houses of Jeroboam I (14:13) and Ahab (2 Kgs. 3:2), the final prophecy of doom comes to a king who is comparatively good. Wisdom does not save Israel from division; Torah, even when kept with incomparable faithfulness, cannot reverse the effects of generations of idolatry. The message of the reign of Josiah is not that the temple must yield to Torah, but that Torah is as impotent as the temple for saving the people of Yahweh. The law is powerless to purify the idolatries of Judah, and Judah is doomed to exile. As Habakkuk says, the law has "become impotent" (Hab. 1:4), and Josiah points to Jesus largely because of his failure, by showing that the law is weak and by leaving Israel desperately hoping for a greater king to perform what the law cannot accomplish.

Why then, as Paul might ask, the law? Paul answers at length in Romans. He begins with the announcement that the gospel reveals God's righteousness, from faith to faith (1:16–17). God's righteousness includes his faithfulness to his promises to Israel, his promise to bless the nations through Abraham and his seed, but righteousness also means something like "right order" and indicates God's commitment to establishing right order in his sin-damaged creation. Thus, the coming of righteousness is often equivalent to "salvation" (Isa. 51:4–11). When God brings righteousness, he comes to scatter the wicked and all his enemies, to rescue his chosen ones, and to establish harmony and right order in creation. Jesus embodies the righteousness of God, and the good news about Jesus unveils God's commitment to Israel and through Israel his commitment to bring his creation to its proper goal. God is determined to make his goodness—and the goodness of his creation—manifest by rescuing his good creation from tyranny of sin and death.

As Romans moves on, however, Paul shows that there is an obstacle to the fulfillment of these promises: the general obstacle of human sin and the more specific obstacle of Israel's sin. Israel, intended to be God's agent for restoring creation and regathering the nations to the Lord's house, instead causes Yahweh's name to be blasphemed among the Gentiles (2:17–29). Israel lies under a curse, specifically the curse of exile, which is the curse of death, and unless the curse on Israel is broken through, unless the curse of death is swallowed up in life, unless there is a true seed of Abraham, there is no hope that blessing will flow out to the Gentiles.

The sequence from Rom. 4–8 is similar to the sequence in Gal. 3–4 and addresses the question of the law's role in redemptive history. Abraham was justified by faith and not by the works of the law (in any sense of that disputed phrase). Why then was the law added? Paul says in Gal. 3:19 that the law was added because of transgressions, and in Romans, especially Rom. 7, Paul argues emphatically that the law cannot bring life. Because of sin and the dominance of flesh, the person who receives the law is radically divided (see the commentary on 2 Kgs. 17:1–41), schizophrenic, in a state of living death, torn apart between inward desire to obey God and total inability to do so. In Rom. 7, Paul, a representative Torah-loving Israelite, is on the rack, stretched out and desperate for deliverance. Torah is good and gives shape to love for God. But if the heart is not right, the law kills. As noted above (see the commentary on 2 Kgs. 21:1–26), the law drives to Christ and to faith in him. The law comes to genuine realization only in faith, and the law therefore exalts the glory and power of God who raises the dead. The law is realized through an incarnate Word-Torah made flesh.

Romans 8 brings these themes to a climax. In stark contrast to the world Paul describes in 1:18–32, a world under wrath, full of idolatry and sin, Rom. 8 describes the effects of God's action to restore creation and humanity, his righteous restoration of the world, his manifestation of his own infinite goodness. What the law is incapable of doing—transforming flesh into Spirit, overcoming the reign of sin and death that is the effect of God's condemnation—God does in the Son and Spirit. Only through the work of the Spirit does it become possible for sinners to fulfill the righteousness of the law (8:3–4), because only through the Spirit does a person become, as Adam was, drunk with joy and love for God. This is why the salvation of sinners is by faith and not by works: God must do what we are incapable of doing, just as Abraham was dependent upon God to give him a child when he and Sarah were too dead to bear children. This is the gospel of 1–2 Kings and of 2 Kgs. 22–23 in particular, as these chapters reveal the impotence of the law and the absolute need of an incarnate word who shares his Spirit.

2 KINGS 23:31–25:30

Overall, the historical books can be read as a fulfillment of the promise and threat of the Torah, and there are intriguing structural parallels between the Torah and the historical books. Together, Joshua and Judges form a new Genesis: Joshua recounts Israel's inheritance of the land promised to Abraham, and Judges tells of twelve judges, who correspond to the twelve sons of Jacob. In 1–2 Samuel, David appears as a new Moses who leads the people out of bondage to Philistia, conquers the city of Jerusalem, sets up a tent for the ark, and receives a promise that establishes new covenantal arrangements for Israel (2 Sam. 7). In many respects, 1–2 Kings corresponds with the book of Numbers: the rebellion of Jeroboam I repeats Israel's golden-calf rebellion (Exod. 32), and periodic revolts and destructions mark 1–2 Kings, as also in Numbers, while the end of 2 Kings corresponds with Deuteronomy, which climaxes with predictions of exile and return (Deut. 28–33).

At the same time, the end of 2 Kings is also structurally connected to the beginning of the book, as everything established during the golden age of Solomon begins to unravel. Under Solomon, Egypt entered a marriage alliance with Judah, but in the end Egypt conquers Judah (23:31–37). Solomon received tribute, but his descendants pay it. Solomon's accumulated masses of gold and silver steadily flow out of Israel and Judah over the centuries, and Nebuchadnezzar removes the last of it (25:15). The temple built by Solomon is burned down, as are the palace and much of the city of Jerusalem (25:9). Judah no longer possesses land extending to Solomonic and Abrahamic boundaries (1 Kgs. 4:21). Instead, Nebuchadnezzar does (מנחל מצרים עד־נהר־פרת) (2 Kgs. 24:7).

The final section of 2 Kings also continues parallels between the northern and southern kingdoms and particularly highlights similarities between the end of the Omride and Davidic dynasties (Leithart 2005a). Though a righteous king,

Josiah's death is reminiscent of Ahab's: both are killed during battles with a Gentile power, and both are taken from the battlefield to the capital city to be buried (1 Kgs. 22:34–37; 2 Kgs. 23:28–30). Both Ahab and Josiah hear a prophecy of doom on their dynasties, but both are told that judgment will fall during the reign of their sons and not during their lifetimes (1 Kgs. 21:20–29; 2 Kgs. 22:15–20). Beyond this, Ahab and Josiah live in similar periods of history with respect to their dynasties and kingdoms. Within a generation of Ahab's death, his son is overthrown by Yahweh's avenger, Jehu (2 Kgs. 9–10), who slaughters the royal family and destroys the temple of Baal in Samaria. Two of Ahab's sons reign over Israel (Ahaziah [2 Kgs. 1] and Jehoram [2 Kgs. 3:1; 9:14–16]) and, though several kings follow Josiah (Jehoahaz, Jehoiakim, Jehoiachin, Zedekiah), the dynasty goes only two generations past Josiah (Jehoahaz and Jehoiakim are both sons of Josiah [23:34], and Jehoiachin is his grandson). The fall of Samaria likewise sets the pattern for the fall of Jerusalem. Both cities suffer three sieges, each from two different enemies. Samaria is twice besieged by the Arameans (1 Kgs. 20:1; 2 Kgs. 6:24) and once by Assyria (17:5), while Jerusalem is besieged once by Assyria (2 Kgs. 18–19) and twice by the Babylonians (24:10; 25:1). For both cities, attacks come because the kings of Israel and Judah break alliances with powerful Gentiles (Provan 1995, 278–79). In each case, the city is delivered during the first sieges, but ultimately falls in the last.

As in the most tumultuous periods of Israel's history, the kings of Judah who put themselves on the throne last only a brief time, while those installed by Gentiles last longer, though many eventually rebel. Over the course of little more than two decades, Judah falls from the heights of Josiah into exile, as the north falls precipitously between Jeroboam II and Hoshea, cast out from the face of Yahweh.[1] As Cohn points out, the last days of Judah follow a neat schema that points to order within the chaos of the history being recorded (2000, 163–64):

2 Kings 23:31–24:2	2 Kings 24:8–25:1
Jehoahaz for three months	Jehoiachin for three months
Jehoahaz imprisoned by Pharaoh	Jehoiachin imprisoned by Nebuchadnezzar
Pharaoh places Eliakim on throne and changes his name	Nebuchadnezzar sets Mattaniah on throne and changes his name
Pharaoh takes Jehoahaz to Egypt; Jehoahaz dies in Egypt	Nebuchadnezzar takes Jehoiachin to Babylon; Jehoiachin does not die in Babylon

1. Jehoahaz reigns a mere three months following the death of Josiah (23:31), but his brother Eliakim/Jehoiakim, set up as a puppet of Pharaoh Neco, reigns for eleven years (23:36). Jehoiakim rebels (24:1), and in response Yahweh sends in Chaldeans, Arameans, Moabites, and Ammonites (24:2), so that the very peoples subdued by David and Solomon make a comeback. Because of the sins of Judah and especially Manasseh, Judah becomes virtually a Canaanite nation: why not move the Canaanites back in? When Jehoiakim dies, his son replaces him, but Jehoiachin is no sooner on the throne than the Babylonians are at the gates, ending his reign after only three months (24:8). Nebuchadnezzar puts Jehoiachin's uncle Mattaniah/Zedekiah in his place, and he reigns for eleven years before rebelling (24:18–20).

2 Kings 23:31–24:2	2 Kings 24:8–25:1
Jehoiakim reigns eleven years	Zedekiah reigns eleven years
Jehoiakim rebels against Nebuchadnezzar	Zedekiah rebels against Nebuchadnezzar
God brings attackers	Yahweh rejects Judah[2]

Comparing these sequences, we can see that Judah's dealings with Egypt foreshadow its dealings with Babylon, and this suggests that the writer of 1–2 Kings is operating within Isaiah's notion of a "second exodus" from Babylon that recapitulates the exodus from Egypt. The final chapters of 1–2 Kings also complete a larger pattern of sevens that runs through the history of Judah:

> six kings and then Athaliah interrupts the dynasty
> six kings and then Manasseh reigns as the worst Davidic king ever
> six kings and then Nebuchadnezzar destroys the city and the temple

At the end of this triple "sabbatical" sequence, Judah, Yahweh's new creation within humanity, is systematically decreated, and Yahweh gives the remnant of his people into the hands of their enemies. Since Egypt is the model for Babylon, Judah has some hope for restoration after a period of exile, as the author of 1–2 Kings leaves open the hope of an "eighth" day following the Sabbath of judgment.

The systematic decreation of the temple and kingdom of Judah is evident also in Nebuchadnezzar's plundering of the temple, the seventh in the history of 1–2 Kings (Davis 2005, 207):

1. Shishak of Egypt (1 Kgs. 14:26)
2. Asa (1 Kgs. 15:18)
3. Joash (2 Kgs. 12:17–18)
4. Jehoash of Israel (2 Kgs. 14:13–14)
5. Ahaz (2 Kgs. 16:7–8)
6. Hezekiah (2 Kgs. 18:14–16)
7. Nebuchadnezzar (2 Kgs. 24:13–14)

With Nebuchadnezzar's invasion, the temple is ruined and emptied, and the land has rest from Judah's idolatry and the shedding of innocent blood. Ignored and abused for centuries, the temple is sent into exile, as Yahweh predicts already to Solomon (1 Kgs. 9:6–9). In this, the ruined temple foreshadows the human temple, the dwelling of God in flesh, who is also abused and ruined,

2. Hobbs (1985, 360) suggests a neat outline for 2 Kgs. 25:
  A king (25:4–7)
    B city (25:8–12)
      C temple (25:13–17)
      C′ leaders (25:18–21)
    B′ people (25:22–26)
  A′ king (25:27–30)

who endures the exile of crucifixion in the confidence that he will be rebuilt after three days, vindicated by his Father (John 2:19–22).

By the reckoning of the Old Testament prophets (Dan. 2; 7), Babylon is the first in a series of Gentile empires to exercise sovereignty over Israel—and to guard them—until the coming of the Messiah. After the times of the Gentiles will come a fifth monarchy, the monarchy of the Son of Man who will receive all the dominion and authority and power of the four beasts and will rule over an everlasting kingdom (Dan. 7:9–22). Time is no longer reckoned by the reigns of Davidic kings, but by the reign of the Babylonian emperor (2 Kgs. 25:1, 8, 27). The fall of Jerusalem occurs in the ninth year of Zedekiah (25:1), and by that time, Nebuchadnezzar's regnal years are the only ones left. Gedaliah, the governor appointed by Nebuchadnezzar, has no years: he is killed in the "seventh month," but of what year we are not told (25:25). The times of the Gentiles begin, which is the time of empire (Nelson 1987, 263).

George Orwell's *1984* was prophetic in a subtler way than many readers or imitators realize. Contrary to the fears of some, 1984 has come and gone, and, Orwell notwithstanding, there is no sign of Big Brother. Lovers can still hold hands in public and make love in private, children can still learn nursery rhymes and sing in the streets, no telescreen monitors every breath and heartbeat, and no Thought Police threaten to burst into homes on midnight raids. Orwell was, however, prophetic about what in my view was the central theme of the novel. The focus of *1984* was not exclusively totalitarian restrictions of individual freedom. Though that is clearly an important emphasis, Orwell was at least equally concerned with how the state, totalitarian or not, blunts memory and rewrites history.

History occupies a central place in Orwell's novel. The hero, Winston Smith, works for the "Ministry of Truth," where he spends his days updating old newspaper reports and tossing the originals down a memory hole. Winston's updated version of history becomes the official record, as all contrary reports are replaced and destroyed. One of the central pillars of the party philosophy is the "mutability of history"; history is what the party says it is. The prerevolutionary world exists only in the minds of those who are alive, and they are considered insane. There is no documentation that anything has ever been different, and Winston is not even certain that the year is 1984.

The party rewrites history, first, because it forces everyone to accept current conditions by removing any standards by which the present can be judged and, second, because it protects the infallibility of the party. The party never admits any change in policy or any error in its projections of future economic conditions. All the records show that the standard of living continues to rise. In one instant, Oceania, where Winston lives, is at war with Eurasia and at peace with Eastasia; in the next, it is at war with Eastasia and at peace with Eurasia. But the party never admits that any change has taken place. Oceania, the party insists, has always been at war with Eastasia, and thanks to the Ministry of Truth the party has the documents to prove it.

Historical understanding among Americans and American Christians is weak, and there are many disturbing signs not only of ignorance of the past, but a deliberate suppression. Europe seems eager to expunge any record of Christianity from its past (Weigel 2005), and this rewriting of history is evident in both obvious and subtle ways. For centuries, the West, believing that Christ had indeed inaugurated a new creation, placed Christ at the center of history; Christ's death and resurrection marked *the* turning point, the date from which all other events are dated. The time after Jesus was the time of Jesus, the years of our Lord. Scholars in the last century have ceased to use the old Christian BC and AD system of dividing history and have adopted BCE and CE in their place. Commonness, toleration, detente, and democracy replace the reign of the Lord Christ as the fundamental defining characteristics of our age. The date remains the same, but the cross is tossed down a memory hole. Chronology is sovereignty, and Nebuchadnezzar's taking over for the kings of Judah is a sign of Judah's exile. The triumph of non-Christian chronology is likewise a sign of the church's exile in the contemporary world.

Nebuchadnezzar completes the removal of the glories of Solomon from the land. He begins with the gold of the temple (2 Kgs. 24:13) and later comes to remove all the bronze (25:13–17). The narrator gives particular attention to the destruction of the monumental pillars Jachin and Boaz, ironically providing the dimensions of the pillars as they are being disassembled and cut into pieces. Long before, Pharaoh Shishak had invaded Jerusalem and removed the gold but left the bronze (1 Kgs. 14:25–28), but at least Rehoboam's kingdom could boast of bronze. No more. Not only has the golden age deteriorated into the bronze, but even the bronze age is at an end. Parallel to the removal of temple vessels is the removal of people. Initially, Nebuchadnezzar removes the skilled inhabitants of Jerusalem (2 Kgs. 24:14–15), the "gold" of the nation, leaving the poorest. Ultimately, he removes the poor as well.

When Zedekiah rebels against Nebuchadnezzar, the Babylonians return and show no mercy. Zedekiah ("Yah is righteous") is captured, blinded, and taken to Babylon, where we hear nothing more of him. That he is blinded after witnessing the deaths of his sons (25:7) not only highlights the cruelty of the Babylonians but alludes back to an earlier devastation at Shiloh. At the battle of Aphek, the sons of the blind priest Eli are killed, and then Eli himself dies. But the most grievous aspect of that battle is that the Philistines capture the ark of the covenant of Yahweh. Here, a king witnesses the deaths of his sons and is then deported, and in the surrounding context the entire house of Yahweh is dismantled. The tragedy of Shiloh is happening all over again (Jer. 7).

The city, once so full of people, is a widow in tears (Lam. 1:1–2), yet in the midst of weeping there is a note of hope. In the middle of a seventy-year exile, in the thirty-seventh year, the king of Babylon removes Jehoiachin from prison (2 Kgs. 25:27–30), as Pharaoh brought Joseph from his prison long before. A change of clothes is a change of status and role, and Jehoiachin moves from prisoner to king's favorite to eat at the table of the king of Babylon. Someday, Judah will be raised up from the prison house of exile, given garments of glory and beauty, and set in the land to receive portions from King Yahweh all the days of its life.

Through the course of 1–2 Kings, Yahweh's people, especially those of the Davidic dynasty, are never without hope. But the focus of their hope is progressively refined, chastened, and sifted. For those who would trust in the wisdom of a king, 1–2 Kings records the cautionary tale of Solomon, the wisest of all kings but ultimately an idolater. For those who would trust in Torah, there is the frustrating tale of Josiah, the perfect Torah keeper whose obedience is insufficient to reverse the decline of Judah. And for those who cry "the temple of the Lord, the temple of the Lord, the temple of the Lord," there is the story of the temple's final destruction. Yet, it is precisely through these failures that Yahweh intends to achieve Israel's salvation, which always lies in new life beyond the grave. The book of Kings is from one angle the story of a temple ignored, rejected, and ultimately dismantled and sent out of the land. Yet, the dispersion of that temple is also the dispersion of the people of God, as the living river of Judah (including such stars of heaven as Daniel and Ezekiel) flows to the four corners of the earth. Israel's destruction brings blessing to the nations, as centuries later living water flows from the human temple of Yahweh, torn on a cross, when the temple veil is rent and a sword pierces his side (John 19:31–37).

Though pointing to the history of the last Adam, the history of Judah is in itself an Adamic history, a feature captured by an important detail early in 2 Kgs. 25. The flight of Zedekiah recapitulates the flight of Ahaziah in 2 Kgs. 9. In both cases, a king of Judah flees an enemy—Ahaziah from Jehu, and Zedekiah from Nebuchadnezzar and the Chaldeans. In neither case does the king escape. Ahaziah is killed, and Zedekiah is captured, blinded, and led away to exile. In both cases, the death or capture of the king is followed by an interruption of the Davidic line of kings. After Ahaziah is killed, Athaliah takes the throne in Jerusalem, the only non-Davidic ruler in Judah through the whole of the monarchy, and after Zedekiah is killed no Davidic ruler rises to take his place.

The two stories are also tied together by two gardens. Second Kings 9:27 informs us that "when Ahaziah king of Judah saw, he fled by the way of the garden house [דרך בית הגן]," and a similar description appears in the account of Zedekiah's flight from the encroaching armies of Nebuchadnezzar: "All the men of war fled by night by way of the gate between the two walls beside the king's garden [על־גן המלך]" (25:4).[3] Garden motifs are common in the Bible, but the word "garden" does not occur often and is very rare in the historical books of the Old Testament. Between Gen. 3 and 1 Kings, in fact, the word is used only once, in Deut. 11:10, and the first time it is used

---

3. Though 2 Kgs. 25 does not explicitly say that the king is in the company of those who flee, this may be inferred from (a) 25:4–5, which records the flight of the "men of war" through the Arabah and the subsequent capture of the king in the plains of Jericho, which is part of the Arabah; and (b) the description of the pursuit and capture of the king immediately after the flight of the "men of war," leaving the suggestion that the parties being pursued in 25:5–6 are the same ones who escape in 25:4.

in 1–2 Kings it refers to Naboth's vineyard, which Ahab wants to turn into a "vegetable garden" (1 Kgs. 21:2). Naboth's vineyard is clearly in view in 2 Kgs. 9:21, when Jehu throws the body of Joram, the grandson of Ahab, on the field of Naboth (9:25), and the garden along the way of escape in 2 Kgs. 25 is a reminder of the blood of Naboth crying for vengeance, which has now been mingled with the blood of Manasseh's victims.[4]

Eden provides the deep background to these garden references. Zedekiah is an Adam driven from the garden and a Cain whose brother's blood stains the land. As descendants of David, the kings of Judah are Adamic kings, inheriting the gift of a garden land. Because they listen to the voice of the tempter and persistently indulge in idolatry, they are sent out, along with the new Eve, Israel. Once they break covenant, the curse of death will come. Yahweh waits patiently for the sins of the Amor-Israelites to mature, but when that day comes he does not hold back his hand. The Davidic Adam will be cast from the garden to the east, and cherubim will block his return until the Lord pleases.

In the commentary on 1 Kgs. 17:1–24, I was careful to distinguish between the remnant and the renewal movement led by Elijah and Elisha. In Old Testament usage, there is a remnant only after a judgment that threatens utterly to destroy Israel, and the remnant is not a portion of Israel but the whole Israel that survives the judgment. Important as this distinction is, it is also important to recognize that in important respects there are continuities between the prophetic movements in the history of Israel and the remnant community that eventually returns to the land as if risen from the dead. This is particularly apparent in the later history of Judah when we read the history of 2 Kings from the perspective of Jeremiah.

Living through the latter days of Judah, Jeremiah is a sharp critic of all forms of zealotry, all vain efforts to stave off the Babylonian invasion and conquest. Rather than resist, Jeremiah prophesies, Judah should surrender to Nebuchadnezzar, whom Yahweh has raised up as his agent (Jer. 27). Surrender and seek the peace of Babylon, Jeremiah urges, and you will survive (Jer. 29). Those who listen to Jeremiah survive and even prosper in exile (e.g., Daniel), but those who resist Nebuchadnezzar are destroyed. In short, those who allied themselves with Yahweh's prophet survive the Babylonian invasion and became part of the renewed, remnant Israel that returns from exile. In exile, those who hear Torah faithfully and listen to the prophets serve the peace of the city where they are exiled, but also keep themselves from idols. Living among Gentiles, the faithful are not swallowed up in the culture or worship of Gentiles. The

4. Hobbs (1985, 360) suggests a neat outline for 2 Kgs. 25:
    A king (25:4–7)
      B city (25:8–12)
          C temple (25:13–17)
          C′ leaders (25:18–21)
      B′ people (25:22–26)
    A′ king (25:27–30)

prophetic communities of renewal, while not identical to the remnant, prepare the way for the future remnant. Likewise, renewal movements in the church, while not identical to the true church or a remnant, prepare the way for the remnant that will eventually emerge from exile. When the Lord purges his church, those who cling to the Lord of the church in faith will be saved and will be reunited with those who emerge from the ruins of other churches, blinking in the sunlight, those who have also faithfully listened to the great prophet, obeyed the incarnate Torah, prayed toward the living temple.

Death in exile is Yahweh's means for reuniting Israel, and Yves Congar is one who recognizes the parallels between Israel's exile and ecclesial reunion. In an article exploring the figuration of Christian division within the history of Israel, he speculates, "one is tempted to ask what trials or deportations will perhaps be necessary before Christians find themselves united once more . . . one begins to wonder what price we shall perhaps have to pay for the grace of reunion" (quoted in Radner 1998, 36n61).

Without laying claim to a prophetic mantle, I think it plausible that Congar was living through the very trials he wondered about and that the church has been paying the price for reunion for several centuries. Modernity is, arguably, the Babylonian exile of the church, its (often voluntary) marginalization and retreat from the cultural and political engagement inherent in the evangelical proclamation that Jesus is Lord. If modernity seems a rather comfortable exile, we should remember the hundreds of thousands, perhaps millions, of believers slaughtered by people in the grip of manic modern ideologies; we should remember the vicious wars of religion that decimated Europe in the seventeenth century and the systematic efforts at de-Christianization that occurred during the French Revolution; we should recall that Christians too were killed in Nazi death camps and that believers were imprisoned, tortured, and murdered in various Marxist gulags; we should contemplate the piles of skulls in Idi Amin's Uganda and the Christians in the killing fields of Cambodia. If modernity seems a rather comfortable exile, it is so only because we have become too self-absorbed to see the cost that others have been paying for our sophistical idolatries and the divisions that they have produced.

The notion that modernity is the church's Babylonian exile is ultimately a heartening thought, for it seems clear that the modern project is collapsing everywhere. The modern world has been drinking the cup of wrath to the dregs and beginning to stumble like a drunkard (Jer. 25). And while modernity staggers in its death throes, there are signs that the centuries-long estrangement of the church from itself is ending and that in this exile, as in Israel's, the Lord has been quietly binding the stick of Judah to the stick of Israel to bring both back from the grave together.

The book of Kings leaves Israel east of Eden, awaiting a return that is not yet come. And so it leaves us, a divided Christendom exiled in modern secularism, enduring the times of the Gentiles. It leaves us in exile, but it does not leave us without hope of return.

BIBLIOGRAPHY

Ackerman, James S. 1990. "Knowing Good and Evil: A Literary Analysis of the Court History in 2 Samuel 9–20 and 1 Kings 1–2." *Journal of Biblical Literature* 109.

Allison, Dale. 1993. *The New Moses: A Matthean Typology*. Minneapolis: Fortress.

Anderson, Fred, and Andrew Clayton. 2005. *The Dominion of War: Empire and Liberty in North America, 1500–2000*. New York: Viking.

Appler, Deborah A. 1999. "From Queen to Cuisine: Food Imagery in the Jezebel Narrative." *Semeia* 86.

Augustine. 1983. *Ennarations on the Psalms*. Nicene and Post-Nicene Fathers 1.8. Reprint, Grand Rapids: Eerdmans.

———. 1997. *On Christian Teaching*. Translated by R. P. H. Green. World's Classics. Oxford: Oxford University Press.

———. 1998. *The Trinity*. Translated by Edmund Hill. Works of Saint Augustine: A Translation for the 21st Century. Hyde Park, NY: New City Press.

Bacevich, Andrew. 2004. *American Empire: The Reality and Consequences of U.S. Diplomacy*. Cambridge: Harvard University Press.

Barth, Karl. 1939–69. *Church Dogmatics*. 4 vols. Translated by Geoffrey Bromiley. Edited by Thomas F. Torrance. London: Clark.

Bauman, Zygmunt. 2005. *Liquid Life*. Cambridge: Polity.

Berger, Peter. 1979. *The Heretical Imperative: Contemporary Possibilities of Religious Affirmation*. Garden City, NY: Doubleday.

Blenkinsopp, Joseph. 1992. *The Pentateuch: An Introduction to the First Five Books of the Bible*. London: SCM.

Boersma, Hans. 2004. *Violence, Hospitality, and the Cross: Reappropriating the Atonement Tradition*. Grand Rapids: Baker.

Bonhoeffer, Dietrich. 2004. *Creation and Fall: A Theological Exposition of Genesis 1–3*. Translated by Martin Ruter and Ilse Todt. Dietrich Bonhoeffer Works 3. Minneapolis: Fortress.

Borg, Marcus. 1998. *Conflict Holiness and Politics in the Teaching of Jesus*. Harrisburg, PA: Trinity.

Breck, John. 1994. *The Shape of Biblical Language*. Crestwood, NY: St. Vladimir's Seminary Press.

Brodie, Thomas L. 1999. *The Crucial Bridge: The Elijah-Elisha Narratives as an Interpretive Synthesis of Genesis-Kings and a Literary Model for the Gospels*. Collegeville, MN: Liturgical Press.

Brown, Francis; S. R. Driver; and C. A. Briggs. 1980. *The New Brown-Driver-Briggs-Gesenius Hebrew and English Lexicon*. Lafayette, IN: Associated Publishers & Authors.

Brueggemann, Walter. 2000. *1 and 2 Kings*. Smyth and Helwys Bible Commentary. Macon, GA: Smyth & Helwys.

Calvin, John. 1960. *Institutes of the Christian Religion.* 2 vols. Translated by Ford Lewis Battles. Edited by John T. McNeill. Library of Christian Classics 20–21. Philadelphia: Westminster.

———. 1983. *An Admonition, Showing the Advantage Which Christendom Might Derive from an Inventory of Relics.* Edited and translated by Henry Beveridge. Selected Works of John Calvin: Tracts and Letters. Grand Rapids: Baker.

Cavanaugh, William. 1998. *Torture and Eucharist.* Challenges in Contemporary Theology. London: Blackwell.

———. 2002. *Theo-political Imagination: Discovering the Liturgy as a Political Act in an Age of Global Consumerism.* London: Clark.

Charry, Ellen. 1993. "Academic Theology in Pastoral Perspective." *Theology Today* 50.

Chesterton, G. K. 1986. *Orthodoxy.* Collected Works 1. San Francisco: Ignatius.

Coakley, Sarah. 1996. "What Does Chalcedon Solve and What Does It Not? Some Reflections on the Status and Meaning of the Chalcedonian 'Definition.'" In *The Incarnation.* Edited by Stephen T. Davis. Oxford: Oxford University Press.

Cohn, Robert L. 1982. "The Literary Logic of 1 Kings 17–19." *Journal of Biblical Literature* 101.

———. 1985. "Convention and Creativity in the Book of Kings: The Case of the Dying Monarch." *Catholic Biblical Quarterly* 47.

———. 2000. *2 Kings.* Berit Olam. Collegeville, MN: Liturgical Press.

Colson, Charles. 2002. "A New Century of Martyrs: Anti-Christian Intolerance." http://www.bereanpublishers.com/Persecution_of_Christians/a_new_century_of_martyrs.htm.

Davis, Dale Ralph. 2002. *The Wisdom and the Folly: An Exposition of the Book of First Kings.* Fearn, Ross-shire, England: Christian Focus.

———. 2005. *The Power and the Fury: 2 Kings.* Fearn, Ross-shire, England: Christian Focus.

Deurloo, K. A. 1989. "The King's Wisdom in Judgment: A Narration as Example (1 Kings iii)." *Old Testament Studies.*

Dillard, Ray. 1999. *Faith in the Face of Apostasy: The Gospel according to Elijah and Elisha.* Phillipsburg, NJ: P&R.

Dulles, Avery. 1987. *Models of the Church.* Expanded edition. New York: Doubleday.

Eire, Carlos M. N. 1989. *War against the Idols: The Reformation of Worship from Erasmus to Calvin.* Cambridge: Cambridge University Press.

Ellul, Jacques. 1972. *The Politics of God and the Politics of Man.* Translated by Geoffrey Bromiley. Grand Rapids: Eerdmans.

Fretheim, Terence. 1983. *The Deuteronomistic History.* Nashville: Abingdon.

———. 1999. *First and Second Kings.* Westminster Bible Companion. Louisville: John Knox.

Frisch, Amos. 1991. "Structure and Its Significance: The Narrative of Solomon's Reign (1 Kings 1–12:24)." *Journal for the Study of the Old Testament* 51.

Gay, Craig. 1998. *The Way of the (Modern) World; or, Why It's Tempting to Live as If God Doesn't Exist.* Grand Rapids: Eerdmans.

Gierke, Otto. 1987 [1900]. *Political Theories of the Middle Age.* Translated by F. W. Maitland. Cambridge: Cambridge University Press.

Girard, René. 1986. *The Scapegoat.* Translated by Yvonne Freccero. Baltimore: Johns Hopkins University Press.

———. 2001. *I See Satan Fall Like Lightning.* Translated by James G. Williams. Maryknoll, NY: Orbis.

Goldberg, Elkhonon. 2005. *The Wisdom Paradox: How Your Mind Can Grow Stronger as Your Brain Grows Older.* New York: Gotham.

Gowan, Donald E. 1998. *Theology of the Prophetic Books: The Death and Resurrection of Israel.* Louisville: Westminster John Knox.

Gray, John. 1970. *I and II Kings: A Commentary.* Second edition. Old Testament Library. London: SCM.

Harnack, Adolf von. 1895–1900. *History of Dogma*. Translated by Neil Buchanan. 7 vols. London: Williams & Norgate.

Hart, David Bentley. 2003. *The Beauty of the Infinite: The Aesthetics of Christian Truth*. Grand Rapids: Eerdmans.

Heaney, Seamus, trans. 2000. *Beowulf*. New York: Norton, 2000.

Henry, Matthew. 1708. *Matthew Henry's Commentary on the Whole Bible*. 6 vols. Reprint, Iowa Falls, IA: World Bible.

Herntrich, V., and G. Schrenk. 1967. "Λεῖμμα κτλ." In *Theological Dictionary of the New Testament*, vol. 4. Edited by G. Kittel. Translated by Geoffrey W. Bromiley. Grand Rapids: Eerdmans.

Heschel, Abraham J. 1955. *The Prophets*. 2 vols. New York: Harper & Row.

Hobbs, T. R. 1985. *2 Kings*. Word Biblical Commentary 13. Waco: Word.

Hodge, Charles. 1986. *Systematic Theology*. 3 vols. Reprint, Grand Rapids: Eerdmans.

Hollerich, Michael. 2004. "Carl Schmitt." In *The Blackwell Companion to Political Theology*. Edited by Peter Scott and William T. Cavanaugh. London: Blackwell.

Horne, Mark. 2003. *The Victory according to Mark*. Moscow, ID: Canon.

Irenaeus. 1981. *Against All Heresies*. Ante-Nicene Fathers. Reprint, Grand Rapids: Eerdmans.

Jacobs, Jane. 2004. *Dark Age Ahead*. New York: Random.

Jones, Peter. 2003. "The Paganization of Biblical Studies." http://tcrnews2.com/biblical studies.html.

Jordan, James B. 1988a. *Through New Eyes: Developing a Biblical View of the World*. Nashville: Wolgemuth & Hyatt.

———. 1988b. *Thoughts on Jachin and Boaz*. Tyler, TX: Biblical Horizons.

———. 1990a. "Confusion among Kings." *Biblical Chronology*.

———. 1990b. *The Meaning of Clean and Unclean*. Studies in Food and Faith 10. Tyler, TX: Biblical Horizons.

———. 1990c. "The Mysterious Numbers of Edwin R. Thiele." *Biblical Chronology*.

http://www.biblicalhorizons.com/ch/ch2_09.htm

———. 1991. "The Abomination of Desolation, part 4a: Abominable and Detestable." *Biblical Horizons* 31. http://www.biblical horizons.com/bh/bh031.htm.

———. 1998. "The Third Word." *Rite Reasons* 60. http://www.biblicalhorizons.com/rr/rr060.htm.

Kagan, Robert. 2004. *Of Paradise and Power: America and Europe in the New World Order*. New York: Vintage.

Kant, Immanuel. 1960. *Religion within the Limits of Reason Alone*. Translated by Theodore M. Greene and Hoyt H. Hudson. Second edition. LaSalle, IL: Open Court.

Keil, C. F. 1965. *The Books of the Kings*. Translated by James Martin. Biblical Commentary on the Old Testament. Reprint, Grand Rapids: Eerdmans.

Kierkegaard, Søren. 1983. *Fear and Trembling/Repetition*. Translated by Howard V. Hong and Edna H. Hong. Kierkegaard's Writings. 6. Princeton: Princeton University Press.

Kim, Jean Kyoung. 2005. "Reading and Retelling Naaman's Story (2 Kings 5)." *Journal for the Study of the Old Testament* 30.

Klawans, Jonathan. 2000. *Impurity and Sin in Ancient Israel*. Oxford: Oxford University Press.

Kline, Meredith G. 1986. *Images of the Spirit*. South Hamilton, MA: privately printed.

Knaut, Ernst Axel. 2000. "Does 'Deut. Historiography' (DtrH) Exist?" In *Israel Constructs Its History: Deuteronomistic Historiography in Recent Research*. Edited by Albert de Pury et al. Journal for the Study of the Old Testament Supplement Series 306. Sheffield: JSOT Press.

Knoppers, Gary N. 1994. *Two Nations under God: The Deuteronomistic History of Solomon and the Davidic Monarchies*, vol. 2: *The Reign of Jeroboam, the Fall of Israel, and the Reign of Josiah*. Harvard Semitic Museum Monograph 53. Atlanta: Scholars Press.

LaVerdiere, Eugene. 1994. *Dining in the Kingdom of God: The Origins of the Eucharist according to Luke*. Chicago: Liturgy Training Publications.

Leithart, Peter J. 2000a. *A House for My Name: A Survey of the Old Testament*. Moscow, ID: Canon.

———. 2000b. "Making and Mis-Making: Poiesis in Exodus 25–40." *International Journal of Systematic Theology* 2.

———. 2001. "Nabal and His Wine." *Journal of Biblical Literature* 120.

———. 2003a. *From Silence to Song: The Davidic Liturgical Revolution*. Moscow, ID: Canon.

———. 2003b. "The Gospel, Gregory VII, and Modern Theology." *Modern Theology* 19.

———. 2003c. *The Priesthood of the Plebs: A Theology of Baptism*. Eugene, OR: Wipf & Stock.

———. 2003d. *A Son to Me: An Exposition of 1–2 Samuel*. Moscow, ID: Canon.

———. 2005a. "Counterfeit Davids, Davidic Restoration, and the Architecture of Kings." *Tyndale Bulletin*.

———. 2005b. "Old and New in Sacramental Theology New and Old." *Pro Ecclesia*.

———. 2005c. "Still Our Ancient Foe." *Touchstone*.

Leithart, Peter J., and James B. Jordan. 1995. "At the Center of the Book of Kings." *Biblical Horizons* 79. http://www.biblicalhorizons.com/bh/bh079.htm.

Lemke, W. E. 1976. "The Way of Obedience: I Kings 13 and the Structure of the Deuteronomistic History." In *Magnalia Dei, the Mighty Acts of God: Essays on the Bible and Archaeology in Memory of G. Ernest Wright*. Edited by F. M. Cross et al. Garden City: Doubleday.

Lewis, Naphtali. 1983. *Life in Egypt under Roman Rule*. Classics in Papyrology. Oxford: David Brown.

Locke, John. 1963. "A Letter concerning Toleration." In *The Works of John Locke* 6. New edition. Reprint, Aalen, Germany: Scientia Verlag.

Long, Stephen. 2004. "God Is Not Nice." In *God Is Not. . . .* Edited by D. Brent Laytham. Grand Rapids: Brazos.

Marshall, Bruce. 2005. "Quod scit una uetula." In *The Theology of Thomas Aquinas*.

Edited by Rik van Nieuwenhove and Joseph Wawrykow. Notre Dame: University of Notre Dame Press.

Masuzawa, Tomoko. 2005. *The Invention of World Religions*. Chicago: University of Chicago Press.

Mead, James K. 1999. "Kings and Prophets, Donkeys and Lions." *Vetus Testamentum* 49.

Meier, Heinrich. 1998. *The Lesson of Carl Schmitt: Four Chapters on the Distinction between Political Theology and Political Philosophy*. Translated by Marcus Brainard. Chicago: University of Chicago Press.

Milbank, John. 1990a. "The End of Dialogue." In *Christian Uniqueness Reconsidered: The Myth of a Pluralistic Theology of Religions*. Edited by Gavin D'Costa. Maryknoll, NY: Orbis.

———. 1990b. *Theology and Social Theory: Beyond Secular Reason*. London: Blackwell.

———. 1991. *The Religious Dimension in the Thought of Giambattista Vico, 1668–1744*, part 1: *The Early Metaphysics*. Studies in the History of Philosophy 23. Lewiston, NY: Mellen.

———. 1995. "Can a Gift Be Given: Prolegomena to a Future Trinitarian Metaphysics." *Modern Theology* 11.

———. 1997. *The Word Made Strange: Theology, Language, Culture*. London: Blackwell.

———. 1999. "Knowledge: The Theological Critique of Philosophy in Hamann and Jacobi." In *Radical Orthodoxy*. Edited by John Milbank, Catherine Pickstock, and Graham Ward. New York: Routledge.

Milgrom, Jacob. 1970. *Studies in Levitical Terminology*. University of California Publications: Near Eastern Studies 14. Berkeley: University of California Press.

———. 1991. *Leviticus 1–16*. Anchor Bible 3. New York: Doubleday.

Minear, Paul. 2004. *Images of the Church in the New Testament*. New Testament Library. Louisville: Westminster John Knox.

Molnar, Thomas. 1988. *Twin Powers: Politics and the Sacred*. Grand Rapids: Eerdmans.

Moltmann, Jürgen. 1974. *The Crucified God: The Cross of Christ as the Foundation and Criticism of Christian Theology*. Translated by R. A. Wilson and John Bowden. New York: Harper & Row.

Mulder, Martin J. 1998. *1 Kings*, vol. 1.1: *Kings 1–11*. Historical Commentary on the Old Testament. Leuven: Peeters.

Nelson, Richard. 1987. *First and Second Kings*. Interpretation. Louisville: John Knox.

Neusner, Jacob. 1979. *From Politics to Piety: The Emergence of the Pharisaic Traditions*. Second edition. New York: Ktav.

Niebuhr, Reinhold. 1932. *Moral Man and Immoral Society*. New York: Scribner.

———. 1963. *An Interpretation of Christian Ethics*. San Francisco: Harper & Row.

Nietzsche, Friedrich. 1982. *The Portable Nietzsche*. Edited and translated by Walter Kaufmann. New York: Viking Penguin.

———. 1988. *The Antichrist*. Translated by H. L. Mencken. Costa Mesa, CA: Noontide.

Nisbet, Robert. 1988. *The Present Age: Progress and Anarchy in Modern America*. San Francisco: Harper & Row.

Noth, Martin. 1957. *Überlieferungsgeschichtliche Studien: Die sammelnden und bearbeiten Geschichtswerke im Alten Testament*. Second edition. Tübingen: Niemeyer.

O'Donovan, Oliver. 1996. *Desire of Nations*. Cambridge: Cambridge University Press.

Pannenberg, Wolfhart. 1989. *Christianity in a Secularized World*. New York: Crossroad.

Pelikan, Jaroslav. 1971. *The Christian Tradition: A History of the Development of Doctrine*, vol. 1: *The Emergence of the Catholic Tradition (100–600)*. Chicago: University of Chicago Press.

Pickstock, Catherine. 1998. *After Writing: On the Liturgical Consummation of Philosophy*. Oxford: Blackwell.

Pritchard, James B., ed. 1969. *Ancient Near Eastern Texts Relating to the Old Testament*. Third edition. Princeton: Princeton University Press.

Provan, Iain W. 1995. *1 and 2 Kings*. New International Biblical Commentary. Peabody, MA: Hendrickson.

Rad, G. von. 1953. *Studies in Deuteronomy*. Translated by David Stalker. Studies in Biblical Theology 9. Chicago: Regnery.

Radner, Ephraim. 1998. *The End of the Church: A Pneumatology of Division in the West*. Grand Rapids: Eerdmans.

Reno, Russell R. 2001. "American Satyricon." *First Things* 116.

Roberts, Kathryn L. 2000. "God, Prophet, and King: Eating and Drinking on the Mountain in First Kings 18:41." *Catholic Biblical Quarterly* 62.

Robinson, Marilynne. 1980. *Housekeeping*. New York: Bantam.

Romer, Thomas, and Albert de Pury. 2000. "Deuteronomistic Historiography (DH): History of Research and Debated Issues." In *Israel Constructs Its History: Deuteronomistic Historiography in Recent Research*. Edited by Albert de Pury et al. Journal for the Study of the Old Testament Supplement Series 306. Sheffield: JSOT Press.

Rousseau, Jean-Jacques. 1968. *The Social Contract*. Translated by Maurice Cranston. New York: Penguin.

Sarna, Nahum M. 1986. *Exploring Exodus: The Origins of Biblical Israel*. New York: Schocken.

Sayers, Dorothy. 1949. *Creed or Chaos?* New York: Harcourt, Brace.

———, trans. 1955. *The Comedy of Dante Alighieri: Purgatory*. London: Penguin.

Schweitzer, Albert. 1952. *The Quest of the Historical Jesus: A Critical Study of Its Progress from Reimarus to Wrede*. Translated by W. Montgomery. London: Black.

Sider, Ronald. 2005. "The Scandal of the Evangelical Conscience." *Books and Culture*. www.ctlibrary.com/bc/2005/janfeb/3.8.html.

Stivers, Richard. 2004. *Shades of Loneliness: Pathologies of a Technological Society*. Lanham: Rowman & Littlefield.

Sweeney, Marvin A. 2001. *King Josiah of Judah: The Lost Messiah of Israel*. Oxford: Oxford University Press.

Tanner, Kathryn. 2004. "Trinity." In *The Blackwell Companion to Political Theology*. Edited by Peter Scott and William T. Cavanaugh. London: Blackwell.

Tertullian. 1964. *Tertullian's Homily on Baptism*. Translated by Ernest Evans. London: SPCK.

———. n.d. *Against Marcion*. Ante-Nicene Fathers 3. Reprint, Grand Rapids: Eerdmans. http://www.ccel.org/fathers2/ANF03/anf03-01.htm#TopOfPage.

Thiele, Edwin. 1983. *The Mysterious Numbers of the Hebrew Kings*. Revised edition. Grand Rapids: Zondervan.

Thomas Aquinas. 1920. *The Summa theologica of St. Thomas Aquinas*. Second and revised edition. Translated by Fathers of the English Dominican Province. http://www.newadvent.org/summa.

———. 1993. *Light of Faith: The Compendium of Theology*. New York: Book-of-the-Month Club.

———. 2003. *On Evil*. Translated by Richard Regan. Oxford: Oxford University Press.

Van't Veer, M. B. 1980. *My God Is Yahweh: Elijah and Ahab in an Age of Apostasy*. Translated by Theodore Plantinga. St. Catherines, ON: Paideia.

Vaux, Roland de. 1961. *Ancient Israel: Its Life and Institutions*. Translated by John McHugh. London: Darton, Longman & Todd.

Walsh, Jerome T. 1989. "The Contexts of 1 Kings xiii." *Vetus Testamentum* 39.

———. 1996. *1 Kings*. Berit Olam. Collegeville, MN: Liturgical Press.

———. 2001. *Style and Structure in Biblical Hebrew Narrative*. Collegeville, MN: Liturgical Press.

Weaver, J. Denny. 2001. "Violence in Christian Theology." *Cross Currents* 51. www.crosscurrents.org/weaver0701.htm.

Weigel, George. 2005. *The Cube and the Cathedral: Europe, America, and Politics without God*. New York: Basic Books.

Wellhausen, Julius. 1885. *Prolegomena to the History of Israel*. Translated by J. Sutherland Black and Allan Menzies. Edinburgh: Black.

Wenham, Gordon J. 1979. *The Book of Leviticus*. New International Commentary on the Old Testament. Grand Rapids: Eerdmans.

Westbrook, Raymond. 2005. "Elisha's True Prophecy in 2 Kings 3." *Journal of Biblical Literature* 124.

Williams, Rowan. 2005. *Grace and Necessity: Reflections on Art and Love*. Harrisburg, PA: Morehouse.

Wink, Walter. 1998. *The Powers That Be: Theology for a New Millennium*. New York: Galilee.

Wiseman, Donald J. 1993. *1 and 2 Kings*. Tyndale Old Testament Commentaries. Downers Grove, IL: IVP.

Worth, Roland H. 1997. *The Sermon on the Mount: Its Old Testament Roots*. New York: Paulist Press.

Wright, N. T. 1993. *The Climax of the Covenant: Christ and the Law in Pauline Theology*. Minneapolis: Fortress.

———. 1996a. *Jesus and the Victory of God*. Christian Origins and the Question of God 2. London: SPCK.

———. 1996b. "Jesus' Self-Understanding." In *The Incarnation*. Edited by Stephen T. Davis. Oxford: Oxford University Press.

———. 1996c. "Paul, Arabia, and Elijah (Galatians 1:17)." *Journal of Biblical Literature* 115.

Yeago, David. 1996. "The Catholic Luther." In *The Catholicity of the Reformation*. Edited by Carl E. Braaten and Robert W. Jenson. Grand Rapids: Eerdmans.

———. 1998. "Martin Luther on Grace, Law, and Moral Life: Prolegomena to an Ecumenical Discussion of Veritatis Splendor." *Thomist* 62.

SUBJECT INDEX

SCRIPTURE INDEX

Lamentations

Leviticus